W9-AYD-127

God's World Science Series

God's World Science Series

God's Inspiring World

Grade 4

with special reference
to the
Book of Job

Teacher's Manual

Rod and Staff Publishers, Inc.
P.O. Box 3, Hwy. 172, Crockett, Kentucky 41413
Telephone: (606) 522-4348

Rod and Staff Publishers, Inc.

P.O. Box 3, Hwy. 172, Crockett, Kentucky 41413

Printed in U.S.A.

ISBN 978-07399-0612-5

Catalog no. 14491

6 7 8 9 10 — 24 23 22 21 20 19 18 17 16 15

In Appreciation

For the greatness of God and His inspiring world, we give thanks and praise. From the biggest star to the smallest seed, we see the power and wisdom of God. To inspire our children with these wonders, that they might love and fear God, is a sacred privilege and responsibility. We are thankful for the freedom, ability, and resources to have Christian schools. We are thankful for the vision to publish textbooks that exalt God and are based on the truth of His Word. We are thankful for the church to whom God has given gifts to produce this science textbook, *God's Inspiring World.*

We are grateful to God for enabling Sister Naomi Eicher Lapp to do most of the original writing. Brother Jonathan Showalter wrote the electricity unit. Many were involved in reviewing, classroom testing, and revising. Brother Lester Showalter served as editor. Brother Lester Miller and Sister Barbara Schlabach drew the illustrations. As each did his part in response to the Lord of the church, there was a blending of efforts, for which we are thankful.

The publishing of this text does not yet meet its objective. These pages have not served their purpose until they become a tool for increasing knowledge about God's created world and, with that knowledge, inspiring the rising generation to worship and serve their Creator. As God has blessed the efforts to produce this textbook, may He further bless the teachers and students who use it.

—The Publishers

Photo Acknowledgments

Lester Showalter supplied all the photos except those listed below.

Bentley, Wilson: 33
©Comstock.com Images: 97
©Eric Martin/Iconotec.com: 16
Hoover, Samuel: 14
Miller, Elaine: 52
Shank, Kevin: 49 (top left and bottom), 223 (right)
Showalter, Mervin: 172, 219
Showalter, Joseph: 13 (left)

Front cover: A rural scene in Vermont

Contents

In Appreciation 5
Photo Acknowledgments 5
Introduction 7

Unit One: God Gives Us Weather
Introduction 10
1. Different Climates 11
2. Wind and Weather 18
3. Clouds and Rain 25
4. Kinds of Precipitation 32
5. Do You Remember? 36

Unit Two: God Created the Animals
Introduction 40
1. Animals With Skeletons 41
2. God Created Birds 47
3. God Created Fish 55
4. God Created Mollusks 61
5. Animals with Strange Bodies 67
6. Do You Remember? 73

Unit Three: The Stars Inspire Wonder
Introduction 76
1. Star Pictures 77
2. The Stars Move 83
3. Learning the Constellations 89
4. Stars Are Useful 96
5. Do You Remember? 102

Unit Four: God Heals Our Diseases
Introduction 106
1. Causes of Sickness 107
2. Fighting Germs 113
3. Getting Well 118
4. Protection From Disease 123
5. Do You Remember? 130

Unit Five: God Made Light
Introduction 134
1. "Let There Be Light" 135
2. Reflecting Light 141
3. Bending Light 147
4. Using Lenses 153
5. Our Eyes 159
6. Do You Remember? 165

Unit Six: Electricity Is From God
Introduction 168
1. Parts of a Circuit 169
2. Different Circuits 177
3. Electricity Is Useful 184
4. Using Electricity Safely 190
5. Do You Remember? 197

Unit Seven: God Gave Us Plants
Introduction 202
1. Seed-Producing Plants 203
2. Roots and Stems 209
3. Leaves Make Food 215
4. Flowers, Fruits, and Seeds 221
5. Plants Can Multiply 227
6. Do You Remember? 233

Tests T–236
Star Guide T–258
Constellation Flash Cards T–261
Index T–269

Introduction

"The heavens declare the glory of God," and every part of creation reveals a wise and powerful Creator. Therefore, the study of science can be very *inspiring;* hence the title of this science textbook, *God's Inspiring World*. To be a teacher of science to fourth graders is a privilege and should be entered into with prayer and a desire to inspire these young people with the glory and greatness of God.

Goals for the Study of Science

1. *Fourth graders should grow in their awareness of the greatness and wisdom of God as seen in the world He created.* The scope of this fourth grade science textbook includes a unit of study about the stars. Before starting to school, your students knew there were stars. But now they are old enough to learn the patterns of the stars in the constellations and the reason they appear to move the way they do. This movement involves distance and motion on a very large scale. Only God could have brought such a universe into existence and ordained laws to keep the giant stars in their places.

Some of the inspiring wonders of creation are so small that no one has ever seen them. The unit about electricity opens to the student the wonders of moving electrons. Small though electrons are, great is the use that can be made of them.

The unit about light is an introduction to a wonder so mysterious that only God knows all the answers to the questions that can be asked about it. Through study, the students should be inspired by the marvels of something as ordinary as light. The design of the eye is one of a multitude of examples that show that we are "fearfully and wonderfully made."

Living things, both plants and animals, are yet another dimension of the created world to inspire the students with the greatness and wisdom of God. This textbook focuses on birds, fish, and strange-bodied animals. The third grade unit about animals included the amphibians, reptiles, and mammals.

This year the students will examine the wonders of seed-producing plants. The fifth grade textbook takes up the study of algae, molds, and mushrooms. The wonders of creation are so great that they cannot all be studied in 1 year, 10 years, or even a lifetime. Yet to focus on various areas helps to magnify God in our eyes.

Weather is of interest to even an unbeliever. For trusting children and believing adults, the study of wind, clouds, and rain speaks of a loving God who has wisely planned for our welfare. Probably you will begin the year with this inspiring study in the first unit.

Where is inspiration in the study of disease? When we learn the cause of disease, we marvel that God has made our bodies that they do not get sick more often than they do. We also marvel that when we do get sick, God heals us. The white blood cells and medicines are part of God's creation to work for healing.

Consideration of God's inspiring world should bring forth the same confession that it brought forth from Job: "I have heard of thee by the hearing of the ear: but now mine eye seeth thee" (Job 42:5).

2. *Fourth graders should grow in their knowledge of the practical facts and order of the created world.* The Bible tells us the origin of the world and God's will for its proper use. But the Bible does not tell us much about the facts and concepts we need to know to make practical use of the natural world. God gave man the ability to discover such truths. Each generation is expected to pass on practical science knowledge and skills. For example, you will be helping your students to learn the following practical information.

—The presence of cirrus clouds often means that rain will soon come. (Unit 1)
—The skeletons of sponges are useful for holding water for washing. (Unit 2)
—Our calendar is set by the position of the sun in relation to the stars. (Unit 3)
—Flu germs can be carried in tiny droplets that go into the air during a sneeze. (Unit 4)
—A convex lens can focus light to make a clear picture of what is in front of it. (Unit 5)
—Parallel is the best way to put two lights in the same electric circuit. (Unit 6)
—New willow trees can be started by putting a branch in water until it grows roots. (Unit 7)

3. *Fourth graders should grow in their interest in God's created world.* Many things in creation will go unnoticed unless they are called to our attention. Often we need help to get started in observing nature. The stars are a good example. This year you will start your students on their way to learn the constellations. You hope that this will not be the end of their interest in learning more about the stars, but only a beginning. Do not feel unable to teach that unit if you do not know the constellations yourself. Let the textbook be your teacher, and learn the stars together with your students.

Middle grade students enjoy collecting. Science can give order and purpose to such collecting. Perhaps a student already has some seashells collected in a box. This year will be a good time to begin identifying, labeling, and displaying those shells. A seed collection could be taken up as a class project. The students may find inspiration in making a collection-list of constellations identified or birds sighted. As a teacher, you have a good opportunity for directing your students into areas that could well become lifelong, special interests.

Fourth graders are mature enough to handle scientific devices carefully. They can well profit from hands-on use of mirrors, lenses, batteries, switches, and wire. An actual plant in the room can be very instructive, provided that plant is used for study and experiment. Many suggestions for projects and demonstrations are given throughout the student text.

Be an Inspiring Teacher

This textbook, *God's Inspiring World*, is designed to help you make science an *inspiring* study for your students. But no textbook can replace an enthusiastic teacher. As you teach the various units this year, make the students' study your study. The effort to bring new insights and demonstrations to the class will be rewarded with interest and good learning from your students.

Do not ignore the suggestions for activities in both the teacher's manual and the student book. The students who can easily learn their lessons can well be challenged to do some of the activities and share them with the class.

Find out what equipment is available at your school. Add to that collection charts, specimens, light materials, and electrical devices. If the school does not have *A Star Guide,* you may want to order one from Rod and Staff Publishers at the beginning of the year so you will have it for Unit Three.

Do not neglect the use of the Bible in teaching science. The Bible is the inspired Word of the One who created the inspiring world. Let its truths about the natural world set a sober and uplifting tone to your classes. The non-Christian teacher gives a vain inspiration to his science teaching by lauding great men of scientific discovery. But those men have died, and their lives are often far from good examples. The Christian teacher of science should magnify God who created it all, provides a perfect example, and lives forever. God "doeth great things past finding out; yea, and wonders without number" (Job 9:10).

The Textbook Theme

The theme and title of this book is *God's Inspiring World.* In a number of places throughout the book, this theme is related to the Book of Job. Job was a wise and prosperous man. But God allowed Satan to touch Job's life and reduce him to a poor sick man who did not have the answers. A number of places in Job's discussion with his friends, the subject of the natural world is mentioned. Elihu especially calls attention to weather in a moving discourse in chapters 36 and 37. This is followed by the climax of God speaking in four chapters full of questions about the created world. This makes the Book of Job very good to use for inspiration for a science textbook.

Be sure your students understand the relation of their text to the Book of Job. You may want to give a series of morning devotional talks from Job to provide a background for their science study. You can introduce this theme by using the introduction of Unit One. Tell the students to be on the lookout for Scripture verses from Job. Every unit makes reference to this inspiring Book.

Recommended Teaching Plans

Time is an important factor in teaching. For good learning, it is best to extend a study over a period of time and have much review. Before you start the school year, you should consider the rate you will need to use the lessons to be able to complete the book in one year. Here is a tabulation of the study exercise groups, review lessons, and tests.

Science 4 Exercise Groups

	Unit 1	*Unit 2*	*Unit 3*	*Unit 4*	*Unit 5*	*Unit 6*	*Unit 7*	
Lesson 1:	2	2	2	2	2	2	2	
Lesson 2:	2	2	2	3	2	2	2	
Lesson 3:	2	2	2	2	2	2	2	
Lesson 4:	1	2	2	3	2	2	2	
Lesson 5:		2			2		2	
Reviews:	1	1	1	1	1	1	1	
Tests:	1	1	1	1	1	1	1	
Total:	9 +	12 +	10 +	12 +	12 +	10 +	12	= 77

In all but one lesson, the exercises are divided into groups. This subdivision will help the students, since they will not need to search for their answers over so much reading material. This grouping of the exercises will also help the teacher by breaking the lesson into segments.

If you have a 36-week school year and schedule two science classes per week, you will have a total of 72 science classes. To cover the entire book in a year, there will need to be five times that two study exercise groups will need to be used for one science class. Having science two times per week will not give much time to do extra activities and will limit the review to one session.

A better plan is to have three science classes per week, even if they are shortened to 20 minutes. This will give a total of 108 class sessions. This would permit using only one study exercise group per class, two sessions for each review, and 24 extra classes for unit introductions and extra activities.

Yet another plan would be to have two science classes per week for half a year and three science classes per week the remainder of the year. This would give a total of 90 class sessions, which is 13 more than the needed 77. This would give two extra class sessions for all but one unit.

Each unit is self-contained, and the units can be studied in any order. Each review of former lessons has questions on only the former lessons of the same unit. These review questions can be assigned along with the last study group of each lesson. Or they may be used as part of the regular science class time.

The exercises are numbered consecutively through the study groups of each lesson. A grade can be taken on each lesson, or the points totaled and a homework grade computed for an entire unit. However, for the fourth grade level, it is better to give the students more frequent feedback of their progress.

An effort has been made to have the answers to the exercises be rather specific and therefore easy to grade. However, this kind of question does not promote exploratory thinking. Try to make the class discussion practical and challenging. Ask questions that stimulate insight that goes beyond the facts given in the book. Encourage questions and discussion about the practical applications of the lesson. Be a teacher of science and not just a textbook administrator. Let the textbook be a tool in teaching and not your slave.

Provide for Frequent Review

The quizzes for each lesson in the teacher's guide can be used to discuss the vocabulary words for the lesson. They can be used later by way of review. The quizzes for a particular unit could be used in combination to make a review over the vocabulary of the entire unit. The more often the new words are used and recalled, the better they will be learned. Repetition is a law of learning.

Beginning with the second lesson of each unit, a five-question "Reviewing What You Have Learned" exercise is included in the student text. Even though the concepts and vocabulary covered are not thorough, just the recall of these specifics will be valuable review to keep the general subject matter fresh in the students' minds. These questions can be assigned along with the last study exercise group of each lesson. At the end of the unit, you can use all of these review questions as a closed book oral review.

These short review exercises do not cross into other units. That makes it possible to study the units in any order. However, it would be good to occasionally assign or use the "Reviewing What You Have Learned" exercises from past units. This would not include items from the last new study lesson of each unit. You may want to add some questions about those lessons.

How to Use the "Extra Activities"

You should not feel obligated to do everything suggested in "Extra Activities." Neither the study exercises nor the tests depend in any way on doing these activities. However, demonstrations and experiments can do much to stimulate interest and broaden insight. It is recommended that at least some of the activities for each unit be used. You may want to do different activities from year to year. You can then report on the results of some activities that were used in the past, to enrich the lesson without actually doing the activity.

God has given some students the ability to learn easily. "Extra Activities" can be assigned to them with the follow-up of a demonstration or report.

You may want to require that each student do an extra activity of his choice once a unit, semester, or year. The research, organization, handicraft, and public speaking involved in such work can be valuable education beyond the knowledge of science acquired in the process of doing an activity.

Of course, it will be good to do some activities as a class with everyone becoming involved and contributing. Cooperation and other social graces can be cultivated by such working together.

Remember the Theme While Teaching

The Book of Job has much to say about the created world. By the questions God asked Job, it is apparent that God intends for a study of creation to be inspiring. Many questions can be asked. Men have learned many things by investigating the natural world. But the world is such that there is no end to the questions, and some of the questions are so hard that man can never hope to have the answers. All of this contributes to making science inspiring. Do not miss communicating this inspiration to your students.

Pupil's Book Introduction

"Hearken unto this, O Job: stand still, and consider the wondrous works of God" (Job 37:14).

All of the wonderful things that you see and use are the works of God; He made them. Sometimes we are so busy and in such a hurry that we do not see how wonderful the works of God really are.

There may be some beautiful clouds in the sky, but you do not see them, because you are going for the mail and are watching that you do not trip over something. Mother calls out, "Look at the interesting shapes of the clouds." You stop and look up. Yes, they are wonderful! You watch them drifting across the sky, slowly changing their shapes. You try to think what kind of clouds they are. You wonder what kind of weather they foretell. You remember that rain comes out of the clouds. You think about how the water in the clouds was once in the ocean. You consider that the clouds are an important part of the way God waters the earth. You are doing what Job was asked to do: "Stand still, and consider the wondrous works of God."

Considering the wondrous works of God is called science. This year you will be studying science with the help of this science textbook. In the first unit, you will be studying about clouds and the weather. Later you will study about animals, stars, light, and electricity. God made all of these things. It is good for you to stand still and consider these wondrous works of God.

Your science textbook is called *God's Inspiring World.* When something stirs up good thoughts and feelings, it is inspiring. Many things about God's world stir up good thoughts and feelings. God's world is very inspiring.

Many times in this book, you will find Bible verses from the Book of Job. God used the wonderful things in creation to inspire Job with how great and wonderful God is. He wanted Job to trust Him completely and not to worry about being sick. God wants you to trust Him too. Considering God's wondrous works can inspire you to trust in God, as it did Job.

Unit One

God Gives Us Weather

"Canst thou lift up thy voice to the clouds?" (Job 38:34).

Weather is a gift from God. We cannot make rain and sunshine. We must wait until God gives us these different kinds of weather.

In the Book of Job, we read: "Fair weather cometh out of the north: with God is terrible majesty" (Job 37:22). "Majesty" means that God is great and wonderful. "Terrible majesty" means that God is so great and wonderful that we are afraid of His power. Only God has the power to make a storm that can uproot trees and blow down buildings. Only God can cause the wind to change and bring beautiful fair weather. We trust in God's wisdom to give us weather.

Remember the story of Job? He lost his great riches, his children, and his good health. Job felt sad. He wanted God to explain why He let this happen.

God did not tell Job why. Instead, God asked Job questions about His creation. "Canst thou lift up thy voice to the clouds, that abundance of waters may cover thee?" (Job 38:34). In dry weather, farmers wish for rain. It would be foolish for them to call to the clouds, but they can call to God who controls the weather.

God wanted Job to trust Him. The weather teaches us to trust God. We can learn from Job's lesson. The beautiful, orderly earth God made reminds us of His greatness. God knows so much more than we do. He does not explain everything to us. God is good even when He lets sad things happen to us.

Unit One

For Your Inspiration

The Book of Job includes several references to weather. In fact, Job 38 records God's own words on this subject. Here He asks Job a series of questions on various aspects of weather to inspire him with the greatness and wisdom of God. Read the following selections about weather from this chapter, not only to receive spiritual truth but also to enjoy their poetic beauty.

Or who shut up the sea with doors, when it brake forth,
as if it had issued out of the womb? (v. 8)
When I made the cloud the garment thereof,
and thick darkness a swaddlingband for it, (v. 9)
And said, Hitherto shalt thou come, but no further:
and here shall thy proud waves be stayed? (v. 11)
Hast thou entered into the treasures of the snow?
or hast thou seen the treasures of the hail? (v. 22)
Who hath divided a watercourse for the overflowing
of waters,
or a way for the lightning of thunder; (v. 25)
To cause it to rain on the earth, where no man is;
on the wilderness, wherein there is no man; (v. 26)
To satisfy the desolate and waste ground;
and to cause the bud of the tender herb to spring
forth? (v. 27)

Canst thou lift up thy voice to the clouds,
that abundance of waters may cover thee? (v. 34)
Canst thou send lightnings, that they may go,
and say unto thee, Here we are? (v. 35)
Who can number the clouds in wisdom?
or who can stay the bottles of heaven, (v. 37)
When the dust groweth into hardness,
and the clods cleave fast together? (v. 38)

Lesson 1

Different Climates

New Words

arid climate (ar′·id), the yearly weather pattern that has very little rain in a year.

atmosphere (at′·mə·sfir′), the layer of air around the earth.

climate, the kind of weather a place has from year to year.

polar climate, the yearly weather pattern that does not get warm enough in the summertime to raise crops.

temperate climate, the yearly weather pattern that has a warm summer and a cold winter.

tropical climate (trop′·i·kəl), the yearly weather pattern that has warm weather all the time.

weather, the condition of the atmosphere from day to day, such as sunny or stormy.

Men live on almost all of the earth. God made the earth as a place for men to live. Over most of the earth, men can find enough to eat. They have enough water to drink. They can keep warm enough and do not get too warm. The earth is a very good place for us to live.

Only a few places on the earth do not make a good home for men. Some of the desert areas are too hot and dry to be good places to live. In the Far North and at the South Pole, it is too cold to be a good place to live. Some of the mountains are so high that the air is too thin and cold to be a good place to live. But in most places, people find what they need. The earth was created by God as a home for you and all living creatures.

Weather happens in the atmosphere. The earth is covered with a thick layer of air called the ***atmosphere.*** You breathe the air of the atmosphere. Birds and airplanes use the air against their wings to fly. Another very important use of the atmosphere is to give us our weather.

Lesson 1

Concepts to Teach

- God gave the earth various climates, which make it a good place to live.
- The atmosphere is the air covering the earth, which brings our weather.
- Weather is the condition of the atmosphere, which changes from day to day.
- Climate is the pattern of weather that can be expected at a particular place.
- Four basic climate types are temperate, tropical, polar, and arid.
- The climate we have is a result of distance from the equator, distance from the ocean, height above sea level, and surrounding landforms.

Introducing the Lesson

Have the students read the unit introduction in class. Emphasize God's wisdom in making the weather. The subject of weather is often discussed. Sometimes men complain about the weather being too hot, too cold, too wet, or too dry. This is not right. Rather, men should be thankful for the weather and should talk about the greatness of God in giving us weather.

Lead the students to see the difference between weather and climate. People who live in the same area talk to each other about the changes in weather from day to day. But if you talked to someone from an area farther north or south, you would probably talk about the differences in the kind of weather throughout the year. A person from Ohio

How many parts of weather can you see on this picture?

We put thermometers into the air to find the temperature. Weathervanes tell us the direction the wind is blowing. We look up into the atmosphere to see the clouds. Rain gauges measure the amount of rain that comes out of the atmosphere. Temperature, wind, clouds, and rain are all part of the ***weather.***

You know that the weather changes very often. Some days are bright and sunny. Others are cloudy and rainy. One day of spring may be warm and pleasant. The next day may be cold and windy. These changes of weather are God's way of giving us different things that we need.

Climate remains the same. Even if the weather changes from day to day, you know that you get about the same weather from year to year. If you live at one place for several years, you learn what kind of weather to expect at each season of the year. If you live in Pennsylvania, you can expect to get some snow each winter. If you live in the Philippines, you would not expect to get snow all year around. In the Philippines you would expect the rainy season to begin in June. Pennsylvania and the Philippines have two different kinds of ***climate.***

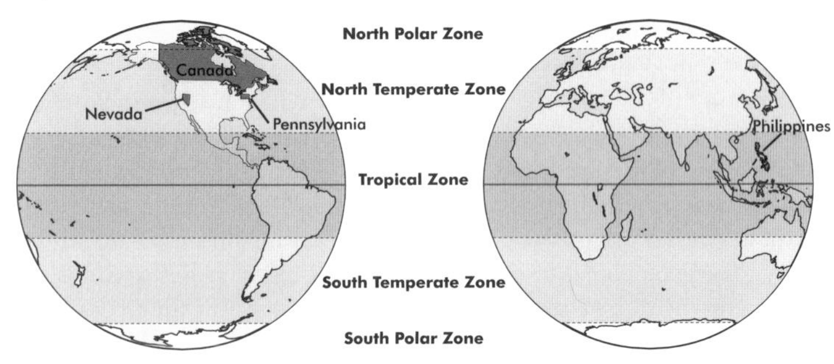

The climate zones of the earth

may say that during some winters there are two feet of snow on the ground. A person from Florida may say that it never snows where he lives. These persons would be comparing their climate.

If one of the children has lived in a different climate, have him tell what that climate is like. Then have a student tell what the weather was like yesterday. Explain that one of the children was telling about climate and the other was telling about weather.

Did you know—

...that the word *climate* comes from the Greek word for slope? The ancient Greeks believed that south of the Mediterranean Sea the earth "sloped" increasingly toward the sun, making the climate progressively warmer down to the southern end of the earth, which they thought was too hot for humans to survive. They believed the opposite was true for the north.

...that since large-scale irrigation of the Great Plains has been practiced, rainfall has increased by 10%?

...that on a typical summer day at the U.S.–Mexican border, the temperature of the U.S. side at Arizona is 5°–6°F cooler than the temperature of the Mexican side? This seems to be because the American side, which is grassland, retains its moisture longer than the Mexican side, where overgrazing of cattle has produced stony, degraded land.

Note: Because of the first of the above "Did You Know?" items, world climates were at one time divided into three groups according to latitude: frigid, temperate, and torrid. This classification emphasized the temperature factor and reflected

Pennsylvania has a ***temperate climate.*** This means that the weather is about half way between hot and cold. People who have a temperate climate have a warm summer season when they can grow crops. Then they have a cold winter season when the trees and fields are bare. There are two main areas of temperate climate. Pennsylvania is in the North Temperate Zone. The North Temperate Zone is

A soybean field of Paraguay in February

a belt around the earth about half way between the equator and the North Pole. There is a South Temperate Zone about half way between the equator and the South Pole. The people of Paraguay live in a temperate climate of the South Temperate Zone.

The Philippines has a ***tropical climate.*** The tropical climate is found in a wide belt around the

Plants grow well in the tropical climate of the Philippines.

center of the earth with the equator running through the center. It is warm all year around in a tropical climate. They do not have a winter with snow in a tropical climate. There is often a wet and a dry season. Crops and trees grow all year around. Bananas and mangoes grow well in this climate. Tropical countries with a lot of rain often have thick jungles containing many interesting animals, such as parrots and monkeys.

People in upper Canada live in the ***polar climate.*** This land is so far north that the ground beneath the surface stays frozen all year

the attitude that the Far North is unbearably cold and the equatorial region is unbearably hot. Recent classifications include the moisture factor and recognize that climates are not strictly effected by latitudes. A simplified classification is being used in this lesson with some of both the old and the new classifications being used. There does not seem to be a good name for the climate having distinct winter and summer seasons. The word *temperate* is used for this, borrowed from the older terminology.

Quiz

Write the New Words on the chalkboard. Call on students to say the word when you give one of the meanings below.

1. All the air around the earth *(atmosphere)*
2. The kind of wind, heat, and water in the atmosphere today *(weather)*
3. The usual weather patterns every year *(climate)*
4. Cold weather around the year *(polar climate)*
5. Warm weather around the year *(tropical climate)*
6. Cold winters and warm summers *(temperate climate)*
7. A climate with very little rainfall *(arid climate)*

long. The winters are very long. The summers are so short and cool that only some very hardy plants will grow. High mountains can also have a polar climate even if they are far from the North or South Pole.

Deserts are caused by a climate that has very little rainfall. Such places have an ***arid climate.*** Most of Nevada has an arid climate, which means that the climate is dry. There is often less than eight inches of rainfall each year in Nevada. Grass grows so poorly that people sometimes cover their yards with crushed stones. In such desert and partly desert lands, much of the ground is bare sand. Because the sky is often clear in an arid climate, the temperature can get very high during the daytime and very low during the night.

Sand dunes in a Nevada desert

People live in all of these different climates. Different people like different climates. Someone raised in a tropical climate may not like the cold winters of a temperate climate. A person raised to like the refreshing snow of winter may be very uncomfortable in a tropical climate. God gave us many kinds of climate. Each climate has its own special yearly weather pattern.

Test Your Reading (Group A)

For each sentence, write the missing word from your lesson.

1. God wisely gave us all we need to live on the ———.
2. One day the ——— may be sunny, and the next day it may be raining.
3. The yearly weather pattern at the same place is called ———.
4. If you have a cold winter and a long-enough summer to grow crops, then you have a ——— climate.
5. People who live in a ——— climate have no winter.
6. People who live in a ——— climate have no summer that will grow crops.
7. An ——— climate has hot days, cool nights, and very little rainfall.

Lesson 1 Answers

Group A

1. earth
2. weather
3. climate
4. temperate
5. tropical
6. polar
7. arid

(7 points thus far)

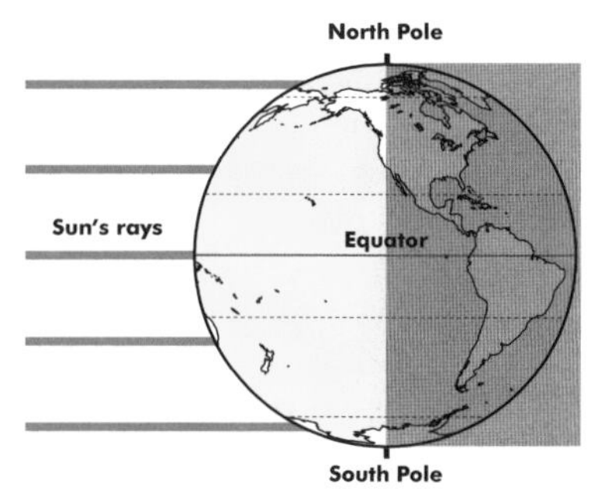

Distance from the equator affects climate.

What causes different climates? The kind of climate you have depends on four important things.

First, the distance from the equator makes a big difference in the climate. If you look at the map above, you see that the equator circles the middle of the earth. There the sun is shining straight down. This makes warm temperatures. The warmest climates are those near the equator. The coldest climates are those near the North Pole and the South Pole. There the sun is shining at a slant, and the ground does not warm up very much.

Second, the distance from the ocean makes a difference in the climate. If you live near the ocean, your climate is probably neither very hot nor very cold. The water of the ocean stores the heat of summer and gives off heat in the winter. If you live far from the ocean, you probably have hotter summers and colder winters. For example, the gardens in Delaware produce food earlier than in Pennsylvania. Delaware has water on both sides of it.

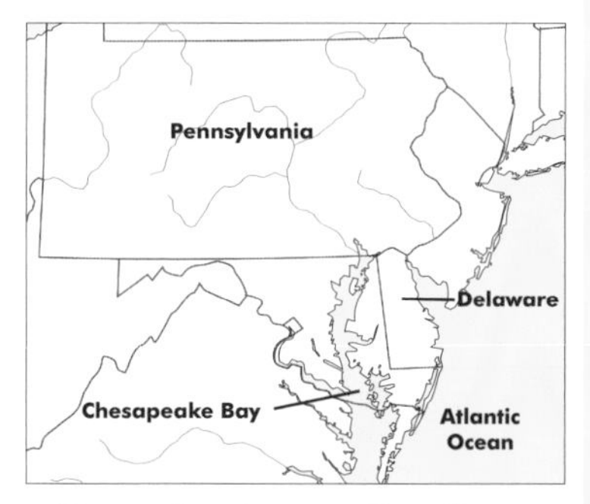

Distance from the ocean affects climate.

Third, the height above sea level makes a difference in the climate. The higher you go up a mountain, the colder the climate is. Some high mountaintops have snow on them all year even though they are close to the equator. In the highlands of Guatemala, the climate is springlike all year around. The lands near sea level have a hot, tropical climate.

Height above sea level affects climate.

Fourth, the land around you makes a difference in the climate. Mountains, deserts, and cities all help cause differences. The tall mountain range in California causes rain to fall on its west side. East of the mountains, it is very dry. That is why Nevada has an arid climate. Deserts and cities are likely warmer than grasslands and forests.

God made the sun, wind, mountains, oceans, and deserts all work together to give us the climates of the earth. It is interesting to learn about weather and climate. God gave us the ability to understand some things about climate and weather. But we shall never understand everything. Only God understands everything!

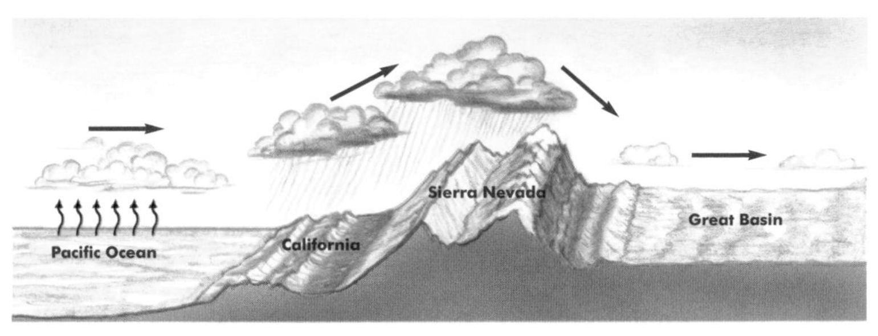

Surrounding land affects climate.

Test Your Reading (Group B)

Choose the best answer.

8. A tropical climate will be
   a. near the equator.
   b. far from the equator.
   c. half way between the equator and a pole.

Group B
8. a

9. Living near the ocean will make your climate
   a. colder all the year.
   b. cooler in the summer and warmer in the winter.
   c. warmer in the summer and colder in the winter.
10. There could be a cool climate near the equator if
    a. the land was very near the ocean.
    b. the land was close to a mountain.
    c. the land was very high.
11. If you live close to a very big mountain range, your climate could be
    a. cool in the summertime.
    b. very different from those on the other side of the mountain.
    c. more like those who live close to the ocean.

9. b
10. c
11. b

Answer the following question.

12. What four things help to make the climates different from one place to another?

12. the distance from the equator; the distance from the ocean; the height above sea level; the land around you (4 points)
(15 points total)

Extra Activities

1. Read about your state or country in an encyclopedia. Be sure to read the sections about your climate. Find out whether you live close to or far from the equator and ocean, how high you are above sea level, and what kind of land is around you. Find information about the climates of the world. What other places of the world have the same climate that you have?
2. Write a description of your climate that would be interesting to someone in a different climate. Be sure to include what seasons you have and what the weather is like in each season. Tell the highest and lowest temperatures you can expect to have in the year. Do you have frost and snow? Do you expect any storms? Do you have much rainfall?

   Send your description to a school in a country that has a very different climate from yours. Ask them to write back and tell you about their climate. Perhaps you can send to some Christian school in a country where your church has missionaries.

Extra Activity Comments

2. An alternative to this activity would be to have someone visit your class who has lived in another climate. Prepare the students to ask questions that would help them learn what the yearly weather pattern is in the different climate.

Lesson 2

Wind and Weather

New Words

cyclone (sī′·klōn), a large circle of moist, warm air that is slowly turning.

hurricane (hėr′·i·kān′), a storm with wind moving in a large circle.

prevailing westerlies (pri·vā′·ling wes′·tər·lēz), wide belts of winds that blow from the west.

thunderstorm (thun′·dər·stôrm′), a storm with wind, thunder, and lightning caused by rapidly rising warm air.

tornado (tôr·nā′·dō), a storm with wind circling at high speed in a small area.

trade winds, wide belts of winds that always blow from the east next to each side of the equator.

If there were no wind, the weather would be almost the same day after day. There would be no rain over the land because the moist ocean air would stay over the ocean. Part of God's wise plan for the weather was the wind.

A weathervane telling a west wind

What is the wind? Wind is simply air moving across the earth. Sometimes it is so soft you hardly feel it. At other times it is strong enough to uproot trees and smash houses.

Jesus said that the wind goes where it will and you can hear the sound of it, but you cannot tell where it is coming from or where it is going (John 3:8). We cannot see the wind. We know that wind is blowing by the rustling sound as it passes through the trees. We see how it moves a weathervane to tell which direction the wind is blowing.

Lesson 2

Concepts to Teach

- The wind is caused by the sun's uneven heating of the earth.
- The winds move in circles.
- The trade winds next to each side of the equator blow from the east.
- The prevailing westerlies blow from the west in belts north and south of the trade winds.
- Many cyclones develop over large bodies of water.
- A cyclone brings us rain with its warm, moist air.
- A hurricane is a large storm with the wind moving in a circle.
- Tornadoes are storms covering small areas with very fast winds.
- Thunderstorms are produced by the rapid rising of warm air.
- Storms show us the greatness of God and test our faith to trust in God.

Introducing the Lesson

Job well knew the strength of wind. Rehearse with your students how "a great wind from the wilderness . . . smote the four corners of the house," killing his children.

Remind the students of the song "The Wise Man Built His House Upon a Rock." In telling the parable, Jesus said, "The rain descended, and the floods came, and the winds blew, and beat upon that house." One house fell, and the other did not. When the wind blows, a house can stand firm if it is built on a rock. Jesus used this story to teach that a man's life can stand firm against the storms of life if he builds on the Lord.

Use a globe or large world map to show the general belts of westerlies and trade winds. Be sure the students know where the poles and equator are.

What makes the wind blow? It is the sun! Although the same sun shines over the earth, the earth heats up unevenly. Places near the North and South Poles stay cold because the sun stays low in the sky like our evening sun. Places near the equator stay warm because the sun shines straight down. So the air near the equator stays warm, and the air near the Poles stays cold.

You know that warm air rises and cold air sinks. In a room that is heated with a stove, the air rises above the stove and cold air moves toward the bottom of the stove. This makes a big circle of air in the room so that the entire room can be heated. This is called convection.

The same thing happens in a much bigger way in the atmosphere. The light, warm air rises. The heavy, cold air sinks and pushes the warm air. This pushing or moving air is the wind blowing. The air circles around and around through the atmosphere, heating and cooling again and again. Year after year, the winds follow the same paths, all because of the sun!

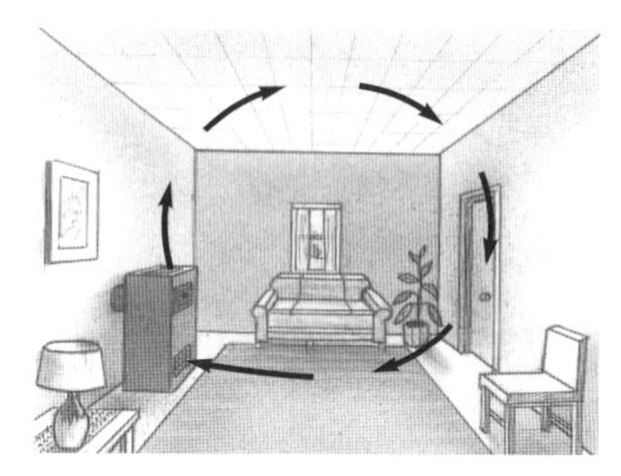

Convection that moves the air in a room causes the wind to blow on the earth.

Thousands of years ago, King Solomon clearly described these wind patterns or cycles. "The wind goeth toward the south, and turneth about unto the north; it whirleth about continually, and the wind returneth again according to his circuits" (Ecclesiastes 1:6). How did Solomon know so much about the wind? He got his wisdom from our wise God who rules the wind.

Which way do the winds blow? If the cold air blows toward the equator from the North and South Poles, most winds come from the north and south, right? Wrong. They might if the earth were holding still. But since the earth spins on its axis, the winds curve and blow mainly east and west.

The winds that blow from the west are called ***prevailing westerlies.*** The prevailing westerlies blow around the earth in two great belts.

With the globe or map, show the general path and size of a cyclone over North America. Have your finger circling counterclockwise as you travel from the Pacific Ocean to the west coast or from the Gulf of Mexico to the northeast across America.

Materials needed:

- globe or large world map

Did you know—

...that the troposphere, which is the lowest part of the atmosphere, contains most of the air. It is about 11 miles (18 km) thick over the equator but only about 5 miles (8 km) thick over the poles?

...that hurricanes are called "typhoons" in eastern Asia?

...that the warm chinook winds of northwestern North America have been known to raise temperatures 30°–40°F (15°–20°C) in three hours?

...that jet streams, the 65–200 mph (105–320 kmph) winds of the upper atmosphere, save much flight time and fuel for airplanes flying along with them?

Demonstration: Prevailing Winds

Using finger or tempera paint and a globe, show why the rotation of the earth deflects the prevailing winds. Have one child move a finger (with paint on it) slowly from the North Pole due south to the equator while another child rotates the globe toward the east. Notice the crosswise path. Explain that this is partly why large air masses moving south from the North Pole actually blow from the east.

Materials needed:

- finger or tempera paint
- globe

Can you find them on the map? Much of North America, Europe, and Asia lies in the path of these west winds.

The two wide wind belts next to each side of the equator that blow from the east are called ***trade winds.*** They blow across South America, Australia, and southern Africa. The two wide belts of trade winds are on both sides of the equator.

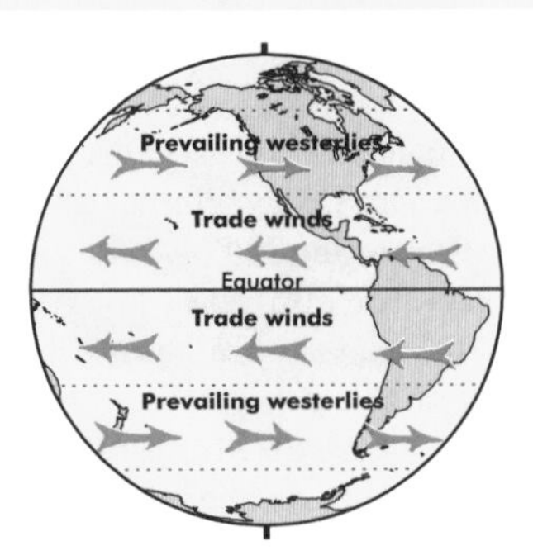

Wind belts of the earth

Lesson 2 Answers

Group A

1. c
2. f
3. e
4. g
5. d
6. b
7. a

8. pole
9. prevailing westerlies
10. trade winds
11. equator
12. trade winds
13. prevailing westerlies

(13 points thus far)

Test Your Reading (Group A)

Choose the best ending for each sentence. Write the letter on your paper.

1. The sun
2. The air at the Poles
3. Warm air
4. Moving air
5. A trade wind
6. Earth's spinning on its axis
7. A prevailing westerly

a. blows over most of the United States.
b. gives wind an east or west direction.
c. causes the wind to blow.
d. blows from the east year after year.
e. is light and rises.
f. receives little heat from the sun.
g. is called wind.

Match each number on this map of the earth with one of the words at the right. Some words get used more than once.

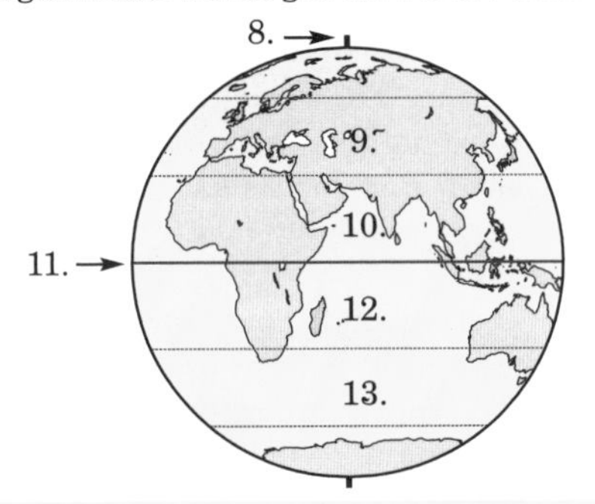

equator

pole

trade winds

prevailing westerlies

Quiz

Write the New Words on the chalkboard. Call on students to say the word when you give one of the meanings below.

1. It is a huge circle of air slowly turning. *(cyclone)*
2. These large bands of wind always blow from the west. *(prevailing westerlies)*
3. These winds always blow from the east next to each side of the equator. *(trade winds)*
4. It is a circling storm covering a large area. *(hurricane)*
5. It is a small circling storm. *(tornado)*
6. It is a storm of wind and lightning caused by rapidly rising warm air. *(thunderstorm)*

Cyclones bring us rain. Within these wind belts are some smaller patterns of wind called ***cyclones.*** A cyclone is a large circle of moist air that is warmer than the air around it. It is often a few hundred miles across. A cyclone is like a huge "top" of warm, moist air slowly spinning.

A cyclone often begins circling over an ocean or a gulf. Much water evaporates from the ocean and makes the air humid. Then, full of warm, moist air, it moves over the land. As the cyclone moves along, it drops its water, bringing us the rain we need. This is how God planned for the water of the ocean to supply us with the precious rain we need.

We can tell when a cyclone is coming because the direction of the wind changes. If you live in the prevailing westerlies, the wind usually blows from the west. But when a cyclone is coming, you begin to have a south or east wind. When that happens, you know that you may have rain in a day or so.

Men knew about this weather sign for a long time. They knew that the direction of the wind could be used to predict the weather. One of Job's friends described the direction of the wind and the weather: "Out of the south cometh the whirlwind: and cold out of the north. . . . Fair weather cometh out of the north" (Job 37:9, 22).

Strong winds are storms. Most of the time the wind blows gently. But sometimes the wind begins moving very fast. These stormy winds can uproot trees, blow roofs off houses, or even destroy whole houses.

Often the winds of a storm move in a circle. If the circle is very big so that it covers an entire state, it is called a ***hurricane.*** If the spinning air is only as wide as your schoolyard, we call it a ***tornado.*** A tornado is much smaller than a hurricane, but the wind is going faster in a tornado.

A tornado

A common kind of storm is called a ***thunderstorm.*** The air in a thunderstorm is very warm and moist. It rises rapidly and makes the wind blow fast. The wind of a thunderstorm does not blow as fast as a tornado, but it can be fast enough to blow a big tree down. Thunderstorms get their name from the loud thunder we hear after the lightning during these storms.

When we see that a storm is coming, we close the windows and doors. We go inside a building and maybe even to the basement. We know that a storm has great power. During a storm we think about the greatness of God. God made the sun that gives the storms their power. God controls the storms, and He has good reasons for allowing storms.

Job knew what a storm could do. One day while his children were eating in a house, a storm blew the house down and killed all of Job's children. God allowed this storm as a test for Job's faith. When we are in a storm, it is a test of our faith to see if we trust in God.

Test Your Reading (Group B)

Answer the following questions.

14. How do the winds move in a cyclone?
15. Where do cyclones often begin?
16. What do cyclones bring to us?
17. How can we tell that a cyclone is coming?
18. How are a hurricane and a tornado the same?
19. In what two ways is a tornado different from a hurricane?
20. What causes the strong wind in a thunderstorm?
21. What do storms teach us about God?
22. What should we do when we are afraid in a storm?

Reviewing What You Have Learned

1. Climate is the weather patterns we have
   a. from day to day.
   b. for one year.
   c. from year to year.
2. Places with a cold winter and a warm summer have a ——— climate.

Group B

14. in a large circle
15. over an ocean or a gulf
16. rain
17. The wind changes direction.
18. They both have very fast wind going in a circle.
19. A tornado is much smaller than a hurricane. The wind is going faster in a tornado. (2 points)
20. rapidly rising warm air
21. His greatness
22. trust in God

(23 points total)

Review Answers

1. c
2. temperate

3. True or false? People in a tropical climate live close to the equator.
4. The higher a land is above sea level, the ——— will be the climate.
5. The distance from the equator, the height above sea level, and the land around you help to make your climate what it is. What is the fourth thing that makes a difference in your climate?

3. true
4. colder
5. the distance from the ocean

(5 additional points)

Extra Activities

1. Start keeping a weather record by making a chart like the one below. For this lesson, do only the *Date* and *Wind Name and Speed* sections. You will do the other sections in later lessons.

   To find the name and speed of the wind today, look at the *Wind Description* on page 24. Which sentence most nearly describes the wind today? Choose one, then find the *Wind Name and Speed* across from it. Write it on your own chart, just like the chart below shows. Keep doing this every day about the same time each day.

My Weather Record

Date	*Wind Name and Speed*	*Clouds*	*Precipitation*
Sept. 10	gentle breeze, 8–12 mph		

Wind Description	Wind Name and Speed
Smoke rises straight up	Calm, less than 1 mph (2 kmph)
Smoke drifts with the air	Light air, 1–3 mph (2–5 kmph)
Leaves rustle; wind can be felt	Light breeze, 4–7 mph (6–11 kmph)
Leaves and small twigs move	Gentle breeze, 8–12 mph (12–20 kmph)
Small branches sway; dust blows	Moderate breeze, 13–18 mph (21–29 kmph)
Small trees sway	Fresh breeze, 19–24 mph (30–39 kmph)
Large branches sway	Strong breeze, 25–31 mph (40–50 kmph)
Whole trees sway; walking is difficult	Moderate gale, 32–38 mph (51–61 kmph)
Twigs are broken from trees	Fresh gale, 39–46 mph (62–74 kmph)
Loose shingles and siding, etc. are blown from buildings	Strong gale, 47–54 mph (75–87 kmph)
Trees are uprooted	Whole gale, 55–63 mph (88–101 kmph)
Much widespread damage	Storm, 64–73 mph (102–117 kmph)
Severe destruction	Hurricane, 74 mph (118 kmph) and above

2. Read about hurricanes. What is a hurricane-like storm called that comes from the Pacific Ocean? How are hurricanes named? What do people do to their houses if they know a hurricane is coming? What direction do hurricanes move? Which parts of the United States have hurricanes? Tell or write about what you learned.
3. Read about tornadoes. What do tornadoes look like? How do they move? What should a person do if there is danger of a tornado? What parts of the United States have the most tornadoes? What is a tornado called if it is over water? Tell or write about what you learned.

Lesson 3

Clouds and Rain

New Words

cirrus clouds (sir′·əs), feathery clouds high in the sky.
cumulus clouds (kyüm′·yə·ləs), fluffy, heaped-up clouds.
fog, a thick mist or cloud just above the ground.
front, the line where warm air meets cold air.
humid (hyü′·mid), damp or moist.
stratus clouds (strā′·təs), thick, gray, low-hanging clouds.

If the sky was clear and there were no clouds, would you expect it to rain? Of course not. You know that rain comes from clouds. You also know that clouds do not always give rain. You are glad for the shade that clouds give you when you are working hard in the garden. Clouds are beautiful. Their fluffy shapes against a blue sky add to the beauty of the outdoors. A sunset is made more beautiful as the bars of clouds glow with red and orange. Clouds are part of the wonderful world God made for us to live in.

Questions about clouds. "Who can number the clouds in wisdom? or who can stay the bottles of heaven?" (Job 38:37). These are questions God asked Job. Who indeed can count the clouds and hold water in the "bottles" of the clouds? Only God can do that! He does it with wise laws He made for weather. These laws explain how clouds are formed.

What makes clouds? The atmosphere is made of air, and the air holds some water. Water goes into the air by evaporation from plants, rivers, lakes, and oceans. When the air contains much water, we say it is ***humid.***

Because of one of God's laws, when humid air is cooled, some of the water comes out of the air. The moisture comes out of the air as tiny drops of water. A large body of tiny water droplets is a cloud. A cloud is formed when humid air has been cooled to form tiny water droplets. If the cloud is cooled more,

Lesson 3

Concepts to Teach

- Rain is a result of wise laws God set up.
- Clouds are formed when humid air is cooled.
- Rain comes when clouds become so cold they must lose moisture.
- Air is cooled when it is raised by mountains or fronts.
- Most cumulus clouds mean fair weather.
- Large, dark cumulus clouds, called thunderheads, produce heavy rain.
- Low stratus clouds often produce a slow, steady rain.
- Thin cirrus clouds tell us that rain may be coming.
- Weather can be predicted because God made orderly laws.

Introducing the Lesson

Obtain the weather map from a recent newspaper. Use it to make a chalkboard sketch of the weather patterns of your area inside a simple outline of the United States. Put an *X* in the general area where you live.

You might say something like this: "Remember how cloudy and rainy yesterday was? It was because of this front right here." Or if you had no recent precipitation due to frontal activity, point out the location of fronts in other areas. *Front* is a new term for this lesson. It is using the word in a different way from what we mean when we say, "The front of the house." Tell how the cold air of a front causes the warm air to rise and form clouds and perhaps rain.

Emphasize the law and order that God has made to give us the weather He wants us to have more moisture must come out of the air. The droplets get bigger and fall out of the cloud. This is the way God's laws work to make it rain.

What makes the air get cooler? As you learned in Lesson 1, the higher you go above sea level, the colder it gets. When air is pushed upward, it gets cooler. This cooling is what makes clouds form.

One way air is pushed up to get cooler is by mountains. As the wind pushes air up the side of a mountain, the air gets cooler. If the air is humid, clouds are formed and it rains. That is why California gets plenty of rain. After the air has gotten to the top of the mountains, it has lost much of its water. That is why the land on the other side of the mountain has an arid climate.

Another way air is pushed up is by cold air. When warm air meets cold air, the cold air slides under the warm air and the warm air rises over the cold air. This meeting of the air makes a long line called a ***front.*** Fronts often happen in cyclones. This is the way the warm, humid air of a cyclone makes rain. At a front, warm, humid air meets cold air. The warm air rises over the cold air. As it rises, the warm air cools. Cooling humid air causes clouds to form. If the air is cooled enough, the clouds will give rain. In this way, God's laws are at work to bring us needed rain.

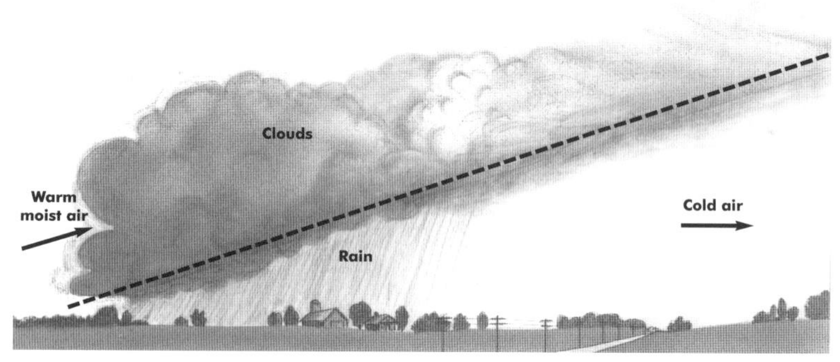

A front

each day. These laws make it possible for us to predict the weather. This is very helpful to the farmer in planning his field work.

Make this lesson practical by having the students observe and identify the clouds and make simple weather predictions.

Materials needed:

- weather map from recent newspaper

Did you know—

...that about 329 cubic miles (1,370 cubic km) of water evaporate each day, and yet water vapor makes up only 0.001% of the world's water?

...that meteorologists sometimes go by the majority vote when they disagree on their forecasts?

...that a thunderhead may be over 11 miles (18 km) tall?

...that weather predictions are made from information collected from over 2,000 weather stations, from airplanes, from high-altitude balloons, and from satellites?

Quiz

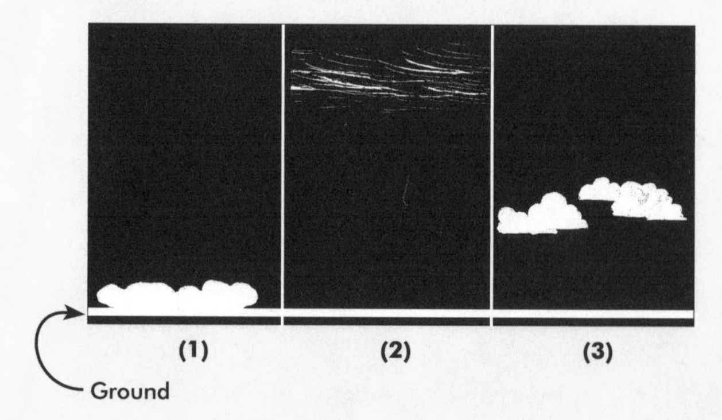

Now we can give a step-by-step process of how the ocean water becomes rain.

1. Heat from the sun causes the ocean water to evaporate into the air.
2. Winds carry the humid air over the land.
3. A mountain or front causes the humid air to rise.
4. As the air rises, it becomes cool.
5. Cooling causes some of the moisture to come out of the humid air to form a cloud.
6. If the humid air is cooled more, enough water comes out to make rain.

We thank God for making the laws to give us rain. Rain is a precious gift from God. We pray to God to send us rain. We thank Him when He sends rain.

Test Your Reading (Group A)

Read each sentence below. Write *true* if the statement is true. Write *false* if the statement is false.

1. God made the laws of rain and weather.
2. All rain comes from clouds.
3. All clouds give us rain.
4. When humid air becomes warmer, it causes clouds and rain.
5. As air is raised, it becomes cooler.
6. Mountains can cause rain to fall.
7. When warm air meets cold air, the cold air rises over the warm air.
8. A front is the line between areas that have much rain and areas that have little rain.

Complete these statements to give the steps of how ocean water becomes rain.

9. The ocean water ——— because of the heat of the ———.
10. The ——— blows the ——— air over the land.
11. The air is ——— by a ——— or a mountain.
12. The air gets ——— as it is forced to ———.
13. Some of the moisture comes ——— of the air in tiny water droplets to form a ———.
14. It will ——— if the humid air is ——— enough.

Lesson 3 Answers

Group A

1. true
2. true
3. false
4. false
5. true
6. true
7. false
8. false

(½ point for each blank)

9. evaporates, sun
10. wind, humid
11. raised, front
12. cool, rise
13. out, cloud
14. rain, cooled

(14 points thus far)

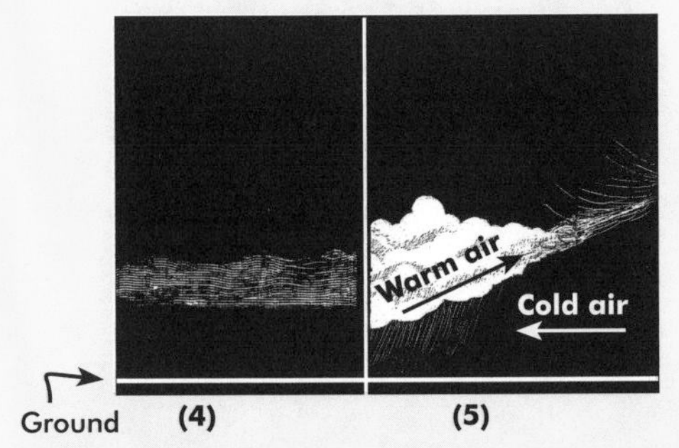

Draw a line near the bottom of the chalkboard to represent the ground. Then use the side of the chalk to draw fog or a cirrus, cumulus, or stratus cloud, and have the class write which one it is. Tell them to notice both the cloud's height and shape.

1. *(fog)*
2. *(cirrus clouds)*
3. *(cumulus clouds)*
4. *(stratus clouds)*
5. *(front)*

Kinds of clouds. As you know, not all clouds bring us rain. Sometimes a cloud is so low that it touches the ground. We call this thick mist a ***fog.*** You know that raindrops do not come out of fog. If you have ever wondered what it would be like to be inside a cloud, now you know. A fog is a cloud that touches the ground.

When you see fluffy clouds like piles of whipped cream against a blue sky, you know that the weather will be fair and sunny. These puffy clouds are called ***cumulus clouds.*** We sometimes call them fair-weather clouds.

Cumulus clouds do not usually bring us rain, but sometimes they do. A thunderstorm develops when cold air pushes the warm air straight upward to form a big, dark cumulus cloud called a thunderhead. Lightning flashes, thunder rumbles, and soon heavy rain showers spill out.

The rain clouds that bring us a slow, steady rain are thick, low-hanging ***stratus clouds.*** They look like a gray blanket or layer above us. *Stratus* means "layer." Stratus clouds are a layer of clouds.

Stratus clouds

Cumulus clouds

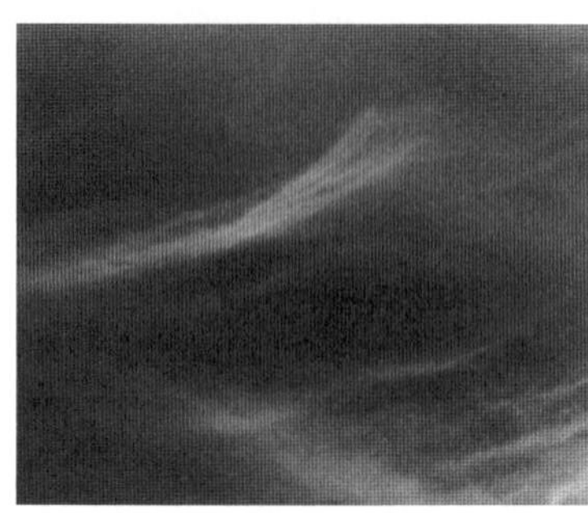

Cirrus clouds

High, thin clouds are ***cirrus clouds.*** They are so high and cold that they are made of fine pieces of ice instead of droplets of water. They look like long, sweeping feathers. They are so thin that you can see the sun through them. Rain or snow does not fall from cirrus clouds, but they give us a clue that rain may be coming.

Weather signs. You can use cirrus clouds to predict the weather. When you see cirrus clouds, you can say, "We'll probably have rain in a few days." Often when we see cirrus clouds, the wind changes from its usual direction. A cyclone is on the way. Now you know two weather signs for rain. The direction of the wind changes, and you can see cirrus clouds.

A ring around the moon predicts rain or snow.

When the moon shines through cirrus clouds, a big ring of light forms around the moon. When the sun shines through cirrus clouds, it can also make a big ring. Sometimes it makes two bright spots in the clouds, one on each side of the sun. We call them sundogs. A ring around the moon, a ring around the sun, and sundogs are more signs that rain may be on the way. The laws of God for the weather are so orderly that they make it possible for us to predict the weather.

Jesus described how we can predict the weather. He said, "When it is evening, ye say, It will be fair weather: for the sky is red. And in the morning, It will be foul weather to day: for the sky is red and lowring" (Matthew 16:2, 3). You have probably heard this poem to help you predict the weather from the evening and morning skies.

Evening red, morning gray,
Sends the traveler on his way.
Evening gray, morning red,
Sends the rain upon his head.

Test Your Reading (Group B)

Choose the correct ending for each sentence. Write the letter on your paper.

15. You know that it is not beautiful inside a cloud because
    a. it is like a rainy day.
    b. fog makes things whitish and hard to see.
    c. it has cooled enough to make droplets of water.
16. If you saw many cumulus clouds in the sky, you could predict
    a. there will be nice weather for the rest of the day.
    b. there will be a thunderstorm before the end of the day.
    c. there is a cyclone coming.
17. On a cloudy day, we cannot see the sun because of
    a. cumulus clouds.
    b. stratus clouds.
    c. cirrus clouds.
18. If you saw a ring around the moon, you would know there were
    a. cumulus clouds.
    b. stratus clouds.
    c. cirrus clouds.
19. We can predict weather because
    a. God has told us what causes the weather.
    b. men have learned to control the weather.
    c. the weather works by the laws of God.

Identify each of the following clouds.

20. 21.

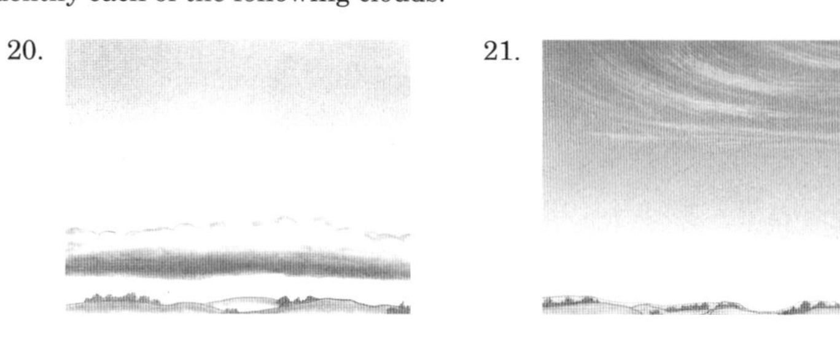

Group B

15. b
16. a
17. b
18. c
19. c

20. stratus
21. cirrus

22.

23.

24.

22. fog
23. cumulus
24. thunderhead

(24 points total)

Reviewing What You Have Learned

1. The weather is the condition of the atmosphere from
   a. day to day. b. year to year. c. country to country.
2. The wind blows because ——— air rises.
3. True or false? The trade winds blow from the east next to each side of the equator.
4. Most of our rains come from
   a. prevailing westerlies.
   b. cyclones.
   c. thunderstorms.
5. The ——— climate has no winter season.

Review Answers

1. a
2. warm
3. true
4. b
5. tropical

(5 additional points)

Extra Activity

Keep working on the weather record you started in the last lesson. Start working on the *Clouds* section. Look at the sky, and decide which kind of clouds you see. Your teacher may also help you decide. Write *cumulus, cirrus, stratus, thunderheads,* or *fog.* If no clouds are in the sky, write *clear* in the space.

Lesson 4

Kinds of Precipitation

New Words

dew, waterdrops that form on grass, etc. at night when humid air cools.

frost, ice crystals that form on grass, etc. at night when humid air cools below freezing.

hail, balls of ice that fall during a thunderstorm.

precipitation (pri·sip′·i·tā′·shən), rain, snow, dew, and other forms of water that come out of the air.

sleet, raindrops that freeze as they fall.

Kinds of precipitation. Rain is not the only way God waters the earth. If the rain freezes on the way down from the cloud, then we have ***sleet.*** Sleet is really frozen rain.

Rain and sleet are two kinds of precipitation. ***Precipitation*** is the name for the forms of water that come out of the air. In this lesson you will be learning about four more kinds of precipitation.

God asked Job questions about some of the kinds of precipitation. He asked Job where rain comes from when He said, "Hath the rain a father?" (Job 38:28). When we have one inch of rain over miles of farmland, that is more water than man can pump with his best irrigation system. Rain is worth thousands of dollars to the farmers, but they do not pay a penny for it. God sends the rain free.

If the clouds are freezing cold, the water comes out of the air as six-sided ice crystals. You know the name of this kind of precipitation. It is snow!

The snowflakes grow from tiny bits of ice into beautiful art patterns. The pattern for each snowflake is a result of the changes in the temperature of the air. Since no two flakes grow in the same temperature changes, no two flakes are alike. We marvel how anything so beautiful can be made high up in

Lesson 4

Concepts to Teach

- Precipitation is formed when humid air is cooled.
- Sleet is frozen rain.
- Hail is formed very high in thunderheads.
- Dew and frost are formed at night when humid air is cooled by the ground.
- Snow and frost are formed below freezing.

Introducing the Lesson

Although the water cycle is not part of this unit of study, you could review the water cycle as an introduction to this lesson on precipitation. The water cycle was studied in *God's Protected World, Science Three,* pages 23–27. God wisely planned that the water of the earth is distributed and purified through the process of evaporation, wind, and condensation in some form of precipitation. We depend on the rain. Even an arid land like Nevada depends on the rain and snow that falls in the mountains. The rivers supply the valuable water for irrigation. Without water, vegetation cannot grow. Without vegetation, people cannot live.

Sometimes children complain about a rainy day that hinders their outdoor play at recess. We should rejoice in precipitation. Even a rain in winter is helping to build up the water table that gives valuable ground water for the summer.

Use the Bible stories of hail in Exodus 9:23–35 and Joshua 10:8–11 to introduce this unusual kind of precipitation. Point out that God is in control of the patterns of weather. "The LORD hath his way in the whirlwind and in the storm, and the clouds are the dust of his feet" (Nahum 1:3).

Photographs of snowflakes: artwork of God

the air even in the dark of night. God is the artist. He loves beauty and can make beauty that is better than what man can make.

God asked Job about snow: "Hast thou entered into the treasures of the snow?" (Job 38:22). Did you ever see snowflakes against your dark coat sleeve? Did you ever look at the flakes with a magnifying glass? If you do this, you are "entering into the treasures of the snow." But even if you examine snowflakes very closely, you will still not understand the way God makes water to freeze into such beautiful patterns.

Hail. God also asked Job a question about hail: "Hast thou seen the treasures of the hail?" (Job 38:22). ***Hail*** is a very unusual form of precipitation because it is balls of ice that drop in the warm summertime. A hailstone starts as an ice crystal or frozen raindrop high in a thunderhead where it is cold. As it falls, it touches cold raindrops, which quickly freeze onto it. The upward wind sweeps the ball of ice high up into the thunderhead again and again. Each time it falls, it meets more raindrops, adding more icy layers and getting bigger. Finally it becomes so heavy that it falls all the way to the ground.

Hailstones are often the size of peas, but sometimes they are as big as potatoes. The larger they are, the more damage they do to crops and buildings.

Did you know—

...that radar in weather stations can detect falling rain or snow over 200 miles (320 km) away?

...that some dry, tropical areas such as Lima, Peru, receive more dew than rain?

...that 6 inches (15 cm) of wet snow or 30 inches (75 cm) of dry snow can equal 1 inch (2½ cm) of rain.

Quiz

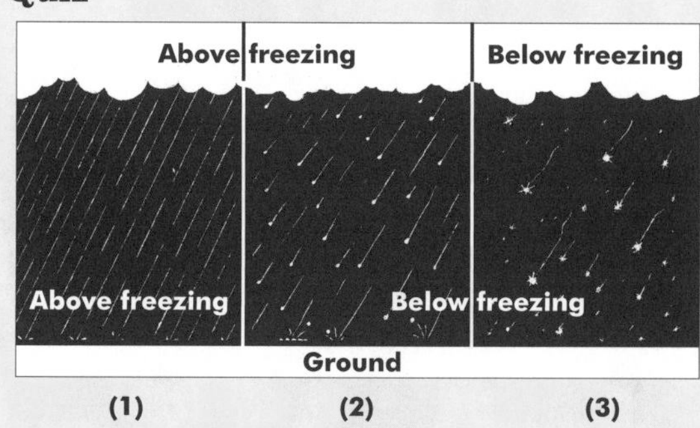

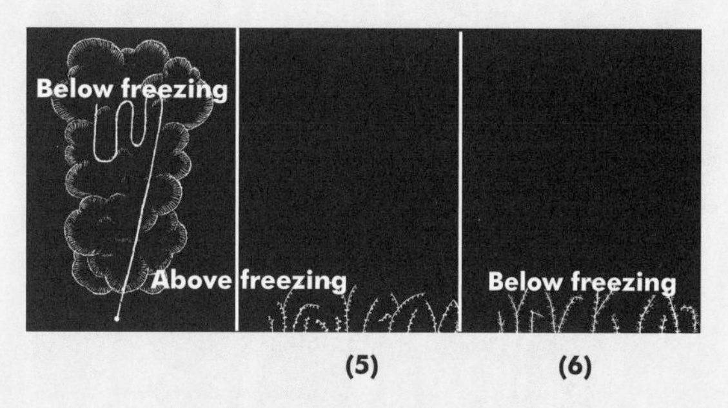

Draw clouds, and write *above freezing* or *below freezing* in the cloud or on the ground to illustrate what makes the different kinds of precipitation. Draw streaks, beads, or fuzz to represent rain, sleet, hail, frost, etc. Have the class guess each kind you illustrate.

1. *(rain)*
2. *(sleet)*
3. *(snow)*
4. *(hail)*
5. *(dew)*
6. *(frost)*

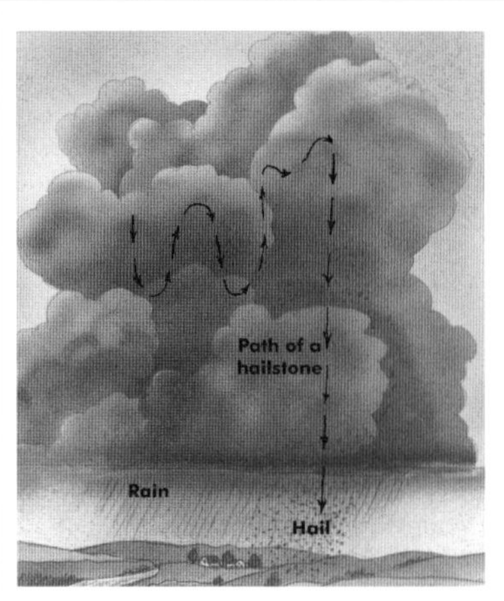

Hail is formed by traveling up and down in a thunderhead.

Nighttime precipitation. God asked Job about two more kinds of precipitation: "Who hath begotten the drops of dew?... and the hoary frost of heaven, who hath gendered it?" (Job 38:28, 29). Both ***dew*** and ***frost*** are kinds of precipitation that happen at night. Both happen on the ground. Two things must be true to have dew or frost. The air must be humid, and the ground must be cold.

At night the ground loses heat and becomes cold. If it becomes cold enough and the air is humid enough, water will come out of the air and make beads of water on the grass. You have seen water come out of the air onto the side of a cold glass of water on a humid day.

If the ground is below freezing, the water comes out of the air as frost. The frost gives the outdoors a fuzzy coat of ice crystals. It paints feathery swirls and lacy designs on our windows.

We need precipitation. Again and again these kinds of precipitation bring water to thirsty plants, animals, and people. We need the water for drinking and cleaning. How glad we should be for God's wise plan for the earth! By His wisdom He keeps the water moving from sea to land and then back again for our good.

Test Your Reading

For each sentence, write *rain, sleet, snow, hail, dew,* or *frost.* The number after each sentence will show you how many answers are needed.

1. It comes from clouds that are cold but not freezing. (1)
2. It is made of ice balls or crystals. (4)
3. It is made of beautiful, six-sided crystals. (1)
4. It is rain that freezes as it falls. (1)

Lesson 4 Answers

1. rain
2. sleet, snow, hail, frost
3. snow
4. sleet

5. It falls during thunderstorms. (2)
6. It is made of several layers of ice. (1)
7. It only forms during a cool night from humid air. (2)
8. It forms on ground that is freezing. (1)
9. It is a form of precipitation that waters the earth. (6)

Answer the following questions.

10. How are snowflakes formed?
11. How are hailstones formed?

Reviewing What You Have Learned

1. A place may have a polar climate because it is high above sea level or because it is far from ———.
2. Which of the following is true?
   a. Trade winds blow from the west.
   b. Cyclone winds blow from the north.
   c. Hurricane winds blow in a circle.
3. The ——— causes the wind to blow.
4. Clouds are formed when
   a. humid air is forced to rise.
   b. evaporation from the ocean makes the air humid.
   c. a front causes the humid air to mix with cold air.
5. True or false? When you see cumulus clouds, you know that it may rain before long.

Extra Activity

Keep working on the weather record. Start filling in the *Precipitation* section. If there is any precipitation, write *rain, sleet, snow, hail, dew,* or *frost.* You will need to check for dew or frost early in the morning. If it rains or snows, give the amount.

5. rain, hail
6. hail
7. dew, frost
8. frost
9. rain, sleet, snow, hail, dew, frost

(19 points thus far)

10. Snowflakes begin as tiny pieces of ice that grow into different patterns with the changes of temperature. (Answers may vary.)
11. Hailstones begin as ice crystals or frozen raindrops that grow as more water freezes on them. The hail travels up and down in the cloud, getting bigger and bigger, until they are too heavy to be blown back up. Then they fall to the ground. (Answers may vary.)

(21 points total)

Review Answers

1. the equator
2. c
3. sun
4. a
5. false

(5 additional points)

Lesson 5

Do You Remember?

Match each letter to the correct number.

1. A cloud on ground level
2. A layer of clouds
3. Wide, slowly rotating warm air that may bring rain
4. A climate without winter
5. The air around us
6. Frozen rain
7. Wide belts of wind
8. Strong winds in a wide circle
9. Water in the air

a. atmosphere
b. cyclone
c. fog
d. humid
e. hurricane
f. prevailing westerlies
g. sleet
h. stratus
i. tropical

From the word box, find and write the correct word for each blank.

arid	front	precipitation	thunderstorm
climate	frost	snowflakes	tornado
dew	hail	sundogs	weather
equator	mountain		

10. The ——— can be rainy, sunny, or windy.
11. Your ——— is the kind of weather you usually have each year.
12. A ——— can cause some land to have very little rain.
13. When there are cirrus clouds, you may see ———.
14. A ——— can do great damage in a narrow path.
15. Warm air meets cold air along a ———.
16. The tropical climate is close to the ———.
17. A desert would be found at a place where the climate is ———.
18. The dark cumulus clouds of a ——— are caused when warm air is pushed up.
19. The different patterns of ——— are made by differences of temperature.

Lesson 5 Answers

1. c
2. h
3. b
4. i
5. a
6. g
7. f
8. e
9. d
10. weather
11. climate
12. mountain
13. sundogs
14. tornado
15. front
16. equator
17. arid
18. thunderstorm
19. snowflakes

Lesson 5

Reviewing the Unit

As an inspirational overview of the unit, read the selections from Job 38 given in this teacher's manual on page 10. Before you begin, remind your students that this is God speaking to Job about His creation, the earth.

Review the unit as a class by paging through each lesson and noting the key points. Discuss the importance of each student also spending time individually in studying for the test.

20. On cool nights in the summer, ——— may form on the grass.
21. ——— will not form unless the ground is freezing.
22. During thunderstorms, sometimes icy ——— falls to the ground.
23. Rain, sleet, and frost are forms of ———.

Choose the best answer to finish each sentence.

24. Weather can be predicted because
    a. we have the same weather year after year.
    b. the weather is controlled by the laws of God.
    c. the Bible gives us weather signs.
25. The wind blows because
    a. the sun heats the air more at some places than at others.
    b. the air is more humid over the land than over the ocean.
    c. the air is cooled as it rises.
26. Winds that blow from the east next to each side of the equator are
    a. trade winds.
    b. prevailing westerlies.
    c. cyclones.
27. When warm air meets cold air,
    a. the warm air goes under the cold air.
    b. the warm air goes above the cold air.
    c. the cold air goes around the warm air.
28. Clouds form and rain falls when
    a. a cold air mass becomes warmer.
    b. ocean water evaporates.
    c. humid air is raised and cooled.
29. Cumulus clouds look like
    a. piles of whipped cream.
    b. long, sweeping feathers.
    c. layers of blankets.
30. A steady rain comes from
    a. cumulus clouds.
    b. stratus clouds.
    c. cirrus clouds.

20. dew
21. Frost
22. hail
23. precipitation

24. b
25. a
26. a
27. b
28. c
29. a
30. b

31. b
32. c

31. We can tell that a cyclone is coming when
    a. the air cools off.
    b. the wind's direction changes from the usual.
    c. there is a fog in the early morning.
32. Cirrus clouds are a good
    a. source of snow.
    b. beginning for a thunderhead.
    c. sign that rain may be coming in a few days.

33. false
34. true
35. false
36. true
37. true
38. true
39. false
40. false

Write *true* if the sentence is true; write *false* if it is not true.

33. God asked Moses many questions about the weather.
34. God uses storms to show us His greatness and to test our faith.
35. Because the earth rotates on its axis, the winds blow mainly north and south.
36. The winds follow the same paths around the earth year after year.
37. We receive precipitation according to God's laws for weather.
38. When warm air is pushed up, dark cumulus clouds may be formed.
39. Stratus clouds cause a ring around the moon.
40. Snow is made when raindrops fall through freezing air.

41. cirrus clouds
42. fog

Label the pictures with these words: *cumulus clouds, thunderhead, cirrus clouds, fog,* or *stratus clouds.*

41. 

42. 

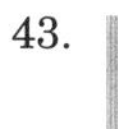

43.

44.

45.

43. cumulus clouds
44. stratus clouds
45. thunderhead

Answer these questions.

46–49. What four things make the kind of climate a land has?

50. What wind belt blows over the United States most of the time?

46–49. the distance from the equator; the distance from the ocean; the height above sea level; the land around you

50. prevailing westerlies

(50 points total)

Unit Two

God Created the Animals

"The LORD God formed every beast of the field, and every fowl of the air" (Genesis 2:19).

Are you glad God made butterflies, puppies, robins, and deer? Many people like these animals. They look pretty or are friendly. These animals are good and important animals.

Are you glad God made flies, spiders, snails, and worms? Some people do not like such animals because of how they look or crawl or feel. Yet these are also good and important animals.

All the animals are important. Each fits into God's wise plan. How are animals important to us? Animals eat plants or other animals. Later, they become food for other animals or people. Their dead bodies help make the soil richer. The rich soil feeds the plants that feed the animals and people.

Can you see the beauty of God's plan? The animals and plants work together on the earth. Each one does what God planned for it. But people do not always use animals and plants wisely. How does God want us to treat animals? God wants us to be kind to them. We may eat their meat and use their hides for shoes. We may kill insects that ruin our garden plants and bother us inside our houses. But we should not kill animals just for fun.

God cares about the animals. When an animal dies, God notices it. Jesus, the Son of God, said, "Are not two sparrows sold for a farthing? and one of them shall not fall on the ground without your Father" (Matthew 10:29).

Unit Two

For Your Inspiration

All Things Bright and Beautiful

All things bright and beautiful,
All creatures great and small,
All things wise and wonderful,
The Lord God made them all.

Each little flower that opens,
Each little bird that sings,
God made their glowing colors,
He made their tiny wings.

The purple-headed mountain,
The river running by,
The sunset, and the morning
That brightens up the sky:

The cold wind in the winter,
The pleasant summer sun,
The ripe fruits in the garden,
He made them every one:

He gave us eyes to see them,
And lips that we might tell
How great is God Almighty,
Who has made all things well.

—Cecil Frances Alexander

Lesson 1

Animals With Skeletons

New Words

backbone, the main bone of the back in animals and humans.

characteristic (kar′•ək•tə•ris′•tik), a special way a living thing is made or acts that is different from other living things.

exoskeleton (ek′•sō•skel′•i•tən), the tough shell or covering of insects and other animals.

skeleton (skel′•i•tən), the hard parts of an animal's body that protect and support the body.

vertebra (vėr′•tə•brə), one of the small bones that make up the backbone.

Animals in the Book of Job. God talked to Job about a very large animal. He said, "Behold now behemoth, which I made with thee. . . . His bones are as strong pieces of brass; his bones are like bars of iron" (Job 40:15, 18). God created large animals with strong bones to hold up their big bodies.

Many different animals are mentioned in the Book of Job. Sheep, camels, lions, peacocks, grasshoppers, and hawks are just a few of them. All of these have something in common except the grasshopper. Do you know how the grasshopper is different from the other animals?

Animals with skeletons. Animals have soft body parts such as the brain, heart, and stomach. Many animals also have hard body parts made of hard materials. All the hard body parts together make up the animal's ***skeleton.*** The hard skeleton protects the soft body parts from bumps and cuts. The skeleton also supports the body. The hard parts that support and protect many animals are bones. You have bones in your body that hold you up and protect your brain, heart, and other soft parts.

The skeletons of some animals are on the outside. The grasshopper does not have bones

Lesson 1

Concepts to Teach

- Skeletons protect soft body parts and give support.
- Some animals have external skeletons. Insects, spiders, centipedes, millipedes, lobsters, and crabs are in this group.
- Some animals have internal skeletons and backbones. Fish, amphibians, reptiles, birds, and mammals are in this group.
- The backbone is made of many vertebrae that have holes to protect the spinal cord.

Introducing the Lesson

Read the unit introduction together; then leaf through the unit. Meanwhile, have each student point out some animal or animal group in this unit that he thinks will be especially interesting to study. Some of this lesson will be review of the study of animals in *God's Protected World,* grade 3.

Remind the class that they were taught in the last unit that God created the air, land, and sea to work together in harmony. Likewise, in this unit they can see how God made the animals all work together to fulfill His plan for them. Each animal does the activities God designed for it, whether flying, swimming, creeping, digging, or even stinging. We should be thankful that God made animals a part of His plan for the earth.

A cicada skeleton. Some insects shed their old exoskeletons and grow new ones. You may have found these empty skeletons clinging to tree trunks.

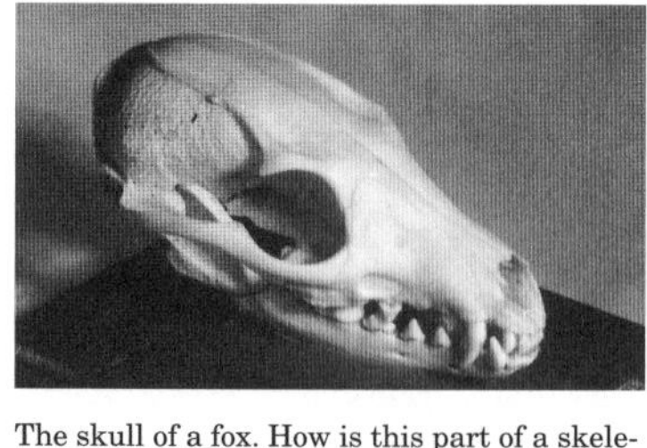

The skull of a fox. How is this part of a skeleton like the cicada shell? How is it different?

inside its body. Its skeleton is a hard shell on the outside. Such a skeleton is called an ***exoskeleton.*** The prefix *ex-* means "out" as in *exit.* Animals with exoskeletons do not have bones on the inside, but stiff, horny material on the outside. Now you know how the grasshopper is different from many other animals mentioned in the Book of Job. The grasshopper has an exoskeleton.

You often see animals with exoskeletons. They are in your back yard and even in your house. Flies, ants, butterflies, grasshoppers, and all other insects have exoskeletons. So do spiders, centipedes, and millipedes (sometimes called "hundred leggers" or "thousand leggers"). Some animals with exoskeletons, such as shrimp, crabs, and lobsters, live in the ocean. Their exoskeletons are thicker and tougher than those of insects and spiders.

Many common animals have skeletons inside their bodies. The inside skeletons allow these animals to be larger in size than animals with exoskeletons. An elephant can be almost 12 feet (4 meters) tall and weigh over 6 tons! Giant bones inside its body hold up this weight and allow the elephant to walk.

A very important part of an inside skeleton is the ***backbone.*** The backbone passes down the back of the animal's body. Like other bones, it helps to support the animal's body.

The backbone is not just one bone. It is made up of many little bones. Each one of these bones is a ***vertebra.*** The vertebrae give the back many joints that allow it to bend and turn. You use these joints when you stoop over and when you turn to see something behind you.

Did you know—

...that a shark's backbone is waxy cartilage instead of bone?

...that of a child's 33 vertebrae, 9 fuse together when he becomes an adult, leaving him with only 26 vertebrae?

...that the human skeleton has 206 bones, of which 60 are in the hands and arms?

Unit Project: Classifying Animals

Put these captions on a wall or bulletin board.

Animals With Bony Skeletons
Animals With Exoskeletons
Animals Without Skeletons

Divide the class into two or three teams and ask them to find pictures to put under each caption. Give examples of animals that would belong in each group. (For small animals such as insects or spiders, the real animals could be dried and mounted on thin cardboard.) Have one or more students be in charge of attaching a label to identify each animal or picture.

To motivate your students, you could decide that only one picture of each kind of animal will be accepted. You may also assign these point values: one point for each animal with a bony skeleton, two points for animals with exoskeletons, and three points for animals without skeletons. Each team could try to get the most points.

Quiz

Ask the children to write the correct New Word as you read each sentence below. Some will be used more than once.

1. It is the large bone made of many small bones. *(backbone)*
2. This supports a beetle's body. *(exoskeleton)*
3. It is one small bone of the many that protect the spinal cord. *(vertebra)*

Look at the picture of the vertebra. Do you see the vertebra shaped like a triangle? Do you see the hole in it? All vertebrae have holes in the center. The holes are in a line down the back. The animal's main cord of nerves, called the spinal cord, passes through the hole of each vertebra. God made the strong backbone to protect the soft spinal cord. God made the backbone strong to hold up the body. If a vertebra of the backbone is broken, it is very serious. The spinal cord may be cut, and the animal may not be able to move parts of the body below the break. The animal may die.

Skeletons are God's wise plan to support and protect the bodies of animals. For some animals, an exoskeleton is best. For other animals, it is best to have an inside skeleton with a backbone.

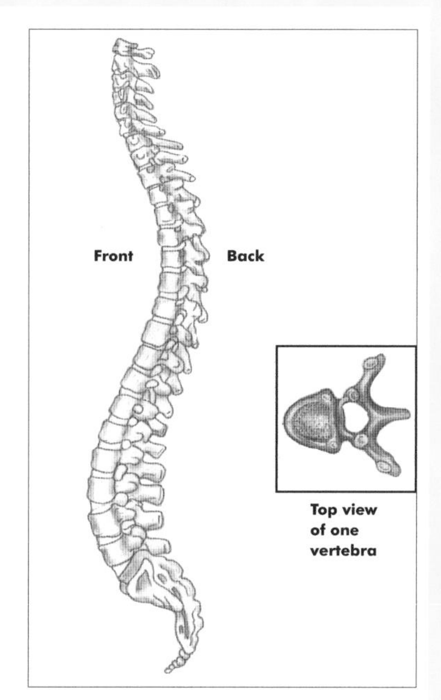

The human backbone is made up of 33 vertebrae that allow you to bend your body forward and turn it from side to side.

Test Your Reading (Group A)

Write the missing words.

1. An animal's skeleton is important for ——— and ———.
2. Flies, spiders, and crabs have ———, which means that their skeletons are on the outside of their bodies.
3. The skeletons on the inside of animals' bodies are made of hard parts called ———.
4. A backbone is made of many bones called ———.
5. The backbone is important to ——— the body and to ——— the spinal cord.

4. It is a hard, tough covering for animal bodies. *(exoskeleton)*
5. It is the main bone of the back of fish, alligators, and horses. *(backbone)*
6. It is the inner part of an animal's body that supports and protects it. *(skeleton)*
7. It is a special way that a living thing is made or acts that makes it different from other living things. *(characteristic)*

Lesson 1 Answers

Group A

1. protection, support (2 points)
2. exoskeletons
3. bones
4. vertebrae
5. support, protect (2 points)

6. bend (*and/or* turn)
7. The vertebrae have holes for the spinal cord to run through.
8. A broken back can cut the spinal cord so that the animal cannot use the body below the cut.

(10 points thus far)

Answer the following questions.

6. What do the many vertebrae of the backbone allow you to do?
7. How are the vertebrae made to protect the spinal cord?
8. Why is a broken back very serious?

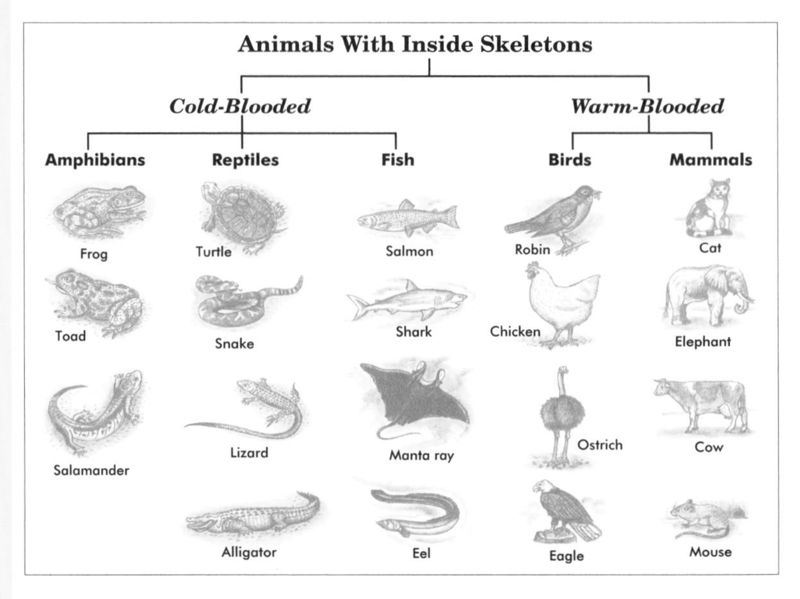

Animal groups. The animal group with inside skeletons is divided into several smaller groups: mammals, birds, reptiles, amphibians, and fish.

Last year you studied about amphibians, reptiles, and mammals. Can you still name some animals in each group? Could you put snakes, chipmunks, frogs, cows, and turtles in the right group? In this unit you will have a special study about birds and fish. But before we study those lessons, we shall review each of the other three groups of backbone animals. We divide the animals into groups by their special characteristics. A ***characteristic*** is the special way a living thing is made or acts that is different from other living things.

Amphibians. Frogs, toads, and

The Study of Animals in *God's World Science Series*

While this unit takes an overview of many kinds of animals, it especially deals with certain groups. The following list of groups of animals and where they are studied in this science series will help you to know which animals your students should have already studied and when they will study other groups. Unit Eight: "Life on the Earth" of *God's Orderly World, Book One* contains a survey of both plant and animal life. That study is intended for seventh or eighth grade.

Animal Group	Examples of Group	Grade and Unit in Series
Protozoa	amoeba, paramecium	not included
Porifera	sponge	Gr. 4, Unit 2, Lesson 5
Coelenterata	jellyfish, hydra, sea anemone	Gr. 4, Unit 2, Lesson 5
Platyhelminthes (flatworms)	planarian, tapeworm, trematode	Gr. 4, Unit 2, Lesson 5
Nemathelminthes (roundworms)	trichina, hookworm	not included
Annelida (segmented worms)	earthworm, leech	Gr. 4, Unit 2, Lesson 5
Echinodermata (spiny-skinned)	starfish, sea cucumber	Gr. 4, Unit 2, Lesson 5
Mollusca	snail, clam, oyster	Gr. 4, Unit 2, Lesson 4
Arthropoda	crayfish, insect, spider	Gr. 5, Unit 2
Aves	bird	Gr. 4, Unit 2, Lesson 2
Pisces	fish	Gr. 4, Unit 2, Lesson 3
Amphibia	frog, toad	Gr. 3, Unit 6, Lessons 2, 3
Reptilia	turtle, snake, alligator	Gr. 3, Unit 6, Lessons 4, 5
Mammalia	cat, cow, whale	Gr. 3, Unit 6, Lessons 6, 7

salamanders have the characteristics that put them in the animal group called amphibians. An amphibian lives part of its life in water and part of its life on land. In the tadpole part of a frog's life, it lives in the water. Then it loses its tail and grows legs and can live on land. All amphibians are cold-blooded. So when the water or air gets cold, the body of a frog gets cold too.

Reptiles. Reptiles are also cold-blooded. Their bodies are covered with plates or scales. Turtles are covered with horny plates. The bodies of snakes, lizards, and alligators are covered with scales. Scales and plates are characteristics of the reptile group of animals.

Mammals. All mammals drink their mothers' milk when they are babies. That is a characteristic of mammals. They have hair and are warm-blooded. *Warm-blooded* means that their body temperature is warm and will stay warm even if the surrounding air or water is cold. Mammals include dogs, cats, elephants, deer, bears, cows, monkeys, and mice.

All of these animals have skeletons inside their bodies. All of them have a backbone with a spinal cord going through it.

Man. God created man a special living thing in a group of his own. None of the animals were given a living soul. You are not an animal, but you do have an inside skeleton with a backbone. Your bones support and protect your body in the same way as those of backbone animals. Yet an animal does not know that God made it. It cannot choose to praise God. But you can!

Test Your Reading (Group B)

Use each animal on this list twice to match with the groups and characteristics.

cat   frog   grasshopper   snake

9. A reptile
10. An insect
11. A mammal
12. An amphibian
13. Feeds its babies milk
14. Lives some of its life in water and some on land
15. Covered with scales
16. Has an exoskeleton

Answer the following questions.

Group B

9. snake
10. grasshopper
11. cat
12. frog
13. cat
14. frog
15. snake
16. grasshopper

17. A warm-blooded animal has a body temperature that is warm and stays warm even if the air or water around it is cold.
18. You have a living soul. (*or* You can know that God made you. You can choose to praise God.) *(20 points total)*

Extra Activity Comments

1. Point out that when the student uses his hand inside the puppet, the hand is doing the work of a skeleton. Plan to use the puppets during science class (and perhaps recess). Then have them put away so the students are not tempted to disturb class or study time with them.
2. You may want to start a school collection of bones that can be studied year after year. Label each bone as to which animal it comes from and which bone it is.

   As a result of studying bones, the students should see that the bones are made to support the animal by being hard, not easily broken, and long.

17. What does being warm-blooded mean?
18. What characteristic do you have that makes you different from an animal?

Extra Activities

1. You can see for yourself why an animal's skeleton is important. You need an animal puppet that is large enough for you to put your hand inside. You also need a large balloon and some water.

   Fill the balloon about half full of water. Knot the opening so that the balloon is watertight. (You may need an adult to help you.) Then put the balloon inside the puppet. Try to make the animal sit or stand up. What happens? Now put your hand inside the animal puppet. Make it nod its head and move its legs. How is this different from having the balloon inside?

   Materials needed:
   - animal puppet
   - large balloon
   - water

2. Try to find a bone to study. Perhaps someone in the class can bring a chicken leg bone. Try to break it. Cut it with a saw. Examine it with a magnifying glass. Cut near the end of the bone and look for the spongy bone that protects the end of the bone. In what ways is the bone made to do its job of supporting the animal?
3. If you can find a grasshopper, examine its exoskeleton. Notice how the body and legs are covered with a hard layer. How is the exoskeleton made at the joints that allows it to bend?

Lesson 2

God Created Birds

New Words

beak, the bill of a bird.

down, soft, fluffy feathers that help birds stay warm.

gizzard (giz′·ərd), a part of the stomach that has strong muscles to crush food.

instinct (in′·stingkt′), a ready-made ability to do a difficult task without learning.

markings, colored patterns, such as stripes or patches, on birds.

perching, sitting on a high place such as a branch.

preen, to arrange or smooth the feathers with the beak.

quill, the long, stiff center tube of a feather.

streamlined, having a long, smooth shape that can move easily through air or water.

God made birds to fly. We admire birds because they can do something we cannot do. They can fly! "Doth the hawk fly by thy wisdom, and stretch her wings toward the south?" (Job 39:26). The flight of birds is a wonder of God's creation.

Why did God make birds to fly? God gave flight to birds in order to protect them from their enemies. Most birds are too small to fight with enemies, such as cats or foxes. They cannot run fast enough to get away, but they can fly away.

Most birds use flying to get their food. Hawks have very good eyesight and can drop out of the air very fast to catch mice or rabbits.

How can a bird fly? God designed a bird's body to be streamlined so that it can move easily through air. A ***streamlined*** shape is long, smooth, and somewhat pointed at each end. As a bird flies, the air flows easily over the streamlined shape without much resistance. Most birds also have lightweight bodies with many hollow bones. This

Lesson 2

Concepts to Teach

Emphasize the marvelous way God designed birds to fly.

- In order for a bird to fly, its body design has to be just right.
- The bones and quills of birds are strong but hollow, making the bird lightweight.
- The bird's body is streamlined, allowing it to glide easily through the air.
- Baby birds hatch from eggs laid in a nest.
- Nest building is an example of an instinct, a God-given ability to do a difficult task without learning.
- Down insulates the birds in cold weather.
- God gave birds special beaks and feet for their special needs. A bird uses its beak to gather food and its gizzard to grind the food.
- A bird can sleep while perching on a branch.
- Birds preen their feathers, and some oil them to make them waterproof.
- We identify birds by their markings.
- We appreciate birds for their singing and for the insects and weed seeds they eat.

Introducing the Lesson

Discuss some of these old sayings.

"A little bird told me." (See Ecclesiastes 10:20.)

"Birds of a feather flock together."

"A bird in the hand is worth two in the bush."

"It was like water running off a duck's back."

Point out that some sayings in relation to birds may not be correct. For example, someone who hardly eats enough is said to "eat like a bird." A bird might not seem to eat much, but it eats a lot

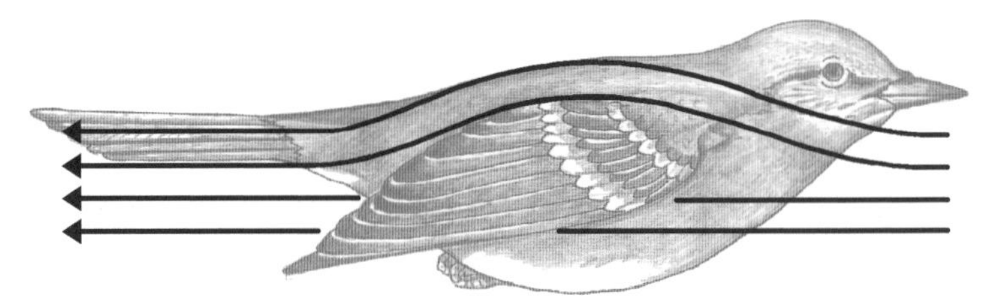

The streamlined shape of the bird's body helps it to move easily through the air.

makes their skeletons light and yet strong enough to support and protect them.

God gave birds strong wings and long feathers. Each feather is made stiff by a strong, hollow center tube called a ***quill.*** The branches coming out from the quill have barbs that hook the branches together to form a flat surface. With a microscope, you can examine this marvelous design. No bird could fly without long feathers with smooth surfaces and stiff quills.

In order to get off the ground, a bird must beat its wings rapidly. A small bird keeps beating its wings as it flies, but some larger birds, such as eagles, fly without much beating of the wings. They do this by riding on strong, steady winds high in the sky.

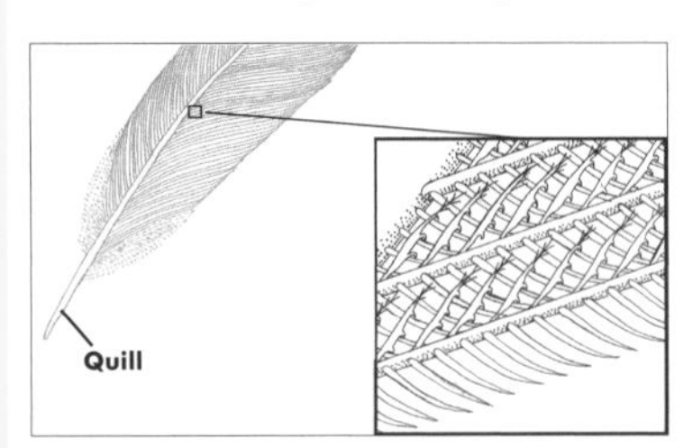

The design of a feather shows the wisdom of God.

Men have copied the birds to make airplanes. Highly educated men spend hours designing a new airplane. Many experiments are done to test out new ideas. Millions of dollars are needed to design and make airplanes. In many ways, an airplane is like a bird. Both have wings. Both have streamlined bodies. Both can take off from the ground and land. But compared to a bird, an airplane is clumsy and wastes fuel. An airplane cannot change direction as quickly as a bird. An airplane cannot take off and land as easily. An airplane is dead; a bird is alive. Men design airplanes, but God designed birds.

for its size. In fact, many birds eat their weight in food each day. They need so much food because of the great amounts of energy used to stay warm and to fly.

Did you know—

...that a bird may have up to 25,000 feathers?

...that the smallest bird, the bee hummingbird, measures 2 inches (5 cm) long, weighs 1/10 ounce (3 g), and builds a nest the size of a half walnut shell?

...that the ostrich is both the largest and the fastest-running bird? It may grow 8 feet (2½ m) tall, weigh 300 pounds (135 kg), and run 40 mph (65 kmph).

...that common swifts and canvasback ducks can fly 70 mph (110 kmph), and that duck hawks and golden eagles dive at speeds of 180 mph (290 kmph)?

Illustrating Wing Movements

To give the students some understanding of the wing movements of birds, have them practice with their hands. Tell them to pretend to be birds, pushing the air downward with their hands for wings. Show them with your own hands, having your fingers held together on the downstroke but spread apart on the upstroke. Have them start slowly and build up speed to imitate flying. This shows the children one reason why birds eat so much food: they spend such great amounts of energy beating their wings.

As the children are beating their hands up and down, ask, "Can you feel much air moving around your hands?" Of course, they are not likely to feel much movement. Explain that their hands are too different from wings.

Who designed each? Which has the best design?

Birds hatch from eggs. Have you ever watched a baby chick or duck hatching from an egg? First, you see a few cracks in the shell. You hear a soft tapping from inside the shell. The cracks grow larger as the baby bird keeps pecking away. Finally the egg splits apart, and the baby chick or duck struggles out into its bright new world.

All baby birds hatch from eggs. Usually the eggs are laid in a nest. God made each kind of bird to build its own special nest just the right size and shape. The ability to do a difficult task without learning is called an ***instinct.*** God gives animals various instincts. A robin has an instinct to make a good robin nest the first time it tries. It does not need to see a robin nest to make one. How God makes instincts to work is still His secret. It is a miracle to us. God reminded Job of these facts when He asked, "Doth the eagle mount up at thy command, and make her nest on high?" (Job 39:27).

A robin's nest

How do birds grow and live? When they are hatched, chicks, ducks, and many other baby birds have soft, fluffy feathers called ***down*** over their bodies. The down helps them stay warm. As they

Now ask some students to stand a few feet away as you rapidly wave cardboard up and down. Can they hear and feel air movement? Explain that the cardboard is working somewhat like a bird's wings, and that it can push more air than their hands can.

Materials needed:

- 2 pieces of 6″ x 12″ cardboard

Writing About Birds of the Bible

Using the section "Birds of the Bible" in a Bible dictionary, assign a bird to each student as a writing assignment. Or assign two birds if they are not mentioned often in the Bible.

Have the students look up their birds in the Bible, a dictionary, and an encyclopedia. Their essays can be fastened together to make a booklet for all to read, or the students can read their essays to the class.

Quiz

Ask the children to write the correct New Word as you read each sentence below.

1. A bird has this in each feather to keep it stiff. *(quill)*
2. We look at these to see what kind of bird it is. *(markings)*
3. This kind of shape moves easily through air or water. *(streamlined)*
4. A bird picks up its food with this. *(beak)*
5. Many birds do this to rest on a branch or wire. *(perch)*
6. This part of a bird does the same work our teeth do. *(gizzard)*
7. A bird needs this to stay warm during the winter. *(down)*
8. A bird does this to smooth its feathers. *(preen)*
9. A bird has this to be able to make a nest. *(instinct)*

grow older, they grow quill feathers so they can fly. But they still have down close to their bodies to keep them warm. Birds are warm-blooded. In fact, birds have a higher body temperature than you do. The human body temperature is 98.6°F (37°C); birds have a body temperature from 101° to 112°F (38° to 44°C). You would be sick if your temperature was that high.

Birds use their ***beaks*** to gather their food. Woodpeckers have pointed beaks for drilling holes in trees to find insects. Sparrows have short, strong beaks for cracking seeds. Ducks have broad beaks called bills for gathering plants and insects for food from water. Birds do not have teeth to chew their food as we do. So God gave them special stomachs called ***gizzards.*** The birds swallow small stones for the strong muscles in their gizzards to use to grind their food. Birds that eat seeds have gizzards strong enough to crush seeds. God gave the birds everything they need.

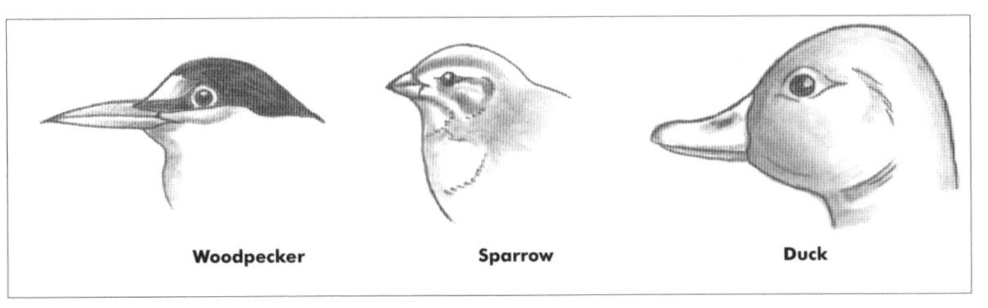

Why do these beaks have different shapes?

Lesson 2 Answers

Group A

1. d
2. g
3. f
4. h
5. b
6. e
7. a
8. c

Test Your Reading (Group A)

Find the correct ending that completes each sentence.

1. God gave birds wings and feathers
2. God gave birds hollow bones
3. God gave birds streamlined bodies
4. God gave birds the instinct
5. God gave birds down
6. God gave birds quills
7. God gave birds gizzards
8. God gave the birds beaks

a. to grind their food.
b. to keep warm.
c. to gather their food.
d. to fly.
e. to have stiff, light feathers.
f. to glide through the air.
g. to be lightweight.
h. to build nests for their eggs.

Write the correct answers.

9. What makes the flat, smooth surface of the feather?
10. What is an instinct?
11. How does a baby bird hatch, or come out of its egg?
12. Give an example of how God gave a bird a special beak for a special use.

Feet are for sleeping and swimming. Of course, birds walk on their feet. But just as God gave special beaks to the birds, so He also gave them special feet. For example, God gave the chicken special feet for ***perching.*** Its feet have three toes in front and one behind. These feet can lock around a branch. The chicken can even go to sleep up in a tree away from danger while its toes are locked around a branch. Many other common birds, such as robins, cardinals, and blackbirds, are also perching birds.

Woodpeckers cling onto the sides of trees while they peck the bark for insects. God gave them feet with two toes in front and two behind. Each toe has a sharp claw for fastening into the tree. Owls also have sharp claws. They use their claws for holding mice and other small animals that they catch.

God designed the duck's feet for water. He made them with webs between the toes for swimming. They are like small paddles that help the duck swim across streams and ponds.

Feathers for floating. Birds use their beaks for smoothing their feathers. This is called ***preening.*** Ducks not only preen their feathers, but they also add oil. The oil is produced by an oil gland near the tail. A duck smoothes the oil over its feathers with its beak. Water will not stick to oil, so it keeps the duck dry and allows it to float for hours

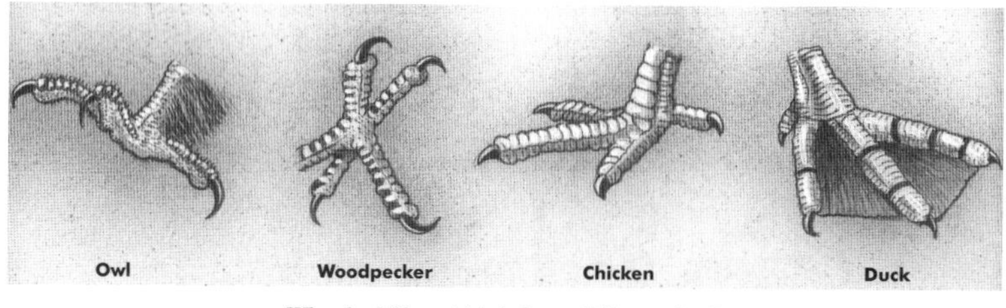

Why do different birds have different feet?

9. The branches of the feather have barbs that hook into each other.
10. An instinct is the God-given ability to do a difficult task without learning.
11. The baby bird pecks the inside of the egg until it cracks the shell and splits it apart. Then it crawls out.
12. (Any of the following.)
    Sparrows have short beaks to crack seeds.
    Woodpeckers have pointed beaks to drill holes in trees to find insects.
    Ducks have broad beaks to gather food from water.

    Examples not given in text:
    Herons have long, pointed beaks for catching fish.
    Flamingos have big bills with "combs" for straining mud out of food it gets from water.

(12 points thus far)

without water soaking the feathers. A duck must keep adding oil to its shiny raincoat to keep it watertight.

Birds are interesting creatures. They lay eggs, fly, swim, perch, preen, and sing. They are beautifully designed and colored. No wonder many people have a hobby of bird watching.

Bird watching. Do you like to hear birds singing? Can you tell the kind of bird by its songs? Can you identify a bird by its ***markings,*** or patterns of color? Do you notice the shape of the tail and beak? Do you know which birds swoop as they fly and which soar high overhead? If so, you make a good bird watcher. Who does not look up to see the V-shaped pattern of a flock of geese, honking as they fly north or south?

One good way to watch birds is to feed them. They need food especially in the wintertime when plants are not growing. You can put sunflower seeds and bread crumbs in a bird feeder. Hang the feeder on a bush or tree that is near your house. That way you can watch birds close up.

Birds eating sunflower seeds

Birds tend to be very excitable. A little noise or movement will send them flying away. A bird watcher needs patience. Often he uses a binocular to be able to get a good look at the markings of a bird that is at a distance.

A bird book is helpful to the bird watcher. Whenever you see a bird that is new to you, notice the bird's markings. Try to remember the shape of its head, body, and tail. Then find the same bird in a bird book to learn its name.

The farmer's friend. Sometimes when birds are eating our peas or cherries, we wish they would go away. But on the whole, birds help the farmer and gardener. They eat harmful insects and weed seeds. One bird might eat dozens of insects or thousands of weed seeds in a single day.

We have many reasons to thank God for the birds. We like birds because they sing. They are colorful and interesting to watch. They are helpful to gardens and farms. They call our attention to the wise God who made them.

Test Your Reading (Group B)

Copy and complete the following chart about birds' feet. The first one is done for you.

	Description of Feet	Special Use for Feet
Robin	*three toes in front, one behind*	*perching*
13. Woodpecker	a. ———	b. ———
14. Owl	a. ———	b. ———
15. Duck	a. ———	b. ———

Choose the best answer.

16. A duck can float on water because
    a. it can paddle with its feet to get it up.
    b. oil on the feathers keeps out the water.
    c. the bottom of the duck's body is very light.
17. If you saw a duck preening, you would see it
    a. rubbing its feathers with its beak.
    b. moving its feet over its feathers.
    c. fluffing its feathers by flapping its wings.
18. A good way to attract birds to your house is to
    a. plant pretty flowers around the house.
    b. keep bird feed in a bird feeder.
    c. wait patiently under a tree.
19. If you want to identify a strange bird you saw,
    a. you need a binocular.
    b. you need some bird food.
    c. you need a bird book.
20. A farmer can be glad if blackbirds are in his field as he disks it because
    a. then they can get close enough for him to shoot them.
    b. he knows that he will have less problem with insects.
    c. they give him something interesting to watch while he works.

Group B

13. a. two toes in front, two behind, with claws
    b. clinging onto the side of a tree while pecking for insects
14. a. claws on its toes
    b. holding mice and other small animals it catches for food
15. a. webs between the toes
    b. paddling to swim in water

16. b
17. a
18. b
19. c
20. b

(23 points total)

Review Answers

1. a
2. protect
3. vertebrae
4. b
5. a

(5 additional points)

Extra Activity Comments

2. Your students may also enjoy working toward the goal of collectively sighting 30, 50, or 100 different birds during this school year. You could discuss which goal is reasonable for your class. (It depends on the size and motivation of your class and the number of different birds in your environment.) Perhaps you could reward them with a nature hike when the goal is reached.

Reviewing What You Have Learned

1. The backbone is part of the
   a. skeleton. b. exoskeleton. c. spinal cord.
2. Skeletons ——— the soft parts of animals.
3. The small bones that protect an animal's spinal cord are called ———.
4. Which group of animals all have external skeletons?
   a. amphibians, reptiles, birds
   b. crabs, centipedes, insects
   c. mammals, millipedes, spiders
5. Which group of animals all have backbones?
   a. amphibians, reptiles, birds
   b. crabs, centipedes, insects
   c. mammals, millipedes, spiders

Extra Activities

1. Use a bird book or an encyclopedia to study the different kinds of bird feet and bills. Find out how each bird is designed for getting a certain kind of food.
2. Keep a class record of the birds you see this year. Write a list of birds commonly seen in your area down the left side of a paper with lines. Leave room below the list for additional birds. You and your classmates can sign your initials the first time you see that kind of bird.
3. Try writing with a quill as people did long ago before there were pencils and ballpoint pens. You need a bottle of ink and a stiff feather. Ask an adult to sharpen the feather to a point with a knife. Now dip the tip of the quill into the ink and try to finish a lesson assignment.

   Materials needed:
   - bottle of ink
   - stiff feather
   - knife
4. Look at feathers with a microscope. Pull some of the branches apart so that you can see the barbs that hold the branches together to form a clothlike covering. Notice the order and beauty God has used in making feathers.

Lesson 3

God Created Fish

New Words

air bladder, a small sack of air inside a fish's body.

fins, the fanlike body parts of a fish, which it uses to swim.

gills, the body part with which a fish breathes underwater.

scales, the many small, tough plates covering the body of a fish.

Fish live all their lives in water. They do not have legs to walk on the land. They do not have wings to fly in the air. God did not make them to live on land or in the air. In many ways, we can see how they are designed to live in water.

Fish swim. Did you ever see a fish swish its tail? Perhaps you watched a goldfish in an aquarium. The fish wags its tail in order to swim. Strong muscles in the sides of the fish move the tail back and forth. The wagging tail pushes the fish forward through the water. Fish can move quickly through the water. A goldfish can go 4 miles (6 kilometers) per hour. That is fast for such a small animal. Some fish can go 30 miles (50 kilometers) per hour.

A fish swims fast for two reasons. First, it must catch its own food. It might be after a worm or a smaller fish. Second, a fish swims fast to escape its enemies. Big water birds, bigger fish, or fishermen may be looking for some good fish for food.

Do you wonder why fish have so many enemies? Both people and animals like to eat fish. God planned that we may eat fish to get some of the materials our bodies need for good health. Some of Jesus' disciples were fishermen. Fishing is still an important occupation for many people who supply us with this healthful food.

Fish can swim fast because God designed their bodies to move easily through the water. Most fish are covered with many thin, hard ***scales.*** The scales provide a smooth

Lesson 3

Concepts to Teach

- A fish pushes itself through water by moving its tail back and forth.
- Fish are a good and healthful food.
- The body surface of most fish is protected with tough, smooth scales and a slippery coating.
- A fish glides easily through water because its body is streamlined.
- Fins help to guide the fish as it swims and to keep its balance.
- A fish uses its air bladder to float at different levels.
- A fish uses its gills to get oxygen from the water.

Introducing the Lesson

Watching live fish is an excellent way to create interest in this lesson. Starting an aquarium at school is one of the suggested activities in the pupil's book. You may want to let the students help set up one for your class, or you may want to introduce the lesson with an actual fish observation.

Perhaps you could ask a student beforehand to bring a fish in a jar of water from his aquarium at home. (Take care not to cover the jar longer than necessary for moving it.) You may use a large picture of a fish if no live ones are available.

Ask the students if they can identify any body parts, such as the head, tail, fins, and gill openings. Point out how the body scales overlap like roof shingles.

body surface just right for swimming. They are tough enough to protect the fish from cuts and scrapes.

A slippery liquid comes out between the fish's scales. It forms a coating all over the fish's body. This slippery coating allows a fish to glide smoothly through the water. The fish's enemies must work hard to hold such a slippery body.

Streamlined fish. Another important part of God's design for a fish is its streamlined shape. The pointed head, sleek body, and thin tail help the fish glide through the water. The water easily flows around the fish. Fish are streamlined to swim easily through the water just as birds are streamlined to fly easily through the air. Today man copies God's art of streamlining in making boats and ships. Airplanes and cars are streamlined for fast travel through the air. Without their streamlined shape, these vehicles would use more fuel because they would have to push harder. You know how hard it is to ride against the wind on a bicycle. If you lower your head to make yourself more streamlined, it is easier to ride against the wind.

Fish have ***fins*** to help them swim. Most fins have a fanlike shape with skin stretched over thin bones. The fin on the end of the tail helps give the fish speed. This tail fin is also used in steering. Fins on the top and bottom help the fish to keep balanced so that it stays right side up. A pair of fins on the side are used to steer and stop.

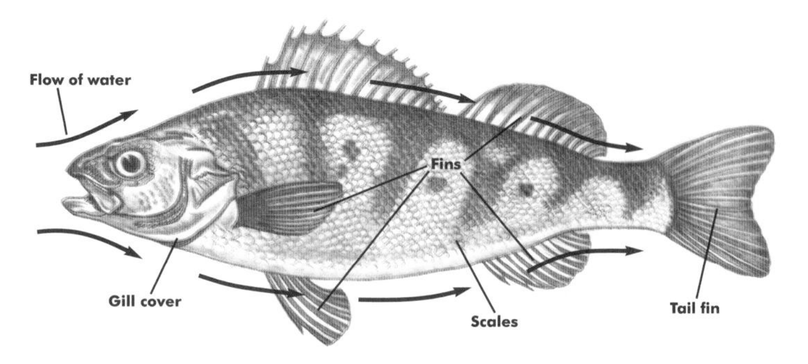

The body of a fish, the handiwork of God

With a live fish, call attention to the wagging tail that propels the fish. Also notice that the mouth continually opens and closes. If the students wonder why, tell them they will find the answer as they study the lesson. Point out that the eyes stay open because a fish has no eyelids.

Can the fish smell and hear? Yes, it depends greatly on its sense of smell. A fish smells with an internal organ connected to nostril pits near its upper lip. It hears with organs inside its head. Many fish also have a line of sensitive scales along each side of their bodies that is sensitive to low-frequency vibrations, such as footsteps.

Materials needed:

- live fish in a jar of water
- large picture of a fish

Did you know—

...that newborn fish are called fry?

...that the bladderwort plant traps and digests fish?

...that the largest fishing nets are almost a mile (1,600 m) long and 600 feet (180 m) deep?

...that a flying fish can glide 150–1000 feet (45–300 m) through the air, using its strong tail and large side fins?

Class Project

You may want to remind the students about the use of fish for food by serving some fish at lunchtime. You could prepare some tuna salad or fried fish cakes. You could also buy a whole fish at a supermarket and study the features of the fish while preparing it for frying. The students could then feel the slippery scales and the fins. Perhaps you could find the air bladder for them.

Test Your Reading (Group A)

Write the missing words.

1. The fish pushes itself forward with its ———.
2. Fish have many enemies because they are good ———.
3. It is good that fish can swim fast so that they can get their ———.
4. The hard cover of ——— makes the outside of the fish smooth and protects the skin of the fish.
5. The outside of the fish is made ——— by a material that comes out between the fish's scales.
6. The ——— shape of the fish helps it glide easily through the water.
7. Most fins have ——— stretched over thin ———.
8. The fins on the top and bottom of the fish help the fish keep its ———.
9. If a fish wants to stop, it can put out its side ———.

More ways God made fish to live in the water. In water, objects usually sink to the bottom or float to the surface. A swimming fish does not want to do either of these things. To be able to stay in the middle of the water, its weight and size must be just right. God gave most fish an ***air bladder,*** a sack of air inside its body. The air bladder is used to adjust the size of the body so that it does not sink or float.

As the fish goes deeper, the pressure of the water increases. More air must be added to the air bladder to keep up the size of the fish. This air is added by the blood. If the pressure would not increase in the air bladder, the

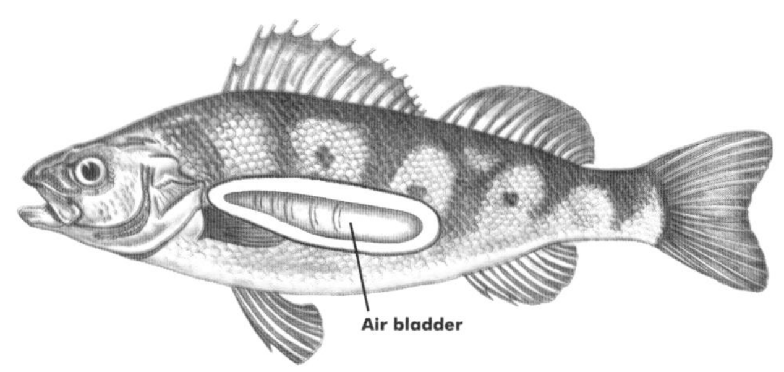

The size and location of the air bladder

Quiz

Ask the children to write the correct New Words as you read each sentence below. Some will be used more than once.

1. A fish needs these to breathe. *(gills)*
2. A fish's body is protected with many of these smooth, little plates. *(scales)*
3. A fish uses this when it rises or sinks in the water, to stay at a certain depth. *(air bladder)*
4. A fish uses several of these to turn, stop, and keep its balance. *(fins)*
5. These two are outside the fish's body. *(fins, scales)*
6. These two are inside the fish's body. *(air bladder, gills)*

Lesson 3 Answers

Group A

1. tail
2. food
3. food
4. scales
5. slippery
6. streamlined
7. skin, bones (2 points)
8. balance
9. fins

(10 points thus far)

water pressure would squeeze the body of the fish and make it sink to the bottom. God made the body of the fish to make changes in the air bladder without thinking, just as you do not need to think to make your heart beat. Everywhere we look in the natural world, we see the wisdom of God. One of those wonders is the air bladder of a fish.

How does a fish "breathe"? Man and animals need oxygen to live. You get oxygen from the air when you breathe. Your lungs take oxygen from the air and put it in the blood. But a fish does not rise to the water surface for air. If a fish is taken out of the water, it will soon die.

Instead of breathing air, fish get their oxygen from the water. That is why air is bubbled into fish aquariums. The oxygen of the air goes into the water so that the fish can breathe. A fish breathes by opening and closing its mouth. It takes in water through its mouth and forces it through its ***gills.*** The water then goes out through the gill openings found on each side of its head.

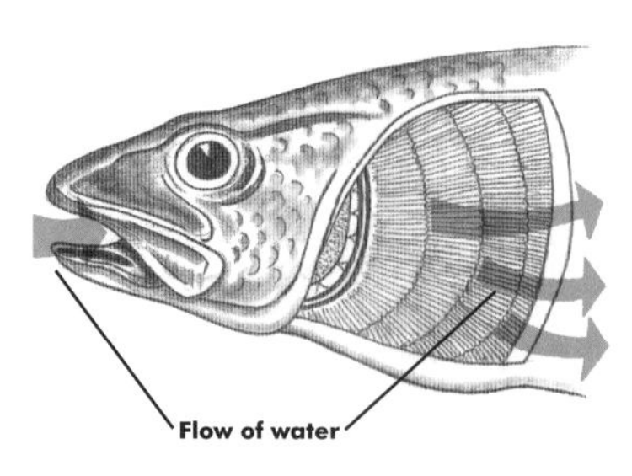

Fish breathe with gills.

The gills are made of several layers of threadlike fingers. Each tiny finger has blood flowing through it. This gives much surface for the oxygen in the water to get into the blood. This oxygen then circles throughout the fish's body where it is needed. The gills continually take oxygen from the water, just as your lungs take oxygen from the air. Gill-breathing is just as normal to a fish as lung-breathing is to you.

Because fish use up the oxygen in the water, oxygen must be replaced in the water of an aquarium, or the water must be changed often. One way of replacing the oxygen is to bubble air into the water from an air pump. Another way is to have many green water plants growing in the aquarium. As green plants grow in light, they give off oxygen. The oxygen from the green plants is just what the fish need to breathe.

Fish are cold-blooded animals. The body temperature of a fish becomes the same as the water it lives in. That way it does not need a layer of insulating fur or down to keep it warm. A layer of insulation would make its body fat and harder to move through the water. The thin, streamlined body of the fish is just right for swimming in water. If fish were warm-blooded, they would need to eat more food to make the extra heat.

God was able to make warm-blooded sea animals. The whale is warm-blooded, but then it is very large. It has a thick layer of fat that is insulation for its body. A whale is not a fish. It is a mammal that breathes air. That is why a whale must come to the surface of the water to breathe. It has a hole on the top of its body so that it does not need to come out of the water very far to breathe. The whale has everything it needs to stay alive. A fish has everything it needs to stay alive. Both were made by God.

The more we study fish, the more we see that they were designed by Someone much wiser than man. Job must have known this because he said, "The fishes of the sea shall declare unto thee. Who knoweth not in all these that the hand of the LORD hath wrought [made] this?" (Job 12:8, 9).

Test Your Reading (Group B)

Read each sentence below. Write *true* if the statement is true. Write *false* if the statement is false.

10. A fish stores oxygen for breathing in its air bladder.
11. The pressure in the air bladder changes because of changes in the depth of the fish.
12. Air is bubbled into an aquarium to supply air for the fish's air bladder.
13. The gills do the same thing for a fish that lungs do for you.
14. The gills are made of many flat, platelike fins.
15. Putting green plants in an aquarium helps the fish get oxygen.
16. Being cold-blooded allows the fish to have a thin body.
17. The whale is a very large, warm-blooded fish.

Group B

10. false
11. true
12. false
13. true
14. false
15. true
16. true
17. false

(18 points total)

Review Answers

1. true
2. preens
3. c
4. gizzard
5. a

(5 additional points)

Reviewing What You Have Learned

1. True or false? A skeleton gives an animal its support.
2. A bird ——— its feathers when it smoothes them with its beak.
3. God designed birds to fly by giving them
   a. fluffy down.
   b. feet that can perch.
   c. hollow bones and quills.
4. A ——— takes the place of teeth in a bird.
5. A good bird watcher
   a. carefully looks for a bird's markings.
   b. carefully counts the insects a bird eats.
   c. carefully watches a bird preening its feathers.

Extra Activities

1. Find "Fish" in an encyclopedia or get a library book about fishes. Try to find as many pictures of different kinds of fish as you can. Then compare the pictures. In what ways are all fishes alike? In what ways are they different?

   Now read your encyclopedia article or library book. What are some new things you learned? Tell or write about them.
2. A fish aquarium is an interesting way to learn about fish. Perhaps you could borrow an aquarium and some tropical fish for your classroom. Learn how to feed them. Do not overfeed the fish. You will need an air pump to supply oxygen for the water. Why? If you do not supply oxygen with an air pump, you will need to change the water every few days. Putting green water plants in the aquarium will help to supply the needed oxygen. You will need to keep the water clean for the fish.

   Read in an encyclopedia or pet book how to best care for tropical fish.

Lesson 4

God Created Mollusks

New Words

clam, a water mollusk with a two-part shell and a hatchet-shaped foot.

mollusks (mol′•əsks), a group of animals with soft bodies, many of which are protected by shells.

octopus (ok′•tə•pəs), a sea mollusk having eight arms with sucking pads.

oyster (oi′•stər), a mollusk that makes pearls and has a rough, two-part shell.

slug, a common garden mollusk without a shell.

snail, a land or water mollusk with a spiral shell and a wide foot.

Animals with no skeletons. In Lesson 1 of this unit, you learned that some animals have skeletons inside their bodies and some have exoskeletons. You have already studied birds and fish, which have skeletons and backbones. Now we shall study animals that have no skeletons at all. The ***mollusks*** are a group of such animals.

Do you remember seeing a snail with its round shell, moving slowly across the ground and leaving a slippery trail? A ***snail*** is an example of a mollusk.

The mollusks have soft, moist bodies. Most of them live in the water. How does God protect them from hungry enemies? A few kinds of mollusks can swim fast like a fish, and a few can sting their enemies

One-part shells were beautifully designed by God.

Lesson 4

Concepts to Teach

- God in wisdom provided hard shells for many of the mollusks with soft bodies.
- Most mollusks have either one-part or two-part shells.
- The order and beauty of shells shows the glory of God.
- A slug is a kind of snail without a shell.
- Clams and oysters are mollusks with two-part shells that are used for food.
- A pearl grows around an irritating grain of sand inside an oyster.
- Octopuses have 8 long arms with sucking pads.

Introducing the Lesson

Bring a variety of shells to exhibit to the class. If possible, bring both halves of a two-part shell and show how the two halves are connected by a hinge. Demonstrate how the mollusk would have opened the halves slightly. Point out the shiny mother-of-pearl that lines the inside of many shells. Explain that the whole shell, including the mother-of-pearl, is made of materials from the mollusk's body.

If necessary, use an encyclopedia or other reference book to identify the shells you are exhibiting. The students may also enjoy helping you find the proper name for each shell.

If you have an aquarium in the classroom, it would be interesting to secure some water snails from a pet store to put in it. The students will enjoy watching the snails "walk" up the sides of the glass.

Materials needed:

- variety of shells
- two-part shell
- water snails in a jar of water

with poison. But most of the mollusks cannot do these things.

Shells. God gave many of the mollusks hard, strong shells around their soft bodies. A mollusk's shell is so hard and strong that most animals cannot break or open it. The round, hard covering on the back of a snail is its shell. The seashells that you can find on the seashore are the shells of mollusks that lived in the ocean.

Mollusk shells are also beautiful and neatly made. Each shell has its own shape and color design. Some are spirals, and some have butterfly shapes when open. Some look as if they were painted with reds, oranges, and yellows. Mollusk shells show us that God likes beauty and order.

Mollusks with one-part shells. The largest group of mollusks has shells all in one piece. We call such a shell a one-part shell. Snails have one-part shells. A one-part shell has a spiral pattern that winds toward the center.

A mollusk with a one-part shell has a kind of foot at the opening of the shell. The mollusk uses its wide foot in a wavelike motion to slowly push its body forward. You know how slow it is if you have ever watched a snail creeping. But no wonder it is so slow. It makes its own slippery road!

The snail's road, or trail, is sticky, slippery slime, made inside the snail's body. The slime allows the snail to slide forward easily. It protects the snail's soft body from rough twigs and stones. In fact, the snail could crawl right across the sharp edge of a knife without being cut.

Snails are sometimes put into aquariums to keep the glass clean. They crawl over the glass, eating the green algae as they go. One kind of snail does not have a shell at all. It is called a ***slug.*** You may have seen slugs on lettuce and other garden vegetables. They move slowly over slippery trails like other snails.

A snail makes its own trail.

Did you know—

...that a mollusk's shell grows as long as the animal lives?

...that clam and whelk shells were used as money by the American Indians, as were cowrie shells by peoples of the Far East?

...that in Bible times, Romans and Phoenicians used Murex snails to make purple dye, and that purple cloth was considered more valuable than gold? (Remember Lydia, a seller of purple in Acts 16:14?)

Discussion Idea: Pearls

Use an encyclopedia to show pictures of pearls. Discuss the value of pearls to many people. Then have students find and read these Scripture verses: Matthew 13:45, 46; 1 Timothy 2:9; Revelation 17:4; and Revelation 21:21. Discuss these verses to impart a Biblical perspective of pearls and other precious stones.

Quiz

Ask the children to write the correct New Words as you read each sentence below.

1. It is well known for its tasty meat and shiny pearls. *(oyster)*
2. It is a kind of snail that does not have a shell. *(slug)*
3. It moves on a path of slime and has a spiral shell. *(snail)*
4. It is a group of soft-bodied animals that are often protected by shells. *(mollusks)*
5. The meat of this mollusk with a two-part shell is almost as well liked as oyster meat. *(clam)*
6. It is a mollusk without a shell, having 8 long arms with sucking pads. *(octopus)*

Test Your Reading (Group A)

Find the correct ending for each sentence, and write the letter on your paper.

1. Mollusks are a group of animals that have
   a. smooth, tough skin.
   b. soft, moist bodies.
   c. hard inside skeletons.
2. God protected many mollusks with
   a. hard shells.
   b. streamlined bodies.
   c. strong fins.
3. All mollusk shells
   a. have no exact shape.
   b. are thick and leathery.
   c. show that God is orderly.
4. The mollusk group containing snails has shells
   a. in three pieces.
   b. in two pieces.
   c. in one piece.
5. You could see where a snail has walked by
   a. a rounded groove.
   b. a slimy path.
   c. a line of rough ground.
6. A snail uses slippery slime
   a. to trap other mollusks.
   b. to protect its body from sharp objects.
   c. to keep its shell watertight.
7. A slug is a snail without
   a. a shell. b. a foot. c. a slippery trail.

Answer the following questions.

8. In what way does a seashell show that God likes beauty and order?
9. How does a snail move?
10. What mollusk with a one-part shell may you see in a garden?

Lesson 4 Answers

Group A

1. b
2. a
3. c
4. c
5. b
6. b
7. a
8. A seashell has beauty and order in its colors and design.
9. A snail moves with a wavelike motion of its muscular foot.
10. snail

(10 points thus far)

Two-part shells were beautifully designed by God.

Mollusks with two-part shells. Many mollusks have two matching shells, or a two-part shell. ***Clams*** and ***oysters*** are in this group. The two shells are connected by hinges. They are usually kept slightly open. But when the clam becomes frightened, it snaps the shells shut with a strong muscle. This is the way God made it to protect itself.

The mollusks with two-part shells all live in water. They creep along with a foot shaped like a hatchet. They eat small plants or animals as the other mollusks do. Both oysters and clams are used for food. Clams can be dug from mud along the seashore.

Many oysters are harvested from underwater "farms" for food. The oyster farmer spreads old shells or clay tiles over the sea bottom. He then "plants" baby oysters. The oysters fasten themselves on the sea bottom and grow. In about three years, the farmer can harvest his crop of oysters and sell them for food.

The outside of oyster shells is rough, but oysters can make shiny, round pearls on the inside. An oyster does not know that pearls look pretty. It makes a pearl because something inside is hurting. Perhaps a grain of sand gets stuck inside the oyster's body. Of course, the oyster has no hands to get it back out. So the oyster coats the grain of sand with layers and more layers of shiny material, thus forming a pearl. The smooth, round pearl does not bother the oyster as the grain of sand did.

Another kind of mollusk is a strange sea animal called the ***octopus.*** *Octo-* means "eight." An octopus has 8 long arms. These arms are lined with many sucking pads to catch food. The arms wrap around the captured animal and pull it to the mouth. Strong jaws tear and crush it. An octopus is usually about the size of a softball, but big ones can have arms over 12 feet (4 meters) long.

An octopus has 8 arms.

Like other mollusks, the octopus has a soft body. But it does not have a shell. It has two other ways to protect itself. It can shoot water forward so that it moves backward like a jet airplane. The octopus can also shoot a black inklike liquid into the water to make a dark cloud. This hides the octopus until it can escape from its enemy.

What interesting creatures God made! The soft-bodied mollusks are only one group of the many animals God created. Some have one shell, some have two shells, and some have no shells at all. But all are given what they need to live and grow.

Test Your Reading (Group B)

Match each word with the best description.

11.	The shape of the foot of a clam	a.	jet
12.	Raised on "farms" for food	b.	octopus
13.	Grown around a grain of sand	c.	hatchet
14.	Dug from mud on seashore	d.	pearl
15.	Mollusk with long arms and strong jaws	e.	*octo-*
16.	Eight	f.	black liquid
17.	Used to move quickly	g.	oyster
18.	Used to hide from enemy	h.	clam

Group B

11. c
12. g
13. d
14. h
15. b
16. e
17. a
18. f

19. The two parts are pulled together with a strong muscle.
20. The oyster farmer spreads old shells or clay tiles over the sea bottom. Then he "plants" baby oysters. (2 points)

(21 points total)

Review Answers

1. b
2. down
3. c
4. true
5. tail

(5 additional points)

Extra Activity Comments

Your students would likely enjoy making a classroom shell display. If you do this, ask that each shell be labeled with its name and owner.

Answer the following questions.

19. What pulls the parts of a two-part shell together?
20. What two things does an oyster farmer do to grow oysters?

Reviewing What You Have Learned

1. When a bird sits or sleeps while grasping a branch, we say it is
   a. preening.
   b. perching.
   c. streamlining.
2. Baby birds are covered with ——— to keep them warm.
3. Fish get oxygen from the water with their
   a. scales. b. fins. c. gills.
4. True or false? An air bladder helps a fish stay in the middle of the water.
5. A fish moves through the water by wagging its ——— from side to side.

Extra Activities

1. Often homes have some shells that were found along a seashore. Some may even have large souvenir whelk shells. Bring various shells to school and make a labeled display of them. Use reference books to identify them.
2. Hunt for shells and start a collection! If you live close to a seashore, you will have a good source for shells. For the sake of safety, always take someone else along with you to the seashore. If you do not live along a sea, you can look for shells in streams and ditches.

   Label each shell neatly with its name and the date and place you found it. You may want to display your shells on a shelf or table. Another good method is to lay them on a bed of cotton in a large, shallow wooden frame, and lay a glass cover on top. (If sharp glass edges are exposed, be sure to tape them.)

Lesson 5

Animals With Strange Bodies

New Words

earthworm, a brown, segmented worm that lives in the soil.

jellyfish, a swimming sea animal with stinging tentacles.

planaria (plə•nar′•ē•ə), a harmless flatworm that lives in ponds and streams.

regeneration (ri•jen′•ə•rā′•shən), the ability to grow missing body parts.

sponge, a plantlike sea animal having a rubbery or soft skeleton.

starfish, a star-shaped, spiny-skinned sea animal, having five or more arms.

tentacles (ten′•tə•kəlz), stringlike body parts that contain stinging cells.

God has made so many different animals that you could study them all year and still not learn about all of them. In the last lesson, you learned about the octopus, which has a strange body. In this lesson you will be learning about five more strange animals.

The earthworm. If you dig in a garden, you will find brown ***earthworms.*** The long body of an earthworm is divided into more than 75 pieces or segments. The earthworm is an example of a segmented worm. Except for the first and the last, each segment has eight short bristles on the sides and bottom.

The earthworm has muscles that squeeze it out long and others that pull it up short. The earthworm pushes forward and holds its

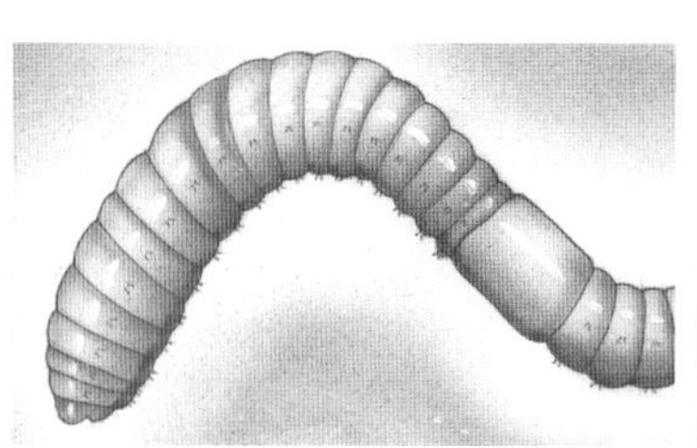

How does the earthworm use its bristles to move?

Lesson 5

Concepts to Teach

- The earthworm is a common segmented worm.
- The earthworm improves the soil.
- Planaria are common flatworms that live in freshwater streams and ponds.
- Sponges have tiny holes and rubbery skeletons.
- The jellyfish get their food by using stinging tentacles.
- The starfish is an example of a spiny-skinned animal.
- The starfish has tubelike feet to move around and open oyster shells.
- Starfish have the power of regeneration: they can replace missing arms or even half of the body.

Introducing the Lesson

Bring a dry starfish or animal sponge to class. Let the students feel the rough and spongy texture of these animals. If these are not available, show a manmade sponge and encyclopedia pictures of animal sponges. Explain that only some kinds of sponges have soft skeletons suitable for washing purposes. Other sponge skeletons are hard, being made of glass or limestone.

Define the term *regeneration*. You could add that the human body does have limited powers of regeneration. It regenerates hair, nails, skin, and a few other tissues. But if a finger or an ear is cut off, the body cannot grow a new one.

Materials needed:

- dry starfish
- animal sponge
- manmade sponge

head end with front bristles. Then it pulls its tail end up and holds its tail with back bristles. Then it is ready to push its head forward again. As it tunnels through the soil, it eats the soil. It digests dead plant material and passes the rest out of its body.

As earthworms tunnel through the soil and digest it, they make the soil better. If you have many earthworms in your garden, you know that you have good soil and that it is being made better. The tunnels help to make the soil loose. The digestion helps to fertilize the soil. Earthworms are very helpful to us.

Planaria. ***Planaria*** are harmless flatworms that live in freshwater streams and ponds. They are about ¼–1½ inches (6–38 millimeters) long, with a triangular head at one end and a rounded tail at the other. In the head are two eyespots that let them see light or darkness.

If you lift a dead leaf or a stick from a stream, you may find some of these tiny black, white, or brown animals. You will enjoy seeing them glide over a surface if you put them in a dish with a little water. They do this gliding motion with many small hairs on their undersides.

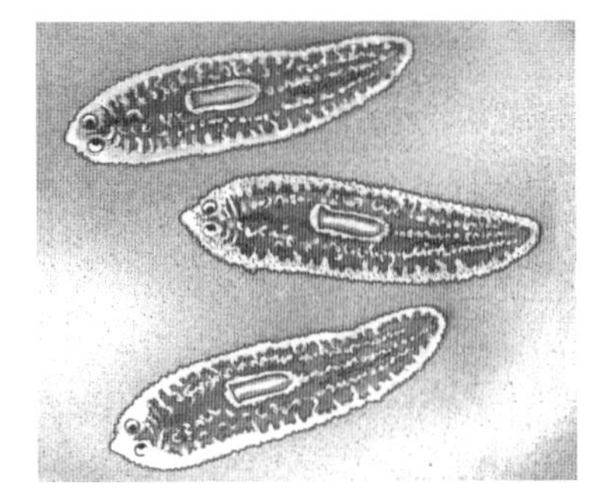

Planaria can be found in streams.

Planaria are just one of the many kinds of small moving creatures that live in the mud and along the banks of streams. They help to eat the dead plants and animals that fall into the water. They make the streams an interesting place to study.

Sponges. Have you ever scrubbed a car or bathtub with a sponge? You probably used a manmade sponge. But if you used a real sponge, you were scrubbing with the skeleton of an animal! The sponge skeleton is soft and rubberlike. It has many small holes that can hold a large amount of water. That is why it is useful for cleaning and scrubbing things.

A live ***sponge*** is like slippery, raw liver. It is plantlike and does not move, for it is fastened to the

Note: The name *planaria* is actually plural with *planarian* being singular. However, textbooks tend to use the word *planaria* for both the singular and plural as the word *fish* is used for both singular and plural.

Did you know—

...that earthworms vary in size from less than ⅛ inch (4 mm) long to several yards (m) in length?

...that both the earthworm and the planaria have enough of a nervous system that they can be "taught" somewhat to make the right choice in a maze?

...that jellyfish and sponges have no blood?

...that jellyfish are no match for weak-looking sea slugs called nudibranchs? (*Nudibranch* rhymes with *bank.*) The colorful slug eats a jellyfish without being stung, yet uses the jellyfish's stinging cells to shock would-be attackers.

...that the Portuguese man-of-war is actually a colony of animals acting as a single jellyfish? People that brush against the tentacles, which may grow 165 feet (50 m) long, suffer painful welts, shock, or fever.

...that some starfish with 50 arms are called sun stars?

...that oyster fishermen used to chop up starfish and throw the pieces back into the water, only to compound their problem because of the starfish's power of regeneration.

...that sponges have the remarkable ability to reunite severed parts? Some zoologists have tested this by pressing a sponge through a fine mesh to separate the cells. When the zoologists put the cells together in water, the cells rearranged to form a normal sponge again.

ocean bottom. Without a head or gills, how can it eat or breathe? Thousands of tiny, threadlike whips inside the sponge keep sweeping seawater throughout its body. The ocean water contains oxygen and bits of food, which the sponge uses to keep it alive. The sponge has a strange body, and yet men have found use for its skeleton.

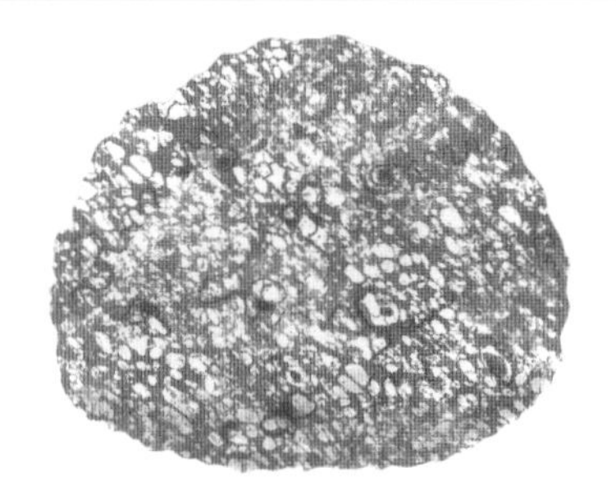

A sponge sweeps seawater through the many holes in its body.

Test Your Reading (Group A)

From the word box, find and write a word for each blank.

bristles	fertilize	segments
dead	flatworm	skeleton
earthworm	glide	sponge
eyespots	planaria	

1. The rubbery ——— of a sponge is useful for washing and scrubbing.
2. The planaria is a ———.
3. The earthworm is an example of a worm with ———.
4. The earthworm uses ——— to hold itself when making a tunnel.
5. You can see a planaria ——— over a surface with the many small hairs on its underside.
6. The earthworm helps to ——— the soil.
7. Both the planaria and earthworm help to use up ——— plants.
8. The planaria have two ——— in its head to see light.
9. The ——— stays fastened at one place on the ocean floor.
10. You can find an ——— by digging in the garden.
11. You may find ——— by looking on the undersides of dead leaves in freshwater streams.

Lesson 5 Answers

Group A

1. skeleton
2. flatworm
3. segments
4. bristles
5. glide
6. fertilize
7. dead
8. eyespots
9. sponge
10. earthworm
11. planaria

(11 points thus far)

"Strange Animals" Bible Project

Your students may enjoy finding Bible references to coral (Job 28:18; Ezekiel 27:16) and sponges (Matthew 27:48; Mark 15:36; John 19:29). A Bible dictionary gives some additional information on their importance in Bible times.

Quiz

Ask the children to write the correct New Words as you read each phrase below.

1. Streamers or threads that sting *(tentacles)*
2. A bloblike stinging animal that floats around the sea *(jellyfish)*
3. A segmented worm that helps to make soil better *(earthworm)*
4. Being able to grow new body parts *(regeneration)*
5. A spiny-skinned animal with five arms *(starfish)*
6. A small freshwater flatworm *(planaria)*
7. A plantlike animal with a useful, rubbery skeleton *(sponge)*

What use does the jellyfish make of its long tentacles?

Jellyfish. The ***jellyfish*** looks like an umbrella floating in the water with frilly streamers and long, stringlike ***tentacles.*** Though the body of the jellyfish is jellylike and has no skeleton, it is not weak. Its tentacles contain stinging cells, which are dangerous. If you ever see a blob of jelly along a seashore, do not touch it. It could give you very hurtful stings.

As the jellyfish swims in the water, its tentacles may brush against a small fish. They sting the fish so that it cannot swim away. Then the jellyfish can eat the fish.

Some jellyfish are so small you can hardly see them. Others are over 6 feet (2 meters) across with tentacles spreading out more than 20 feet (6 meters).

The starfish is a spiny-skinned animal.

Starfish. The ***starfish*** are in a group of strange animals called spiny-skinned animals because of their hard, rough skins.

The starfish gets its name from its star shape. Most starfish have five arms. Each arm has many tiny, tubelike feet with sucking pads on them that work somewhat like those on an octopus. These arms are all fastened to the center like spokes on a wheel.

How does a starfish get food? The starfish slowly pulls its body along the ocean bottom until it finds a clam or an oyster. With the sucking pads, it holds each side of the shell and begins to pull. The clam or oyster is much stronger than the starfish and clamps its shell shut. The starfish keeps pulling and pulling until the mollusk becomes tired. The shell opens just a crack. The starfish pushes its baglike stomach into that small crack and eats the mollusk inside its own shell. What a strange animal! Starfish are a problem to oyster farmers.

If a starfish loses an arm, it can grow a new one. The ability to grow missing body parts is called ***regeneration.*** Even one arm with some of the center can regenerate the missing parts and become a new starfish. Animals such as planaria, sponges, and octopuses have this ability of regeneration too. Your body cannot regenerate missing parts. If you should lose your arm, no new arm will grow in its place.

Each kind of animal is made to show God's glory in its own way. The strange and interesting animals you studied in this lesson are the work of God. They fit into God's wise plan. They teach us about the wisdom of God.

Test Your Reading (Group B)

Answer the following questions.

12. Where do jellyfish get their name?
13. Why should you not pick up a jellylike mass along a seashore?
14. How do jellyfish use their tentacles to get food?
15. Where do starfish get their name?
16. What kind of covering do starfish have to protect their bodies?
17. What does a starfish have on its arms that can hold to something?
18. How does a weaker starfish open the shell of a stronger oyster?
19. What does it mean that starfish have the power of regeneration?
20. Why would it be unwise for oyster fishermen to cut up starfish they catch and throw them back into the water?

Reviewing What You Have Learned

1. Which group has streamlined bodies?
   a. birds, fish
   b. amphibians, reptiles
   c. snails, slugs
2. The parts of a two-part mollusk shell are held together by a ———.

Group B

12. Jellyfish look like blobs of jelly floating along the seashore.
13. You may get stung by the tentacles of a jellyfish.
14. The tentacles sting small fish as they swim by. Then the fish cannot swim away. The jellyfish can then eat them.
15. The bodies of starfish are shaped like stars, most with five arms. (Although *fish* is in their name, they are not actually fish.)
16. Starfish have hard, rough, spiny skins.
17. A starfish has tubelike feet with sucking pads on them.
18. The starfish keeps pulling on the oyster's shell until it becomes tired and lets its shell come open a little.
19. If a starfish loses an arm, it can grow a new one.
20. This would make more starfish, since each piece that has part of the center would grow into a new starfish.

(20 points total)

Review Answers

1. a
2. muscle

3. true
4. gills
5. c

(5 additional points)

3. True or false? An oyster makes a pearl when a grain of sand bothers it.
4. Fish get oxygen from the water with their ———.
5. An octopus can move rapidly by
   a. running on its eight arms.
   b. swimming with special fins.
   c. shooting water.

Extra Activities

1. Read more about the strange animals in your lesson in an encyclopedia or library book. You might look for the titles "Earthworm," "Planaria (Planarian)," "Sponge," "Jellyfish," and "Starfish." Share with the class interesting facts about these animals that are not given in your textbook.
2. Dig in a garden to find some earthworms. Pull an earthworm gently over your finger to feel the bristles. Watch an earthworm crawl. Notice how it squeezes its body and makes it thin when it makes itself long. Be sure to give the earthworms moist leaves and soil to live in. Earthworms breathe through their moist skin. You should return them to the soil so that they can continue to help build up the soil.
3. Try to find some live planaria in a pond or stream. They are often on the undersides of dead tree leaves. Put some with a few dead leaves in a dish. Watch how they glide over the surface of a leaf. Examine them with a magnifying glass or a microscope. Notice their eyespots.

   Planaria have the power of regeneration. With a sharp razorblade, cut a planaria in two. Check it each day. Notice how the head end will grow a tail and the tail end will grow a new head.

Lesson 6

Do You Remember?

Match each letter to the correct number.

a. clam	d. mollusks	g. slug
b. earthworm	e. oyster	h. snail
c. jellyfish	f. planaria	i. sponge

1. A sea animal that makes pearls
2. A slippery-path maker with a one-part shell
3. A group with soft bodies usually protected by shells
4. A floating sea animal that is like an umbrella
5. An animal that digs tunnels through soil
6. A flatworm that lives in ponds and streams
7. A mollusk with a hatchet-shaped foot found in mud
8. A common land mollusk that has no shell
9. An animal with a rubbery skeleton used for washing

From the word box, find and write a word for each blank.

air bladder	gills	regeneration
backbone	gizzard	scales
beak	markings	streamlined
down	perch	tentacles
exoskeletons	preen	vertebrae
fins	quills	

10. Insects, spiders, and lobsters have stiff ——— to support their bodies.
11. The spinal cord of a horse is protected by a strong ———.
12. Many small ——— connected together form the backbone.
13. A bird needs stiff ——— in its feathers in order to fly.
14. The small, soft feathers that keep a bird warm are called ———.

Lesson 6 Answers

1. e
2. h
3. d
4. c
5. b
6. f
7. a
8. g
9. i
10. exoskeletons
11. backbone
12. vertebrae
13. quills
14. down

Lesson 6

Reviewing the Unit

Read Genesis 1:20–25 and 2:19, 20. Have the students mention as many animal groups from this unit as they can remember. Discuss on which day each animal group was formed. (It is difficult to establish exactly on which day the animals such as snails and worms were created, since some kinds live on land and others in the water.)

Your class might also enjoy a question chain. Have each student prepare two or more questions and their answers from this unit. Then start a chain: ask a question and ask all students who think they know the correct answer to raise their hands. Call on one of them. If he answers correctly, he asks one of his questions to the class. Go on in this way for a stated length of time (perhaps 10 or 15 minutes). Request that no question be asked more than once.

15. streamlined
16. beak
17. perch
18. markings
19. preen
20. gizzard
21. fins
22. gills
23. scales
24. air bladder
25. regeneration
26. tentacles

15. Birds, fish, cars, and ships need to be ——— for easy travel through air or water.
16. A woodpecker uses its ——— to find its food.
17. A chicken will ——— on its roost and sleep without falling off.
18. We can learn to tell birds apart by studying their ———.
19. Ducks and geese ——— their feathers by smoothing them.
20. A robin's ——— grinds up the hard food in its stomach.
21. A goldfish uses its ——— to turn, slow down, and stop.
22. A salmon or any other fish needs its ——— in order to get oxygen from the water.
23. A tough covering of ——— protects the outside of a fish's body.
24. When a fish wants to swim at a higher or lower level, it uses its ——— to rise or sink.
25. Octopuses and starfish have the power of ——— to grow missing body parts.
26. Jellyfish use their stinging ——— to get food.

Choose the best answer to finish each sentence.

27. b
28. b
29. a
30. c

27. The animal groups with inside skeletons and backbones include
    a. mammals, reptiles, and insects.
    b. fish, birds, and amphibians.
    c. reptiles, worms, and mammals.
28. In order to fly, a bird must have
    a. hollow bones and perching feet.
    b. strong wings and stiff feathers.
    c. oily feathers and hollow quills.
29. A fish moves forward by
    a. wagging its tail.
    b. squeezing its air bladder.
    c. opening its gills.
30. A clam has
    a. an inside shell.
    b. a one-part shell.
    c. a two-part shell.

31. An oyster's enemy is the
    a. starfish.
    b. jellyfish.
    c. sea anemone.

Write *true* if the sentence is true; write *false* if it is not true.

32. God designed the bodies of most birds especially for flying.
33. Baby birds hatch from eggs laid in a nest.
34. The meat of fish is a healthful food.
35. Many earthworms in a garden are a sign that the soil is poor.
36. Jellyfish float around the sea, but sponges and starfish fasten themselves to rocks.
37. The octopus has five arms with sucking pads on them.

Copy and finish each sentence correctly.

38–39. Two reasons why many animals need skeletons are ———.
40. God made a bird's bones to be hollow because ———.
41. Geese, ducks, and swans need oiled feathers in order to ———.
42–43. We like birds for these two reasons: ———.
44. The way the bodies of animals are made reminds us of ———.
45. The starfish's arms can hold tightly with feet that have ———.

31. a
32. true
33. true
34. true
35. false
36. false
37. false
38–39. Two reasons why many animals need skeletons are to protect soft body parts and to support their bodies. (2 points)
40. God made a bird's bones to be hollow because hollow bones are more lightweight for flying.
41. Geese, ducks, and swans need oiled feathers in order to float (*or* stay dry).
42–43. We like birds for these two reasons: they sing, and they eat harmful insects (*or* they eat weed seeds and are colorful and interesting). (2 points)
44. The way the bodies of animals are made reminds us of the glory of God (*or* the wisdom of God).
45. The starfish's arms can hold tightly with feet that have sucking pads.

(45 points total)

Unit Three

The Stars Inspire Wonder

Have you ever wondered how big the stars really are? Do you ever think about how far away they are from the earth? Do you think about the One who keeps each star in its place?

"Canst thou . . . loose the bands of Orion?" (Job 38:31).

God wants us to ask such questions about the stars. While we learn to know the stars, we can also learn about God. The great number and size of the stars teach us of God's power. The vast distances between the stars teach us of God's greatness. The position and movement of the stars teach us of God's order.

Even though Job lived thousands of years ago, he saw the very same stars that we see today! God asked Job some questions about the stars to teach Job of God's greatness and Job's weakness.

When God talked to Job about the stars, He said their names. Notice the names in the following verses: "Canst thou bind the sweet influences of *Pleiades,* or loose the bands of *Orion*? Canst thou bring forth *Mazzaroth* in his season? or canst thou guide *Arcturus* with his sons?" (Job 38:31, 32). In this unit you will study most of these star names.

In these questions God was asking Job, "Can you change any of the stars? Can you keep them in their proper places?" Of course, Job knew that he could never take care of the stars. Only God could do that.

God wanted to remind Job that only God was great enough to take care of the stars. Only God was great and wise enough to take care of Job. God wanted Job to trust and obey Him, just as He wants us to trust and obey Him today.

Unit Three

For Your Inspiration

Have you noticed how God's Word links stars with angels and with Jesus? "Or who laid the corner stone thereof; when the morning *stars* sang together, and all the sons of God shouted for joy?" (Job 38:6, 7). It seems that the chief occupation of these angels or morning stars has always been rejoicing! They glorify God with all their heart.

Often stars are used as a figure of speech referring to angels or important men. One such brilliant star chose not to glorify God as the other stars did. Isaiah 14:12–14 reveals the sorry details: "How art thou fallen from heaven, O Lucifer, son of the morning! how art thou cut down to the ground, which didst weaken the nations! For thou hast said in thine heart, I will ascend into heaven, I will exalt my throne above the *stars* of God: I will sit also upon the mount of the congregation, in the sides of the north: I will ascend above the heights of the clouds; I will be like the most High." Lucifer's anarchy grew as more angels followed suit. "And his tail drew the third part of the *stars* of heaven, and did cast them to the earth" (Revelation 12:4).

God was far from defeated by these traitors. Jude tells their fate: "And the angels which kept not their first estate, but left their own habitation, he hath reserved in everlasting chains under darkness unto the judgment of the great day." Jude also describes Lucifer's followers as "wandering *stars,* to whom is reserved the blackness of darkness for ever" (Jude 13).

How did God defeat Lucifer? In the fullness of time, He sent His precious Son to earth just as He had planned from the beginning of time. "There shall come a *Star* out of Jacob, and a Sceptre shall rise out of Israel" (Numbers 24:17).

The holy angels were thrilled with joy at God's

Lesson 1

Star Pictures

New Words

Big Dipper, a group of stars forming a picture of a large dipper.

constellation (kon′·stə·lā′·shən), a group of stars that forms a picture.

Little Dipper, a group of stars shaped like a small dipper.

Orion (ō·rī′·ən), a large constellation shaped like a hunter.

Pleiades (plē′·ə·dēz′), a cluster of six bright stars said to be sisters.

God made the stars. Can you tell how the stars got into the sky? Of course—God put them there! The Bible says that God made the stars on the fourth day of the Creation week. "And God made two great lights [the sun and moon]; . . . he made the stars also" (Genesis 1:16).

Job knew that God created the stars. Job said, "By his spirit he hath garnished [or decorated] the heavens" (Job 26:13).

Job also knew that God set each star in its position. The order of the stars is very exact. Tonight you can see the same star pictures that Job did.

Star study is very old. Ever since God made the stars, people have studied them. They wanted to learn the positions of the stars. But it was hard to learn the many, many stars one by one. It was easier to learn groups of stars.

So the bright stars were put into groups called ***constellations.*** Each constellation was named for the picture it seemed to form, such as a man, a fish, or a rabbit. In this way, people divided the sky into star pictures called constellations. Then they learned the name of each constellation and its neighbor constellations. When they talked about a certain star, they named the constellation to which it belonged. That made it easier to tell in which part of the sky the star was.

good work. Luke 2:13, 14 says, "And suddenly there was with the angel a multitude of the heavenly host praising God, and saying, Glory to God in the highest, and on earth peace, good will toward men."

God used a star to guide the wise men to the greatest Star. "And, lo, the *star,* which they saw in the east, went before them, till it came and stood over where the young child was. When they saw the *star,* they rejoiced with exceeding great joy" (Matthew 2:9, 10).

Today wise men still seek this *Star* "until the day dawn, and the day *star* arise in your hearts" (2 Peter 1:19). May we all be wise men who joyfully adore the One who has said, "I am the root and the offspring of David, and the bright and morning *star*" (Revelation 22:16).

Joyful, joyful, we adore Thee,
God of glory, Lord of love;
Hearts unfold like flowers before Thee,
Hail Thee as the sun above.
Melt the clouds of sin and sadness;
Drive the dark of doubt away;
Giver of immortal gladness,
Fill us with the light of day!

All Thy works with joy surround Thee,
Earth and heaven reflect Thy rays,
Stars and angels sing around Thee,
Center of unbroken praise;
Field and forest, vale and mountain,
Blossoming meadow, flashing sea,
Chanting bird and flowing fountain,
Call us to rejoice in Thee.

Mortals, join the mighty chorus
Which the morning stars began;
Father-love is reigning o'er us,
Brother-love binds man to man.
Ever singing, march we onward,
Victors in the midst of strife;
Joyful music lifts us sunward
In the triumph song of life.

—Henry van Dyke

Can you see the relation of the stars in Orion to an imagined picture of a hunter?

Today we still use this same method to learn the star positions. We still imagine that we can see pictures in the constellations. We still use some of the same star and constellation names that Job and other men did long ago.

Two familiar constellations. One of the brightest star groups is the ***Big Dipper.*** Can you guess what picture it forms? Yes, if you draw lines from one star to the next, it looks like a large dipper with a bent handle.

The ***Little Dipper*** is smaller than the Big Dipper. Most of the stars in the Little Dipper are dim. But three of the stars of the Little Dipper are bright—the end of the handle and the side of the dipper.

You can use the Big Dipper to find the Little Dipper. Look at the picture below. Do you see the two "pointer stars" at the side of the Big Dipper? Imagine that they form a straight line. Then follow that line until you reach a bright star. This bright star is the end of the Little Dipper's handle. The handle of the Little Dipper curves backward. The Big and Little Dippers can be seen on a clear night any time of the year. They are always in the northern part of the sky.

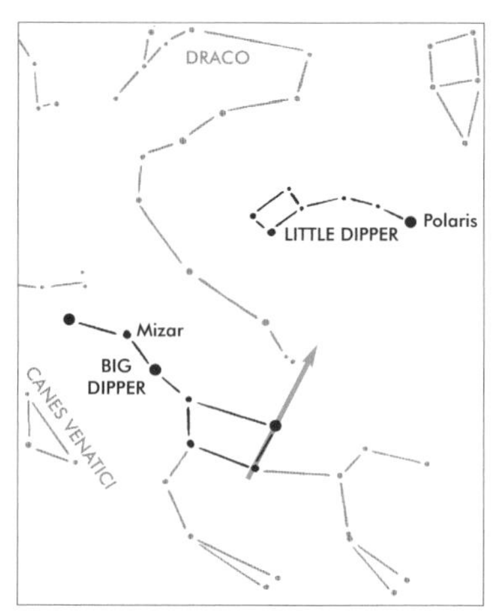

The two dippers

Note: A fourteen-inch-square "Star Guide," available from Rod and Staff Publishers, Inc., will be helpful in teaching this unit. Lesson 3 includes a study of the star guide. A mask that comes with the guide can be set for any day of the year and any time of the night to reveal the part of the starry heavens that is visible at that time. This is a great help in learning the constellations without an assistant.

The booklet *Discovering God's Stars,* available from Rod and Staff Publishers, Inc., gives additional information about star study and tells how to use the "Star Guide."

A smaller blackline star guide is given on pages 258 and 259. Permission is given to copy this star guide for students using this textbook. It will be best to copy this on heavy paper. The students will need to cut out the mask for use with the star map.

Lesson 1

Concepts to Teach

- God set the stars in the sky.
- Constellations help us learn the star positions.
- Anyone can learn constellations with some effort and time in viewing the night sky.
- Some of the constellations are easy to locate.

Introducing the Lesson

Before you begin an overview of the new unit, your class could sing a song about stars such as "Can You Count the Stars?" or "Twinkle, Twinkle, Little Star." For the last line of the latter song, you could sing, "Twinkle, twinkle, little star; God has made you what you are."

This lesson may be the first that your students will be taught to identify star groups. Seek to inspire them with the wonder of the starry heavens and a reverence for God, their Creator.

Test Your Reading (Group A)

Choose the best answer.

1. Job said that he knew that God
   a. made the night sky beautiful with stars.
   b. created the stars on the fourth day with the sun and moon.
   c. gave the constellations their names.
2. When you find a constellation, you will see
   a. many stars to form a milky patch of light.
   b. several stars in a row to form lines.
   c. bright stars that look like a picture.
3. The names we use for stars and constellations
   a. are sometimes the same as the names used in the Bible.
   b. were given by God at Creation.
   c. were made by modern scientists.
4. The Big and Little Dippers can be seen
   a. best at midnight.
   b. all year around.
   c. in the southern sky.
5. Two stars of the Big Dipper are called "pointer stars" because
   a. they form the handle of the dipper.
   b. they can be used to find a bright star in another constellation.
   c. they are easy to point to in the sky.

Give the name for each of these constellations.

6. 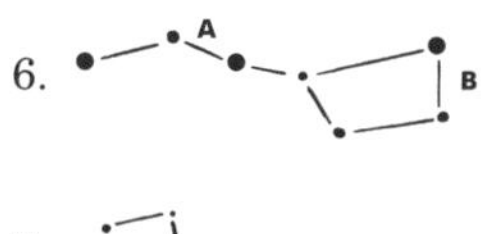

7. C D

8. Which letter is beside two stars that are dim?
9. Which letter is beside two stars that are "pointer stars"?

Lesson 1 Answers

Group A

1. a
2. c
3. a
4. b
5. b
6. Big Dipper
7. Little Dipper
8. D
9. B

(9 points thus far)

Did you know—

...that the Big Dipper is actually an asterism instead of a constellation? An asterism is a familiar star group or pattern that is only part of a constellation. The Big Dipper is a star figure that is part of the larger constellation Ursa Major. The Little Dipper is an asterism of the constellation Ursa Minor. The Keystone is an asterism of Hercules. The Northern Cross is an asterism of Cygnus. Pleiades is an asterism of Taurus.

...that the constellation names are in Latin? Latin was at one time the language of the scholars. These Latin names are the ones used by astronomers and in books about the stars. The King James Version of the Bible uses these names. It will be good for your students to learn both the Latin name and the common name, for example, Orion, the hunter.

...that the Greeks named only 48 constellations? With the exploration of the Southern Hemisphere, 23 constellations were added to cover that part of the sky. The present 88 constellations were decided on by the International Astronomical Union in 1928.

Constellation Flash Cards

Make flash cards of all the constellations named in this unit from the master copies on pages 261–268. Some of the cards have the lines between the stars; some have the stars only. You could make teams and keep score this way: two points for naming each constellation without lines and one point for each constellation with lines.

An easy constellation to find. When you first try to find constellations, you will see that some of them are small and some are made of dim stars. But the constellation ***Orion*** is big and made of bright stars. That makes it easy to find. Orion is a marvelous and inspiring constellation. Be sure to find it in the sky.

Look at the map of Orion. What shape or picture do the stars form

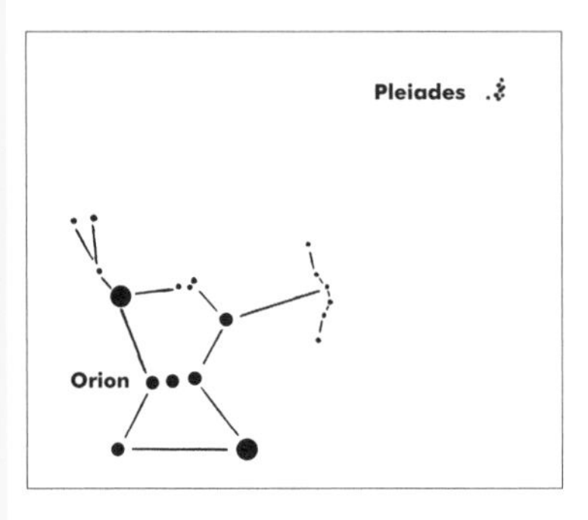

in your mind? People long ago thought these stars looked like a hunter with a belt of three stars and a bow or shield. This beautiful constellation is called Orion, the hunter. As you learned, the Big and Little Dippers can be seen in the northern sky all year around. But many constellations can be seen in the evening sky during only part of the year. Orion is such a constellation. It can be seen best during the winter months.

A star cluster. Not far from Orion is a patch of stars called ***Pleiades,*** the seven sisters. Perhaps the star watchers long ago could see seven bright stars, but today we see only six. If you have sharp eyes, you can see all six stars in the sky on a clear night. To you, they might look like a fuzzy patch of light. Like Orion, Pleiades is seen during winter evenings.

Look for the constellations. Both the Big Dipper and Orion are made of very bright stars. This makes these star groups two of the easiest ones to find. Try it for yourself on a clear night. Look for the Big Dipper toward the north. If it is a winter evening, look in the southeast sky for the three bright stars in a row that form Orion's belt. Then find the rest of the constellation. Next, try to find Pleiades almost overhead.

God is pleased when we study His stars and praise Him for His great works. It is not hard to learn some stars and constellations. All you need is some time to look at the night sky and some patience to keep

Quiz

Have the students say or write the correct New Word for each sentence below.

1. It is shaped like a small gravy ladle. *(Little Dipper)*
2. It is a star picture in the sky. *(constellation)*
3. It is shaped like a large gravy ladle. *(Big Dipper)*
4. It is a patch of stars called the sisters. *(Pleiades)*
5. It is a large, bright winter constellation that looks like a hunter. *(Orion)*

trying. It is helpful to have someone with you who can show you where to find some constellations.

Job knew about Orion and Pleiades. Twice in the Book of Job, these star names are mentioned. Job said that it is God who "maketh . . . Orion, and Pleiades, and the chambers of the south" (Job 9:9). God asked Job, "Canst thou bind the sweet influences of Pleiades, or loose the bands of Orion?" (Job 38:31). How exciting it is to look in the sky and see groups of stars that Job could see! How wonderful it is to look at the constellations and know that our great God put them there!

Test Your Reading (Group B)

Write the missing words.

10. The bright constellation named ——— looks like a hunter.
11. Three stars in a row form the ——— of Orion.
12. Orion can be seen in the evening sky during the ——— months.
13. One cluster of stars is called ———, the seven sisters.
14. God asked Job if he could "loose the bands of ———."
15. To learn the constellations, you need to spend ——— watching the night sky.
16. As you learn the constellations, be sure to ——— God for His marvelous works.

Extra Activities

1. Is the sky clear? Is the moon dim? If so, tonight is a good night for star watching. You may ask someone who knows the stars to go with you. Take a strong flashlight along to help you find your way in the dark and to use as a pointer in the sky.

   Follow the instructions in this lesson to find the Dippers toward the north and Orion toward the south and southeast. In the fall months, Orion will not be in the east until 1 A.M. (2 A.M., D.S.T.) in September, 11 P.M. (12 midnight, D.S.T.) in October, and 9 P.M. in November.

Group B

10. Orion
11. belt
12. winter
13. Pleiades
14. Orion
15. time
16. praise

(16 points total)

Extra Activity Comments

Perhaps you could do these and other star-watching activities in later lessons as a class one or more evenings. If it is cold outside, the children should be reminded to dress warmly. The beam of a flashlight makes a very good pointer, especially a flashlight that can be focused. The perspective is such that the beam will appear to point to the same star for everyone even in a scattered group.

You have a wonderful opportunity to develop interest in learning the star and constellation names. If you do not know them yourself, you can learn them along with the students with the help of "A Star Guide" and *Discovering God's Stars,* both published by Rod and Staff Publishers, Inc.

Daylight Saving Time moves the clock time ahead during the summer. For example, 6:00 P.M. Standard Time equals 7:00 P.M. Daylight Saving Time (on the clock). If you want to know what the stars will be like at 7:00 P.M. clock time, you will need to set the star guide back one hour to 6:00 P.M. When you look at the position for 6:00 P.M. on the star guide, you are seeing what stars are visible at 7:00 P.M. according to the clock (Daylight Saving Time).

2. Start a star-watching chart such as the one below. Fill it in each time you go star watching. In the middle column, mark all the stars or star groups you could pick out in the sky. In the right-hand column, write the names of the ones you saw for the first time.

My Star-Watching Chart

Date	*Time*	*Stars or Star Groups I Saw*	*New Stars or Groups*
12-9-98	8:30	Big and Little Dippers	Pleiades
12-9-98	8:30	Orion	

Lesson 2

The Stars Move

New Words

Arcturus (ärk·tůr′·əs), the brightest star of the constellation Boötes.

Boötes (bō·ō′·tēz), a constellation whose name means "herdsman."

Polaris (pə·lar′·is), the North Star, and the brightest star of the Little Dipper.

Ursa Major (ėr′·sə), the constellation meaning "big bear," which includes the Big Dipper.

Ursa Minor (ėr′·sə), the constellation meaning "little bear," which includes the Little Dipper.

The stars move. You know that the sun rises in the east and sets in the west. You have seen this happen all your life. Do you know what causes this movement? It is not the sun at all, but the earth. The earth is turning on its axis all the time—one turn every day. The turning earth makes it look as if the sun were moving across the sky.

Does the earth stop spinning at night? No, of course not. It keeps rotating just the same, day or night. So, like the sun, the stars rise in the east and set in the west. You can see this for yourself by choosing a bright star to watch some evening. Look at it early in the evening, then again an hour later, and once more another hour later. You will see that it moves from east to west just like the sun.

One star is still. *Polaris* is a special star that hardly moves at all. It is found at the end of the Little Dipper's handle and is the brightest star of the Little Dipper.

Other stars circle around Polaris at night. You can see this in the picture on page 84. This is how far the stars move in one hour. Can you find the stars of the Little Dipper in the picture?

Stars that are closest to Polaris make little circles every night. Stars farther away make bigger circles. Most stars make such

Lesson 2

Concepts to Teach

- Because of the earth's rotation, the stars appear to move around Polaris once a day.
- Because of the earth's revolution, the stars change their positions with the seasons.
- Ancient men could tell the time and season by the position of the stars.

Introducing the Lesson

Read or ask a student to read Amos 5:8 to the class. Ask if anyone can tell (without looking in Lesson 1) what the other name for Orion is, and can give the group name for the "seven stars."

Tell the class that in Lesson 1 they learned the name of a constellation (Orion) and some star groups (the Dippers and Pleiades). In this lesson they will learn the names of two individual stars. Star watchers have given names only to the bright stars. It is impossible for man to name all the stars, but not for God. "He telleth the number of the stars; he calleth them all by their names. Great is our Lord, and of great power: his understanding is infinite" (Psalm 147:4, 5).

Use a globe and a "sun" to review the concepts that the earth's rotation causes day and night and that its revolution determines the length of a year.

Materials needed:

- globe
- object to represent the sun

Did you know—

...that the early Chaldeans (or Babylonians) made a calendar, divided the sky into at least 52 constellations, predicted solar and lunar eclipses fairly accurately, and kept detailed records of the movements of the heavenly bodies? Quite likely, this knowledge was a part of Daniel's schooling under Ashpenaz.

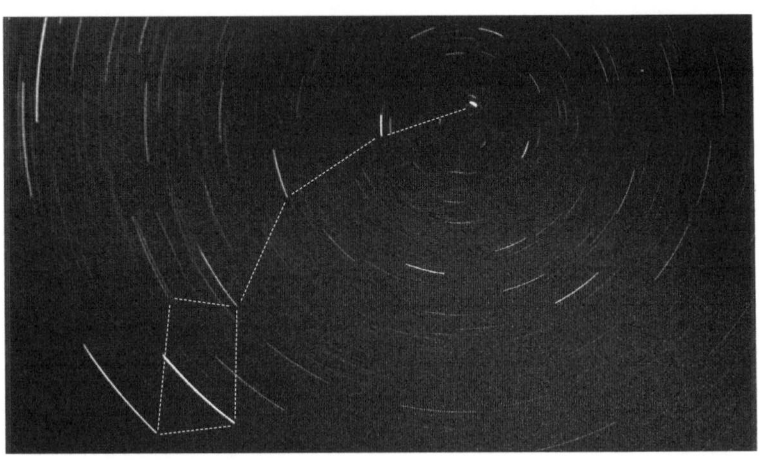

The movement of the stars around Polaris for about one hour. The dashed lines show the Little Dipper.

large circles that we only see part of the circles. That is why we see most stars rise in the east, move across the sky, and set in the west like the sun.

Why does Polaris stay in one spot all the time? Polaris is located in the sky right above the North Pole of the earth. The star Polaris is often called the North Star because it is north, above the North Pole. Just as the earth rotates around the North Pole, so the sky seems to rotate around Polaris, the North Star.

For many years Polaris has been helpful to travelers at night. When they were not sure of their directions, they looked for the North Star. They knew that Polaris was always toward the north. When they discovered which way north was, they could quickly figure out where south, east, or west was.

The stars change through the year. While the earth rotates on its axis, it also revolves around the sun. It makes one big circle, or revolution, around the sun every year. Each day the earth moves a little farther in its circle around the sun.

This daily progress of the earth's revolution causes each star to rise about 4 minutes earlier

...that in 213 B.C. an enraged Chinese emperor ordered all the astronomy books burned because his astrologers failed to accurately predict the future? For this reason, the extent of ancient Chinese astronomy is unknown today, though it is believed that they knew at least as much as the Chaldeans.

...that most ancient peoples such as the Chaldeans, Chinese, and Egyptians studied astronomy chiefly to divine the future using "sky gods"? No wonder, then, that Joseph and Daniel so impressed their rulers with their God-given interpretations of dreams that accurately foretold the future.

...that if the Lord tarries 2000 or more years, the earth's axis will point to other stars, one after the other, as polestars instead of Polaris? At the present speed with which the earth's axis changes direction, it will take 26,000 years to make a complete circle and return to Polaris as the polestar.

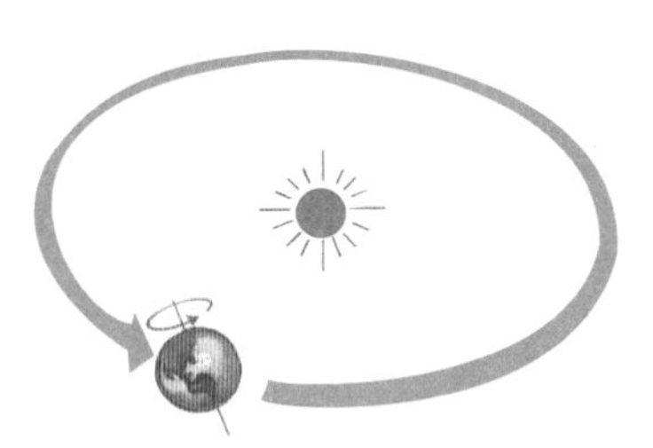
The two motions of the earth

each night than the night before. With all these minutes added up day after day, the stars change in the evening sky through the year. The same stars are not in the evening sky in the summer as in the winter.

Every day some stars disappear into the west before it gets dark, and every day some "new" stars become visible in the eastern night sky. By the end of six months, most of the night sky has completely changed. So most of the stars you see in the summer evening sky will be different from the stars you see in the winter evening sky.

Test Your Reading (Group A)

Decide which of the three choices is best. Write the letter of the best choice on your paper.

1. The stars move
   a. from east to west.
   b. toward the north.
   c. away from Polaris.
2. The stars move during the night because
   a. the stars revolve around the earth.
   b. the sun rises in the east and sets in the west.
   c. the earth rotates on its axis.
3. Polaris hardly moves at all because
   a. it is at the end of the handle of the Little Dipper.
   b. it is above the North Pole of the earth.
   c. the other stars make circles around it.
4. Polaris may be useful to you sometime if
   a. you need to know what time it is.
   b. you need to locate Orion in the sky.
   c. you need to know which direction is west.

Lesson 2 Answers

Group A

1. a
2. c
3. b
4. c

Quiz

Notice that not all the answers are vocabulary words.

1. This constellation is a star picture of a herdsman. *(Boötes)*
2. This star shows us which way is north. *(Polaris)*
3. This constellation looks like a big bear, but it is easier to see it as a big dipper. *(Ursa Major)*
4. This means the spinning of the earth. *(rotation)*
5. This bright star is seen during spring and summer. *(Arcturus)*
6. This word means the earth's circle around the sun. *(revolution)*
7. This constellation is often called the Little Dipper. *(Ursa Minor)*

5. Every night the stars rise 4 minutes earlier in the east because
   a. the earth rotates on its axis.
   b. the stars revolve around the earth.
   c. the earth revolves around the sun.
6. If you can see a constellation high overhead this evening, in six months
   a. it will not be visible in the evening sky.
   b. it will be farther west in the evening sky.
   c. it will be farther south in the evening sky.

5. c
6. a

Answer the following questions.

7. How does the earth move in its rotation?
8. How does the earth move in its revolution?
9. Which of these motions makes the stars move during the night?

7. It rotates around its axis.
8. It revolves around the sun.
9. the rotation

(9 points thus far)

Telling time by the stars. The people who lived in Job's time long ago knew how the stars change. They could tell time by looking at the sun and stars. During the day they looked at the sun. They noticed where it was in the sky. The sun told them the time of day.

At night the stars told these people the time of year. They knew the constellations very well. They knew which stars could be seen on spring evenings, on summer evenings, on autumn evenings, and on winter evenings. When they began to see Orion and Pleiades, they knew that winter was there to stay. When they saw ***Arcturus*** in the east, they knew that spring had come.

Arcturus is a very bright star. In the summertime after the sun sets, Arcturus is one of the first stars you can see. Arcturus is the brightest star in the constellation ***Boötes,*** which means "herdsman."

Dippers or bears? God talked to Job about Arcturus. He

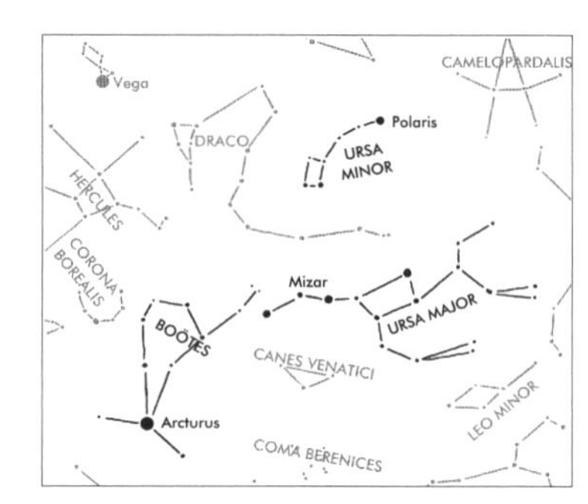

What other names do you know for two constellations on this map?

said, "Canst thou guide Arcturus with his sons?" (Job 38:32). The name *Arcturus* means "bear keeper." The "sons" of Arcturus may have been the bears, Ursa Major and Ursa Minor. In the language used long ago, *ursa* meant "bear." *Major* means "big," and *minor* means "little." So ***Ursa Major*** and ***Ursa Minor*** are the constellation names for the big bear and the little bear.

Ursa Major is actually the Big Dipper with some extra stars. Likewise, Ursa Minor includes the Little Dipper. The handles of the Dippers were supposed to be the tails of the two bears even though bears do not have long tails. Since the star patterns look more like dippers than bears, many people call them by their dipper names. Scientists and star watchers still use the proper constellation names: Ursa Major and Ursa Minor.

When God made the sun, moon, and stars, He planned that they would be used to measure time. God said, "Let there be lights in the firmament of the heaven to divide the day from the night; and let them be for signs, and for seasons, and for days, and years" (Genesis 1:14). Today God's plan for timekeeping still works. The rotation of the earth makes our day. The revolution of the earth makes our year. These two movements help men to use the sun, moon, and stars to measure time just as God said they would.

Test Your Reading (Group B)

Choose the best ending for each sentence.

10. Stars can be used
11. Arcturus can be used
12. Boötes is the constellation
13. *Ursa* is an old name
14. *Ursa Minor* is the proper name
15. *Major* is a word
16. *Ursa Major* is the proper name
17. The revolution of the earth makes
18. God gave the sun and stars

a. where you find Arcturus.
b. one year.
c. for the Big Dipper.
d. for days and years.
e. for a calendar.
f. meaning "big."
g. meaning "bear."
h. for the Little Dipper.
i. to tell when spring has come.

Group B
10. e
11. i
12. a
13. g
14. h
15. f
16. c
17. b
18. d

(18 points total)

Review Answers

1. c
2. constellation
3. true
4. Pleiades
5. a

(5 additional points)

Extra Activity Comments

The students may also enjoy having you as a teacher fill out a star-watching chart. Your own enthusiasm will influence your students' interest in this and other projects.

It will be good for you to make firsthand observations and then tell your students in which directions to look for the stars and constellations for the time of the year you are in.

Reviewing What You Have Learned

1. Two stars of the Big Dipper will help you find
   a. Orion. b. Pleiades. c. the Little Dipper.
2. Orion is a ——— that looks like a hunter.
3. True or false? The Bible uses names for the stars that we use today.
4. One small group of stars is called ———, the seven sisters.
5. The best way to learn the constellations is
   a. to use patience and time hunting constellations.
   b. to read books about the stars.
   c. to listen to your teacher talk about constellations.

Extra Activities

1. Would you like to see Arcturus? Though you cannot see Arcturus on a winter evening, you can see it in the early morning sky. Be sure to get up while it is still very dark. First find the Big Dipper. Follow the curving arc of the Big Dipper's handle on out to the first bright star. The bright star at the end of the arc is Arcturus.

   Now look for Boötes (bō·ō′·tēz), the constellation to which Arcturus belongs. Arcturus is brighter than the rest of the stars in Boötes. Notice on the map on page 86 that the end of Boötes's arm is near the Big Dipper.

   If you started keeping a star-watching chart, fill it in after doing this activity or the next one.
2. For a bigger challenge, find Serpens, probably the "crooked serpent" mentioned in Job 26:13. Use Arcturus and the next brightest star beside it to form an imaginary line pointing east. Follow that line to the first clump of stars, which is the head of Serpens.

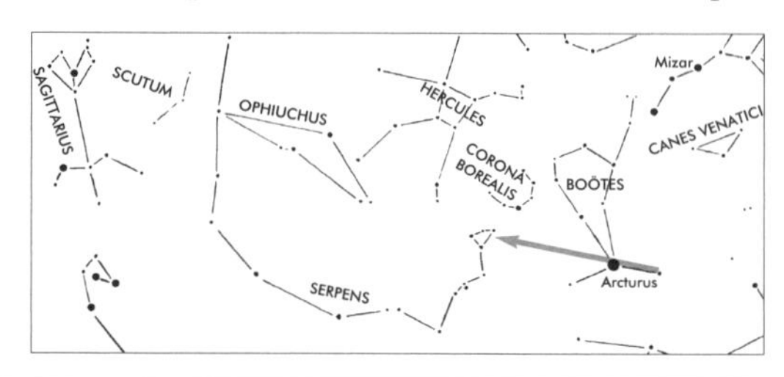

Lesson 3

Learning the Constellations

New Words

Cassiopeia (kas′·ē·ə·pē′·ə), a W-shaped constellation that was named after a queen.

Cygnus (sig′·nəs), a cross-shaped constellation whose name means "swan."

Gemini (jem′·ə·nī′), a bright winter constellation whose name means "twins."

Hercules (hėr′·kyə·lēz′), a summer constellation named after a giant.

horizon (hə·rī′·zən), the line where the sky seems to meet the earth.

Leo (lē′·ō), a spring constellation whose name means "lion."

Pegasus (peg′·ə·səs), a boxlike constellation named after a winged horse.

zenith (zē′·nith), the point that is directly overhead in the sky.

The star calendar. When we want to know what time of the year it is, we look at a calendar hanging on the wall. God gave us a much greater calendar. Would you like to use this calendar? God's calendar is the stars!

Whenever you see Orion high in the evening sky, you know it is wintertime. Since the earth revolves around the sun, Orion rises 4 minutes earlier each evening. In the summertime Orion is not in the evening sky at all. But by December, you can see it in the east a few hours after the sun goes down.

Other constellations are in the sky in different seasons. Each season has its special constellations in the evening sky. If you want to see all the constellations you can possibly see from where you live, you should study them

Lesson 3

Concepts to Teach

- Each season has its own set of constellations that are best visible in the evening sky.
- In one year's time, you can see all the constellations in the evening that are visible from your latitude.
- Stars are clearer at the zenith than at the horizon.
- A star guide can help you learn the constellations on your own.
- When using a star guide, it is helpful to begin with the stars at the zenith.
- Some constellations are known by a special shape that they contain.

Introducing the Lesson

Show the class a star guide with a mask and explain how to use it. First, find the words *north, east,* and *west* on the star mask; then point in each direction. Hold the star mask and guide overhead so that the words match the proper directions. Help them match the time of day with the calendar day, and show how the mask must be moved around the star map as time moves on. On the star guide, all times are interpreted as standard time.

As you move the mask around in a circle, have them watch the Dippers: they never get covered by the mask, which means they are visible year around. Then have them watch Orion "rise" and "set" under the mask.

Explain that the stars said to be of a particular season are those seen right after it gets dark. Later in the night, the next season's stars are visible.

during all four seasons. In this lesson you will learn about two constellations for each of the four seasons.

Winter constellations. To learn the star calendar, you will need to learn which constellations can be seen during the evenings of each season. You

Winter constellations

already know that Orion is a winter constellation.

Another bright winter constellation is ***Gemini,*** which means "twins." The twins are standing side by side near Orion. In fact, Orion's upraised arm points to the feet of Gemini.

Spring constellations. What constellations can you see during spring evenings? Orion and Gemini have moved toward the west. But Boötes, the herdsman, has risen in the east. Remember that the bright star Arcturus is at Boötes's feet. Boötes seems to be reaching for the handle of the Big Dipper, which is the tail of Ursa Major, the big bear.

Watch out, Boötes! A lion is nearby. ***Leo,*** the lion, is south of the

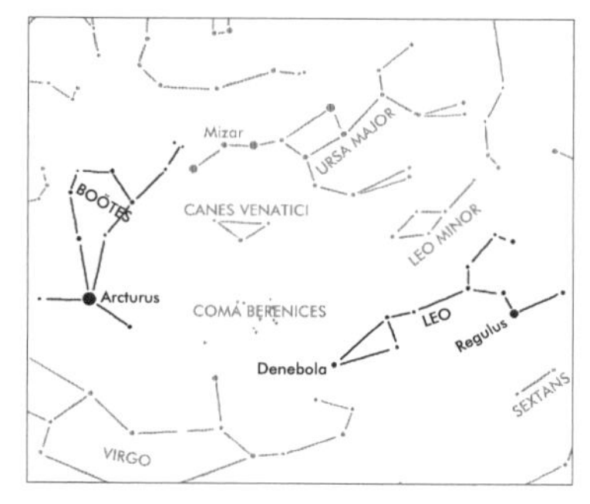

Spring constellations

Big Dipper and directly west of Arcturus. In the springtime Leo is almost overhead.

Summer constellations. During summer evenings, Boötes and Leo have moved west. Then ***Hercules,*** the giant, is overhead, just east of Boötes.

Boötes, the herdsman, is like David in the Bible. On one side are a lion and a bear. On the other side

Materials needed:

- "A Star Guide" with mask from Rod and Staff Publishers, or photocopies of reproducible "Star Guide" and mask on pages 258 and 259.

Note: If you already know how to locate the constellations mentioned in this lesson, you will feel comfortable teaching the students. But if these are strange names to you, you may feel that it will be too hard for the students to learn. Determine that you will learn these constellations with the students. You will be surprised how familiar they can become, and you will soon be calling your students' attention to them with enthusiasm. Do not neglect to give God credit for this majestic splendor.

Did you know—

...that if the sun were eclipsed for 24 hours, we could see the constellations of all 4 seasons in one day?

...that though the constellations were familiar to ancient peoples, the precise boundaries of each one were not defined until 1930?

...that the relative brightness of stars in constellations is shown with the Greek alphabet? The brightest star in each constellation is called alpha, the next brightest is beta, the third brightest is gamma, and so on. The top star of Cygnus is alpha, the brightest. The bottom star of the cross is beta, the next to the brightest. (In a telescope, Beta Cygnus is a lovely double star, one bluish and the other golden.)

is a giant. Maybe David gazed at these constellations and was reminded to say, "Thank You, God, for helping me fight a bear, a lion, and a giant."

Directly east of Hercules is another summer constellation called ***Cygnus.*** Cygnus is often called the Northern Cross because its five brightest stars form a cross. But the name *Cygnus* really means "swan." Think of it as flying, with the lower part of the cross its long neck and head. The upper stars of the cross are the swan's tail and outstretched wings.

Autumn constellations. What constellation tells you that autumn is here? The boxlike shape of ***Pegasus*** overhead is a good clue. Pegasus was the name of a winged horse. Even though there is really no such animal, the people long ago imagined they saw a horse with wings in the stars of Pegasus.

Also overhead is ***Cassiopeia,*** the queen. Cassiopeia looks like a W. Cassiopeia is found half way between Pegasus and Polaris, the North Star. In fact, Cassiopeia is close enough to Polaris that it can be seen in the sky at any time of the year. But it is best seen in the evening when it is high in the sky during the autumn months.

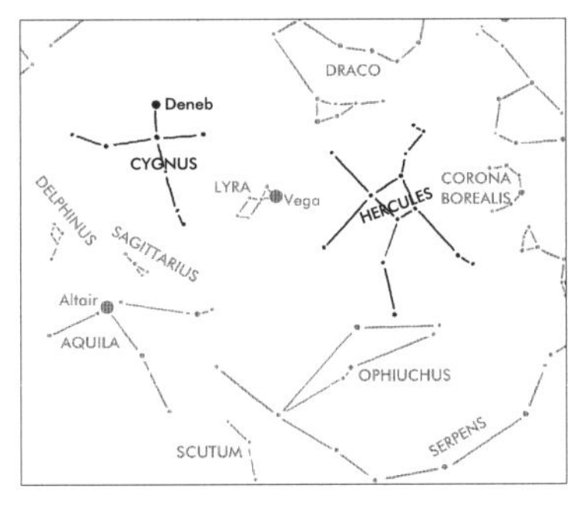

Summer constellations

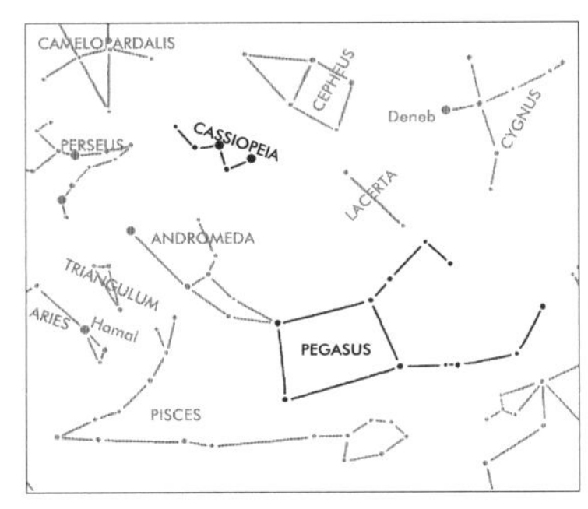

Autumn constellations

Find the Zenith Constellation

Help your students find the zenith and the zenith constellation on a star map. On the Rod and Staff "A Star Guide," with mask in place, the zenith is the center of the oval shape left by the mask. On some star maps, a symbol with the word *zenith* is marked at the center.

You could ask them to find the zenith constellation for July 3 at 8 P.M. (Boötes), the one for September 15 at 9 P.M. (Cygnus), and the one for March 27 at 7 P.M. (Gemini) to give them practice.

Also encourage them to go outside on a clear evening with a star guide and match the zenith constellation shown on the star map with the stars they see directly overhead.

Quiz

Have the students say or write the correct New Word for each sentence below.

1. Here the sky seems to touch the earth. *(horizon)*
2. This winter constellation looks like twins. *(Gemini)*
3. This autumn constellation has a large box in it. *(Pegasus)*
4. This is called the Northern Cross. *(Cygnus)*
5. This autumn constellation is called a queen. *(Cassiopeia)*
6. It means the sky straight above you. *(zenith)*
7. This spring constellation looks like a lion. *(Leo)*
8. This summer constellation is named for a mighty giant. *(Hercules)*

Lesson 3 Answers

Group A

1. Pegasus, winged horse, autumn
2. Cassiopeia, queen, autumn
3. Cygnus, swan, summer
4. Leo, lion, spring
5. Gemini, twins, winter
6. Boötes, herdsman, spring
7. Hercules, giant, summer

(21 points thus far)

Test Your Reading (Group A)

Label each constellation with its name. After each constellation, write the common name, and then write *spring, summer, autumn,* or *winter* to tell which season it is seen best in the evening. The first one is done for you.

Orion, hunter, winter

1\.

2\.

3\.

4\.

5\.

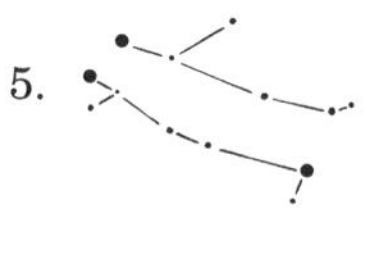

6\.

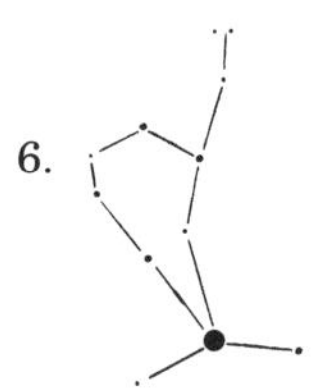

7\.

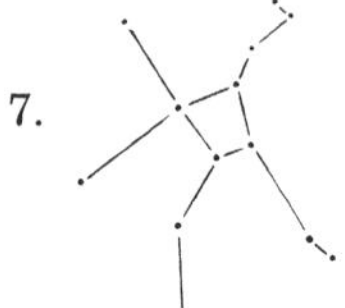

Finding your way in the sky. Four times already in this lesson, the word *overhead* is used. The spot directly overhead is called the ***zenith.*** *Zenith* means "the highest point." To see zenith stars, you must look straight upward to the highest point in the sky. Zenith is easy to find, and so it is easy to find stars at the zenith.

The stars are brighter at the zenith than at the ***horizon,*** where the sky seems to meet the earth. A star near the horizon is harder to see. Its light travels through much more air and looks blurred and dim.

The star guide. If you want to learn the constellations, it is helpful to use a ***star guide,*** or star map. The stars seem to be moving, slowly circling Polaris. At one time Boötes is at the zenith, and at another time it is near the horizon. This might seem confusing without a star guide. The star guide shows you where and when you can see any star or constellation. The star guide is made so that you can set it to show the sky for any time of the night and any day of the year. A mask covers the stars that are not in the sky. The oval shape inside the mask shows the stars you can see.

With a star guide, you can find which stars are at the zenith. On a star map, the zenith is the center of the oval shape left by the mask. First, you find what constellation is at the zenith on the map and then you find that constellation in the sky by looking straight overhead. This is a good way to begin learning where to find the constellations.

Another good method is to look for a bright star group you already know. Next, find one of its neighbors on the map and look for the same star shape in the sky.

Often constellations are remembered by a special figure made by the stars. Here is a list of the special figures in some of the constellations you have learned.

Orion—Three stars form a **belt** (called "bands" in God's question to Job).

Leo—Six stars on the right form the shape of a **sickle.**

Boötes—The body forms the shape of a **kite.**

Hercules—The body has a **keystone** shape.

Cygnus—Four stars one way and three the other way form a **cross.**

Pegasus—The main part is in the shape of a big **square.**

Cassiopeia—The constellation forms a big W.

When you find the constellations, you are, like Job, looking at the handiwork of God. God asked Job questions about Orion, Pleiades, and Arcturus. By now, you should know what stars these name.

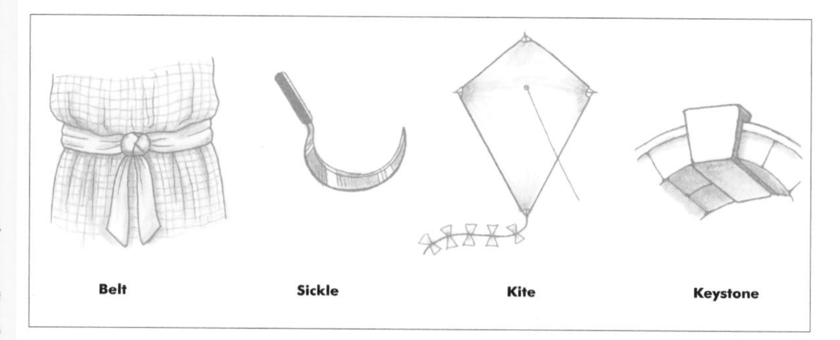

Test Your Reading (Group B)

Answer the following questions.

8. Where is the zenith in the sky?
9. Why are stars easier to see at the zenith than at the horizon?
10. What does the mask of a star guide do?
11. Where are the zenith stars on a star guide?
12. If you can find Orion easily, how can you learn the constellations around Orion?
13. What constellation is in the form of a cross and is sometimes called the Northern Cross?
14. Arcturus, a star of Boötes, is at the bottom of what shape of stars?
15. If you were not sure if you had found Leo, you could look to see if it had what shape?
16. What shape would you look for to find Pegasus?

Group B

8. The zenith is straight overhead.
9. The light of the stars at the zenith does not go through as much atmosphere as the light from the stars near the horizon.
10. The mask covers the stars that cannot be seen at a certain time.
11. The zenith stars on a star guide are in the center of the oval left by the mask.
12. Look on a star guide to see what constellations are near Orion.
13. Cygnus
14. kite
15. sickle
16. square

17. What letter is formed by Cassiopeia?
18. God asked Job if he could loosen what special group of stars in Orion?
19. If you saw a keystone of stars high in the summer sky, what constellation would you see?

17. W
18. "bands," or belt
19. Hercules

(33 points total)

Reviewing What You Have Learned

1. The stars appear to travel around the earth once a day because
   a. the earth revolves around the sun.
   b. the earth rotates on its axis.
   c. the stars revolve around the earth.
2. Orion, Ursa Major, and Boötes are names of ———.
3. If you were lost, you could find which direction was north by finding the star named ———.
4. Which of the following names is wrong?
   a. Arcturus, the bear keeper
   b. Pleiades, the twin sisters
   c. Orion, the hunter
5. True or false? Each night the stars rise ten minutes later than the night before.

Review Answers

1. b
2. constellations
3. Polaris
4. b
5. false

(5 additional points)

Extra Activities

1. If the sky is clear tonight, find the constellations for this season. You may also see the next season's constellations if you get up early in the morning before sunrise. You could ask another star watcher to help you find the constellations and use the star guide. Do not forget to record your sightings on your star-watching chart.
2. Compare the stars overhead with the stars near the horizon. Can you see which ones appear clearer and brighter? Stay outside long enough for your eyes to become adjusted to the darkness.
3. Find out what baby swans are called. Compare this word with the name for the swan constellation.

Lesson 4

Stars Are Useful

New Words

observatory (əb·zėr′·və·tôr′·ē), a place with telescopes for studying the stars.

sextant (sek′·stənt), a tool for measuring the angle between the earth and a star.

Sirius (sir′·ē·əs), a very bright star near the constellation Orion.

telescope (tel′·i·skōp′), a tool for seeing faint stars and other distant objects.

The star calendar. Long ago the farmers of Egypt watched for the star Sirius. ***Sirius*** is a very bright star that rises in the east about an hour after Orion. The Egyptian farmers knew that after they saw Sirius, the Nile River would begin to flood and they could soon plant their fields and gardens. Without much rain to water the land, how glad the farmers were for the Nile River! How glad they were for Sirius to show them every year when the Nile would water the land! The stars were a calendar to them to tell them what time of the year it was.

Today some farmers still use the star calendar. In South America, some farmers use the stars to tell them the right time to plant their yams, a vegetable much like a sweet potato. They watch for the night when Pleiades sets just after the sun. Pleiades tells the farmers the right time to plant their yams.

Our calendars are set by the stars. Today most farmers use printed calendars. But even these calendars need the stars. Men need the stars to measure the exact time it takes the earth to revolve around the sun. That tells them exactly how long a year is.

Men have special places to study the stars. Such a place to *observe* stars is an ***observatory.*** Observatories have ***telescopes*** to

Lesson 4

Concepts to Teach

- The sun, moon, and stars are used to determine exact time and special days of the year.
- There are special observatories to accurately measure time by the stars.
- Navigators use sextants to determine their location by measuring the angles between the stars and the horizon.
- Stars show us the glory of God by their beauty and greatness.
- Telescopes show us even more wonders in the sky than we can see with our eyes alone.
- The stars should inspire worship to God, but should not be worshiped themselves.

Introducing the Lesson

Read Acts 27:20 to the class and explain the setting: the apostle Paul was in a ship during a long, terrific storm. Ask the class to scan quickly through Lesson 4 to discover why it was so important to the sailors to see the sun or the stars. Have them raise their hands as soon as they find the reason.

Then read Acts 28:11, a further account of Paul's ocean journey. Explain that Castor and Pollux are the head stars of Gemini. The sailors did not trust God to keep them safe on the stormy ocean, but instead hoped that their "lucky stars," Castor and Pollux, could help them. This was and still is a common form of idol worship.

Palomar Observatory in California

A telescope shows faint objects more clearly.

see faint stars and other distant objects in the night sky. Some special observatories have special telescopes to measure time by the stars. The stars are used to find out exactly how long the year is. The sun, moon, and stars set the dates on our calendars.

Many calendars tell the first day of each season. The first day of winter is close to December 21. The first day of spring is close to March 21. These days are set by the position of the sun compared with the position of the stars. Many calendars also give the days for the changes of the moon. They tell on which day the moon will be a quarter moon or a full moon. Our calendars are set by what is happening in the sky.

September

Sun	Mon	Tue	Wed	Thu	Fri	Sat
	1 ● New Moon	2	3	4	5	6
7	8	9 ◐ First Quarter	10	11	12	13
14	15	16 ○ Full Moon	17	18	19	20
21	22 Beginning of Autumn	23 ◑ Last Quarter	24	25	26	27
28	29	30				

A calendar page showing phases of the moon and the first day of a season

Did you know—

...that according to one report, Australian aborigines have long used Arcturus's appearance at sunset to signal termite-hunting season, and Vega's position to determine the hunting time for mallee hen eggs?

...that the Stonehenge in England, built around 2000 B.C., is the oldest existing structure that is known to have been an observatory?

...that in 1582, the year needed to be shortened by 10 days to make the calendar agree with the seasons according to the stars? This was because of an accumulative error over the years due to having too many leap years.

Quiz

Some of the vocabulary words are used more than once.

1. You would expect to find telescopes at this place. *(observatory)*
2. This tool helps a sailor figure out the position of his ship. *(sextant)*
3. With this, you can see stars too faint to see with your eye alone. *(telescope)*
4. This is a place where star watchers study stars. *(observatory)*
5. This is a bright star that rises in the east about one hour after Orion. *(Sirius)*
6. With this, you could measure the angle between a star and the horizon. *(sextant)*

Lesson 4 Answers

Group A

1. Sirius, Orion (2 points)
2. Pleiades
3. calendars (*or* years)
4. observatory
5. telescope
6. season, moon (2 points)

(8 points thus far)

Test Your Reading (Group A)

Write the missing words.

1. Egyptians used to know when the Nile River would overflow by the star ———, which rises about one hour after ———.
2. Some farmers of South America use the setting of ——— to help them know when to plant their yams.
3. Men use the stars so that they have the right number of days in their ———.
4. At a special place called an ———, men study stars and can use the stars to determine the exact time.
5. A ——— helps men see faint stars and other distant objects.
6. Besides showing the days, weeks, and months, many calendars tell the first day of each ——— and the days for the changes in the shape of the ———.

Sailors use the stars. On the ocean, sailors have no roads or signs to follow. They can use the stars to find out where they are and what direction they are going.

To find his location, the sailor can use a special tool called a ***sextant.*** With a sextant, he measures the angle between the earth and a star, or how far the star is above the horizon. He repeats the process with two other stars. He then uses a book of star tables and the exact time he measured the stars to find out where his ship is on the ocean. God made the position and movement of the stars so exact that sailors can use them to find the position of a ship.

Stars show us God's glory. When we look at the stars and praise God for His wonderful creation, we are using the stars for a good purpose. God is glorified when we study His stars and give Him the credit for their greatness and exactness. The constellations show how God has kept the stars

A sailor using a sextant

in their positions for thousands of years. The motion of the earth that makes the stars appear to move is part of God's wisdom and power. Even our clocks and calendars are set by the stars God created.

Psalm 19 tells us that "the heavens declare the glory of God." As you study about the stars, you can learn about the glory of God that the stars show us. The stars inspire us to worship God.

Star study is a very inspiring hobby. Some people collect butterflies. Many people are bird watchers. Still others enjoy seeing and naming the stars. Like butterflies and birds, stars are the handiwork of God. Stars are beautiful. Stars are so far away that even though they are very big, they look like tiny points of light. With our eyes alone, we can see the greatness and beauty of the stars. With a telescope, we can see even more of the wonders of God's created world. The stars show us the glory of God.

Interesting Telescopic Objects
(in the constellations you know)

Cloud of glowing gas in "sword" hanging at belt of Orion
Blue and yellow double star at bottom end of cross in Cygnus
Cluster of over 100,000 stars on right side of keystone of Hercules

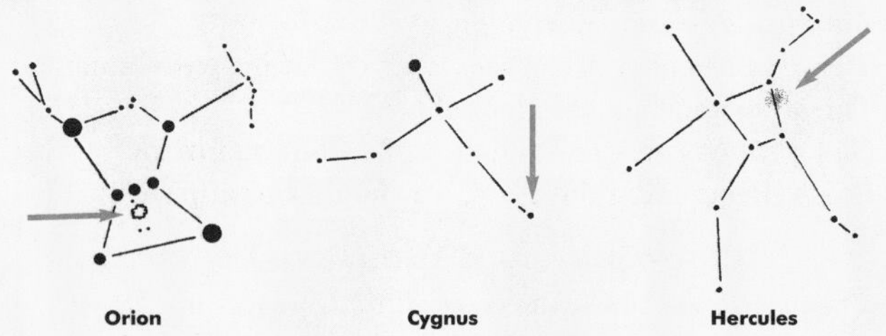

Orion Cygnus Hercules

Wrong use of the stars. Thus far, you have learned some good uses for the stars. But not all star study is good. Some people use the stars to try to foretell the future. They trust in the stars more than they trust God and His Word. In this way they actually worship the stars instead of God.

Job knew that God is Lord over the stars. He knew that it is wrong to worship anything except God, for he said, "If I beheld the sun when it shined, or the moon walking in brightness; and my heart hath been secretly enticed . . . : this also were an iniquity . . . : for I should have denied the God that is above" (Job 31:26–28). We are to worship God who made the stars. It is wrong to worship the stars.

Test Your Reading (Group B)

Answer *true* if the statement is true. Answer *false* if the statement is not true.

7. Sailors can use the stars to find out where they are on the ocean.
8. The sextant tells how far a star is from the zenith.
9. To find where he is, a sailor would need to have a star guide.
10. The motion of the stars shows us God's exactness.
11. Stars look like points of light because the stars are so small.
12. Stars are different colors.
13. Star study is an inspiring hobby.
14. With a telescope, you can see clouds of glowing gases among the stars.
15. The stars show us the glory of God.
16. God gave us the stars to help us foretell the future.
17. Since God created the stars, we should worship them.

Group B
7. true
8. false
9. false
10. true
11. false
12. true
13. true
14. true
15. true
16. false
17. false

(19 points total)

Reviewing What You Have Learned

1. The brightest star of the constellation Boötes is
   a. Arcturus. b. Sirius. c. Polaris.
2. The stars look brightest at the ——— of the sky.
3. Which of the sentences about constellations and seasons is wrong?
   a. Orion is a winter constellation.
   b. Cygnus is a summer constellation.
   c. Pegasus is a spring constellation.

Review Answers

1. a
2. zenith
3. c

4. The stars appear to travel around Polaris because the earth is ——.
5. True or false? Two stars of the Little Dipper point to a bright star in the Big Dipper.

4. rotating
5. false

(5 additional points)

Extra Activities

1. Use a calendar that has special days of the seasons and the moon marked on it. Make a list of the first days of the seasons for this year. Make a list of the days of the new moon, first quarter, full moon, and last quarter for this year. How far is it from one new moon to the next? Check to see if the calendar dates for the moon agree with the actual moon. From new moon to full moon, the moon can be seen in the evening. From full moon to new moon, the moon can be seen in the morning. Do you expect the calendar to agree with the moon? Why? How do the calendar makers know when to put these special days on their calendars?
2. Use an encyclopedia to find out about leap year. Why can we not have the same number of days in each calendar year? What would happen if we did not have leap year?
3. Find out what "sun time" is at your school. Make a simple sundial by driving a metal stake or rod into the ground. Choose a place where the noon sun will shine on it. Make the stake very straight. Your teacher can come to school some evening after dark to find true north by sighting toward Polaris. Have your teacher lay a second rod or stake on the ground, placing one end against the upright stake and pointing the other end toward Polaris. When the shadow of the stake crosses the true north line, that is twelve o'clock noon. Set a clock to run on "sun time." Depending where you live in your time zone, "sun time" will either be ahead or behind standard time. Only if you live in the exact center of your time zone will the two times be the same.
4. What is the closest observatory to you? Some colleges have observatories. See if you can find some information about the United States Naval Observatory in Washington, D.C. Perhaps you can visit an observatory.

Extra Activity Comments

2. The history of bringing our calendar year into step with the star year is interesting. Fast students could be assigned to do research on this and report to the class. The index to the encyclopedia can be used to find the places where this subject is discussed.
3. It would be good to fasten to the classroom ceiling an arrow that is pointing to true north. Such a direction can be established by sighting out the window to Polaris (provided your classroom has a window to the north). True north is usually not the same as magnetic north. The north magnetic pole is not at the true north pole.

Lesson 5

Do You Remember?

From the word box, find and write a word for each blank.

constellation	sextant	telescope
horizon	star guide	zenith
observatory		

1. The stars look dim and blurred near the ———.
2. Learning the ———s helps us remember the arrangement of the stars.
3. A constellation that is directly overhead is at the ———.
4. A ——— measures the angle between a star and the horizon.
5. A ——— is used to see faint objects in the sky.
6. A ——— would help you find the stars that are visible tonight.
7. Men study the stars with a telescope at an ———.

Give the scientific name for these constellations, and then tell what that name means.

8. 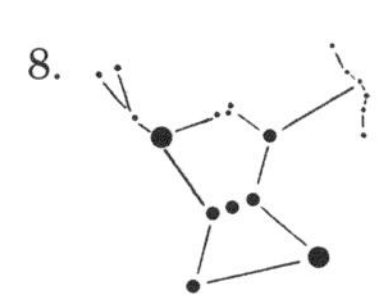

10. 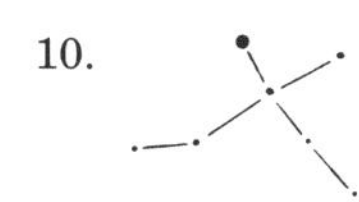

9. 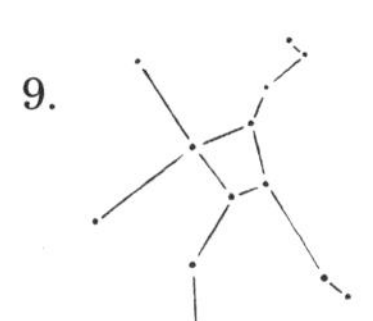

11. 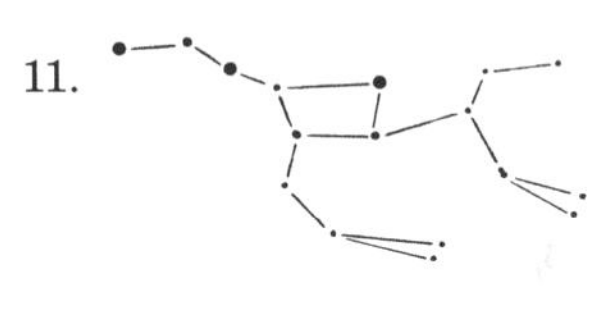

Lesson 5 Answers

1. horizon
2. constellation
3. zenith
4. sextant
5. telescope
6. star guide
7. observatory

(Each part can count ½ point.)

8. Orion, hunter
9. Hercules, giant
10. Cygnus, swan
11. Ursa Major, big bear

Lesson 5

Reviewing the Unit

Have your students take turns reading paragraphs of the unit introduction on page 76. Take note of the concept that our star study should reinforce our awe and reverence for God.

If the students wonder what Mazzaroth is, say that it is believed to be the zodiac. Explain the zodiac as a set of 12 constellations, 2 of which are Leo and Gemini. The sun, moon, and planets pass through these 12 constellations. God made the constellations of the zodiac, but man has linked them with the ungodly practice of fortunetelling called astrology.

Ask the class if they remember what *Arcturus* means and what his "sons" are. If they need help, refer them to Lesson 2. Stress the review of the constellations and stars mentioned in this unit. Be sure the students can identify drawings of each, since this skill is called for in the test.

Review the unit with a question chain, as described on page 73, or with a few of the "Lesson Answers" questions from each lesson. Remind the class that each of them also needs to study thoroughly on his own.

12. 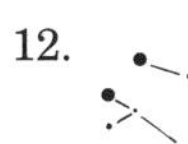

15. 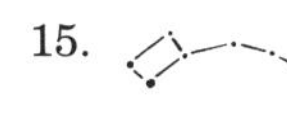

13. 

16. 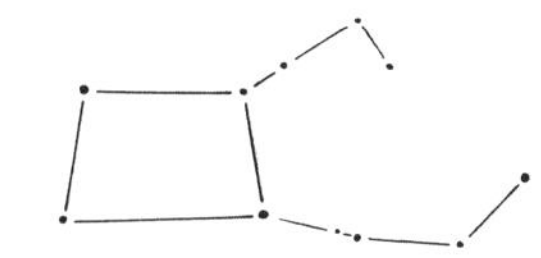

14. 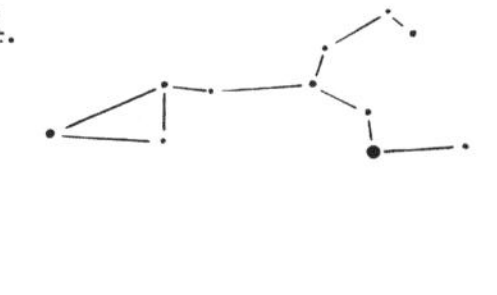

17.

12. Gemini, twins
13. Cassiopeia, queen
14. Leo, lion
15. Ursa Minor, little bear
16. Pegasus, winged horse
17. Boötes, herdsman

Name these stars.

18. The North Star
19. The bright star that comes up about one hour after Orion
20. The star God mentioned to Job that is in Boötes
21. The "seven sisters"

Choose the best answer to finish each sentence.

22. The Northern Cross is the name that is sometimes used for
    a. Cygnus. b. Boötes. c. Hercules.
23. Each day the stars circle around
    a. Sirius.
    b. Arcturus.
    c. Polaris.

18. Polaris
19. Sirius
20. Arcturus
21. Pleiades
22. a
23. c

24. The stars can be used as a calendar because
    a. a constellation rises at the same time year around.
    b. a star sets 4 minutes later each night than the night before.
    c. each different season has its own set of constellations.
25. One of the constellations best seen in spring is
    a. Orion.
    b. Gemini.
    c. Leo.
26. Pegasus can be found by looking for
    a. a big square.
    b. a kite shape.
    c. a keystone shape.
27. Both Ursa Major and Ursa Minor can be seen
    a. in the south.
    b. in the autumn.
    c. all year around.
28. The Bible talks about the bands of
    a. Hercules.
    b. Orion.
    c. Boötes.

Write *true* if the sentence is true, and write *false* if it is not true.

29. You can learn many constellations by taking time to study the stars with a helper and a star guide.
30. The reason most constellations can be seen only part of the year is mostly because of the earth's rotation.
31. God wants us to worship Him rather than the stars.
32. Some observatories use the stars to keep exact time.
33. God wants us to use the stars to tell the future.

Answer these questions.

34. How were the stars helpful to farmers long ago?
35. How could you use the stars if you were lost?
36. Why do the stars appear to be moving around the earth?
37. How can you use the Big Dipper to find Polaris?

24. c
25. c
26. a
27. c
28. b

29. true
30. false
31. true
32. true
33. false
34. Farmers long ago watched for certain stars or constellations to show them the right time of year to plant their crops.
35. You would find Polaris, or the North Star. That would show which direction was north.
36. The stars appear to move around the earth because the earth is rotating on its axis.
37. The two stars on the side of the dipper point in the direction of Polaris.

(37 points total)

Unit Four

God Heals Our Diseases

"And he took him a potsherd to scrape himself withal; and he sat down among the ashes" (Job 2:8).

No one likes to be sick. Neither did Job. All over his body were painful sores called boils. Job felt very tired, yet he could not sleep well. He tossed about during the night and wished for night to end. He said, "My flesh is clothed with worms and clods of dust; my skin is broken, and become loathsome" (Job 7:5). Job was miserable. With a bit of broken pottery, he scraped his hot, crusted body. Perhaps this gave him some relief from itching.

The Bible does not tell us that he had pills or doctors to help him. Job had help that is better than doctors and medicine. God was watching over Job and saw how miserable Job was. He had allowed Satan to make Job sick. Satan had thought that Job's sickness would make him hate God. But God knew that it would help Job know God better and trust Him more.

That is just what happened. Job knew God better after his sickness than he had before. He said to God, "I have heard of thee by the hearing of the ear: but now mine eye seeth thee" (Job 42:5). God healed Job's sickness and made him well again.

Job was thankful that God healed him. This is the same God who heals us. Doctors can help us when we are sick. Medicine can help us. But God heals us.

In this unit you can learn how God heals us when we get sick. You can learn how He has designed your body to stay healthy. You can discover how He has given your body many little "soldiers" to fight disease. You can trust God to help you when you get sick.

Unit Four

For Your Inspiration

Anyone who has had an extended illness as Job did knows that the experience usually involves not only physical suffering but also some degree of emotional pain. There is a natural tendency toward discouragement and depression. This discouragement may be caused by physical exhaustion, by the lack of normal hormonal balance, or simply by the feeling of being useless and unproductive. Sad to say, at times it may be intensified by the thoughtless or unkind remarks of supposed friends, just as Job experienced.

In the following verses, notice how much of Job's suffering was other than physical.

When I lie down, I say, When shall I arise, and the night be gone?
and I am full of tossings to and fro unto the dawning of the day.
My flesh is clothed with worms and clods of dust;
my skin is broken, and become loathsome.
My days are swifter than a weaver's shuttle,
and are spent without hope.

I called my servant, and he gave me no answer;
I intreated him with my mouth.
My breath is strange to my wife,
though I intreated for the children's sake of mine own body.
Yea, young children despised me;
I arose, and they spake against me.
All my inward friends abhorred me:
and they whom I loved are turned against me.

And now am I their song,
yea, I am their byword.
They abhor me, they flee far from me,
and spare not to spit in my face.

—Job 7:4–6; 19:16–19; 30:9, 10

Lesson 1

Causes of Sickness

New Words

diet (dī′·it), the kinds and amounts of food you eat from day to day.

fever (fē′·vər), overheating of the body during sickness.

germs, tiny plants or animals that can cause disease and are seen only with a microscope.

minerals (min′·ər·əlz), iron, calcium, and other materials needed for good health.

symptom (sim′·təm), coughing, sore throat, or another sign of illness.

vitamins (vī′·tə·minz), a group of materials which are needed by the body for good health and are named by letters, such as vitamin A or vitamin C.

A poor diet can make us sick. Long ago many British sailors became sick at sea. But they were not just seasick. Their sickness was called scurvy. This sickness could make sailors very weak and tired. Their joints and mouths felt sore, and their gums bled easily. Cuts and scratches healed very slowly. Some sailors even died of scurvy.

Then some sailors discovered a secret. They found out that if they drank lime juice from time to time, they would not get scurvy. Limes are green fruit shaped about like lemons. Soon the good news spread, and sailors took limes along on their trips. They drank so much lime juice that people started calling the sailors "limeys."

The sailors did not know why lime juice kept them from getting scurvy. They were just glad it did. Neither did they know why they were more likely to get scurvy at sea than at home on land. But today we know these answers.

When the sailors were at home, they ate more vegetables and fruit than when they were out on the

When we are at our weakest and most vulnerable state, Satan tries to exploit the situation to his advantage. Just as surely as he incited Job's wife to advise him to "curse God and die," so he will somehow try to shake our faith in God.

But, praise God, He gives us victory over Satan even while experiencing illness and emotional pain. We need not be overcome by our inclination to discouragement when we rest our case with Him. With Job, we can say, "But he knoweth the way that I take: when he hath tried me, I shall come forth as gold" (Job 23:10).

The apostle Paul is another shining example of victory through suffering, even though he was not healed in this life. Notice the ring of triumph in the last two verses.

And lest I should be exalted above measure through the abundance of the revelations, there was given to me a thorn in the flesh, the messenger of Satan to buffet me, lest I should be exalted above measure.

For this thing I besought the Lord thrice, that it might depart from me.

And he said unto me, My grace is sufficient for thee: for my strength is made perfect in weakness. Most gladly therefore will I rather glory in my infirmities, that the power of Christ may rest upon me.

Therefore I take pleasure in infirmities, in reproaches, in necessities, in persecutions, in distresses for Christ's sake: for when I am weak, then am I strong.

—2 Corinthians 12:7–10

ocean. At sea, they had only dried beef and hard biscuits to eat for months at a time. Beef and biscuits did not supply their bodies with all the vitamins they needed. The sailors got scurvy because their bodies lacked one vitamin called vitamin C. But the lime juice they drank had plenty of vitamin C in it, so it kept them from getting scurvy.

A lime would be good medicine for these sailors sick with scurvy.

Your body needs several ***vitamins*** to stay healthy. They are vitamins A, B, C, and D. Your body also needs some ***minerals*** like iron and calcium. The mineral iron is needed to make blood, and calcium is needed to make bones. You need only a little of each kind of vitamin and mineral. If you get too much of some of them at once, they make you sick. God has put just the right amount of them in vegetables, grains, meat, and milk products. If you eat a wide variety of these good foods, you are likely to get the right amount of vitamins and minerals.

What about foods such as candy, cake, and potato chips? These foods do not contain many vitamins or minerals. If you want to be strong and healthy, you should not eat much of these foods. Instead, you should eat more whole-grain bread, milk, cheese or meat, and plenty of fruits and vegetables.

If you have a wide variety of good food in your diet, you are likely to stay healthy. Your ***diet*** is the kinds and amounts of food you eat from day to day. Your parents care for you by providing many kinds of food for your diet. That is why they have you eat plenty of vegetables and fruit. They do not want you to get sick because of a poor diet that lacks the vitamins and minerals your body needs.

Lesson 1

Concepts to Teach

- Some diseases are caused by a lack of certain materials in our diet.
- Our bodies need vitamins and certain minerals to be healthy.
- Some living things called germs cause disease and are so small that they can only be seen with a microscope.
- Germs make us sick by making poisons and destroying body cells.
- Disease germs and their poisons cause certain signs called symptoms.

Introducing the Lesson

Read and discuss Job 2:3–8. Notice that the reason for Job's sickness was a complete mystery to him. He had no idea of the conversations about him between God and Satan. In fact, we have no indication that God ever explained it to Job while he lived on earth.

But God did inspire the writer of the Book of Job to record at least part of the reason for our benefit. This helps us understand that God has a purpose for sickness in our lives also, even though we may never know it in this life.

Take time for a quick overview of the unit, as usual.

Did you know—

...that 5 of the 13 vitamins the human body needs are manufactured inside it rather than being supplied by food?

...that vitamin K is produced by bacteria in the human intestine?

...that studies of Egyptian mummies have shown that the ancient Egyptians suffered many of the same diseases that we do today?

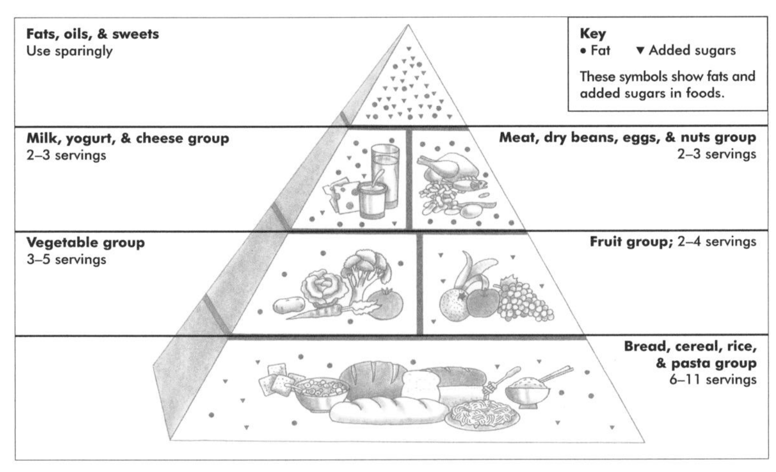

A Food Guide: Eat a variety of foods every day.

Test Your Reading (Group A)

Write the missing words.

1. Sailors used to get a disease called ———, which made their mouths and gums get very sore.
2. The sailors got the disease because they did not get enough vitamin ——— in their diet.
3. When they drank ——— juice, they did not get the disease, because it had the vitamin their bodies needed to stay healthy.
4. Your body needs small amounts of ——— A, B, C, and D.
5. Your body needs some of the ——— iron to make blood.
6. Your body needs some ——— to grow strong bones.
7. ——— put the right amount of vitamins and minerals into the foods we eat.
8. Be sure to eat enough ——— like beans, carrots, and lettuce so that you get the vitamins and minerals your body needs.
9. Your parents provide you with different foods in your ———.

...that because viruses are very simply built and behave as living things in some ways and as nonliving matter in other ways, scientists consider them both living and nonliving?

Quiz

Have the students say or write the correct New Word for each sentence below.

1. It is a sign that you are sick. *(symptom)*
2. We get these materials named with ABCs by eating vegetables. *(vitamins)*
3. It is a common symptom of many diseases. *(fever)*
4. This is a very tiny plant or animal that makes us sick. *(germ)*
5. Our bodies need calcium, which belongs to this group. *(minerals)*
6. We use this word to name the kinds and amounts of food you usually eat. *(diet)*

Lesson 1 Answers

Group A

1. scurvy
2. C
3. lime
4. vitamins
5. mineral
6. calcium
7. God
8. vegetables
9. diet

10. a. yes e. no
b. no f. no
c. yes g. yes
d. yes h. yes
(17 points thus far)

Write *yes* if the food is a good source of vitamins and minerals. Write *no* if the food is not a good source of vitamins and minerals.

10. a. meat
b. candy
c. fruit
d. whole-wheat bread
e. potato chips
f. cake
g. vegetables
h. milk

Germs can make us sick. You may not know of anyone who is sick because of a lack of vitamins and minerals. That is because we eat healthful foods that God has made for us. But maybe you know people who are sick because of germs. ***Germs*** are very tiny plants or animals that can grow in our bodies and make us sick. These living things are so small that a microscope is needed to see them. But they can make even a big man feel very sick.

Germs feed, grow, and multiply, feed, grow, and multiply; and in a single day, one germ can become hundreds of germs! The many germs harm and even kill cells of the body. They make poisons that hurt the body. The more cells they destroy and the more poisons they make, the more sick a person becomes.

How can something as small as germs make a man sick?

Germs cause diseases such as leprosy, strep throat, whooping cough, and scarlet fever. Germs also cause more common diseases such as colds, flu, mumps, measles, and chicken pox.

What are some symptoms of sickness? Whenever germs are multiplying or making poisons inside a person's body, they cause certain signs, or ***symptoms.*** Cold germs may cause the symptoms of coughing, sneezing, a runny nose, and a sore throat. Chicken pox germs cause the symptoms of a rash, sore muscles, a headache, and a fever. The symptoms do not cause the disease; they are signs that a person has a disease. Doctors use these symptoms to decide what kind of disease the person has.

You have likely had a fever already. It is a common symptom of many diseases. A ***fever*** is the overheating of your body because of sickness. It is not the same as feeling hot on a sticky summer day. If you have a fever, you feel hot and sick all over. You may be sweating one minute and shivering the next. This is called "chills and fever."

A fever can be measured by taking a person's temperature with a fever thermometer. If you have only a slight fever, your mother might tell you to rest and drink plenty of liquids. But if you have a high fever, she probably would take you to a doctor. If a high fever is not treated quickly, it can damage the brain.

Job knew what it was like to have a germ disease. Satan "smote Job with sore boils from the sole of his foot unto his crown" (Job 2:7).

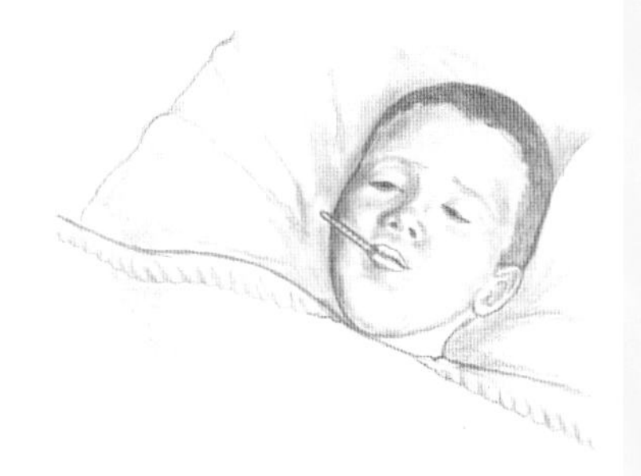

What symptom will the thermometer show?

Boils are one kind of germ disease. It seems that Job had the symptom of fever with his sickness. He said, "My bones are burned with heat" (Job 30:30).

Job was glad when God healed him, just as you are glad when God heals you from a sickness. In the next lessons, you will study some ways God made your body to fight germs. You will learn how you can do your part to get well and stay well.

Test Your Reading (Group B)

Answer the following questions.

11. What are the tiny living things that can make a person sick?
12. How can only a few germs make a person sick in three or four days?
13. What are two ways that germs make the body sick?
14. How do doctors know what disease a person has?
15. What are three symptoms of a cold?

Group B

11. germs
12. They multiply to make hundreds of germs.
13. by destroying cells and by making poisons (2 points)
14. by looking at the symptoms
15. (Any three.) coughing, sneezing, a runny nose, a sore throat (3 points)

16. a symptom
17. hot and sick all over
18. by taking your temperature with a thermometer
19. of having germs

(29 points total)

Extra Activity Comments

1. Some of the vitamins are identified by name, such as thiamine and niacin. A dictionary can be used to determine which are names for vitamins. You can do this activity as a class, seeing how many different vitamins and minerals you can find on food packages. This activity can help the students appreciate the many things God placed in food for us to be healthy.
4. A person's body temperature is slightly higher while exercising vigorously than while resting because the body is burning fuel at a faster rate. But exercising does not cause fever. God gave the body the ability to maintain almost the same temperature at all times.

   You could demonstrate the proper way to take a temperature, and then allow a few students to take their temperatures. Ask if anyone can explain why you need to leave the thermometer in your mouth for a few minutes. Emphasize carefulness with a glass thermometer, for it can break easily. Of course, it should be dipped in alcohol after each use so that germs are not spread.

16. When you tell your mother, "I have a fever," is the fever a disease or a symptom?
17. How will you feel if you have a fever?
18. How can you know for sure if you have a fever?
19. When someone has a boil, is it because he lacks a vitamin or because he has germs?

Extra Activities

1. Find the names for as many vitamins and minerals as you can from food package labels.
2. Learn more about germs. Look up the names *bacteria* and *virus* in a dictionary or encyclopedia. Draw pictures of the different kinds of germs. Label each picture with its name and the disease it causes.
3. Learn more about vitamins and about diseases caused by a poor diet. You could read the articles under "Nutrition," "Vitamin," and "Disease" in an encyclopedia. Tell or write what you have learned.
4. Ask your teacher or mother to help you take your temperature with a fever thermometer. You could take your temperature twice: first after you have been reading or resting quietly for a while, and next after you have been running or working hard. Are both temperatures alike? Can you guess why or why not?

Lesson 2

Fighting Germs

New Words

antibodies (an′·ti·bod′·ēz), materials made by the body to fight germs.

immune (i·myün′), protected from getting a certain disease.

vaccine (vak·sēn′), a mixture of weak or dead disease germs that causes the body to protect itself from the disease.

white blood cells, tiny living parts of the blood that destroy disease germs.

Germs make us sick. One morning you wake up with a sore, scratchy throat. Your eyes hurt. Your bones ache, and you feel hot all over. "I don't feel good at all," you say. "I feel sick!"

A flu germ may be making you sick. There are many other kinds of germs that can make your body sick. If you could see all the germs around you, you would say, "I'm surprised that I'm not sick all the time!"

When God made us, He knew about all these germs. He knows all about keeping us healthy. So He gave us a body that fights hard to stay well.

How does your body protect itself from germs? First of all, God protected your body with a tough wrapping of skin. Germs cannot get inside unless they enter through

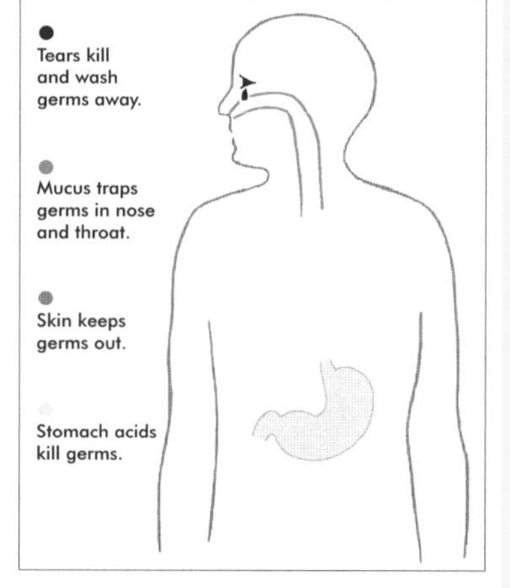

God made it hard for germs to enter the body.

Lesson 2

Concepts to Teach

- Our bodies keep many of the germs out.
- Special cells in our blood fight germs.
- Once the body has fought a disease germ, it is more ready to fight that kind of germ again.
- Your body can become immune to some diseases by producing antibodies.
- A vaccine can help the body to develop immunity.
- The body is somewhat weakened by a disease and can more easily get a second disease.

Explain that we do appreciate and benefit from the work of scientists who have developed vaccines that protect us from many diseases. However, guard against boastful expressions such as "Look at what all we know that those poor people didn't back there" or "Look at what all man has done—in time we may conquer all diseases." Point out that scientists are using their God-given minds to understand and stimulate our God-given immune system. Without the body's natural protections against disease, vaccines are worthless.

Introducing the Lesson

Tell the story of the first smallpox vaccination by Edward Jenner in 1796. During that time smallpox was one of the most feared diseases. Year after year many people died from it. If the disease was not fatal, the victim was often scarred for life.

Dr. Jenner knew that dairymaids who had the mild disease of cowpox were said to be safe from smallpox. So he decided to try a daring experiment. First he found some people who were willing to help him: James Phipps, a healthy, eight-year-old boy, and Sarah Nelmes, a girl who had cowpox from milking cows. Dr. Jenner took a little of the material from a sore on Sarah's hand,

openings in the skin: either through your eyes, nose, and mouth, or through a cut in your skin.

For the germs that do enter in these ways, God made three more protections within your body. He made tears to wash away the germs in your eyes. He made a sticky mucus to trap any germs in your nose and throat. He made stomach liquids to kill germs that you swallow with your food. With your skin on the outside and these three on the inside, most germs around you do not make you sick.

But why do you ever get sick? If you breathe in enough cold or flu germs, some may stay inside your nose or throat and start multiplying. Or if you cut your skin, germs start getting inside right away. Some may find their way into your bloodstream.

Your blood is like a river with many streams that flow to every part of your body. Germs that get into your blood can spread everywhere unless they are stopped.

Lesson 2 Answers

Group A

1. true
2. true
3. false
4. false
5. true
6. false

(6 points thus far)

Test Your Reading (Group A)

Write *true* if the statement is true. Write *false* if the statement is not true.

1. Germs can give you a sore throat.
2. Sometimes you come in contact with germs without getting sick.
3. The skin lets germs get into your body.
4. The tears of the eyes help the germs make you sick.
5. The body has a way to trap or kill germs that enter your nose and throat.
6. Germs enter your stomach through a cut in your skin.

How do white blood cells destroy germs? God put many millions of special cells called ***white blood cells*** in your blood. White blood cells are like tiny soldiers, always ready to fight enemy germs. When your throat or any other body part is hurt by germs, it somehow sends a HELP call to the white blood cells. They rush to the rescue,

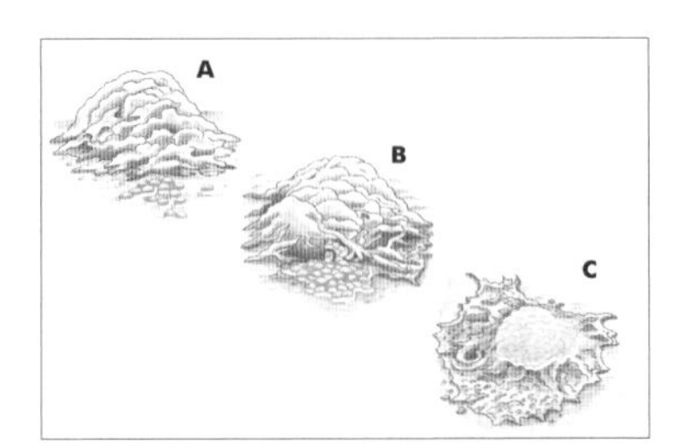

A white blood cell surrounds the germs and then kills them.

which was sure to contain cowpox germs, and put it into two small cuts on James's arm. In a short time, James got cowpox just as Dr. Jenner had expected. He had a few minor sores like those of dairymaids.

Forty-eight days later, Dr. Jenner performed the most dangerous part of his experiment. Into James's arm, he put material from a sore containing smallpox germs. The next days and weeks, they all watched for signs of smallpox, but James did not get it at all. The cowpox germs had caused his body to build up its defenses against the very similar smallpox germs.

Only a few years after this experiment, vaccination became well accepted as a protection from smallpox. Because of vaccination, today there are so few cases of smallpox anywhere that the disease has been officially declared to be wiped out.

Did you know—

...that the white corpuscles can leave the bloodstream and travel to infected tissues as needed?

...that the World Health Organization is responsible for monitoring influenza outbreaks worldwide, and for providing a new vaccine from time to time as a new strain of influenza replaces the old kind?

...that the AIDS virus is so dangerous because it attacks white corpuscles that are vital to the immune system, leaving the body wide open to infectious invaders of any kind?

...that sometimes babies have died because an antibody in the mother's Rh-negative blood has caused clumping of the red blood cells of the child with Rh-positive cells? Today there are several methods doctors can use to help avoid such deaths.

swarm over the disease germs, and eat them up. If necessary, your body quickly makes millions more of these white blood cells to help fight germs.

Some of the white blood cells eat so many germs that they die. You see them in the yellowish pus of a sore. The pus is a mixture of dead white blood cells, dead germs, and body liquids. Wherever you see it, you can be sure that your white blood cells were working hard to get rid of germs.

Sometimes enemy germs sneak inside your body without your body knowing it. Usually the sneakiest germs are those that your body has never fought before. For example, if your body has never fought measles or chicken pox germs before, they sneak right in and make you sick.

How do antibodies fight germs? God created your body to make special materials called ***antibodies.*** When many chicken pox germs attack your body, it starts making chicken pox antibodies. These antibodies find chicken pox germs and either make their poison harmless, kill them, or make it easier for the white blood cells to eat them. Each time your body fights a new kind of germ, it makes antibodies to fight only that kind of germ or germ family.

When you have had measles or chicken pox once, some of the antibodies that your body made stay in the blood. Never again will they let those kinds of germs multiply and make you sick. You have become ***immune*** to them.

But why does not your body become immune to colds and the flu? These germs are tricky. There are many different kinds of germs that cause a cold, and the antibodies for these germs do not last very long. So just having a cold does not make you immune to all cold germs. They can slip inside your body and make you sick again and again.

Test Your Reading (Group B)

Write the missing words.

7. When germs get into the body, the ——— blood cells can kill them.
8. The ——— in a sore shows that germs are being killed.
9. Different diseases are caused by different ———.
10. Your body can best fight the germs of a disease if it has the right ——— against that disease.

Group B

7. white
8. pus
9. germs
10. antibodies

Quiz

Have the students say or write the correct New Word for each sentence below.

1. These cells in your blood fight all kinds of germs. *(white blood cells)*
2. They each fight only one kind of germ. *(antibodies)*
3. This material causes the body to make antibodies for a certain disease. *(vaccine)*
4. It means that your body is already prepared to fight off a certain disease. *(immune)*

11. makes
12. immune
13. cold (*or* flu)

(13 points thus far)

11. When a new germ gets into the body, the body ——— the needed antibody.
12. If you had a certain disease, you may be ——— to it and never get that disease again.
13. The antibodies made for ——— germs do not last very long.

How does a vaccine protect you from germs? For many diseases, there is another way of becoming immune besides having the disease. You can get a vaccine as a shot in your arm or as a liquid to drink. A ***vaccine*** causes your body to make antibodies for a certain disease *before* the live germs get inside.

When you were a baby, you may have gotten some shots of different vaccines. One such vaccine had dead mumps germs in it. Your body could not tell that the mumps germs were harmless. It "thought" that you were actually getting sick with mumps. So it got busy making lots of mumps antibodies. Now, if you get normal mumps germs inside you today, your body is all ready to destroy them. The vaccine has caused you to become immune to mumps.

Why does your body feel weak? Germ fighting does not last long in a small cut on your finger. You hardly notice that there is any battle at all. But sometimes your body must fight longer to get rid of disease germs—maybe a few days, weeks, or even months. During this time, your body is rather weak. And you are more likely to get other diseases. This is why you should take extra good care of your body while you are sick.

In the next lessons, you can learn about taking care of your body to get well and stay healthy.

Test Your Reading (Group C)

Choose the best answer.

14. When you get a vaccine,
    a. your body is given antibodies for a disease.
    b. your body makes antibodies for a disease.
    c. your body gets sick from a disease.
    d. your body gets better from a disease.

Group C

14. b

15. Babies are sometimes given a vaccine for a disease because
    a. they have brothers and sisters who have the disease.
    b. the doctor thinks they have the disease.
    c. this gives the doctor work to do.
    d. they can become immune to the disease without having the disease.
16. After getting better from a disease, you should still take care because
    a. a weak body can more easily get another disease.
    b. the body needs time to make antibodies.
    c. the germs may not all be dead.
    d. you may give the germs to another person.

15. d
16. a

(16 points total)

Reviewing What You Have Learned

1. To be healthy, our bodies need
    a. scurvy and symptoms.
    b. vitamins and minerals.
    c. diet and vaccines.
2. We must use a microscope to see the ——— that cause disease.
3. A poor diet could cause you to get
    a. fever.
    b. chicken pox.
    c. scurvy.
4. True or false? Germs can harm body cells with poisons.
5. When Job said, "My bones are burned with heat," he probably had a ———.

Review Answers

1. b
2. germs
3. c
4. true
5. fever

(5 additional points)

Extra Activities

1. Ask your parents to tell you which vaccinations you have received, and ask to see your health records if you have them at home.
2. Learn more about how your body fights germs by reading articles in an encyclopedia under these titles: "Blood," "Immunity," "Immunization," and "Lymphatic System." Tell or write what you learned.

Lesson 3

Getting Well

New Words

diagnosis (dī′·əg·nō′·sis), the careful study of symptoms to determine which disease one has.

medicine (med′·i·sin), something used to prevent or treat a disease.

prescription (pri·skrip′·shən), written directions used for getting and taking medicine.

God heals our diseases. You know that God is better than any doctor. He did not need pills to heal Job's sickness. At the right time, God simply made Job well.

God and His Son Jesus have made many people well in this way. Think of Moses' sister, Miriam, and of Naaman, whom God healed of leprosy. Think of all the blind, deaf, and lame that Jesus healed. Think of the people that God still heals today.

So whom should you expect to heal you when you are sick? It is God! God sometimes heals right away. Sometimes He heals after a time of waiting. At other times, God does not heal until His children go to heaven. But God always heals His children of their diseases.

Doctors do not heal our bodies. They only give us advice and help to make healing come more quickly and easily. It is God who does the actual healing.

We can help our bodies get well. Although God does the work of healing, He still wants you to do your part when you are sick. First of all, God wants you to trust Him. He wants you to be as cheerful as you can be, even though you are sick. The Bible says, "A merry heart doeth good like a medicine" (Proverbs 17:22). A cheerful, peaceful person is likely to get well faster than one who is worried and grouchy.

God also wants you to take good care of your body while you are sick. During this time you should not work hard. Instead, you need plenty of rest and sleep to get well.

Lesson 3

Concepts to Teach

- The first help we should seek is from God.
- A cheerful attitude does much to help the body recover from disease.
- A good diet and plenty of rest are needed.
- The cards and visits from others are a help in getting well.
- God has made many materials that are used as medicines to help the body fight germs.
- Doctors can be used by God to help us get well.

Introducing the Lesson

Bring some medicines along to class, both prescription and nonprescription. Pass them around the class, having the students notice the purpose for each medicine and the variations in directions. Discuss the importance of following directions properly and of not taking drugs prescribed for someone else. Perhaps you or one of the students can relate an incident when someone accidentally took the wrong pills or when a child's stomach needed to be pumped because he helped himself to medicine.

Be sure to put the medicines away in a safe place after this activity.

Materials needed:

- prescription drugs, such as penicillin and heart medication
- nonprescription drugs, such as cough syrup, Tylenol, or Sudafed

Did you know—

...that for every new drug on the market, about 10,000 are rejected during research and testing?

...that each year a number of American children die from aspirin overdose?

Cleaning a wound and bandaging it are important for healing, but what makes the wound heal?

The ability of the body to heal is a wonderful gift from God. When you cut yourself, the skin will grow back together. When you clean a wound and keep it clean with a bandage, you are helping to keep germs out that would slow down the healing that God made for you.

In some sicknesses we need to give our stomachs and digestion a rest. Then it is best to eat soups, toast, fruit, and custard. We should not eat foods that have much fat in them, such as meat and nuts. During a time of sickness, it is important to drink plenty of liquids. Parts of the body that remove poisons can work better if they have plenty of water.

God does the healing, but we want to be careful that we do not work against that healing by eating a poor diet or by not being clean.

Others can help us get well. When Job was sick, three of his friends visited him. They felt so sorry for Job that they tore their clothes and cried. They did not talk to him for seven days because they saw how sad he was.

But then Job's friends said some unkind things. They said he must be sick because he had done bad things. They said God must be punishing him for his sins. This only made Job feel worse. He said, "Miserable comforters are ye all" (Job 16:2).

Now when you visit a sick person, think of the story of Job. Do not add to their discomfort with unkind or unpleasant talk. Try to bring comfort and cheer to the sick one. Doctors know that if their patient is cheerful, healing can happen faster. Friends can do much to help a sick person be cheerful with cards, gifts, and visits. These help a sick person feel better.

Friends can help a sick person get better, but who does the healing?

...that some poor countries have only 1 doctor for every 25,000–75,000 people, whereas some rich countries have 1 doctor for every 1,000 people?

...that George Washington's doctors treated his fatal illness of "inflammatory quinsy" by draining blood a number of times from his veins? Today doctors believe his disease was strep throat, which of course would only be worsened by removing blood.

...that on an Egyptian scroll of about 1550 B. C. are written more than 800 prescriptions naming about 700 drugs, and that the ancient Romans opened the first drugstore? Most of these drugs were useless except for the Egyptians' use of castor oil as a laxative and the Romans' use of opium for pain relief.

Quiz

Have the students write the correct New Word for each sentence below.

1. It can be a shot in your arm or a pill to swallow to treat your disease. *(medicine)*
2. You take this to a druggist so that he will give you medicine. *(prescription)*
3. Your doctor first makes this before he gives you medicine. *(diagnosis)*

Lesson 3 Answers

Group A

1. c
2. d
3. e
4. g
5. h
6. a
7. b
8. f

(8 points thus far)

Test Your Reading (Group A)

Choose the best ending for each sentence.

1. God
2. Worry and grumbling
3. A sick person
4. A cut finger
5. Soup and toast
6. Plenty of liquids and rest
7. A get-well card
8. A visitor to a sick person

a. help the body remove poisons and become well.
b. can cheer a faraway sick friend.
c. and not the doctor does the healing.
d. may keep us from getting well soon.
e. should trust God for healing.
f. should talk to bring comfort and cheer.
g. will heal slowly if it is not kept clean.
h. give the digestion a needed rest.

Medicine can help us get well. It is often helpful for a sick person to take ***medicine.*** A vaccine is one kind of medicine. Other medicines fight germs. They are poisons to the germs and need to be used only as a doctor directs. Some medicines help weakened body parts work properly. You may know someone who takes stomach or heart medicine. Many medicines simply reduce pain or discomfort. When you have a cold, the medicine you take does not cure the cold, but it helps to lessen the symptoms so you feel better. Some medicines come from materials in plants, animals, and minerals, but some medicines are manmade.

God made all these materials that help the body, but man has to work hard to find them and has to learn how to use them wisely. Each year medical workers learn new ways to fight disease. Each year new medicines are made that seem to work better than the ones used before.

Doctors can help us get well. In most cases a doctor must tell you which medicine to use. First he checks your symptoms, such as a fever, a cough, or swelling. Then he makes his diagnosis. A ***diagnosis*** means that he decides which disease you probably have. The doctor can do this because he has studied many medicines and the symptoms of many diseases. He knows which medicine is likely the best for your illness.

In order to make a proper diagnosis, your doctor may have your blood tested. He wants to know whether your body has made more white blood cells than normal. A high white-cell count tells him that your body is indeed fighting some disease.

When the doctor has made a diagnosis of your disease, he often writes out a ***prescription.*** The prescription tells the name of the proper medicine, how much of it to take, and how often to take it. If the medicine is for a common illness such as a cold or the flu, the doctor might give the medicine to you at his office. Otherwise, he tells you to take the prescription to a druggist, who then gives you the right medicine.

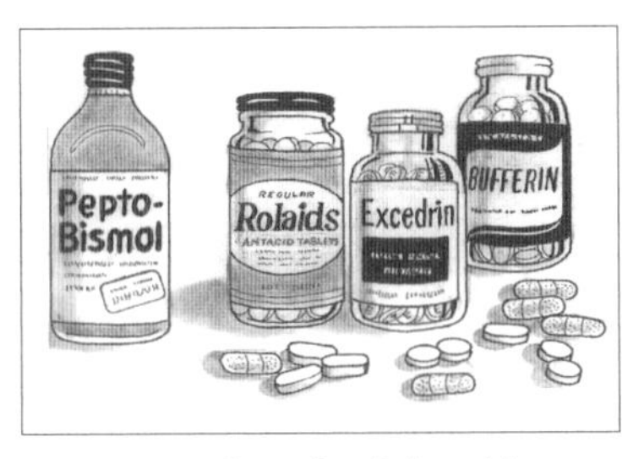

Medicines can do much to help a sick person get better, but what heals the person?

It is important to follow directions when taking any kind of medicine. All medicines can be harmful if used improperly.

You have learned that doctors, medicines, cards and visits, good body care, and a cheerful attitude can all be helpful when you are sick. But do not forget that God's work of healing is the most important. Remember to thank God and others who have helped you to get well again.

Test Your Reading (Group B)

Write the missing words.

9. God has created many plants and minerals that can be used to make ——— that will help you get well.
10. Some medicines, like penicillin, help you get well by fighting the ——— that cause disease.
11. If you have a weak stomach, you might take a medicine to help your stomach ——— properly.
12. Sometimes if you have the flu, you may take aspirin to reduce ———, even though the aspirin does not fight the disease.
13. The doctor looks at the ——— of your disease to help him make the right ——— of your disease.
14. If the doctor does not have the right medicine at his office, he will send you to the drugstore with a ———.

Group B

9. medicines
10. germs
11. work (*or* digest)
12. pain
13. symptoms, diagnosis (2 points)
14. prescription

15. A prescription tells the name of the medicine, how much to take, and how often to take it. (3 points)
16. God heals you.

(19 points total)

Review Answers

1. true
2. c
3. vaccine
4. immune
5. a

(5 additional points)

Answer these questions.

15. What three things does a prescription tell you?
16. Doctors and medicines do not heal you; they only help to heal. How then do you get well?

Reviewing What You Have Learned

1. True or false? Liquids in the stomach kill many germs.
2. White blood cells destroy germs by
   a. making toxins.
   b. sending a HELP call.
   c. eating them.
3. Dead or weakened disease germs are used to make a ———.
4. We do not get the same disease the second time because we are ——— to it.
5. God made your body in a way that
   a. most germs cannot enter it.
   b. most germs are fought with antibodies.
   c. most germs are killed with a fever.

Extra Activities

1. Ask your teacher or parents if you may visit someone who is sick. You could make your own get-well card to give the sick person. First, fold a sheet of white paper once or twice; then draw or paste a cheerful picture on the outside, and write a short Bible verse on the inside.
2. Ask your parents if you can see some prescription medicine bottles that are in your home. Find the three things that a prescription tells. Why are these three things important for the doctor to give?
3. Read about some very useful medicines by looking up "Antibiotic" and "Sulfa Drugs" in an encyclopedia. Tell or write what you learned.

Lesson 4

Protection From Disease

New Words

antiseptic (an′•ti•sep′•tik), an ointment or solution used to kill germs to prevent a wound from becoming infected.

carrier, a person or thing that passes a disease to others.

contagious (kən•tā′•jəs), easily spread around to others.

infection (in•fek′•shən), a sore or sickness because of germs.

sanitation (san′•i•tā′•shen), the prevention of disease by practicing safe garbage disposal and careful food handling.

Contagious diseases can cause death. Have you ever wished that you lived long ago during pioneer times? Then forests were still full of bears, panthers, and other wildlife. The land was less crowded, and the air was much cleaner.

But life was not always better long ago. Children were much more in danger of dying from diseases. For example, only 200 years ago, one out of every three children did not live to grow up.

One reason for this was the lack of vaccines and other medicines. Doctors did not have medicines to fight contagious diseases as they do today. A ***contagious*** disease is any disease that spreads from one person to the next. Measles, chicken pox, and whooping cough are all contagious diseases. Small pox and diphtheria were once dreaded diseases. Many died from these diseases. Today these contagious diseases are so rare that you probably do not know anyone who had them.

How do you get a contagious disease? You get the flu, for example, by being near someone with the flu. This person is a ***carrier*** of the flu germs. When that person coughs or sneezes, he sends small droplets onto his hands or into the air. These droplets are sure to have some flu germs in them. You get the germs from the carrier by touching him,

Lesson 4

Concepts to Teach

- Most disease germs are spread from person to person.
- When we are sick, we should practice extra care that we do not spread the germs.
- Good health habits are both polite and helpful to ourselves and others.
- Wounds should be carefully dressed to avoid infection.
- Cleanliness decreases the spread of disease germs and promotes healthful living.
- Proper food preparation and garbage disposal promote healthful living.

Introducing the Lesson

One of the most important methods of disease control is providing safe drinking water. If most of your students live in a rural area and use well water, discuss the sanitation laws for wells and septic systems. If most of your students live in a city, explain and show pictures of water purification, which can be found in an encyclopedia under "Water (City Water Systems)." The "Sanitation" article may also contain helpful information.

Did you know—

...that in the 1300s, ¼ of Europe's population perished because of a kind of bubonic plague called the "Black Death"? The plague is spread by fleas from infected rats and is still troublesome in parts of Asia and Africa.

...that before the 1900s, all surgical wounds became infected because of unsanitary practices, such as doctors having unwashed hands, unsterilized instruments, and blood-stained robes, and operating before crowds of germ-laden spectators?

touching something he has touched, or even by breathing air in a room where he has been. Some of them stick to the inside of your throat and start multiplying until you become sick. Now you are the carrier of flu germs. You pass them on to someone else, and so it goes on and on.

Animals can also be carriers. Flies and mosquitoes, dogs, cats, mice, and rats are all known to be carriers of disease. Some lands are troubled with terrible, deadly diseases spread by insects and other animals.

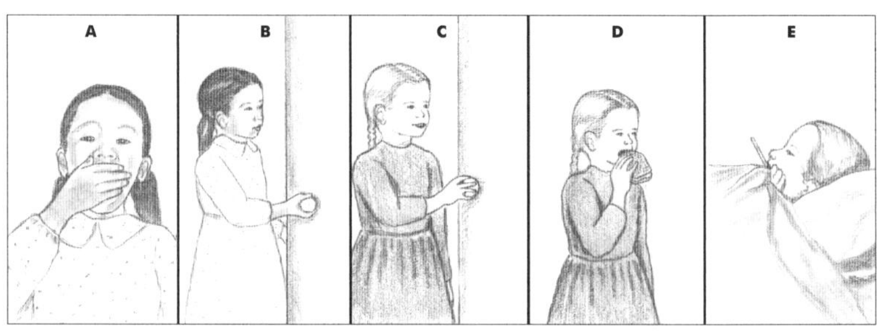

Persons with the flu are carriers of flu germs. What could have been done so the second child would not have become sick?

Test Your Reading (Group A)

Choose the right answer.

1. Years ago, many children did not live to be grown up because
   a. their parents did not care for them.
   b. they did not have medicines for deadly diseases.
   c. the diseases were more contagious in those days.
2. If you have a contagious disease, then
   a. you got the germs from someone.
   b. you did not have the right diet.
   c. you were in the cold air too long.
3. Which of the following diseases is rare today?
   a. chicken pox
   b. flu
   c. small pox

Lesson 4 Answers

Group A

1. b
2. a
3. c

...that in 1900 the average American life span was less than 47 years, but by the 1990s it was 75 years?

...that in the late 1980s, Americans buried 73% of their trash in landfills, recycled 13%, and burned 14%?

Quiz

Ask the students to say or write the correct New Word for each sentence below.

1. You try to avoid this, but sometimes you get it. *(infection)*
2. You may use it on cuts and sores. *(antiseptic)*
3. This word describes measles but not cancer. *(contagious)*
4. We practice this to keep germs under control. *(sanitation)*
5. This can be a fly, a mouse, or you yourself. *(carrier)*

4. If you are a carrier of a disease, then you
   a. are immune to the disease.
   b. can give the disease to others.
   c. can easily get the disease.
5. A bite from a cat can be very serious because
   a. it may be carrying a deadly disease.
   b. the wounds from cats take a long time to heal.
   c. cats can bite very deep.

4. b
5. a

(5 points thus far)

What can you do to avoid getting a contagious disease? In the Old Testament, God told His people to wash and be clean. He knew that they would not have as much problem with disease if they had clean practices. Even in a day with many medicines, you will be less likely to get sick if you practice good health habits. Practice the following rules both to stay healthy and to be polite to those around you.

Good Health Habits

1. Use a handkerchief to cover your nose and mouth when you sneeze or cough.
2. Wash your hands with soap before handling food and after using the restroom.
3. Use your own comb, toothbrush, and drinking glass.
4. Wear clean clothes, and take a bath at least twice a week.
5. Wash your hair at least once a week.

Follow the rules below to avoid giving your disease to others.

Rules During Sickness

1. Be extra careful to follow the "Good Health Habits."
2. Always keep tissues or handkerchiefs handy to catch coughs and sneezes.
3. Wash your hands often with soap.
4. Stay away from others, especially babies and other sick people.

In Lesson 2 you learned that your skin is a God-given protection from germs. Whenever a part of your skin is cut or burned, that part is an open door to germs. The germs cause signs of ***infection,*** such as pain, swelling, and redness.

For a deep cut or serious burn, you need to see a doctor. But you can doctor small wounds yourself. To treat a wound, wash it carefully and apply a clean, dry bandage. You might also want to put a mild ***antiseptic*** liquid or first-aid cream on the wound or bandage. An antiseptic keeps germs from growing.

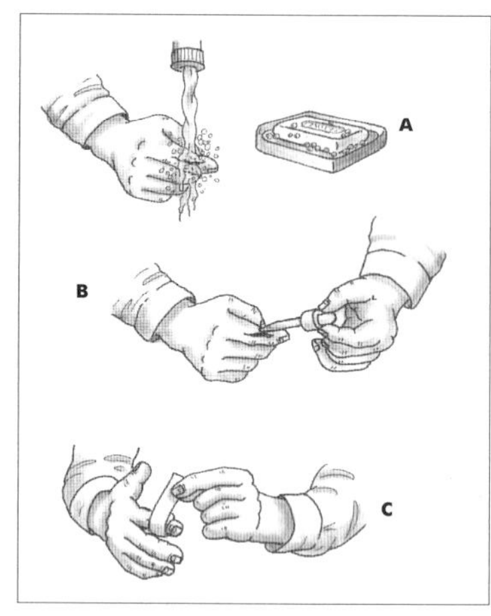

First aid for a wound: Clean the wound, kill the germs, and bandage it to keep it clean.

Group B

6. handkerchief, sneeze (2 points)
7. soap, restroom (2 points)
8. own, toothbrush (2 points)
9. clean, twice a week (2 points)
10. Wash, once a week (2 points)
11. during sickness
12. pain, swelling, redness (3 points)
13. to kill the germs (*or* to keep the germs from growing)

(20 points thus far)

Test Your Reading (Group B)

Study the list of "Good Health Habits." Then supply the missing words from memory.

6. Use a ——— to cover your nose and mouth when you ——— or cough.
7. Wash your hands with ——— before handling food and after using the ———.
8. Use your ——— comb, ———, and drinking glass.
9. Wear ——— clothes, and take a bath at least ——— ——— ———.
10. ——— your hair at least ——— ——— ———.

Answer the following questions.

11. When should you be especially careful to practice good health habits?
12. What are three signs that a wound has become infected with germs?
13. Why should you put an antiseptic on a wound?

How does our community protect us from disease? When you have good health habits, you are doing your part to protect yourself from germs. But there are some important things that you cannot do by yourself. For example, how can you make sure that your drinking water is not polluted with germs? How can you make sure that the meat and milk on your table did not come from a sick cow? You cannot tell just by looking at your water, milk, or meat.

For these problems, the community works together for protection from disease. This is called ***sanitation.*** Providing clean water, milk, and food is a part of sanitation. Another important part is properly getting rid of garbage and sewage. You are practicing sanitation for your family when you help to wash the dishes in hot, soapy water. Sanitation is cleanliness that helps to keep germs from multiplying or spreading.

Some community workers make laws to help keep our water from being polluted with sewage. They also make laws to help keep our milk and food clean. A farmer's milk must pass regular tests if he wants to sell it. A chicken slaughterhouse or soup cannery must also pass regular inspections and follow strict rules of cleanliness. All those who handle food must keep it as clean and germfree as possible, or they are not allowed to sell it. It is important that everyone obeys the sanitation laws.

How are these men promoting sanitation?

Why is it necessary to handle garbage properly? Flies, mice, and rats all thrive at open garbage dumps. Wherever these animal carriers go, they take many germs along and spread diseases. Because of this, garbage is usually buried at a landfill. In large cities, some garbage is burned and the heat energy is changed into electricity. Some garbage such as cardboard, plastic, and glass is used again, or recycled, instead of being wasted.

Many communities in other lands do not have enough money to have good sanitation. As a result, the people have much disease and many health problems. Many young children in such places do not live long. As we have opportunity, let us share with those who are not blessed as we are. Let us thank God for His goodness to us.

Test Your Reading (Group C)

Write *true* if the statement is true. Write *false* if the statement is not true.

14. If you practice good health habits, you can be just as healthy when others are careless as when others are careful.
15. Your water may have germs in it even if it looks clean.
16. Sanitation laws are made to make it hard for the farmers to sell milk.
17. Sanitation is the name used for a community that does not have any sickness.
18. A bakery would need to practice better sanitation than a woodworking shop.
19. Burying or burning garbage helps to have less carriers of disease germs.
20. Recycled garbage is a wasteful use of what we throw away.

Group C

14. false
15. true
16. false
17. false
18. true
19. true
20. false

(27 points total)

Reviewing What You Have Learned

1. True or false? Any kind of antibody will fight any kind of germ.
2. A doctor makes his diagnosis after he knows your
   a. white-cell count.
   b. symptoms.
   c. prescription.
3. "A ——— heart doeth good like a medicine."
4. We need more rest when we are sick because
   a. our bodies work hard to fight germs.
   b. antibodies cannot be made while we work.
   c. medicines work best while we rest.
5. Men use chemicals to make ——— that can help us get well.

Review Answers

1. false
2. b
3. merry
4. a
5. medicine(s)

(5 additional points)

Extra Activities

1. Ask your teacher or parents if you may visit a cannery, slaughterhouse, or dairy farm. Find out how sanitation is being practiced in these places. If you live on a dairy farm, ask your father what sanitation laws must be obeyed. Write a report of these laws, or give an oral report to the class.
2. Take this little test just to see how much you know about disease.
   For each sentence, write *true* if you think it is true, and *false* if you think it is not true. Ask your teacher for the correct answers.
   a. You get one kind of vitamin from being outside in the sunshine.
   b. A person taking cancer treatments should increase his vitamin intake.
   c. Some kinds of bacteria are living inside your body right now.
   d. Cancer is a contagious disease.
   e. Some people get sick from dust and cat hair.
   f. White corpuscles will attack and break up a splinter in your finger.
   g. A newborn baby is immune to many diseases.
   h. The sick who receive loving care need less pain medicine than those who are ignored.
   i. The medicine called penicillin is made from molds that grow on bread.
   j. Most mosquitoes drink human blood and spread disease.

Extra Activity Comments

2. Answers for the mini-test on disease:
   a. true. This is, of course, vitamin D.
   b. true
   c. true. Many bacteria live on the skin, in the nose, throat, and mouth, and in the lungs, stomach, and intestines. They usually do no harm unless the body's resistance is lowered or unless they move to an organ where they are not normally present.
   d. false. Though one virus has been proven to be linked with cancer of the nose and throat, cancer is not spread by germs and is therefore not contagious.
   e. true. This disease is an allergy, in which a substance that would not bother most people is seen as an enemy by the sick person's body.
   f. true
   g. true. God wisely provided for the newborn baby to have a set of antibodies that protect it from infectious diseases for a few months.
   h. true
   i. false. Penicillin is made from a kind of mold, but not bread mold.
   j. false. Most mosquitoes suck plant juices, but only some kinds of female mosquitoes suck human blood.

Lesson 5 Answers

1. c
2. b
3. g
4. h
5. e
6. f
7. a
8. d

9–10. vitamins, minerals
11. germs
12–13. vaccine, immune
14. antibodies
15. diagnosis
16. antiseptic
17. contagious
18. sanitation

Lesson 5

Do You Remember?

Match each word on the right with its meaning on the left.

1. Tiny plants and animals that cause disease	a. carriers
2. High body temperature	b. fever
3. Any signs of sickness	c. germs
4. Disease-fighting blood cells	d. infection
5. Used to treat a disease	e. medicine
6. Directions for medicine	f. prescription
7. Those who spread germs	g. symptoms
8. Sickness from germs	h. white blood cells

For each blank, write the missing word from the word box.

antibodies	germs	sanitation
antiseptic	immune	vaccine
contagious	minerals	vitamins
diagnosis		

9–10. Scurvy and similar diseases are found where people do not get enough ——— and ———.

11. We cannot see disease ——— except with a microscope.

12–13. A ——— causes you to become ——— to a disease without getting it.

14. Mumps ——— watch for and fight against only mumps germs.

15. A doctor wants to know the symptoms of a person's disease in order to make his ———.

16. To avoid getting infection in cuts and sores, you may put an ——— on it.

17. Any disease that spreads from one person to the next is ———.

18. Providing pure water, clean food, and proper waste disposal are important parts of ———.

Lesson 5

Reviewing the Unit

As a reminder of the main theme of each lesson, have the class read the lesson titles in unison. You might also ask each student to say something he has learned by studying this unit.

Perhaps your students would enjoy reviewing with a question chain, as before, or by redoing the quizzes from the teacher's guide.

Decide whether each sentence is true or not true, and write *true* or *false*.

19. Antibodies are blood cells that fight germs by eating them.
20. All germs make us sick if they get inside our bodies.
21. Measles are a symptom of fever.
22. A person's body may fight germs for weeks before getting well again.
23. The sick who trust God get well faster than those who worry.
24. Cards and visits help the sick get well.
25. One way God helps to heal us is by the work of doctors and medicines.
26. Most disease germs spread from animals to people.

19. false
20. false
21. false
22. true
23. true
24. true
25. true
26. false

Choose the best ending for each sentence, and write the correct letter on your paper.

27. These foods have plenty of vitamins and minerals:
    a. candy and cookies.
    b. potato chips and chocolate cake.
    c. carrots and oatmeal bread.
28. Some diseases caused by germs are
    a. colds and chicken pox.
    b. mumps and fever.
    c. flu and scurvy.
29. You are protected from many germs by
    a. cuts in your skin.
    b. the inside of the lungs.
    c. stomach liquids.
30. It is easiest for your body to destroy whooping cough germs
    a. when it has fought them before.
    b. when it is fighting flu viruses.
    c. when it has not fought them before.
31. Being immune to chicken pox means that you will not
    a. get any chicken pox germs inside your body again.
    b. become sick with chicken pox again.
    c. need chicken pox antibodies again.

27. c
28. a
29. c
30. a
31. b

32. a
33. b
34. c

35–36. Germs multiply quickly and make poisons inside the body.
37–38. You can become immune to a disease by getting it or by receiving a vaccine.
39–43.
(1) Use a handkerchief to cover your nose and mouth when you sneeze or cough.
(2) Wash your hands with soap before handling food and after using the restroom.
(3) Use your own comb, toothbrush, and drinking glass.
(4) Wear clean clothes and take a bath at least twice a week.
(5) Wash your hair at least once a week.
44–47.
(1) Be extra careful to follow the "Good Health Habits."
(2) Always keep tissues or handkerchiefs handy to catch coughs and sneezes.
(3) Wash your hands often with soap.
(4) Stay away from others, especially babies and other sick people.
48–50. Garbage can be buried, burned, or recycled.

(50 points total)

Note: Numbers 39–47 should be emphasized, since these rules will be needed for the test.

32. A sick person needs
    a. plenty of liquids and rest.
    b. large meals and proper medicine.
    c. cheerfulness and hard work.
33. Some good foods for a sick person are
    a. cake and ice cream.
    b. soup and toast.
    c. steak and cherry pie.
34. Our food supply is kept clean mainly by
    a. adding chemicals to kill germs.
    b. dumping garbage in faraway ditches.
    c. having workers obey laws for cleanliness.

Write the correct answers.

35–36. Write two things that germs do inside your body when you become sick.
37–38. In what two ways can you become immune to a disease such as measles?
39–43. After studying the five "Good Health Habits," write them from memory.
44–47. After studying the four "Rules During Sickness," write them from memory.
48–50. What are three good ways to get rid of garbage?

Unit Five

God Made Light

"Where is the way where light dwelleth?" (Job 38:19).

Light is very common. Why will you be studying a unit of science about ordinary light? After all, you turn it on in the morning. The sun gives you light during the day. You turn off the light at night. You have known about light since you were a little child.

But there is much for you to learn about light. In this unit you will learn what makes light hot or cold, why light can bounce or bend, what makes a rainbow, how eyeglasses help people, what happens inside your eyes, and why you need two eyes.

If you study this unit so well that you get every answer right on the test, you will know only a little about light. Even a wise man like Job did not know all about light. God asked him a hard question, "Where is the way where light dwelleth?" (Job 38:19). Job did not know the answer. God did not expect Job to answer. God knew that He Himself was the only one who knows everything about light.

Light is from God. Like every good and perfect gift, light "is from above, and cometh down from the Father of lights" (James 1:17).

Unit Five

For Your Inspiration

"Truly the light is sweet, and a pleasant thing it is for the eyes to behold the sun" (Ecclesiastes 11:7). Have you ever wondered why light has always been associated with good, and darkness with evil? For example, why does it seem strange for murder to be committed in broad daylight?

To be sure, physical light and darkness are amoral: in themselves they are neither right nor wrong. But because of our great need for light, and because of the evil that is done in darkness, light is as desirable to us as darkness is undesirable. We like light and dislike darkness.

Thus light and darkness are logical analogies for good and bad spiritual qualities. The Bible contains many such illustrations. Look at some of Christ's own words.

"And this is the condemnation, that light is come into the world, and men loved darkness rather than light, because their deeds were evil" (John 3:19).

"I am the light of the world: he that followeth me shall not walk in darkness, but shall have the light of life" (John 8:12).

"Walk while ye have the light, lest darkness come upon you" (John 12:35).

"If therefore the light that is in thee be darkness, how great is that darkness!" (Matthew 6:23).

The apostles Paul and John used the same kind of imagery in their epistles. Here are a few examples:

"For ye were sometimes darkness, but now are ye light in the Lord: walk as children of light" (Ephesians 5:8).

Lesson 1

"Let There Be Light"

New Words

light, the form of energy by which we can see.

luminous (lü′•mə•nəs), giving off its own light.

ray, a single line of light.

shadow, the dark area formed when an object stops the light coming from a source.

spectrum (spek′•trəm), the band of colors formed when white light is separated into its parts.

Let's think back to a time long, long ago. It was the very first day of the earth. What a strange earth it was! There were no leafy trees or singing birds or busy people. You could not have seen anything, for there was no ***light.*** Everything was as dark as the blackest midnight.

God created light. On the first day of Creation, God said, "LET THERE BE LIGHT" and there was light! (Genesis 1:3). What a wonderful thing God created that day. We like light, and we know that God liked it. The Bible says, "And God saw the light, that it was good" (Genesis 1:4).

Many years later, Job knew that the light was good. He knew that we need light to see where we are going. In thinking about what God does to great men, Job said, "They grope in the dark without light" (Job 12:25). Job knew how important light is in our everyday life.

You know that God created light so that we could see. He also created light to give us heat. We get some light and heat from fire when we burn wood or other fuels. But most of our light and heat comes from a much greater fire. In fact, this fire is a million times larger than the whole earth. It is the sun.

What are luminous objects? God created the sun as our most important source of light. We say the sun is ***luminous*** because it gives off its own light. The moon is

"God is light, and in him is no darkness at all. . . . If we walk in the light, as he is in the light, we have fellowship one with another" (1 John 1:5, 7).

As you study this unit with your students, may you be guided by God's Word, which is "a lamp unto my feet, and a light unto my path" (Psalm 119:105). May you ever "shew forth the praises of him who hath called you out of darkness into his marvellous light" (1 Peter 2:9).

Note: Look ahead to preparing to teach Unit Seven by reading "Plant Study for Unit Seven" on page 203.

Lesson 1

Concepts to Teach

- God created light on the first day of Creation.
- Light gives us heat and lets us see the world around us.
- God created luminous bodies to give us light.
- Light travels in straight rays in all directions from its source.
- Shadows are formed because light cannot bend around the edges of objects.
- Light can be separated into the rainbow colors of the spectrum.

not luminous because it cannot make light. Moonlight is simply sunlight that has bounced off the moon and down to the earth.

Can you think of other things that are luminous? The stars are luminous, for they are burning just like the sun. Flames are luminous, whether on candles, in oil lamps, or in fireplaces. Sometimes heated wires become luminous. For example, a common electric light bulb gives you light because the wire inside is very hot.

Not all luminous things are hot. For example, what "fire" does a firefly use for its light? Maybe you have caught one and watched its yellow-green light blink—blink—blink. Why doesn't the firefly feel hot when it lights up? God made the firefly's body give off cold light: it gives off light without becoming hot. Glowworms and some deep-sea fishes also make cold light.

Whether cold or hot, an object that gives off its own light is luminous.

What makes the light bulb filament luminous?

Cold light from a firefly

Test Your Reading (Group A)

Choose the best answer.

1. God made light on the
   a. first day. b. second day. c. third day.
2. Light was created when God
   a. made the sun.
   b. lighted a fire.
   c. said the word.

Lesson 1 Answers

Group A

1. a
2. c

Introducing the Lesson

Read and discuss a few of the verses given about light in "For Your Inspiration." You might stimulate the students' thinking by asking questions such as: "Why do we need light? How is Jesus like a light? Is light better than darkness?"

Tell the students to page through the unit and tell the class something that they notice will be studied. Ideas could come from headings, pictures, and even extra activities.

Have on hand a source of light to use throughout this unit. A flashlight will be especially helpful in demonstrating principles of light. Do not fail to emphasize the mysterious nature of light. Though light is so common, it is one of the hardest things for men to understand and explain. This proves that God's ways are far above man's ways and that God's ways are past finding out.

Did you know—

...that strictly speaking, we cannot actually *see* light itself? We only see the "photographs" our brain is constantly developing of where light *has been*.

...that light energy exerts a very slight pressure on us which can be measured with very sensitive instruments?

...that decaying leaves can produce light?

...that only 10% of the energy from an ordinary incandescent light bulb is light, while 90% is heat? On the other hand, 90% of the energy produced by a firefly's glowing tail is light. God's knowledge of physics is indeed far superior to man's knowledge.

3. We need light in order to
   a. know who is calling.
   b. know where to walk.
   c. know a surface is rough.
4. Sunlight gives us
   a. heat. b. rain. c. air.
5. Something luminous makes its own
   a. food. b. heat. c. light.
6. Which one is luminous?
   a. the moon b. a star c. a dragonfly
7. Cold light is
   a. light from a luminous object that is not hot.
   b. light from the sun in the winter.
   c. light from a luminous object very far away.
8. The name *firefly* is not best because
   a. a firefly is not always luminous.
   b. a firefly is luminous without heat.
   c. a firefly is luminous while it flies.

3. b
4. a
5. c
6. b
7. a
8. b

(8 points thus far)

How does light travel? When you turn on a lamp in a dark room, how does the light get from the bulb to your eyes? The light moves from the light bulb in straight lines, or ***rays.*** The rays leave the light bulb in all directions so that there is light in every part of the room.

Light travels in straight lines. When you see a classmate on the other side of the room, you know that he is in the direction you see him because light is reflected from him to you in straight lines. Since light rays are straight, if you put your hand between the light and the wall, the rays do not bend around the edge of your hand. Your hand makes a ***shadow*** on the wall. Shadows are made because light rays are straight.

What are these rays of light that come from luminous objects? Only God can answer that question fully.

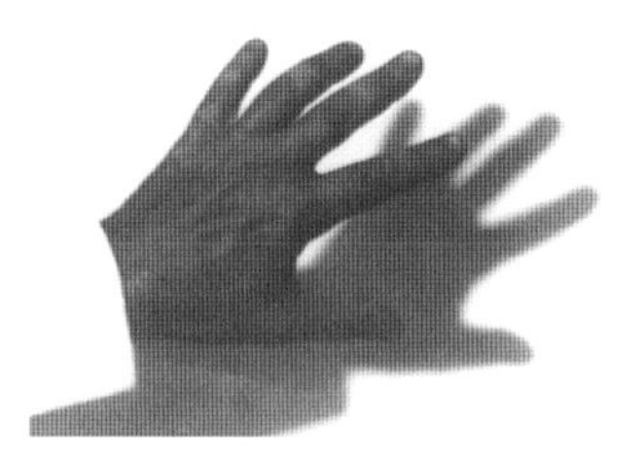

Why does light make shadows?

Test of Luminous Objects

Gather both luminous and nonluminous objects, and have your class examine them. Encourage them to tell which ones they think are luminous and which are not. Then take the objects into a totally dark room and see which ones glow. If the room is too small for your entire class, perhaps you could take several groups.

Here are some suggested objects:

- shiny pan
- bicycle reflector
- reflecting tape
- writing done with fluorescent markers
- numbers on calculators (get two, only one luminous)
- hands and numbers on alarm clocks (again, get two)
- a motto with luminous letters
- a balloon (rubbed against hair for static electricity)

Why the Sky Is Blue

Here is a demonstration that shows why the sky is blue and why a sunset is red. Get an aquarium or glass gallon jar, a flashlight, a teaspoon, and some milk. Fill the aquarium or jar with water, and add a teaspoon of milk. (You may want to experiment with slightly more or less for the best result.)

In a darkened room, shine the flashlight through the water. Show the students that from the side, the light appears bluish, which is like the sky during the day. But on the side opposite the flashlight, the light has a red-orange glow like the evening sky. (Add more milk if you do not get this red-orange glow.)

Now explain why it happens. First remind the class that sunlight is made up of all the colors of the rainbow. As the sunlight travels through the dusty atmosphere (which is like the milky water), the dust scatters the blue light but the red light

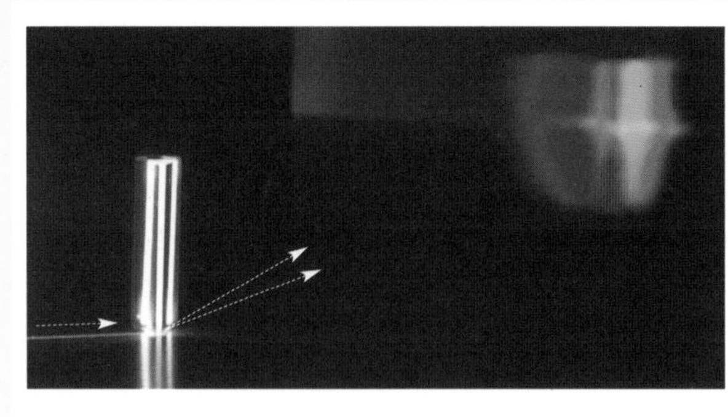

A prism separates sunlight into the colors of the spectrum.

Light is very common; we use it every day, but it is a very great mystery that shows the wisdom of God.

What is the spectrum? The light we get from the sun can be separated into many colors. Sunlight is actually made of the colors red, orange, yellow, green, blue, and purple—the colors of the rainbow. The colors in the order of the rainbow make up the ***spectrum.***

In sunlight the colors of the spectrum are all mixed together. This mixture of light we call white. But when the rays of sunlight pass through raindrops, they separate into a lovely spectrum. Then you say, "Come look at the rainbow!"

Raindrops are not the only things that make light separate into its spectrum. A wedge-shaped glass called a prism will do the same thing. The scales of a fish and the wings of a dragonfly also give off rainbow colors. God has made His world very beautiful with light and color.

Test Your Reading (Group B)

Write the missing words.

9. A ray of light travels in a ——— line.
10. Light fills a room with light because rays travel in all ———.
11. A shadow is formed because light cannot ——— around the edge of an object.
12. All the colors found in sunlight are called the ———.
13. The colors of the spectrum are red, ———, yellow, ———, blue, and purple.
14. A rainbow is formed when sunlight passes through ———.

Group B

9. straight
10. directions
11. bend
12. spectrum
13. orange, green (2 points)
14. raindrops

continues straight through. So during the day, the sky looks blue for the same reason the milky water looks bluish from the side of the aquarium. Then in the evening, we see the red light, which has not been scattered by the dust particles. It looks red for the same reason the milky water looks reddish on the side opposite the flashlight.

You may want to sketch the following drawing on the chalkboard to help them understand how it happens.

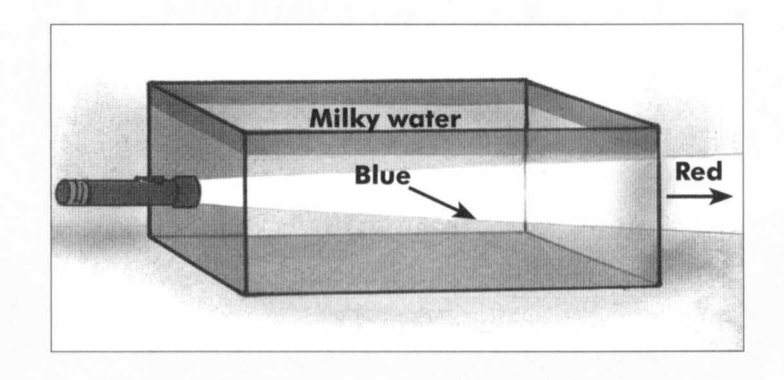

Materials needed:

- aquarium full of water
- flashlight
- teaspoon
- ¼ c. milk

Answer the following questions.

15. Jesus said that men put a candle on a candlestick "and it giveth light unto all that are in the house." What about the travel of light makes this true?
16. What about the way light travels helps us know where to pitch a ball?
17. How is a prism like the wings of a dragonfly?

Extra Activities

1. You can make your own little rainbow to see the spectrum. Go outside during a sunny morning or afternoon, when the sun is not high in the sky. Get a garden hose, and stand with your back to the sun. Spray the water in a fine mist into the air. Through the mist you will see the spectrum.

   Materials needed:
   - garden hose
   - nozzle (to spray in a fine mist)

2. See whether or not light travels in straight lines. Cut a hole the size of a dime in the middle of two pieces of paper. Hold the papers about a foot apart as shown in the drawing.

   Look through the holes at a number on a clock or calendar. How must the holes be placed in order to see the number? What does this tell you about light?

15. Light travels in all directions from a source.
16. Light rays travel in straight lines.
17. Both the prism and the wings of a dragonfly can separate sunlight into the colors of the spectrum.

(18 points total)

Extra Activity Comments

2. Make sure the students understand the significance of this experiment. Because light travels in straight lines, they can see the number only if they line up the holes in the paper between the number and their eye.

Quiz

Write the New Words on the board. Ask the students to choose the correct word for each of the sentences below.

1. We could not see without it. *(light)*
2. We see it when we see a rainbow. *(spectrum)*
3. It means shining with its own light. *(luminous)*
4. It is a straight line of light. *(ray)*
5. It is formed when an object stops light rays. *(shadow)*

Materials needed:
- 2 pieces of paper
- scissors
- clock or calendar

3. Make a pinhole viewer. You may be surprised at what light can do. Cut out most of one side of a cereal box as shown in the picture.

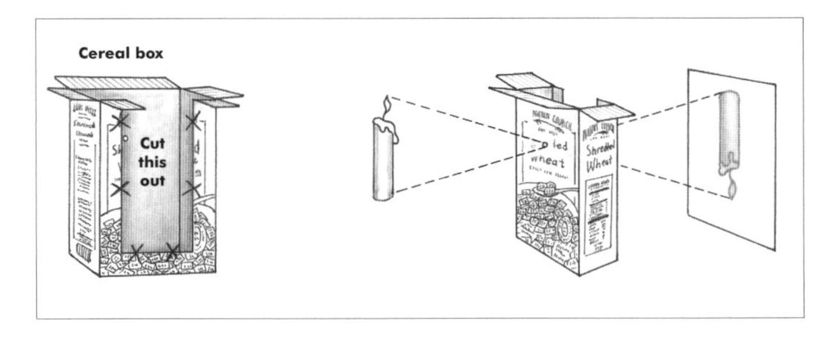

Use a pencil or nail to punch a "pinhole" about this size (o) into the other side of the box. Turn the pencil around a few times to smooth the edges of the hole.

In a darkened room, set up a lighted candle and the box as shown in the picture. Hold a sheet of white paper about eight inches behind the pinhole so that you see the flame's image. What is different about the image on the paper? Can you explain why it is turned this way? (Hint: Remember that light travels in straight lines.)

Move the paper farther away. How does this change the picture of the flame? Why?

Materials needed:
- cereal box
- scissors
- pencil or nail
- a darkened room
- candle
- sheet of white paper

3. The pinhole viewer turns the image upside down. This happens because all the rays must travel through the same small opening. Since they all travel in a straight line, the image is inverted. You may want to illustrate it by sketching this drawing on the chalkboard.

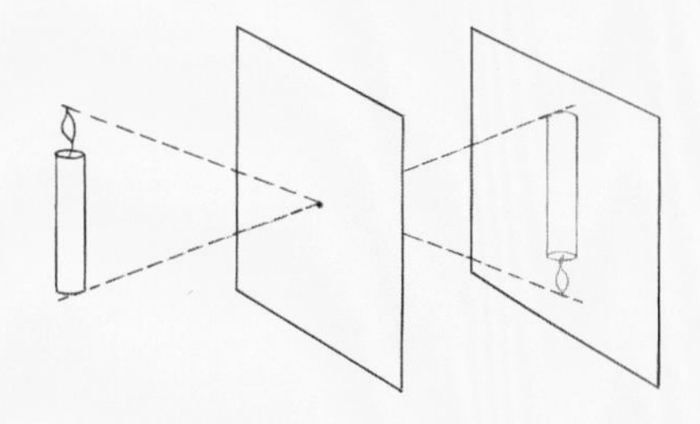

Lesson 2

Reflecting Light

New Words

absorb, to take in instead of reflecting.
mirror, a coated glass in which one's image may be seen.
reflect, to cause light to bounce off.

Let's pretend you have never before seen your own face. Then for the very first time, someone gives you a ***mirror***! What would you do?

You would probably look and look in the mirror. Is that face really yours? You might be surprised to see that you look very much like your big brother—the same brown eyes and straight nose. You blink your eyes and wiggle your nose. The face in the mirror blinks and wiggles too.

If you really had never seen a mirror before, you would want to keep it as a treasure. But to you, mirrors are so common that you may not think much about them. Of course, you need a mirror to comb your hair. You know that the driver of a car needs a rear-view mirror to drive safely. What is so special about a mirror?

A rear-view mirror is necessary for safe driving.

Light can be reflected. A mirror shows us something very important about light. Light can be bounced, or ***reflected.*** Right now, light is reflecting off this page and into your eyes. Look all around you. Light is bouncing off everything in the room and into your eyes. Reflected light allows you to see the things around you.

What if light could not be

Lesson 2

Concepts to Teach

- Mirrors are useful for looking glasses, rear-view mirrors, and reflectors of light sources.
- All surfaces reflect light, the amount depending on the color and smoothness of the surface.
- Dark surfaces absorb more light and change it to heat.
- Some surfaces are smooth enough that they reflect light evenly; in these we can see our own reflections.
- A mirror image is always backward.
- When light is reflected, it bounces off at the same angle it strikes, much like a bouncing ball.

Introducing the Lesson

Choose one of the following demonstrations to direct your students' minds toward the lesson.

1. If the sun is shining brightly, use a small mirror to move a spot of light back and forth across the ceiling. Show that the angle of the light coming toward the mirror is the same as its angle going away from the mirror.

   Materials needed:
   - small mirror
2. Show the students how much more light is reflected from a light-colored object than from a dark-colored object. Get a flashlight, a piece of white paper, and a piece of black paper. Darken the room as much as possible.

reflected? Then you could only see when you looked right at something luminous, such as a lamp or the sun. Everything else would be dark. That would be like having night all the time.

Light-colored objects reflect light. All objects reflect light, but there is a big difference in how much light is reflected. One thing may reflect very little light, while another reflects nearly all the light that falls on it. What makes the difference?

It depends partly on the color of the object. The lighter in color an object is, the more light it reflects. For example, pink and white reflect much light.

Dark colors, such as black and brown, reflect little light. Instead, they take in, or ***absorb,*** most of the light that falls on them. The light energy that is absorbed changes to heat energy.

How can knowing which colors reflect and absorb light be a help to you? On cold winter mornings, you can choose dark-colored clothes. They help you feel warmer because they absorb light and change it to heat. On the other hand, you can wear light-colored clothes during the summertime. They help you feel cooler because they reflect light.

Lesson 2 Answers

Group A

1. false
2. true
3. false
4. true
5. true
6. false
7. true

(7 points thus far)

Test Your Reading (Group A)

Answer *true* if the sentence is true; answer *false* if the sentence is not true.

1. You can see yourself in a mirror because mirrors are luminous.
2. We see objects that are not luminous because they reflect light.
3. A good meaning for *reflect* would be "to pass through."
4. Light that is not reflected is changed to heat.
5. A good meaning for *absorb* would be "to take in."
6. A white coat would help you be warmer on a cold, sunny day than a brown coat would.
7. Dark colors absorb more light than light colors do.

Smooth objects make mirrors. The smoother an object is, the better you can see yourself when you look at it. You may have seen yourself when looking at the side of a very shiny car. Very smooth materials reflect light rays so evenly that you can see your

First shine the flashlight onto the white paper. Hold your hand about 12 inches above the paper as shown in the picture. Ask the students to notice how much light is reflected up to your hand. Then do the same thing with the black paper. Do they notice any difference?

Materials needed:

- flashlight
- white paper
- black paper
- dark room

Did you know—

...that light, heat, and radio waves are simply different forms of one kind of energy, which is electromagnetic radiation?

...that the mirror on a reflecting telescope has its reflective coating on the front and not on the back as with common mirrors? This is so the light is not distorted by needing to pass through the glass.

...that mirrors are used in projectors and cameras, in solar power stations, in sextants on ships, in ophthalmoscopes for doctors, and in range finders for surveyors and photographers, in photocopiers, and by dentists to see the underneath side of upper teeth.

Mirror Angles

Hang a mirror on a wall at eye level with the students. On the floor, tape a 10- or 15-foot length of masking tape parallel to the wall and about 5 feet away from it. Then tape another strip on the floor directly beneath the mirror. Make it meet the first line at a right angle.

Have a student stand on the first line a short distance to the left of the mirror, and another student the same distance to the right. Then ask them to point at each other's reflection in the mirror. Show the students that the angles from which they point are the same, though from different directions.

face in them. Mirrors, shiny metal, and still water are such materials.

Rough surfaces scatter light. If you shine a flashlight on a mirror, it will make a spot somewhere on the wall. If you shine a flashlight on a sheet of paper, the light will be scattered around the room. Only shiny surfaces make mirrors.

Light that is reflected off a mirror bounces back in an equal way. If you shine a flashlight straight at a mirror, the light will be reflected straight back. But if you shine a flashlight at a slant from the side, the light will bounce off in an equal slant away from the flashlight. You know that if you throw a ball slanted at the floor, it will bounce away from you at an equal slant. This is the same equal way light bounces off a mirror. This is a very orderly way God made light to be reflected.

Mirrors are not always flat. Sometimes mirrors are curved inward to fit around a light. The headlights of a car and the searchlights in an airport are made this way. Because of reflection, the lights inside these curved mirrors seem much brighter than they would be by themselves. Some

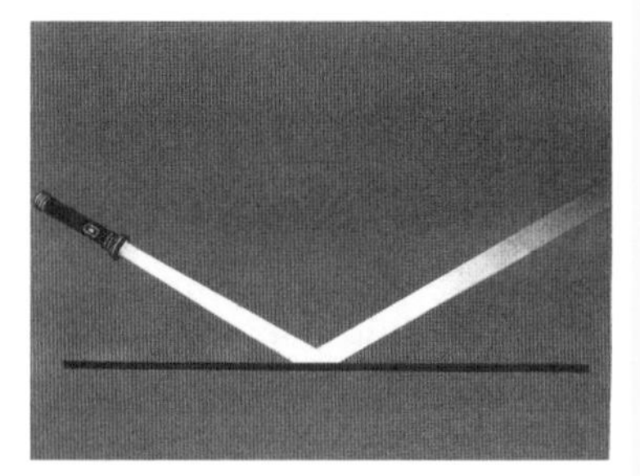

Light leaves a mirror at the same slant that it strikes the mirror.

rear-view mirrors on cars are curved outward. This lets the driver see a much wider view than with a flat mirror.

What you see in a mirror is backward. Did you know that you see yourself backward in a mirror? You are so used to seeing yourself in a mirror that what you see seems turned right to you. To see

What word is written on the front of this fire department truck? Look at it in a mirror to find out.

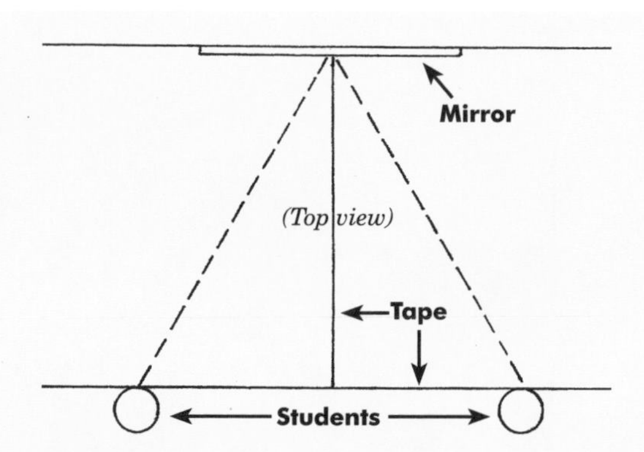

Now have one student move a few steps along the line. Ask the class which way the other student must move in order for them to see each other in the mirror. Try it a few more times.

Materials needed:

- mirror
- masking tape

Bouncing Illustrates Reflection

Checkers or Ping-Pong balls can be used to show the principle of equal angles in reflection. Set up a long, narrow board along the edge of a smooth table. This board represents a mirror. With the end of a stick, push a checker (or Ping-Pong ball) from about a foot against the board at an angle. The path that it takes as it bounces away from the board is the same as the path of a light ray reflecting off a mirror.

Materials needed:

- checker or Ping-Pong ball
- long, narrow board
- stick

how you really look to other people, you must look at a photograph of yourself.

How can you tell that mirrors make things look backward? Just try reading this book or threading a needle while looking at a mirror. Maybe you have seen an ambulance with the name written backward on the front.

The name is written backward so that a driver in front can read it right when he looks in his rear-view mirror. See the picture on page 143.

God made light rays behave in this orderly way. He planned how light would reflect from a mirror.

Group B

8. c
9. e
10. b
11. d
12. a

13. j
14. h
15. f
16. g
17. i

(17 points total)

Test Your Reading (Group B)

Find the right choice that completes the sentence.

8. Still water
9. Rough surfaces
10. Rear-view mirrors
11. Mirrors curved inward
12. Mirrors curved outward

a. give a wide view.
b. are flat or curved outward.
c. reflects light like a mirror.
d. make lights seem brighter.
e. scatter light.

Find the right choice that completes the sentence.

13. A bouncing ball
14. Flat mirrors
15. Reflected light
16. Headlights
17. A backward word

f. enters and leaves a mirror at the same slant.
g. use mirrors that are curved inward.
h. make things look backward.
i. will look right in a mirror.
j. shows the equal way light reflects.

Review Answers

1. light
2. false
3. b
4. heat
5. true

(5 additional points)

Reviewing What You Have Learned

1. A luminous object makes its own ———.
2. True or false? A spectrum is one of the colors of the rainbow.
3. A ray travels
   a. around corners.
   b. in a straight line.
   c. to its source.
4. The sun gives us light and ———.
5. True or false? God created light on the first day of Creation.

Demonstration: Fire in Water

Get a short candle, a clear glass of water, and some flat glass from a small picture or window frame. Prop up the flat glass on a table between several stacks of books. Set the glass of water about four inches away from one side of the flat glass. Place the candle the same distance away from the other side. Darken the room, and light the candle.

Have the students look at the flat glass from the side nearest the candle. The candle seems to be burning underwater!

Next, remove the glass of water and hold your finger at the same place. It appears as though you are calmly letting your finger be burned. Ask the students to explain how reflection helped you do this demonstration.

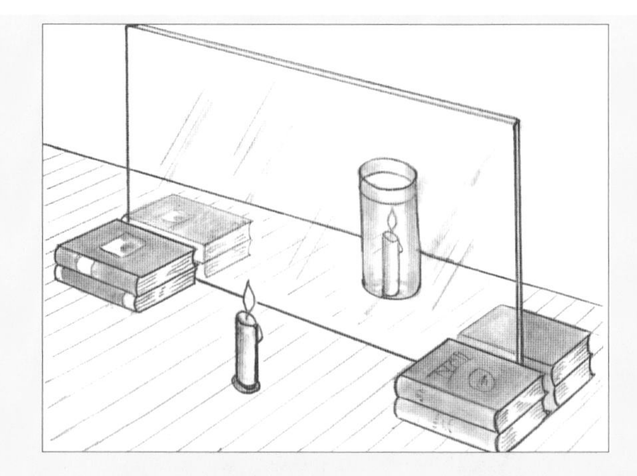

Materials needed:

- short candle
- clear water glass
- pane of glass
- water
- 8 books
- matches

Extra Activities

1. Try this activity using reflection. While looking only at a large mirror, write your name and address on a piece of paper. How fast can you write "backward"?

   Next, put three dots like this on your paper. Looking only at the mirror, quickly connect them with straight lines. Does it look easy? Try it!

   Materials needed:
   - pencil
   - paper
   - large mirror

2. What is the blackest black of all? You can find out. Get a shoebox with its lid and the blackest cloth scrap or paper that you can find. Cut a hole the size of a penny in one end of the box. Cut another hole the same size in the black material. Glue the material to the outside of the box so that its hole is on top of the hole in the box. Put the lid on the shoebox. Now look; which is blackest—the material or the hole? Next, get a mirror and carefully look at the black dot in the center of your eye. Can you explain what makes it so black?

   Materials needed:
   - shoebox
   - black cloth or paper
   - scissors
   - glue
   - mirror

Note: A bright object (the candle flame) is reflected by a very smooth surface (the flat glass). At the same time, the light rays from the water glass are passing through the transparent window glass. The two objects seem to be at the same place.

Quiz

Ask the children to write the New Word they think of when you say the phrases below.

1. To bounce light *(reflect)*
2. A looking glass *(mirror)*
3. A backward image *(mirror)*
4. To take in light *(absorb)*
5. White does it well *(reflect)*
6. Black does it well *(absorb)*

Extra Activity Comments

2. A hole is always blacker than a black surface because no light rays are reflected back; while from a black surface, there are at least a few. The pupil of an eye looks black because it is actually a hole.

3. Periscopes are important tools in submarines. They enable the seamen to observe what is above the surface of the water while the submarine is submerged.

   Scientists also use periscopes to study nuclear energy from a safe distance. One such periscope in Idaho is 90 feet (27 m) long, which makes it the longest periscope in the world.

3. You can make light turn a corner! Cut holes in the side of a cracker box as shown in the picture.

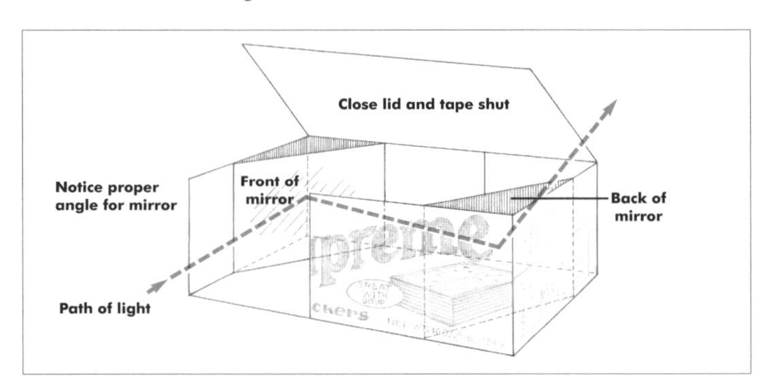

Tape the mirrors across the corners. They must be set at just the proper slant to reflect the light into your eye. Also tape any cracks in the box so that it does not fall apart when you hold it upright.

Now you have made a little periscope! Peek around a corner with it. Use it to help you find your friends when you play hide-and-seek. Ask your teacher to tell you how periscopes are used today.

Materials needed:
- cracker box
- scissors
- 2 pocket mirrors
- tape

Lesson 3

Bending Light

New Words

concave (kon·kāv′), being curved inward so that the thinnest part of the lens is at the center.

convex (kon′·veks′), being curved outward so that the thickest part of the lens is at the center.

focus (fō′·kəs), the point where light rays are brought together.

lens, a piece of glass or other transparent material that has a curved surface to focus or scatter light.

transparent (trans·par′·ənt), being clear, like water or glass, so that objects can be seen through it.

Your last lesson told what light does when it meets an object it cannot pass through. It is either reflected or absorbed. If light meets a shiny, smooth cake pan, much is reflected off the cake pan. If light meets a dark, fuzzy blanket, much is absorbed and changed to heat.

God was wise to make light rays that can be both reflected and absorbed. Both of these ways are helpful to us. Reflected light allows us to see objects that are not luminous. Absorbed light from the sun warms the earth where we live.

When do light rays bend? Light can pass through some materials like glass and clear plastic. When light rays enter a clear material, they bend. Does that sound strange? You learned in the first lesson that light travels in *straight* lines.

Yes, light rays do travel in straight lines most of the time. But when they meet anything clear, or ***transparent,*** such as glass or water, they bend. The light changes direction a little as it enters or leaves the transparent material.

You can easily see that light bends. Look at the picture of the

Lesson 3

Concepts to Teach

- A material that is transparent will allow light to pass through it.
- When a light ray enters or leaves a transparent material at an angle, it is bent.
- A lens is a carefully shaped glass that bends light to do useful things for us.
- A convex lens is curved outward to be thickest at the center.
- A convex lens makes objects look bigger.
- A convex lens can bring light rays to a point called the focus.
- A concave lens is curved inward to be thinnest at the center.
- A concave lens scatters light and makes objects look smaller.

Introducing the Lesson

Have some clear glasses or jars half full of water ready before class. Pick up a glass, and put a pencil into it. Show the class how to look through the side of the glass with the water line at eye level to see the pencil "break." Pass the other glasses around so that each student can try it himself. Explain that the reason for this is that the light bends when it enters a different kind of material.

Then if possible, show one or more convex and concave lenses. Also pass these around, asking the students to try reading a few words through them. They should soon notice that the one lens makes the words look larger and the other one makes them look smaller. Tell them they will find out the special name for each of these lenses in this lesson.

Materials needed:

- clear glasses or jars
- pencil

Put a straight edge along the pencil to see where it is "broken" by water.

pencil in a dish of water. Why does it look bent? It is because the light rays bend sideways when they go from the water into the air.

Light that bends does more interesting things. Sometimes you may be riding in a car on a hot day and see "pools of water" on the highway ahead. But the "water" always disappears before you get there. The hot air above the highway made the light bend and caused you to see something that was not there.

A rainbow is caused by bending light. When sunlight passes through the transparent raindrops, it bends and makes all the colors of the spectrum to appear.

Test Your Reading (Group A)

Choose the best answer.

1. When light rays meet an object they cannot pass through, they will either
   a. be absorbed or bent.
   b. be bounced back or bent.
   c. be changed to heat or reflected.
2. An example of a transparent object is
   a. a door.
   b. a window.
   c. a sheet of paper.
3. When light enters water, it will
   a. change direction a little.
   b. slant back equal to the slant coming in.
   c. move in a curve through the water.
4. You can tell that light bends if you
   a. look at your hand through a window glass.
   b. look at a stick held into water.
   c. look at a tree in the distance.

Lesson 3 Answers

Group A

1. c
2. b
3. a
4. b

Additional helpful materials:

- one or more convex lenses (magnifying glasses)
- one or more concave lenses (from eyeglasses for a nearsighted person)

Note: The following diagrams show how light is bent in going through a lens, making the viewed object appear to be a different size than what it really is.

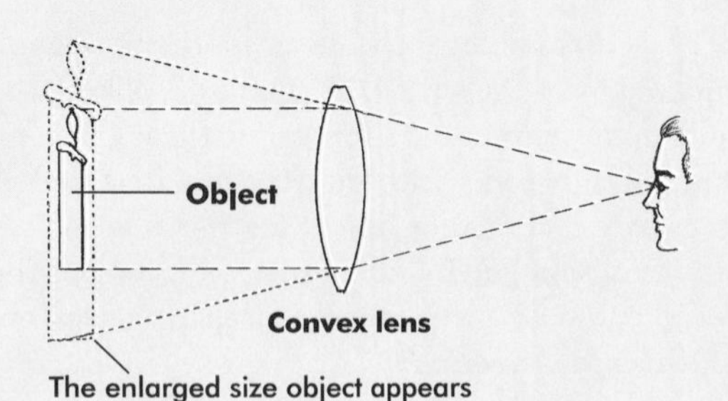

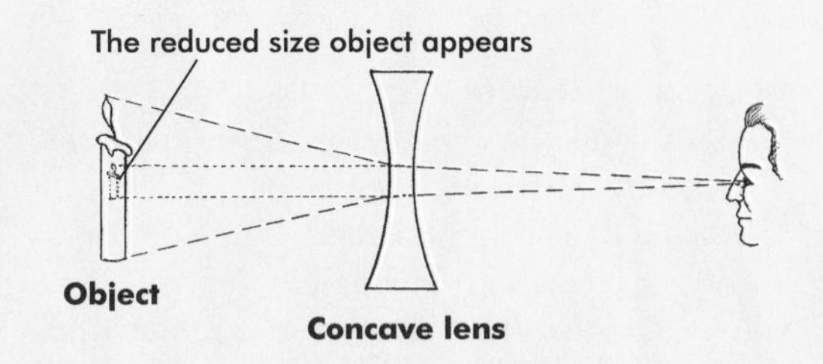

Did you know—

...that you never see the sun, moon, or any star in its true position in space unless it is directly overhead? As the light travels from outer space to the earth, it is refracted by the air around the earth.

...that one kind of mineral called cryolite seems to disappear when placed in water? This happens because it refracts (bends) light exactly the same amount as water does.

5. A wet-looking road may not be wet on a
   a. cold day.
   b. dry day.
   c. hot day.
6. You can see a rainbow because sunlight
   a. is reflected by the clouds.
   b. is absorbed by the rain.
   c. is bent by water.

5. c
6. c

(6 points thus far)

Bending light is useful. A carefully shaped glass is called a ***lens.*** A lens bends light to do useful things for us. One such lens is a magnifying glass. It makes small things look large. With a magnifying glass, we can examine a flower, an ant, or our fingerprints much better than with just our eyes. We can learn new things about our world because light bends while passing through a magnifying glass.

A magnifying glass is a convex lens. A ***convex*** lens is thickest at the center. One or both of its sides are curved outward. All convex lenses make things look larger.

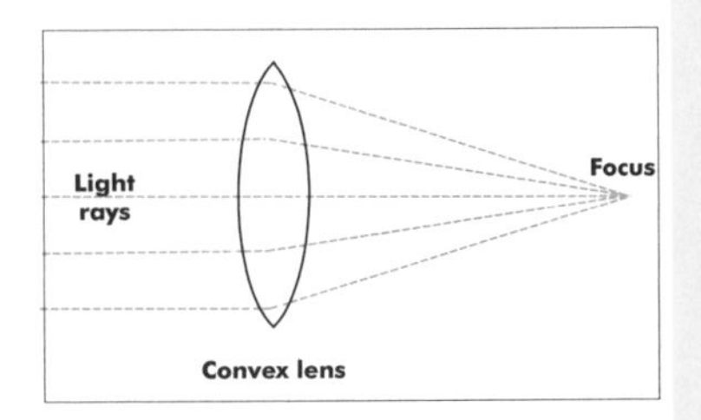

A convex lens always brings light rays closer together. It bends them toward one spot called the ***focus.*** If you hold a magnifying glass in front of a white sheet of

A view through a magnifying glass

The magnifying glass must be just the right distance to make the picture be in focus. Notice that the picture is upside-down.

...that experts measure the amount of refraction in jewels to help determine their quality? Valuable jewels, such as diamonds, refract light more strongly than other gems, which gives them an especially brilliant sparkle.

Focus Sunlight

If it is sunny outside, you can show the students how intense sunlight can be by focusing it on black paper and burning a hole in it. Explain that this is how a solar oven works. Do caution them against doing this on their own without the supervision of an adult.

Materials needed:

- magnifying glass
- black paper

Quiz

Write the New Words on the chalkboard. Call on students to choose the correct one when you give one of the sentences below.

1. It is a glass that has a curved surface to do a special job. *(lens)*
2. It is the spot where light rays come together. *(focus)*
3. It is thinnest at the middle. *(concave)*
4. It is thickest at the middle. *(convex)*
5. It means being clear enough that things can be seen through it. *(transparent)*

paper, it will make a picture of the windows in your classroom if you hold it the right distance away. If you are too close or too far away, the picture will be fuzzy and blurred. But if you have the distance just right, the picture will be in focus.

A ***concave*** lens is just the opposite of a convex lens. One or both of its sides curve inward, so it is thinnest at the center. A concave lens spreads light rays apart.

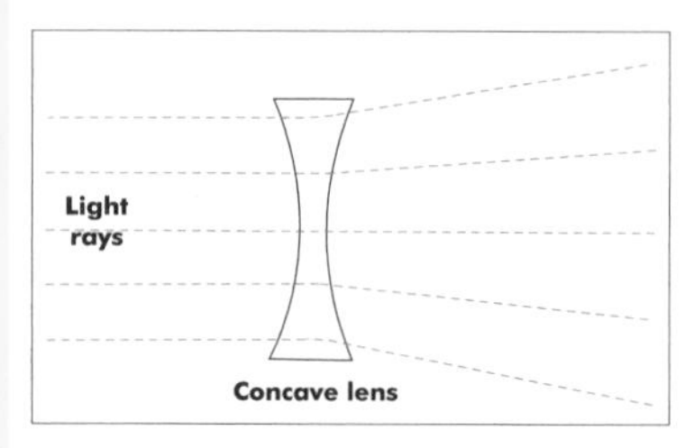

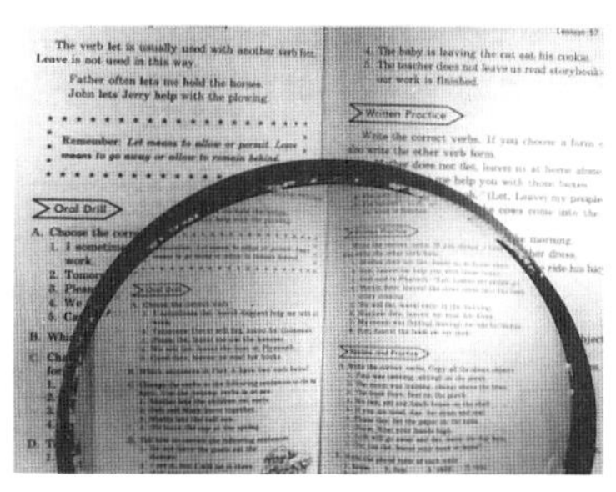

A view through a concave lens

A concave lens makes things look smaller. You can see this if you get a pair of eyeglasses. (Most children who wear glasses have concave lenses.) If you hold the glasses in front of this book, the letters will look smaller.

In the next lesson, you can learn about some important uses of both convex and concave lenses.

Test Your Reading (Group B)

Write the missing words.

7. A glass with curved sides made to bend light in a useful way is called a ———.
8. A magnifying glass makes things look ———.
9. The thickest part of a convex lens is at the ———.
10. A convex lens brings light rays to a point called the ———.
11. A picture can be made on a piece of white paper with a magnifying glass if it is at the right ———.
12. Things look smaller when seen through a ——— lens.
13. The sides of a concave lens are curved ———.
14. A concave lens causes light rays to ——— apart.

Group B

7. lens
8. larger (bigger)
9. center
10. focus
11. distance
12. concave
13. in (inward)
14. spread

(14 points total)

Reviewing What You Have Learned

1. Which group has only luminous objects in it?
   a. fire, fireflies, shiny pan
   b. stars, raindrops, glowworms
   c. sun, light bulbs, candle flame
2. True or false? All objects reflect some light.
3. When light is absorbed by an object, it is changed into
   a. ray energy.
   b. heat energy.
   c. reflected energy.
4. A white shirt will ——— much light.
5. ——— are useful because they reflect light rays so evenly.

Extra Activities

1. Try this with lenses! You need a binocular and a straight line across the floor. Mark it with a string unless the floor already has straight lines in its design. Stand at one end of the string or line. Use the lenses in your binocular by looking through the widest end (the "wrong" end). Look down at your feet. Do they look small and far-away? Now, still watching your feet through the binocular, try walking on the line to the other end. (Do you think it is easy? Try walking up a stairway, but be ready to grab the railing!)

   Materials needed:
   - binocular
   - string or line on floor

2. Watch what a convex lens can do to the view from your window. Is it a sunny day? If so, today is a good day for this experiment.

   Darken the other windows and switch off the lights. Get a magnifying glass and a sheet of white paper. Hold them a few feet away from the window, with the magnifying glass between the paper and the window. (**NEVER** try to look at the sun through the magnifying glass, or you could hurt your eyes.) Move the magnifying glass slowly back and forth until you see a clear image of the landscape on the paper. Which way is the image turned? Can you tell what causes it?

Review Answers

1. c
2. true
3. b
4. reflect
5. Mirrors

(5 additional points)

Extra Activity Comments

2. You may need to help the student hold the paper and lens in the correct position. The magnifying glass, like all other convex lenses, causes the image to be turned upside down and backward.

   The magnifying glass focuses the light of the top of the window view to a point at the bottom of the paper. And the light at the bottom of the window view is focused to a point at the top of the paper. This makes a reverse, or upside-down, image of the window view.

Materials needed:
- magnifying glass
- sheet of white paper

3. The bending of light as it passes from the water into the air causes the penny to appear.

3. Did you know that bending light can make you see a penny where it isn't? Try it.

Ask someone to be your helper. Put a penny in a mug that has sides that are not transparent, then slowly back away. Stop as soon as you no longer see the penny.

Now ask your helper to slowly pour some water into the mug while you watch. What do you see? Can you tell what happened?

Materials needed:
- penny
- mug
- water

Lesson 4

Using Lenses

New Words

eyepiece, the lens that you look through in a microscope or telescope.

microscope (mī′·krə·skōp′), a device with lenses that make tiny things look larger.

telescope, a device with lenses that make stars and other faraway objects seem nearer and larger.

Lenses are used in eyeglasses. Look around at all the people in the room. How many are wearing glasses? Perhaps you are wearing glasses yourself. If you are, your sight is being helped by lenses.

You need concave lenses if you are nearsighted. Without them, you can see only nearby objects clearly. Faraway objects look blurry. Look at the first picture on this page to see what a nearsighted person would see.

On the other hand, you need convex lenses if you are farsighted. Without them, you can only see faraway objects clearly. Nearby objects are out of focus. The picture below

The view of a person who is nearsighted

The view of a person who is farsighted

Lesson 4

Concepts to Teach

- Glasses use lenses to correct eye problems.
- The microscope uses lenses to help us see small things.
- Each lens of a microscope or telescope must be spaced just right to see clearly.
- The microscope lenses are moved back and forth to adjust the focus in order to see clearly.
- The telescope uses lenses to help us see faraway things.
- The telescope and microscope show us hidden wonders of creation.

Introducing the Lesson

Discuss this verse: "O magnify the Lord with me, and let us exalt his name together" (Psalm 34:3). Ask the class what they think this verse means. Should we make the Lord bigger? Develop the thought that a magnifying glass can show us new things about well-known objects, such as flowers or cloth. Likewise, we should keep showing others more things about how good and wonderful God is, even if they already know Him.

Did you know—

...that the ancient Chinese and Middle Eastern people are believed to have made eyeglasses?

...that while microscopes using light can magnify up to 2,500 times, electron microscopes using streams of electrons can magnify a million times?

...that soft contact lenses are made from a special plastic called polyhydroxyethylmethacrylate?

...that telescopes have helped scientists photograph at least a million galaxies in space and have led to the estimate that there are 100 sextillion stars in the known universe?

shows what a farsighted person would see.

Lenses help us see very small things. Men have learned much about God's wonderful world by using lenses. For example, we have learned that our blood is made of very tiny red and white cells. We have learned that we get strep throat and whooping cough because of very tiny germs. Germs are so tiny that thousands of them could fit on the period at the end of this sentence. The details of snowflakes can be seen and photographed (page 33). There are many kinds of tiny animals in a drop of muddy water from the bottom of a stream.

How did lenses teach us these things? They have been used to make the ***microscope,*** which makes tiny things look much larger. The word *microscope* is made of two parts. *Micro* means "small," and *scope* means "to see." A microscope helps us "to see small."

A very strong magnifying glass is a simple microscope. But microscopes usually have several lenses spaced a certain distance apart. With these lenses working together, a microscope makes something small look much bigger than it would with only one lens.

You remember from the last lesson that when using a magnifying glass to make a picture on a paper, you move it back and forth to focus the picture. You use a microscope in much the same way. When you turn the knob, the lenses move up and down. What you see is in focus when the lenses are positioned so that you can see the object clearly. The microscope is then in focus.

The lens or group of lenses at the top of the microscope is called the ***eyepiece.*** It is called the eyepiece because that is where you put your eye to look into the microscope.

Below the eyepiece is the other lens or group of lenses. It is placed above the small object you want to

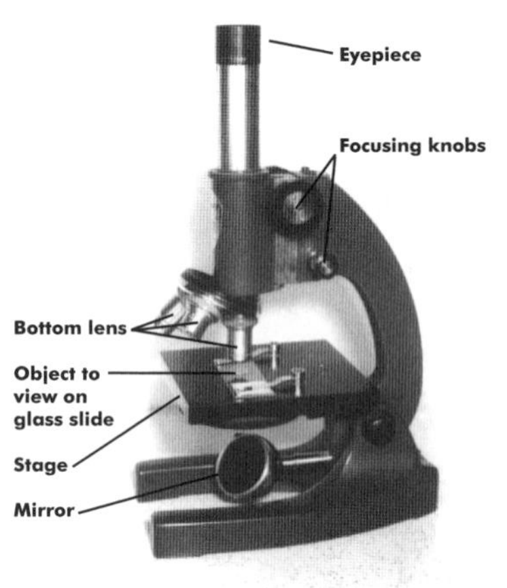

A microscope

Microscope and Telescope Practice

Give your students some hands-on experience with a quality microscope and telescope. If your school does not have them, perhaps they could be borrowed. Point out the various kinds of lenses, and show how to focus them properly.

Use the microscope to examine such things as a stamp, a dollar bill, an insect, a flower petal, a leaf, and a fingerprint on glass.

Perhaps you could arrange an evening for your students to get together to view the night sky with a telescope. It will be much more interesting and worthwhile to them if you or another knowledgeable adult can point out some familiar planets and constellations.

Quiz

Ask the children to write the correct New Word as you read each sentence below.

1. You look into this part of a microscope or telescope. *(eyepiece)*
2. You look at tiny things with it. *(microscope)*
3. You look at faraway things with it. *(telescope)*

see through the microscope. When the lenses in the eyepiece and the lenses below are in focus, you can see a sharp image that is dozens or hundreds of times bigger than the real object.

With the microscope, a Christian can see the very small wonders God has created. These wonders show how wise God is and how carefully He can make even things too small for us to see with our eyes alone.

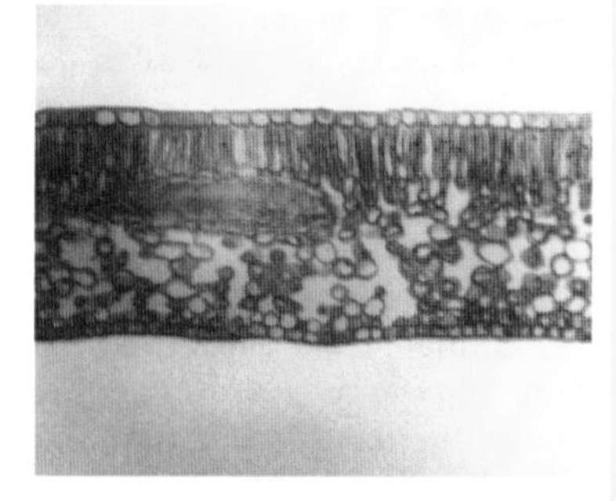

With a microscope, the cells of a leaf can be seen.

Test Your Reading (Group A)

Answer the following questions.

1. What kind of lenses does a person need who cannot see distant things clearly?
2. When would a person need glasses that are thickest in the center?
3. What do the two parts of the word *microscope* mean?
4. On a microscope, what is the name of the place where you look in?
5. If you look in a microscope and what you see is blurred, what must you do to see clearly?
6. What are two examples of things that men have learned with the use of the microscope?
7. What special use would a godly man make of the microscope?

Lenses help us see distant things. Do you ever use a binocular (also called field glasses) to watch wild birds and animals? The binocular helps you clearly see things that are far away. Actually, a binocular is two telescopes in one.

Why would a bird watcher use a binocular?

The word *telescope* is made of

Lesson 4 Answers

Group A

1. concave lenses
2. when he is farsighted (*or* when he cannot see near things clearly)
3. (*micro*) small; (*scope*) to see (2 points)
4. eyepiece
5. You must move the lenses until the image is sharp and clear.
6. (Any two.) The blood contains cells. Germs cause disease. Snowflakes have beautiful details. There are tiny animals in the muddy water of streams. (Give credit for other right answers.) (2 points)
7. to see the very small wonders God has made

(9 points thus far)

two parts. *Tele* means "far off," and *scope* means "to see." The telescope helps us "to see far off."

All ***telescopes*** use lenses to make faraway things look nearer and larger. For example, with a good telescope, you can see the mountains on the moon and the four biggest moons around the planet Jupiter. Thousands of star islands called galaxies have been discovered through the telescope.

A telescope works much like a microscope. It has lenses or groups of lenses spaced just the right distance apart. The one set of lenses in the eyepiece is made the same as the eyepiece of a microscope. But the lenses in the other set are different. They are much wider than those in a microscope. The largest telescope of this kind has a lens that is 40 inches (1 meter) wide.

Today even larger telescopes use mirrors instead of lenses. These mirrors can be made much wider than lenses. One large telescope in California has a mirror that is over 16 feet (5 meters) across!

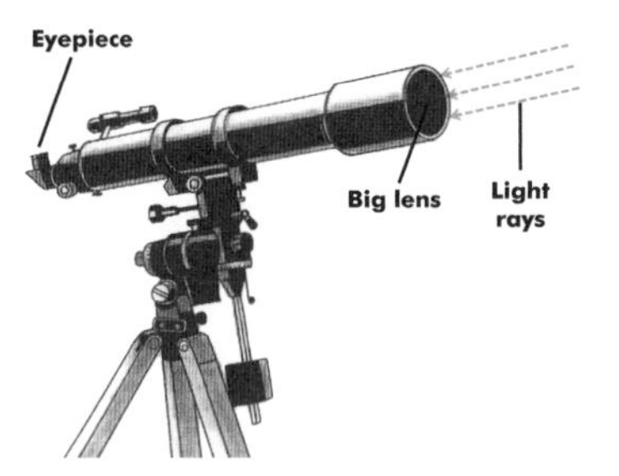

A telescope that focuses light with a large lens

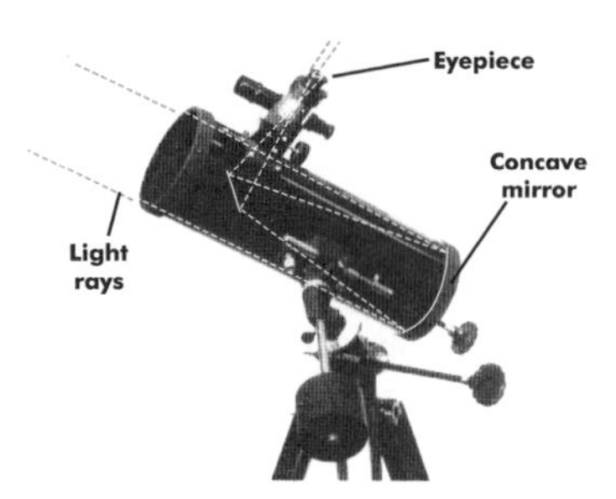

A telescope that focuses light with a mirror

You learned in this lesson that we use lenses in eyeglasses, binoculars, microscopes, and telescopes. There are many more uses for lenses. They are used in cameras and copiers. Lenses help doctors, dentists, and scientists do their work.

Although men have done much with lenses, we must remember to give God the praise He deserves. He made the materials used in glass and plastic lenses. He also gave man a good mind to learn how to make lenses. The things we learn by using lenses should help us honor God and praise His Name.

Test Your Reading (Group B)

Choose the best ending for each sentence below.

8. *Telescope* means
9. A binocular is
10. A telescope eyepiece is
11. The lenses of a telescope are
12. A blurred view is
13. The telescope lens where light comes in is
14. Some very big telescopes use
15. Lenses are also used in

a. spaced the right distance apart.
b. cameras and copiers.
c. mirrors instead of big lenses.
d. like that of a microscope.
e. "to see far off."
f. two telescopes in one.
g. bigger than in a microscope.
h. out of focus.

Answer the following questions.

16. What are two wonders of creation in the sky that can be seen only with a telescope?
17. What two kinds of people use lenses in their work?
18. In what two ways did God make the microscope and the telescope?

Reviewing What You Have Learned

1. Which one will absorb the most light?
   a. a black shirt b. a dark blue shirt c. a gray shirt
2. Lenses thicker at the center than at the edge are ———.
3. True or false? Concave lenses scatter light.
4. When a light ray travels at a slant into a transparent material, it is
   a. focused. b. reflected. c. bent.
5. Raindrops can change light into a
   a. ray. b. spectrum. c. reflection.

Extra Activities

1. Borrow a pair of bifocal eyeglasses from someone. (Older people are more likely to have bifocals than younger people.) Be sure to handle the glasses very carefully. Look at a newspaper or coin and then at a calendar on the wall. Do you see that each half of the glasses has two kinds of lenses in it? How are the two kinds different from each other? Are they both concave, both convex, or is there one of each? How can you tell?

Group B

8. e
9. f
10. d
11. a
12. h
13. g
14. c
15. b

16. (Any two.) mountains on the moon, four moons around Jupiter, thousands of galaxies (Give credit for other right answers.) (2 points)
17. (Any two.) doctors, dentists, scientists (Give credit for other right answers, such as surveyors and watch repairmen.) (2 points)
18. God made the materials that are used to make microscopes and telescopes. God gave men good minds to learn how to make microscopes and telescopes. (2 points)

(23 points total)

Review Answers

1. a
2. convex
3. true
4. c
5. b

(5 additional points)

Extra Activity Comments

1. By seeing if the lenses in the glasses enlarge (convex) or reduce (concave), the students should be able to detect which lenses are convex and which are concave.

Materials needed:
- bifocal eyeglasses

2. If tonight is a clear night, use a telescope or binocular to look at the moon and stars. Find the mountains and craters on the moon, and notice how many more stars you can see this way than you could with your naked eye.

Materials needed:
- telescope or binocular

3. Make your own "microscope with two lenses."

Place a pencil on either side of a postage stamp as shown in the picture.

Lay clear plastic wrap across the pencils, keeping it stretched out. With an eyedropper or a drinking straw, carefully place one drop of water on the plastic wrap above the stamp. Take care not to wet the area around it.

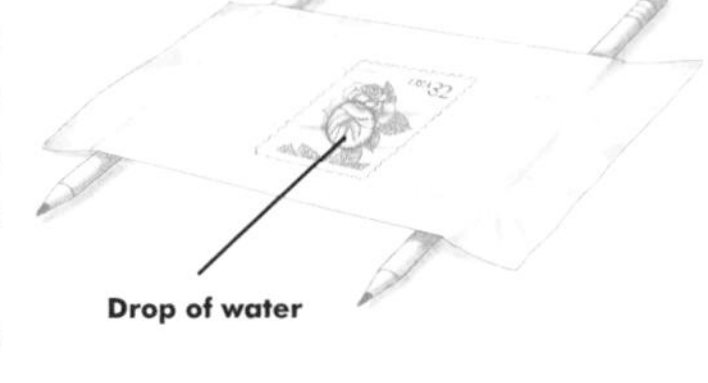

Look through the drop at the stamp. Does the stamp look bigger at that spot? Now hold a magnifying glass above the drop and look through both of them. How does the stamp look now?

Materials needed:
- stamp
- 2 pencils
- clear plastic wrap
- water
- eyedropper
- magnifying glass

3. If the students use a drinking straw rather than an eyedropper, you may need to show them how to transfer just one drop of water onto the plastic wrap. After you have dipped the straw into the water, plug the upper end of the straw with a finger. The water will stay in the straw until you are ready to release it by lifting your finger.

You may need to try more than once in order to get a single, nicely rounded drop onto the plastic wrap.

Lesson 5

Our Eyes

New Words

cornea (kôr′•nē•ə), the clear, outer covering on the front of the eyeball.

iris (ī′•ris), the colored part of the eye that controls the amount of light entering the eye.

optic nerve (op′•tik), the cord of nerves that sends messages from the eye to the brain.

pupil, the black opening in the iris where light enters the eye.

retina (ret′•i•nə), the back inside surface of the eyeball where images form.

What would you do without your eyes? Your eyes can receive messages from trillions of miles away when they see stars. They can also see the six points of a tiny snowflake held just inches from your eyes. Sight is one of the five valuable senses God gave to you.

When you see something, the reflected light travels into your eye and a "sight message" is sent to your brain in an instant. In this lesson we shall pretend to make just one sight message travel very slowly so that we can keep up with it. We shall follow its path through your eye and into your brain. Then you can better understand how you see.

How do we see? Do you see this letter A? How did it get to your brain? First, the light reflected off this page and came straight to your clear cornea. The ***cornea*** is a transparent covering over the front of the eye. If you look at the side of another person's eye, you can see

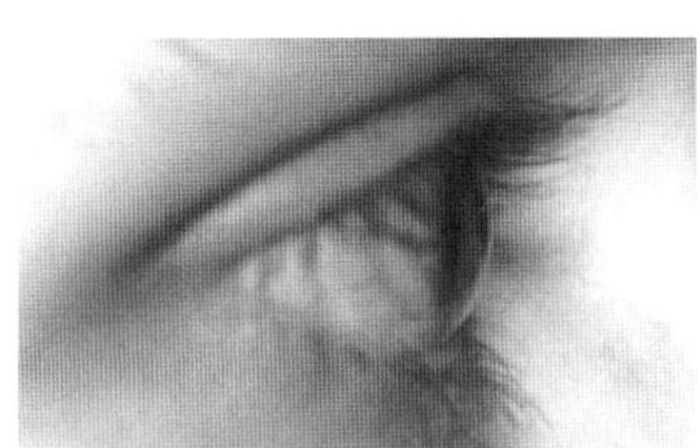

The cornea is the bulging, transparent covering on the front of the eye.

Lesson 5

Concepts to Teach

- Sight is one of the most valuable senses God has given us.
- Our eyes are a marvelous piece of God's handiwork.
- The iris controls the amount of light that enters the eye.
- The lens focuses light onto the retina.
- The optic nerve carries the vision message from the retina to the brain.
- The two eyes work together to give us one wide-angle vision and to help us judge distances correctly.
- The clear cornea protects the front of the eye.
- The eyebrows, eyelids, eyelashes, and tears protect our eyes from dirt and dust.
- The bony eye sockets protect our eyes from injury.
- We must be good stewards of our eyes by protecting them from harm and by using them only for good things.

Introducing the Lesson

Ask your students to clear off their desks and close their eyes tightly. Then with their eyes closed, have each one get his science book, pencil, pen, and eraser and place them on the right side of his desk. Next, ask them to try to find Lesson 5, again without looking. (They can only estimate about how many pages back it is.) This should help them realize afresh how valuable their sight is to them. Discuss the importance of being grateful for this gift from God.

the bulging shape of the clear cornea.

After the light passed through the cornea, it traveled through a watery liquid to your iris. The ***iris*** is the colored circle in your eye. If you say you have brown eyes, you mean that your irises are brown.

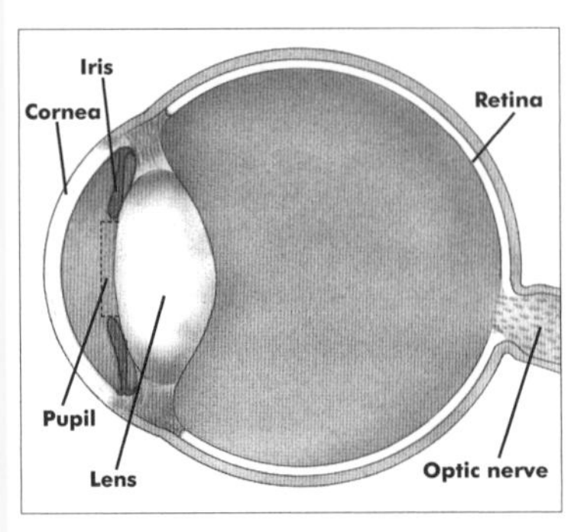

The parts of the eye

In the middle of your iris is a black dot called the pupil. The ***pupil*** is simply a hole or an opening in your iris where light can go through. If you read the letter A in bright light, your iris makes the pupil small and blocks out most of the light. But if you read the A in dim light, your iris opens to make a large pupil. This allows more light to enter your eye so you can see clearly in dim light. God made the iris so it could adjust the amount of light all by itself.

After entering the pupil, the light passed through a convex lens just behind it. This lens focuses the light so that you can see clearly. Like the iris, it can adjust itself by changing its shape. The eye is a marvelous display of God's handiwork.

The light from the lens is focused sharply on the back "wall" of the inside of the eye called the ***retina.*** Your lens causes the A to be focused upside down on your retina. The retina is made of special cells that respond to light. The millions of cells of the retina record the total picture of what you see in front of you.

After the image of the A formed on your retina, the light cells sent the sight message up to your brain through a cord of nerves called the ***optic nerve.*** The optic nerve sped the message to your brain. Your brain did not mind that the A was upside-down, for it knows that all sight messages come that way. It simply turned the A right side up and told you, "That is an A." Then you were all finished seeing that A.

Did you know—

...that just as you are either right-handed or left-handed, so you are either predominantly right-eyed or left-eyed? (This can be tested by observing which eye is used to look into a microscope or telescope.)

...that for some unknown reason, emotional tears contain more protein than reflex tears (those caused by foreign objects in the eye)?

...that you see colored spots in front of your eyes after staring at a bright light because the nerve endings of your retina have become tired?

...that because the retina is just concave enough to counterbalance the convexity of the lens, we can see images that are free from distortion?

...that the retina is sensitive to an incredibly wide range of light intensity? For example, the light from white paper in full sun is 10 million times as intense as the outdoors at night, and 10 billion times as intense as the absolute threshold of vision.

Play Blindman's Buff

At recess time, let the boys and girls take turns playing blindman's buff (or play in separate areas) because it is not suitable to play this game with a mixed group. Choose a certain room or area in which to play. Blindfold one player, and have him count to 50 while the others scatter. They should stand upright somewhere inside the designated area, not on top of chairs or under a table. Once the blindfolded player reaches 50, the other players must freeze wherever they are. They may lean from side to side, but they must not move their feet. The blindfolded player tries to find and identify everyone by the sense of touch. Each person identified leaves the area. The last one found is the winner.

Actually, all this happened in only 1/10 *of a second*!

While you read this lesson, many thousands of sight messages whiz from the page to your eye to your brain just as the A did. Sight is a great gift from God to you. We must thank Him for our eyes and praise Him for the wonderful way He made them.

Test Your Reading (Group A)

Use the names for eye parts given in the box to match with each of the following descriptions and the parts of the drawing. Each word is used more than once.

cornea	lens	pupil
iris	optic nerve	retina

1. It is the colored part of your eye.
2. It is the transparent covering of the eye.
3. It has cells that respond to light.
4. It speeds sight messages from the eye to the brain.
5. It controls the amount of light that enters the eye.
6. It focuses images by changing its size.
7. It is the black dot in your eye.
8. It is a cord of nerves.
9. It is a wall where upside-down images form.
10. It is convex like a magnifying glass.

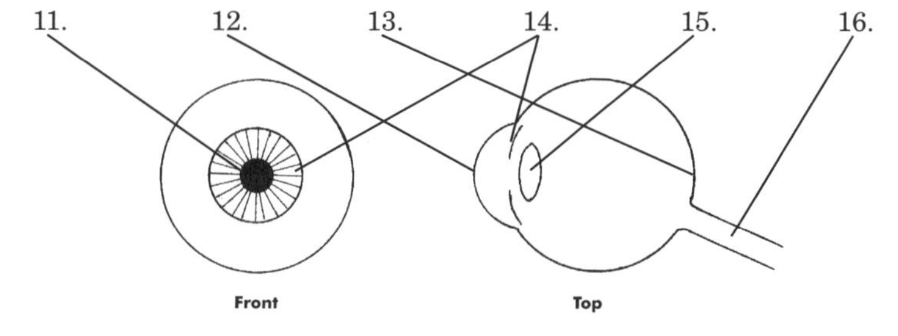

Lesson 5 Answers

Group A

1. iris
2. cornea
3. retina
4. optic nerve
5. iris
6. lens
7. pupil
8. optic nerve
9. retina
10. lens
11. pupil
12. cornea
13. retina
14. iris
15. lens
16. optic nerve

Point out to the students how easy it would be for the blindfolded player to find the other players if he could see. Discuss with the students how a blind person uses other senses and abilities to make up for the lack of sight. These include hearing, touching, smelling, and memory.

Essay Suggestion

Your students can give oral or written reports about blindness, colorblindness, snow blindness, and Seeing Eye dogs. You might help them by setting out appropriate library books and encyclopedias on a shelf or table.

Quiz

Ask the children to write the correct New Word as you read each phrase below.

1. The black opening in your eye *(pupil)*
2. The outer, clear covering on your eyeball *(cornea)*
3. The back wall of the eye where images are formed *(retina)*
4. The cord that carries sight messages to the brain *(optic nerve)*
5. The colored circle in your eye *(iris)*

17. The iris makes the pupil larger.
18. God designed the eye (*or* God created the eye).

(18 points thus far)

Answer the following questions.

17. What happens to the eye to help you see in dim light?
18. How did the eye get its design to be able to work so well?

Two eyes are better than one. You have learned how a sight message goes from one eye to your brain. But why do you need two at the same time? When you use both eyes, you can see a wider area around you than with only one eye. Also with two eyes, you can judge distances better. Since your eyes are a little over two inches apart, each eye sees a view that is just a little different. God has made your brain to be able to take the differences from your two eyes and tell you which objects are near and which are far.

Sometimes persons have had one eye injured so that it goes blind. They are glad that they had two eyes so they still have one eye to see. Sight is a very valuable gift from God. Be very careful that you do not lose your sight.

How did God protect your eyes? God not only gave you eyes to see, but He also provided protection for them so that you can keep on seeing. He gave you eyebrows and eyelashes to catch dust or dirt so it does not enter your eyes. He gave you corneas at the front of your eyes to act as transparent shields for the tender inner parts of the eyes.

If some dirt gets into your eye, you immediately start blinking to get it out. Tears form in your eyes to wash it away. If something comes flying toward you, your eyelids blink to protect your eyes. God made your eyelids close so quickly that you hardly think before you shut them.

Any hard knocks or bumps could seriously damage your soft eyeballs. In order to protect them, God gave you bony eye sockets like walls around the eyeballs. These strong eye sockets can stand much harder blows than your eyes can.

How can you use your eyes wisely? Even with all these protections, your eyes can still be hurt. God wants you to use your eyes wisely by doing your part to protect them. You can be a good steward of your eyes by keeping sharp objects and strong chemicals away from them. You must protect your eyes with a shield or with goggles to keep them from being hit by flying bits of matter from grinders, lawn mowers, or other machines that can throw things. You must not stare at the sun or other bright lights.

You use your eyes wisely when you use them to do good things to please God, who gave them to you. You make good use of your eyes when you read the Bible and other good books. You make good use of your eyes when you do work that is helpful to others.

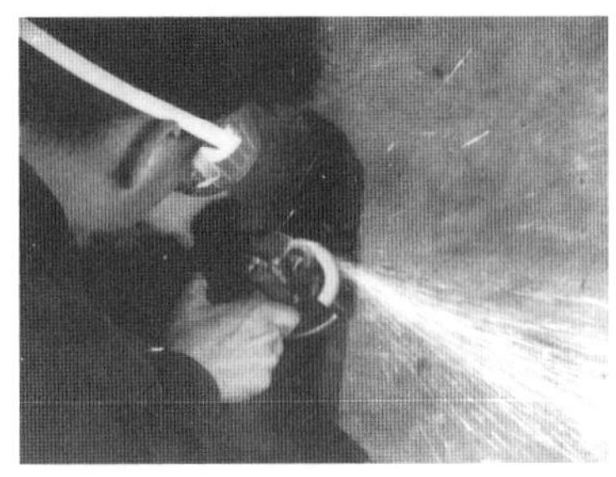

How does this picture show wise use of our eyes?

Job talked about a good use for his eyes. He said, "I was eyes to the blind" (Job 29:15). Do you think he stopped to help a blind person find his way? Do you think he gave blind people food and clothes? We do not know exactly what Job did, but we do know that he was kind to blind people. We can also be "eyes" to a blind person by helping him in any way we can. We use our eyes wisely when we help people who are blind.

You should not use your eyes to learn or do wrong things. You should be so thankful for the gift of sight that you want to use the gift only as it pleases God.

Test Your Reading (Group B)

Write the following lists of things about your eyes.

19. List three reasons why it is good that God gave you two eyes instead of one.
20. Explain five ways God provided protection for your eyes when He made you.
21. List three things that are harmful to your eyes.
22. List three good things you can do with your eyes. (Job tells us about one of them.)

Reviewing What You Have Learned

1. Mirrors are useful because they
   a. absorb light. b. bend light. c. reflect light.

Group B

19. to have a wider view, to judge distance better, to have one eye left if the other is injured (3 points)
20. The cornea is a transparent shield for the inner parts of the eye.
    The eyebrows and eyelashes catch dust and dirt.
    Tears wash any dirt away.
    Eyelids blink shut so quickly if something comes near the eyes.
    The eye sockets are protective walls around the eyeballs. (5 points)
21. (Answers may vary.) sharp objects, strong chemicals, flying pieces (3 points)
22. read the Bible and other good books, do work that is helpful to others, help blind people (3 points)

(32 points total)

Review Answers

1. c

2. focus
3. lenses
4. b
5. true

(5 additional points)

2. A convex lens brings light rays to a point called the ———.
3. Glasses use ——— to correct eye problems.
4. The lenses on a microscope can be moved to
   a. reflect light. b. focus light. c. absorb light.
5. True or false? A telescope has two sets of lenses that must be spaced just right.

Extra Activities

1. Try a test on yourself. Put a chalkboard eraser underneath a chair across the room. Ask someone to time how long it takes you to start from your desk, get the eraser, and return to your desk. Then time how long it takes you to do the same thing blindfolded. How much difference is there in the amount of time? This helps to show how much you depend on your eyes.

   Materials needed:
   - clock or stopwatch
   - scarf or other blindfold

2. Take another test. Find out if your two eyes really are better than one. Close your eyes while a classmate holds a pencil upright not far away. Then open only one eye and quickly touch the top of the pencil with one finger. Could you do it? Try it again; then try it using both eyes. Which was easier?

   Materials needed:
   - pencil

3. You can watch your irises at work. All you need is a dark room and a mirror. First, look at the mirror to notice how small your pupils are right now. Next, ask someone to time you for five minutes while you stay in the dark room. When the time is up, turn on the light while you are looking at the mirror and *immediately* watch the pupils of your eyes in the mirror. What happens? Why?

   Materials needed:
   - dark room
   - mirror

Lesson 6

Do You Remember?

Match each letter to the correct word group.

1. A line of light
2. Rainbow colors
3. A looking glass
4. To bounce off
5. Making light of its own
6. A lens that is thin at the center
7. Being clear
8. Where light could not reach
9. The colored part of the eye
10. A black opening in the eye

a. concave
b. convex
c. iris
d. luminous
e. mirror
f. pupil
g. ray
h. reflect
i. shadow
j. spectrum
k. transparent

For each blank, write the missing word from the word box.

cornea	lens	optic nerve
eyepiece	light	retina
focus	microscope	telescope
heat		

11. We need ——— in order to see.
12. Light that is absorbed changes to ——— energy.
13. A curved glass made to bend light is called a ———.
14. A fuzzy, blurry image is out of ———.
15. Small things look larger when seen through a ———.
16. Faraway things look nearer when seen through a ———.
17. We look into the ——— of a microscope to see small things.
18. Your ——— protects the front of your eye.
19. The convex lens in your eye focuses light onto your ———.
20. Your ——— speeds each sight message to your brain.

Lesson 6 Answers

1. g
2. j
3. e
4. h
5. d
6. a
7. k
8. i
9. c
10. f
11. light
12. heat
13. lens
14. focus
15. microscope
16. telescope
17. eyepiece
18. cornea
19. retina
20. optic nerve

Lesson 6

Reviewing the Unit

Use this lesson as an opportunity to reinforce reverence for God in your students. Let them hear tones of awe and wonder in your voice as you speak of God's wisdom in creating light and the intricate human eye. Tell the class that although light seems very common to them, some aspects of it remain a mystery even to the most-learned scientists.

Remind your students that God created light before there was any sun, moon, or stars to shine. How did He do it? We cannot pretend to know, but we believe that the Bible is true.

Finally, ask for volunteers to tell the class (without looking at their books) something they learned about light in this unit.

21. c
22. a
23. b
24. c
25. b
26. a
27. c
28. c

Choose the best answer for each sentence.

21. God created light on the
    a. third day.
    b. second day.
    c. first day.
22. Something luminous that God created is
    a. the sun.
    b. the moon.
    c. the sky.
23. Which reflects the most light?
    a. a black shingle roof
    b. a shiny tin roof
    c. a gray slate roof
24. Which absorbs the most light?
    a. a green dress
    b. a gray dress
    c. a black dress
25. A mirror image is always
    a. upside-down.
    b. backward.
    c. slanted.
26. A transparent material will
    a. allow light to pass through it.
    b. cause light to bounce off.
    c. change most of the light to heat.
27. When a slanting light ray goes from the air into water,
    a. it is absorbed.
    b. it is reflected.
    c. it is bent.
28. A convex lens brings light rays to a point called
    a. the spectrum.
    b. the contact.
    c. the focus.

Write *true* if the sentence is true; write *false* if it is not true.

29. Light gives us heat when it is reflected.
30. Light travels in rays from the sun.
31. Sunlight is made of many colors.
32. You can sometimes see your reflection in a rough board.
33. The slant that light strikes a mirror is the same slant that it bounces off in the opposite direction.
34. A microscope must be focused to be able to see clearly.
35. A concave lens brings light rays closer together.
36. Lenses in eyeglasses can correct poor vision.
37. The lenses of a telescope must be spaced a certain distance apart in order to focus properly.
38. Your eyes are a marvelous display of God's wisdom.

Copy and finish the sentences.

39. The iris lets just enough ———.
40. Both the iris and the lens of the eye can ———.
41. We need two eyes so that we can ———.
42. Eyelids, eyelashes, and tears protect the eyes from ———.
43. Bony eye sockets protect the eyes from ———.

Write the correct answers.

44–45. Write two ways in which mirrors are useful.

46. Name something that man can see with the microscope that he cannot see without it.

47. Name something that man can see with the telescope that he cannot see without it.

48–50. Name three main ways we can use our eyes wisely.

29. false
30. true
31. true
32. false
33. true
34. true
35. false
36. true
37. true
38. true

39. The iris lets just enough light enter the eye.
40. Both the iris and the lens of the eye can change their shape (*or* work without thinking).
41. We need two eyes so that we can judge distances correctly (*or* see a wider area).
42. Eyelids, eyelashes, and tears protect the eyes from dust and dirt.
43. Bony eye sockets protect the eyes from knocks and bumps.

(Answers may vary.)

44–45. (Any two.) Mirrors are useful for looking glasses, rearview mirrors, reflectors around searchlights and auto headlights, in telescopes. (2 points)

46. With the microscope, man has seen blood cells and germs.

47. With the telescope, man has seen mountains on the moon, Jupiter's four moons, and thousands of galaxies.

48–50. We can use our eyes wisely by protecting them from harm, by doing good with them, and by helping the blind. (3 points)

(50 points total)

Unit Six

Electricity Is From God

It is dark and the night is warm. You are asleep. A bright flash fills your bedroom, and you are startled out of your sleep. For several seconds you lie frozen, afraid to move. The bright light is followed by a loud crack and the echoing boom of thunder. It frightens you, and maybe you wish there was not anything like a thunderstorm. But wait! Do not be afraid. This is a display of the greatness of our God. That bright light and loud boom is made by a huge spark of electricity, much greater than men have ever made.

"He directeth . . . his lightning unto the ends of the earth" (Job 37:3).

Think about Job. Three of his friends told him that the reason he was sick was because he had sinned. It was not because of Job's sin, but because he needed to learn how great God is and how small he was. After these three friends talked, Elihu, another man, spoke. He told Job to think about the greatness of God. As he talked, it seems that a thunderstorm came up, because he asked Job "to hear attentively the noise of [God's] mouth [thunder]. . . . He directeth . . . his lightning unto the ends of the earth." A little later he said that "God thundereth marvellously with his voice" (Job 37:1–5). After Elihu finished talking, God talked to Job out of a whirlwind and Job listened.

So when the lightning flashes and the thunder is loud, do not be afraid. Be like Job. Think about the greatness of God, and listen to God speak.

What does this have to do with electricity? Lightning is electricity—a giant electric spark of about 100 million volts. Only God can make such a giant spark!

Unit Six

For Your Inspiration

Today electricity is a common part of our lives. If our ancestors from before 1900 could visit us, they would be astonished at what we can do with electricity. Electricity lights our homes, it washes our clothes, it freezes our food, it cooks our food, it rings our bells, it starts our cars, it carries our voices over many miles, it calculates our taxes, and it runs our clocks. What to us seems commonplace would be marvel after marvel to them.

In most modern science textbooks, scientists and inventors get the credit and praise. Men have become very proud of what they can do with electricity. They will freely mention the place that men like Benjamin Franklin, Michael Faraday, and Thomas Edison had in the development of electrical discoveries and inventions. They make not one mention of God who created the electron and made electricity possible.

However, one noted inventor, Samuel Morse, was willing to associate God with a notable invention. The first long-distance telegraph message he sent from Washington, D.C., to Baltimore was "What hath God wrought!" (Numbers 23:23). In reality, the many electrical inventions are the work of God. He created the laws and materials of electricity. The possibility for every invention was created by God. Computer chips could not be made but for the special electrical properties of silicon and other special materials. Some materials conduct electricity well, and some not at all, according to the wise plan of God. Both are necessary for our electrical appliances. Only a few materials (iron, cobalt, and nickel) are magnetic. This makes generators, motors, and transformers possible. To God be the glory.

Lesson 1

Parts of a Circuit

New Words

appliance (ə·plī′·əns), a machine or light that uses the electricity in an electric circuit.

battery, one or more cells that contain special chemicals that make an electric current.

circuit (sėr′·kit), the complete circle or path for an electric current to travel in.

conductor (kən·duk′·tər), a material that carries electricity.

insulator (in′·sə·lā′·tər), a material that will not carry electricity and will not allow electricity to pass through.

switch, a part of an electric circuit used to turn the flow of electricity on or off.

When you turn on a light switch in a dark room, can you see what turns the light on? Can you hear anything happening? No; you turn on the switch, and immediately there is light.

Something happened that you could not hear or see. It is the wonder of electricity. We use it so often to turn on lights, fry bacon, drill holes, and feed cows that we may forget that this is a work of our great God.

Electricity moves. First, think of a very small thing, so small that you would not be able to see it even in a microscope. These very small things are called electrons, from which we get the word *electricity.* The moving of these electrons through a wire is what gives us electricity. Since no one can actually see electrons, we shall use something that we can see to help explain them.

Think of a garden hose. We connect the garden hose to a faucet. When we turn the faucet on, water is pushed through the hose by a pump and you see water coming out the other end. Electricity is like that. A battery is like

Even the inventors themselves are a witness to the creative power of God. God created man with the ability to discover the natural laws and to apply those laws in making inventions. Thomas Edison could have invented nothing if God had not given him an inquiring and inventive mind. Behind every inventor is the existence of God who gave him his ability. The creator of the inventor is greater than the inventor himself. To God be the glory.

Electrical inventions come as a result of years and generations of discoveries. Michael Faraday could not have invented a pocket calculator no matter how hard he tried. Invention requires sufficient education, favorable economy, and available resources. All history, including the history of invention, is under the providence of God. He allows the circumstances and birth of particular men that make possible the production of useful devices. It was not our good management to be born into a time that has such wonders available. We should look at them as special gifts from God to use in His service. To God be the glory.

As you teach this unit, do not fail to draw the students' minds to God, who has made all these things possible. Call their attention to the wonder of these things they use every day. Help them understand that when we work with batteries, wire, and light bulbs, we are handling the results of the creative power of God. "What hath God wrought!"

Note: Look ahead to preparing to teach Unit Seven by reading "Plant Study for Unit Seven" on page 203.

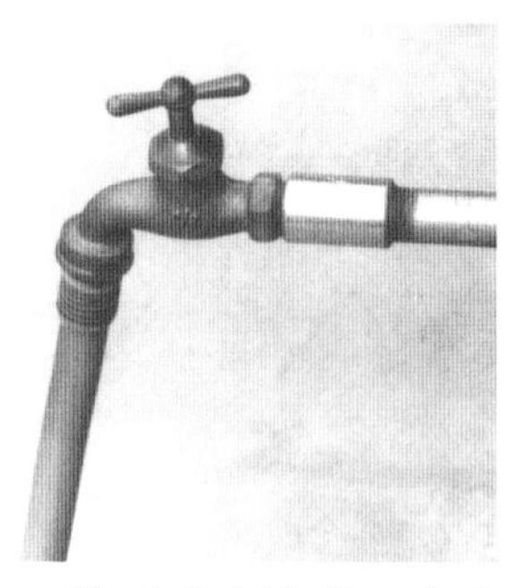

How is electricity like water in a garden hose? How is it different?

a pump that moves electrons. The wire is like the garden hose. The electrons are like the water. The switch is like the faucet. This helps explain how electricity flows through a wire.

But the garden hose does not explain everything about electricity. The water comes out the end of the hose. But electrons in a wire do not work this way. You cannot hook the end of one wire to a battery and have electrons running out the other end.

Electrons move around in a circle. Let us add one more thing to our garden hose picture. If we hook the end of the garden hose to the pump, there will be a complete circle and the water will continue to go around and around.

Electrons flow in a current like this. The wires must make a complete circle, from the battery, to the light bulb, and back to the battery again. We call this a ***circuit.*** One wire carries the electrons to the light bulb, and another wire carries the electrons back to the battery. The electrons will move in a wire only if there is a path to carry them back to where they started.

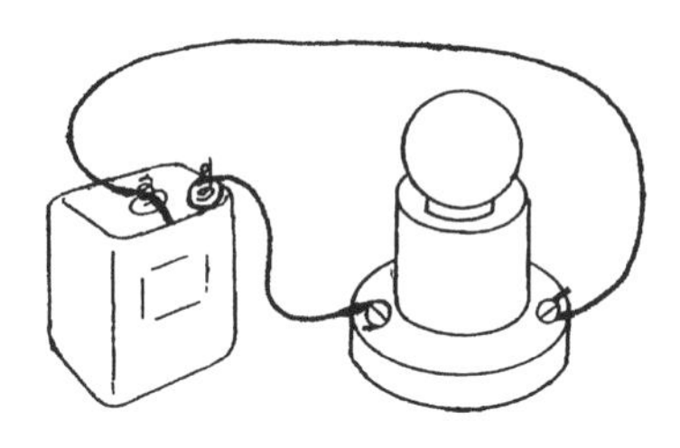

Why must two wires connect the battery and the light bulb?

Use the Chalkboard

Make much use of the chalkboard in teaching the concepts of circuits in this unit. The following simple diagrams for the parts of the circuit can be used.

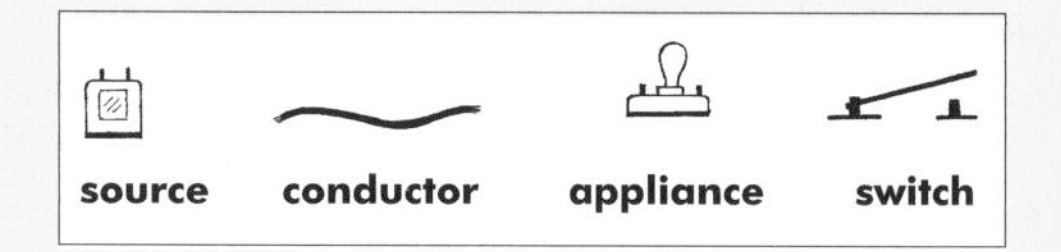

Have the students go to the board and draw the circuits being studied.

Lesson 1

Concepts to Teach

- Electricity must have a complete circuit of conductors for an electric current to flow.
- A complete circuit has four parts: a source, conductors, an appliance, and a switch.
- Some materials are conductors, and some are insulators.
- The conductors must be insulated to keep the electricity in its path.
- A battery and a generator are sources of electricity.
- A switch allows the electricity to be turned on and off.

Electrons move through a circuit of wire as water moves through a garden hose. But the wire does not have a hole through it like the garden hose. The electrons move through solid wire. This is a wonder of electricity, planned and created by God.

Conductors and insulators. Electricity will only move in certain kinds of materials called ***conductors.*** *Conduct* means "to carry." Any material that will carry electricity is called a conductor. Some good conductors God has given us are iron, aluminum, copper, and tin.

There are also many materials that will not conduct electricity, such as wood, plastic, glass, and rubber. Materials that do not conduct electricity are called ***insulators.*** They insulate electricity, or keep the electricity from going through, much as your clothes insulate you when they do not let the cold go through in the wintertime.

Rubber or plastic is the insulating material that covers the cords and wires of the electric machines that you use. To use electricity safely, you must have both conductors and insulators. You can see how wise God is to give us everything we need so that we can use electricity.

Test Your Reading (Group A)

Choose the best answer for each.

1. Electricity is a wonder from God because
   a. only God can make an electric circuit.
   b. electricity works in a way that only God could create and plan.
   c. we can only see electricity at work in lightning that God makes.
2. A circuit means
   a. a path for flowing electrons that comes back to where it started.
   b. the insulating material that covers the outside of a conductor.
   c. the moving electrons inside a wire.
3. All of the following are conductors except
   a. copper.
   b. plastic.
   c. aluminum.

Lesson 1 Answers

Group A

1. b
2. a
3. b

Introducing the Lesson

Begin the study of electricity with some discussion of lightning as God's use of electricity long before man knew how to use it. Read God's own question to Job about lightning (Job 38:35). Remind the students that in Bible times, lightning was a form of electricity they knew about. Perhaps they knew about static electricity, but they would have been amazed if they could have seen our use of electricity. Call the students' attention to God's part in the modern electrical inventions that they use. (See "For Your Inspiration" for this unit.)

Have an appliance that has a switch, such as an electric fan or a table lamp, to show the students. Explain to them the function of a switch. Illustrate how a switch makes and breaks contact by putting your hands together and then taking them apart. Ask them what will be necessary to make the appliance work. They should know that it must be plugged into a receptacle. Plug the appliance in, and ask them why it still does not work. They will know that it must be turned on. It would be good if you would need to use an extension cord to reach a receptacle. Have them say why each part is necessary to make the appliance work. Lead the discussion to the four parts of an electric circuit.

Materials needed:

- appliance with a switch
- extension cord

Did you know—

...that electrons are so small that no one has ever seen them? In fact, the electron must be moving to exist. If we would stop it to look at it, there would be no electron there. This limitation makes the electron a mystery known only to God.

4. An insulator is a material that
   a. keeps a wire warm.
   b. does not let electrons pass through it.
   c. carries electrons well.
5. Which of the following would make a good insulator?
   a. rubber
   b. steel
   c. tin

Answer the following questions.

6. A garden hose is like what part of an electric circuit?
7. Why do we need two wires connected to a light bulb to make it work?

4. b
5. a
6. the conductor (*or* wire)
7. One wire carries the electrons to the light bulb, and the other wire carries the electrons away.

(7 points thus far)

The source of electricity. Every circuit must have four parts: a source, conductors, an appliance, and a switch. You have already read about conductors. Conductors can carry electricity, but they cannot make the electrons move. We must have a source, something that produces electricity. One source of electricity is a ***battery.*** Special chemicals in the battery work together to produce electric current. All batteries must have two places to connect wires. Flashlight batteries have flat conducting surfaces at each end that conductors touch to complete the circuit.

Electric power plants have large generators that are the source of electricity for many homes, schools, and businesses.

Another source of electricity is a generator. A generator looks very much like a big electric motor. The generators that make the electricity for your home and school are taller than a man. Every generator, big or small, must have two places to connect wires: one for the electrons to go

...that the "plus" and "minus" on a battery are only arbitrary names? They could be backward, and it would make no difference so long as all other electrical devices had them backward.

...that the one conductor of an electric fence is the ground? The cow that touches it is the switch that completes the circuit and gets shocked.

...that the birds that sit on one wire of a high-voltage line do not get shocked because they are not part of a circuit?

...that the colder a conductor is, the less resistance it has? If a wire is cooled to near absolute zero (-460°F, -273°C), it has almost no resistance and a current flowing through a circle of wire will continue to do so for some time without a source.

...that the giant switches at power plants have the contacts in a bath of oil (a very good insulator) so that when the switch is opened, an arc does not develop that would burn the contacts?

...that a problem of using aluminum wire for electricity is that with contraction and expansion of heat the wire gets loose in a connection and can cause a fire? Special connectors are used to avoid this.

out and another for the electricity to come back through the circuit.

Appliances use electricity. The electricity that flows through a wire must be used. If it is not used, the electrons will go too fast and make the wire hot. This could start a fire and be dangerous. Something must use this electricity, such as a light bulb, a toaster, a refrigerator, a drill, or a computer. These are called appliances. An ***appliance*** uses the electricity to do something helpful for us. An appliance keeps the wire from becoming too hot. There must be an appliance in every electric circuit.

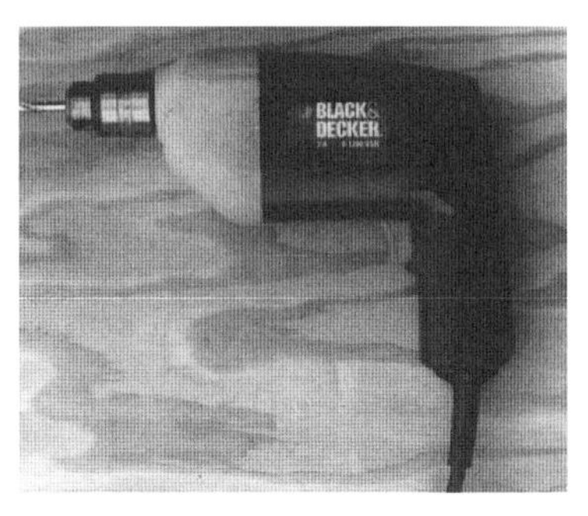

An electric drill is one kind of appliance.

Turning it on and off. One more thing that is needed in an electric circuit is a ***switch.*** A very simple example of a switch is a knife switch. When the blade of the switch is up, the circuit is open, and the electricity cannot flow. The electrons do not move, and the light (or other appliance) is off. When the blade of the switch is put down, it touches the metal of the other part and closes the circuit. The electrons can flow, and the light will come on. The light switches in your house do not look like a knife switch, but they do the same thing.

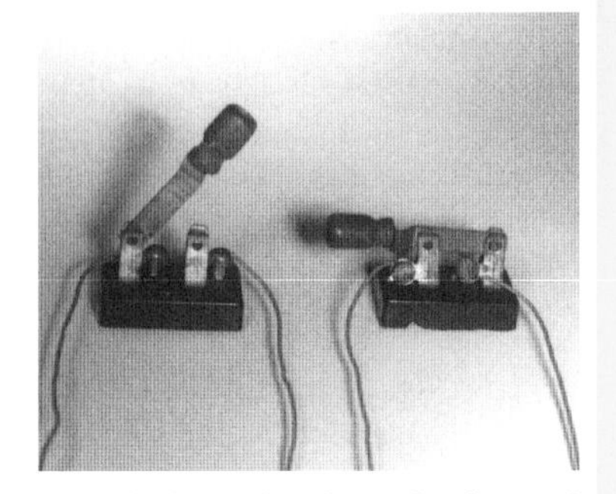
Which knife switch makes a closed circuit? Which makes an open circuit?

An electric circuit needs four parts: a source, conductors, a switch, and an appliance. If any part is missing, it will not work, or it will be dangerous.

Quiz

Have the students say or write the correct New Word for each sentence below.

1. It is a material that is used to cover a wire to keep the electricity in the wire. *(insulator)*
2. It is a source that makes electricity with chemicals. *(battery)*
3. It is the part of an electric circuit that uses the electricity to do something helpful. *(appliance)*
4. It is the complete path that the electricity flows around. *(circuit)*
5. It is the kind of material of which electric wires are made. *(conductor)*
6. It is the part of a circuit that lets you turn the current on or off. *(switch)*

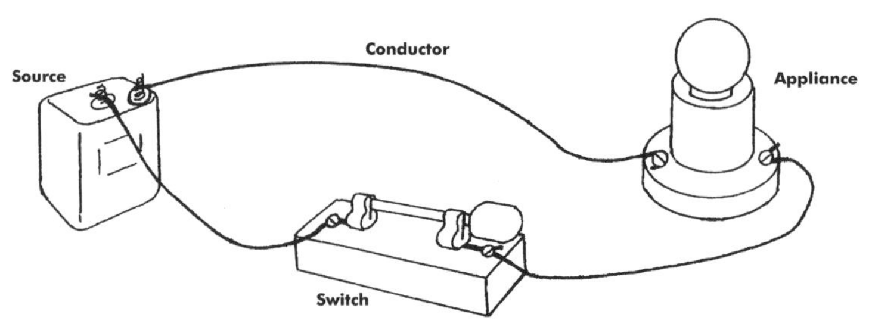

A complete electric circuit

Electricity is a wonder God created. Sometimes He shows us what electricity is like with the giant spark of lightning. At other times when electricity is running machines or lighting light bulbs, we know that moving electrons are making them work. Only God can make electricity possible.

Test Your Reading (Group B)

Write the missing words.

8. A ——— produces electricity with special chemicals.
9. Both a battery and a generator must have ——— places to connect wires.
10. The part of an electric circuit that uses the electricity is the ———.
11. To stop the flow of electricity, the ——— must be open.
12. God shows us what electricity is like with ———.

Answer the following questions.

13. What is the source of the electricity that you use in your house?
14. What are the four parts of an electric circuit?
15. Why would it be dangerous to have a circuit without an appliance?

For each number, choose the correct letter from the drawing on page 175.

16. Carries the electricity from one place to another
17. Provides the source of electricity
18. Uses the electricity

Group B

8. battery
9. two
10. appliance
11. switch
12. lightning
13. generator
14. conductors, a source, an appliance, a switch (4 points)
15. The wire would get hot and could start a fire.
16. b
17. c
18. a

19. Makes a place to stop and start the flow of electricity

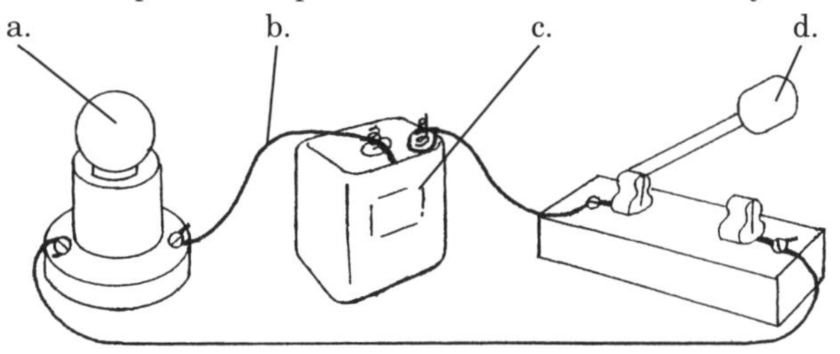

19. d

(22 points total)

Extra Activities

1. Examine a flashlight to find the four parts of an electric circuit. Notice how the one end of the battery is touching the bottom of the bulb. How does the other end of the battery connect with the light bulb? Try to find out how the switch opens and closes the circuit.

   Materials needed:
   - a flashlight

2. Make a conductor tester. On a 4″ x 8″ board, drive in long nails on each side of two flashlight batteries laid end to end. Put one nail at each end to make electrical contact with the battery. Wedge some aluminum foil between the nail and the flat end of the battery to make good contact. Remove 1″ of insulation from the ends of 3 six-inch pieces of wire. Fold a two-inch square of aluminum foil in half twice the same way to make a piece ½″ wide and 2″ long. Place the aluminum strip flat on the board, and fasten it with a thumbtack about ¼″ from one of the ends. Before pushing the thumbtack tight, wrap one of the ends of wire around it.

   Wrap the end of another wire around the base of a flashlight bulb to make contact. Fasten the wire with thumbtacks so that the end of the light bulb is touching the aluminum foil strip. Wrap the other end of the wire around the nail at one end of the batteries.

   Connect one end of the third wire to the opposite battery nail. Your circuit will be connected in this order: wire, nail at one end of

Extra Activity Comments

1. There are different kinds of flashlights, and it would be good to have the students bring in a variety for study. When the case of the flashlight is metal, the case itself is used as the conductor from the bottom of the last battery to the light end. The switch sometimes is simply a metal strip that touches a metal ring around the light bulb holder.
2. With the addition of a knife switch, the four parts of an electric circuit can be illustrated with this activity. The use of an actual miniature light socket would improve this activity. Wire, bulbs, knife switches, and sockets can be purchased from some hardware stores, hobby stores, and electronic stores.

battery, batteries, nail at other end of batteries, wire, light bulb base, end of light bulb held against aluminum strip, wire under tack pushed into aluminum strip. This leaves two free ends of wire to act as a switch. Touch them together. The light bulb should light.

Now use the two free ends of wire to test if materials are conductors or insulators. Place the two free ends on a material but not touching each other. How will you know if the material is a conductor? Test many things, and make lists of conductors and insulators. Try wood, paper, coins, carbon (lead from a lead pencil), rainwater, well water, salt water, sugar water, wet soil, and many other things. For a solution that does not light the bulb, you can tell if it is conducting electricity by seeing if tiny bubbles form on one of the wires in the solution. Test a metal filing cabinet. Try a spot where there is no paint. Explain the results. **WARNING: NEVER CONNECT YOUR TESTER TO ELECTRICITY FROM AN ELECTRICAL OUTLET.**

Materials needed:

- board about 4″ x 8″
- 2 dry cell batteries
- about 6 fourpenny or sixpenny nails
- hammer
- aluminum foil
- about 18″ of insulated bell wire
- several thumbtacks
- flashlight bulb (for use with 2-cell flashlight)
- various materials to test

Lesson 2

Different Circuits

New Words

parallel circuit (par′·ə·lel′), an electric circuit that has more than one appliance and has more than one path for the electricity to follow.

resistance (ri·zis′·təns), that which slows down the flow of electricity in a circuit.

series circuit (sir′·ēz), an electric circuit that has more than one appliance but only one path for the electricity to follow.

Electricity must flow in a complete circuit. You learned this in Lesson 1. Do you remember the example of a battery, wires, switch, and light that we used in Lesson 1? In order for the light bulb to come on, the wire must go from the battery to the light and back to the battery again. This is an example of a very simple circuit.

Now suppose we want to make more than one light bulb to light. Shall we get another battery, another set of wires, and another light and switch? No, we do not need to. We can use the same battery and only add the light to the circuit. But we can choose from two kinds of circuits.

Making a series circuit. One kind of circuit is called a ***series circuit.*** *Series* means "one after the other." Below is a drawing of how the series circuit is wired. The wire connects each part of the circuit one after the other.

Since there is a complete circuit, both light bulbs will light. The electricity goes through a wire from the

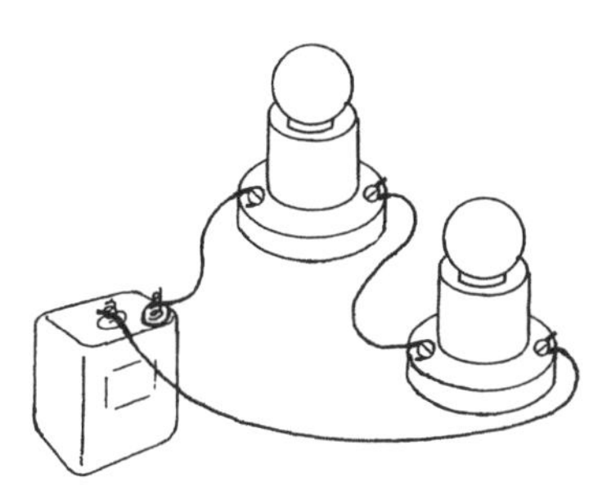

Two bulbs wired in series

Lesson 2

Concepts to Teach

- Appliances are wired in series when the electricity goes through them one after the other.
- Appliances are wired in parallel when the electricity divides and goes through them side by side.
- When appliances are wired in parallel, one can be out and the others will continue to operate.
- Switches are wired in series with the other parts of the circuit.
- Wires and appliances slow down, or give resistance to, the flow of electricity.
- The thinner a wire, the greater the resistance.
- The longer a wire, the greater the resistance.

Introducing the Lesson

Use the lights, receptacles, and switches in the classroom to illustrate how several appliances can operate from the same source. Plug something that lights or operates into a receptacle. Then turn the switch of the room on and off and have them notice that this does not affect what is plugged into the receptacle.

It would be helpful to have a worn-out, complex electrical device, such as an electric fencer, an amplifier, or a battery charger. Remove the covers so that the students can see the wiring. Perhaps one of them will have a circuit board that has the "wires" as copper strips printed on the surface of the board. How does the electricity know where to go in such a mass of wires? God has made laws for the electrons that work perfectly. Men design electrical devices to use these laws. As long as the wires go to the right place, the electricity will go right.

battery, through the first light bulb, then through the second light bulb, and then back to the battery. Each bulb lights as the electricity passes through it.

But there is a problem of wiring lights in series. If one of the light bulbs burns out, the circuit is broken and the other light will go out also. If several bulbs in a shop would be in series and one would burn out, all the lights would go out.

Making a parallel circuit. Instead of using a series circuit, we could use a ***parallel circuit.*** *Parallel* means "side by side." Below is a drawing that shows how two lights would be wired in a parallel circuit. The circuit divides, and the electricity goes through each bulb side by side. Then the circuit comes back together again.

The circuit is complete through each bulb, and both light bulbs will light. The electricity from the battery can go two ways. Some goes through the one light bulb and back to the battery, and some goes through the other light bulb and back to the battery. Really, we have two circuits in one. We call this kind of circuit a parallel circuit.

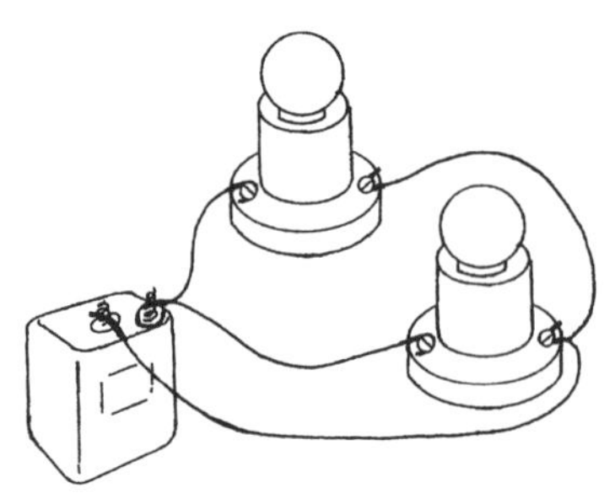

Two bulbs wired in parallel

The parallel circuit does not have the problem of the series circuit. Since each light bulb has its own circuit, if one bulb burns out, the other light bulb will still light. This makes it possible to have many light bulbs on one circuit and to have light even though one of them is burned out.

Test Your Reading (Group A)

Study the following circuits carefully. Decide whether the circuit is *series* or *parallel.* Write the answer for each picture.

1. 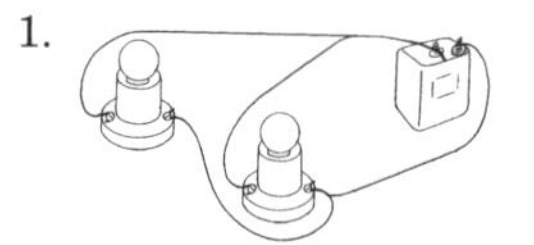

2. 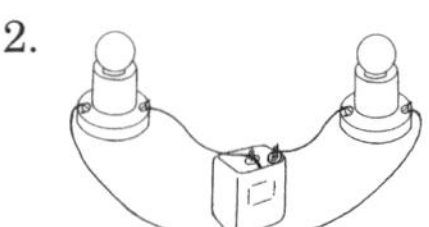

Lesson 2 Answers

Group A

1. parallel
2. series

Materials needed:

- two appliances
- worn-out electrical device

Did you know—

...that some motors are made to run on either 120- or 240-volt current simply by changing the wiring of the windings from parallel to series wiring? Series makes more resistance and will stand the higher voltage.

...that the circuits for many electrical devices are printed on both sides of boards? On one side of the board, the "wires" make connections at right angles with the "wires" on the other side.

...that the different heats of an electric stove are produced by putting the two heating elements in series or parallel with either 120- or 240- volt electricity?

...that the electricity is carried from large generators with bars of copper instead of wire? These are called bus bars.

...that the higher the wattage of a bulb, the less is its resistance? So if a high-watt bulb and a low-watt bulb are put in series, the lower-watt bulb will be brighter since most of the energy will be used pushing the electricity through the higher resistance.

3. 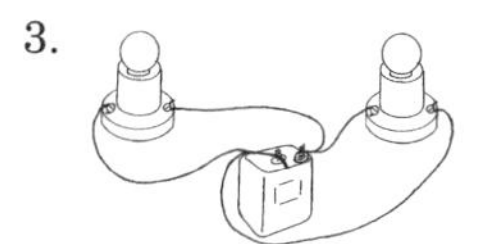

6. 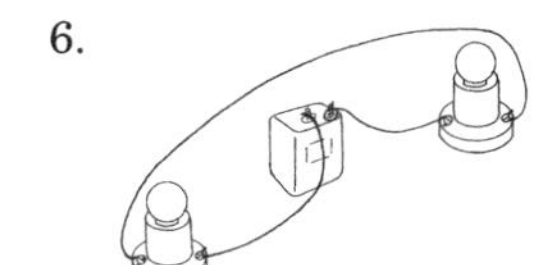

4. 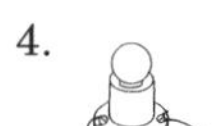

7. 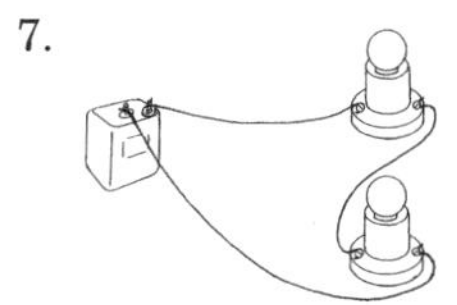

5. 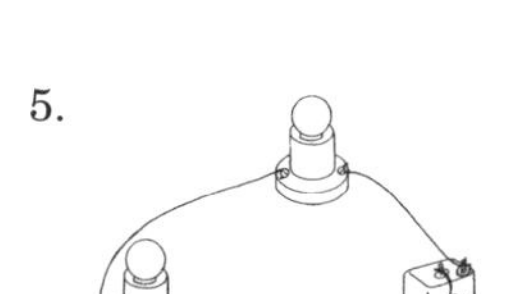

8. 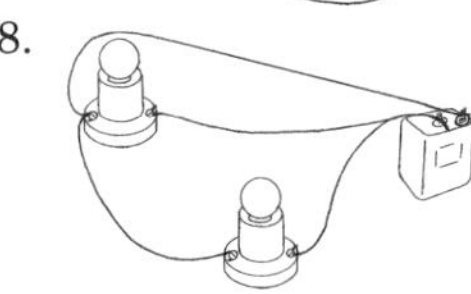

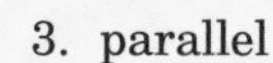

3. parallel
4. parallel
5. series
6. series
7. series
8. parallel

Choose the best ending.

9. The word *series* means
   a. side by side. b. one after the other. c. more than one.
10. You would know that two light bulbs are wired in parallel if
    a. the other went out when you unscrewed one.
    b. they both went out when you opened the switch.
    c. the other stayed on when you unscrewed one.

9. b
10. c

(10 points thus far)

Switches must be wired in series. From these descriptions of the two kinds of circuits, you may say that the parallel circuit is the best. If it is the best, why do we need the series circuit? There are some places where we must use series wiring. For example, switches must be in series.

You remember that a switch turns the electricity on or off. To make the electricity stop in all the lights, it must be put somewhere between the battery and the first light of a series circuit or where the wires divide in a parallel circuit. Then if the switch is off, no electricity can flow to either of the two lights.

Quiz

Have the students say or write the correct New Word for each sentence below. Each vocabulary word will be used twice.

1. It means flowing side by side. *(parallel)*
2. All of the electricity goes through all of the appliances. *(series)*
3. It slows down the flow of electricity. *(resistance)*
4. It means “one after the other.” *(series)*
5. The electricity divides and goes through different appliances. *(parallel)*
6. An appliance has much of this. *(resistance)*

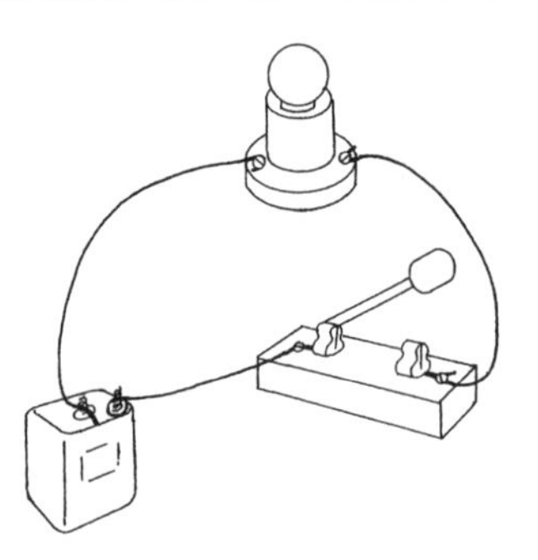

Switches are wired in series.

Wiring a switch in parallel is dangerous. If the switch was in parallel with the lights, all the current would go through the switch. The circuit would then have no appliance. This would be very dangerous since the wire would get hot and could start a fire!

Resistance—slowing electricity down. As we studied in Lesson 1, every electric circuit must have an appliance to use the electricity. An appliance slows the electricity down and keeps it from flowing too fast and making the wires hot. This is called resistance. ***Resistance*** is anything in an electric circuit that slows the electricity down. Appliances give resistance in a circuit. The wires of a circuit also give some resistance.

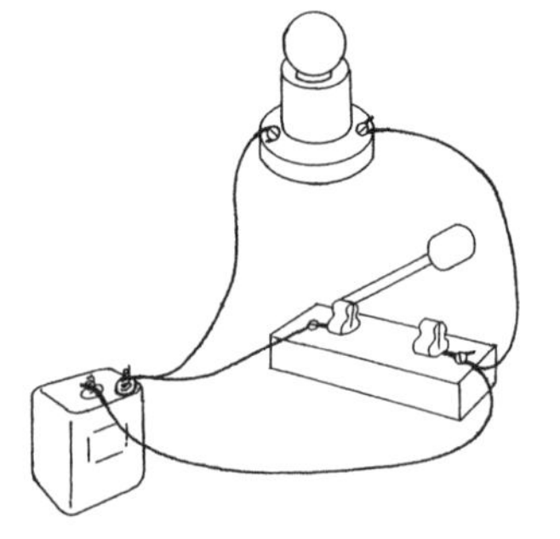

What will happen if the switch is closed?

To understand resistance in a wire, let us think again of water in a garden hose. As the water flows through the hose, some of the water is slowed down by rubbing against the side of the hose. This is resistance. If we made the garden hose smaller, more of the water would touch the sides of the hose and the hose would have more resistance. If the hose were made larger, it would have less resistance and the water would move more easily. A wire is like the garden hose. A small, thin wire has a lot of resistance. A large, thick wire has little resistance.

The length of a wire also makes a difference on the amount of resistance. Just as a long garden hose has much resistance to the flow of water, the longer a wire, the more resistance it has to electricity. The shorter the wire, the less resistance. If only a small amount of electricity is needed, a long, thin wire will work. But if a strong motor that uses much electricity is being used, we need to use a thick wire and to make it as short as possible.

An understanding of circuits and resistance helps us use electricity in the best and safest way.

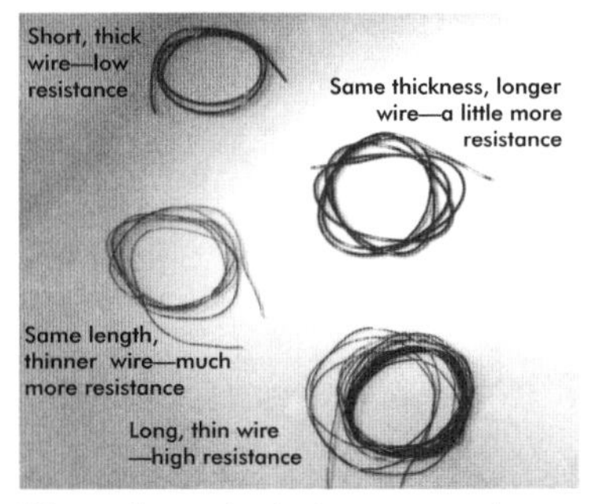

What makes each wire have more resistance than the one above it?

Test Your Reading (Group B)

Look at the switches in these drawings. Some of the switches are wired correctly, and some are wired incorrectly. Write either *correct* or *incorrect* for each drawing.

11.
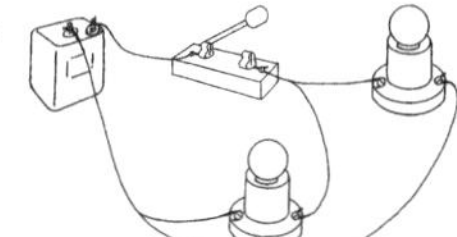

13.
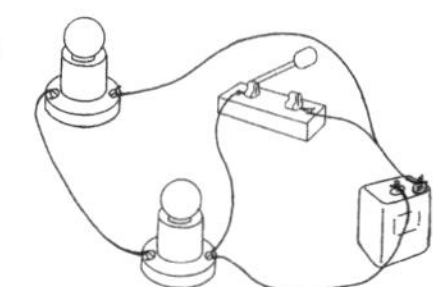

12.
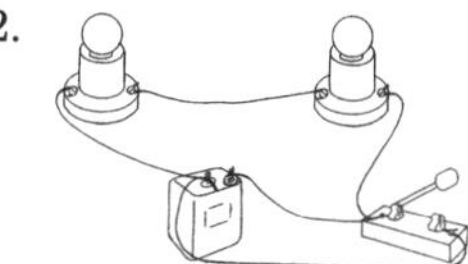

14.
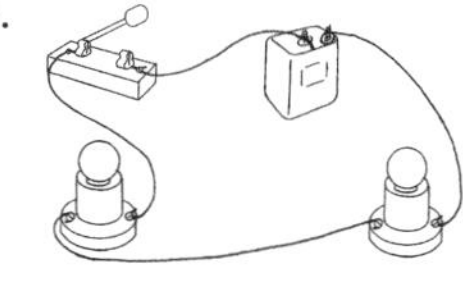

Answer *true* if the statement is true and *false* if the statement is not true.

15. A switch should be wired in series with the lights of a circuit.
16. A short wire has more resistance than a long wire.
17. A thin wire has more resistance than a thick wire.
18. If you want to send electricity for many miles, it would be best to use a thick wire.

Group B

11. correct
12. incorrect
13. incorrect
14. correct

15. true
16. false
17. true
18. true

19. It could cause a wire to get too hot and start a fire.
20. by making it very long; by making it very thin (2 points)
21. two bulbs in series

(22 points total)

Review Answers

1. c
2. circuit
3. true
4. a
5. b

(5 additional points)

Extra Activity Comments

1. Socket bases for screw-type flashlight bulbs would be best for this activity. You can buy them at electronic and hobby stores.

   Answers:
   a. The other bulb goes out.
   b. The other bulb stays on.
   c. the lights in the parallel circuit
   d. between any two of the parts: battery and the two bulbs

Answer the following questions.

19. Why should a switch not be wired in parallel?
20. What two things make a wire have a high resistance?
21. Which would have more resistance—two light bulbs in series or two light bulbs in parallel? Hint: Two bulbs in series would be like hooking two garden hoses end to end. Two bulbs in parallel would be like using a Y connector and hooking two hoses to the same faucet.

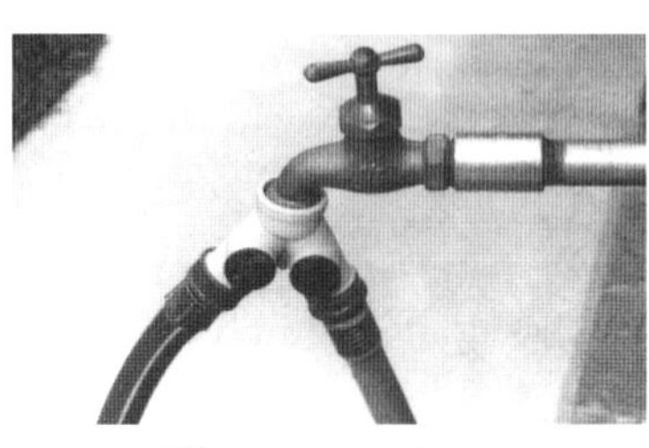
A Y connector on a faucet

Reviewing What You Have Learned

1. Which one does not allow electricity to flow?
   a. appliance   b. conductor   c. insulator
2. A source of electricity, conductors, an appliance, and a switch are needed to make a ———.
3. True or false? Generators produce electricity.
4. Which one uses electricity?
   a. appliance   b. conductor   c. insulator
5. Which set has only materials that will conduct electricity?
   a. glass, copper   b. aluminum, tin   c. iron, rubber

Extra Activities

1. Use batteries and flashlight bulbs to make both series and parallel circuits. With your light bulb circuits, answer the following questions.
   a. What happens to the other bulb of the series circuit if one is taken out?
   b. What happens to the other bulb of the parallel circuit if one is taken out?
   c. Which lights are brighter—the ones in the series circuit or the ones in the parallel circuit?
   d. At what three places can you put a switch in the series circuit?

e. At what two places can you put a switch in the parallel circuit?

Materials needed:

- 2 batteries
- 4 flashlight bulbs
- insulated bell wire

e. between the battery and the place the wires divide on either side of the battery

2. Draw a wiring diagram for the switch, four lights, and two outlets in a room. On a sheet of paper, copy the following drawing of a room with the parts of the circuit. Pretend that the lines on the left side are two wires coming from a source. Then use other lines (wires) to connect the parts so that the lights are in parallel and are all turned on and off by the switch. Then connect the outlets in parallel so that they are on all of the time. Ask your teacher to check your work.

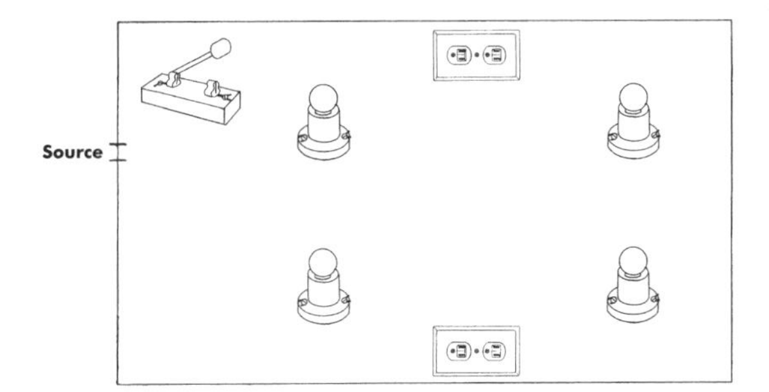

2. The drawings can vary and still be right. Here is an example of a correct solution.

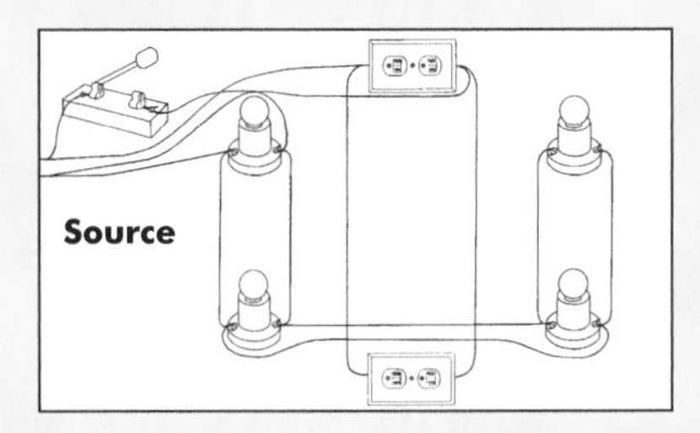

3. Take a tour with your teacher of your school building to see how it is supplied with electricity. Find out where the electricity enters the building. Where is the electric meter that measures how much electricity gets used? Where is the "panel box," where the different circuits are divided? Where are the circuit breakers? What part of the circuit are they? By counting the circuit breakers, you can find out how many circuits are in your school. Are there any three-way switches in your school? Three-way switches allow you to turn a light on or off at more than one place. Often there are three-way switches at the top and bottom of stairsteps.

3. Perhaps you could have one of the board members give this tour. If one of the school patrons is an electrician, he could give a very educational tour of the school.

Lesson 3

Electricity Is Useful

New Words

electromagnet (i·lek′·trō·mag′·nit), a magnet that is made by passing electricity through wire that is wrapped around an iron center.

fluorescent light (flů·res′·ənt), a tube that makes light when electricity travels through a gas.

heating element, a special wire that gives off heat when electricity travels through it.

incandescent light (in′·kən·des′·ənt), a bulb that makes light when electricity travels through a wire.

motor, a machine that uses electricity in electromagnets to make a center shaft turn and make power that can do work.

What would it be like to live without electricity? Just think. We would have no electric lights to turn on with a switch. We would have no freezers or refrigerators to keep our food cold. In the barn or shop, there would be no milk pumps, electric drills, or grinders. There would be no telephones. This is the way your great-grandparents lived.

Electricity is a wonder God created. It is a wonder because of how it works and because of the many useful things it can do.

Electricity can make light. In the first two lessons, we used a light bulb as an appliance in our examples to help explain how circuits work. How does a light bulb use electricity to make light? Do you remember resistance? In most appliances, we do not want wires to have much resistance because we do not want them to become hot. But in an electric light bulb, a wire with much resistance is used. When electricity travels through it, the electricity makes the wire very hot. The wire becomes so hot that it glows and gives off a yellow light. Such electric lights are called ***incandescent lights.*** Most of our

Lesson 3

Concepts to Teach

- The wire in an incandescent light bulb gets so hot that it gives off light.
- In a fluorescent light, electricity passes through a gas, which gives off special rays and makes the chemical coating glow.
- In electric stoves and heaters, a heating element gets very hot when electricity flows through it.
- Insulated wire wrapped around a piece of iron makes an electromagnet.
- In electric bells and motors, electromagnets produce useful motion.

Introducing the Lesson

What would life be like without electricity? Have the students recall a time when the current was off for a while. What problems did this create? What did the family do differently? We take electricity so much for granted that we may forget that up until the early 1900s, many homes did not have so much as an electric light bulb.

On the board, put the headings: Light, Heat, Motion. Have the students give an electrical appliance and tell which heading it would go under. They may have trouble deciding the heading for a welder (heat), a telephone (motion—sound is a kind of motion), a refrigerator (motion—a motor runs the compressor), an alarm clock (motion, light), or a doorbell (motion, light for those with an illuminated button). The calculator and computer are difficult to classify since their main function is high-speed switching in miniature circuits.

What makes the wire inside a light bulb give off light?

houses are lighted with incandescent light bulbs.

Another kind of electric light is the ***fluorescent light,*** which looks like a white, glass tube. Inside this tube is a special kind of gas. As electricity travels through the gas, the gas gives off special rays. These rays make the coating on the inside of the tube to glow white. Fluorescent tubes do not get as hot as incandescent bulbs. They give off more light and whiter light than incandescent bulbs. For these reasons, fluorescent lights are better for schools and big buildings. Perhaps your schoolroom is lighted with fluorescent lights.

Electricity can make heat. An electric stove and a heater use electricity to make heat. Electricity travels through a special wire called a ***heating element.*** The heating element becomes hot enough to cook food or to heat a room. To get more heat from a heating element, more electricity needs to travel through it. The different settings of the dial of your mother's kitchen stove allow different amounts of electricity to pass through the heating element. This makes different temperatures.

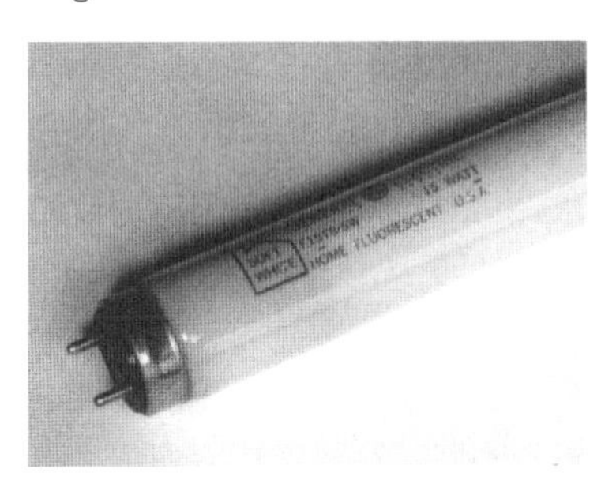

A fluorescent light

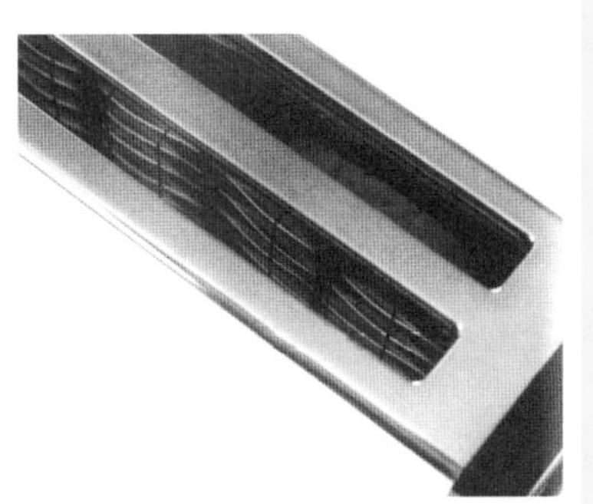

Where is the heating element in this toaster?

Lead the students to understand that electricity has not made life better. People before the age of electricity could be just as happy and godly as they are now. In many ways, some people today are more unhappy and ungodly than in the time when life was less complicated by so many electrical gadgets.

Did you know—

...that the first lighting device using electricity was the carbon arc lamp that was noisy, smoky, too bright, and inefficient?

...that the incandescent light was invented in 1879, and the fluorescent light was invented in 1935?

...that the speed of sewing machine motors is controlled by changing resistance that is wired in series with the motor? The speed of fan motors is controlled by using different wiring within the motor itself.

...that the smallest electric motor is only 1/64 of an inch high and requires a microscope to see it run? A giant electric motor used to pump water for irrigation in Washington State has a rotor weighing 169 tons and develops 65 thousand horsepower.

Lesson 3 Answers

Group A

1. fluorescent
2. incandescent
3. fluorescent
4. heating element
5. heating element
6. incandescent
7. fluorescent
8. incandescent
9. heating element

(9 points thus far)

Test Your Reading (Group A)

On a piece of paper, write *incandescent, fluorescent,* or *heating element* for each of these descriptions.

1. Special rays from gases make a white light with little heat.
2. Its resistance makes a special wire get hot enough to give off light.
3. It is a good kind of light to use in a school or large building.
4. The resistance of a special wire makes heat to cook food.
5. It becomes very hot but does not give off light.
6. It produces much heat along with the light it makes.
7. It has a coating that makes its light white.
8. It is called a light bulb.
9. It can be found in an electric stove.

Electricity can make magnetism. To do so is simple. Take a piece of metal, such as a nail, for an iron center. Wrap 20 feet (6 meters) of thin, insulated wire around the nail. Put the wrapped wire in series with a battery and a switch. Turn the switch on, and you have an ***electromagnet.*** Pick up paper clips, pens, or thumbtacks. When you want to drop your load, turn off the switch; and paper clips or thumbtacks drop to the table.

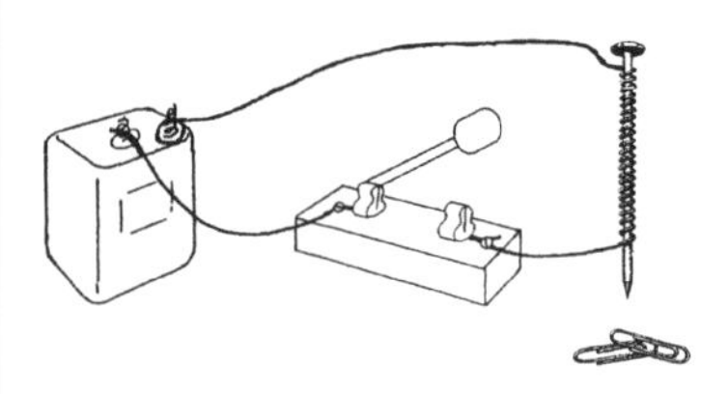

What will need to be done to make the electromagnet pick up the paper clips?

This electromagnet is very small and will pick up only a few light things. Huge electromagnets, with bigger iron centers and more wraps of wire and more electricity, are used to move iron cargo from trucks to a ship, or to carry tons of scrap metal from one place to another in a scrapyard. All it takes is an electromagnet, electricity, and a closed switch. Such a machine can be very useful.

Electricity can make motion. Electromagnets are used in many machines. In an electric bell, an electromagnet pulls an arm against the metal gong to make a ding. Electric bells ring in our telephones. Your school may have electric bells to tell you when to start school or come in from recess. Electric

Quiz

Have the students say or write the correct New Word for each sentence below.

1. It becomes hot enough to cook food when electricity goes through it. *(heating element)*
2. It makes light when electricity passes through a gas. *(fluorescent light)*
3. It uses electricity to produce rotating motion to run saws and pumps. *(motor)*
4. It will attract pieces of iron when an electric current flows through its wire. *(electromagnet)*
5. It makes light with electricity when a wire becomes so hot that it glows. *(incandescent light)*

buzzers work like electric bells except that they do not have the metal bell to make the noise. All you hear is the arm moving rapidly back and forth, making a buzzing sound.

Another machine that uses electromagnets is an electric ***motor.*** When you look at a running electric motor, all you see turning is the short shaft that comes out the end. But what makes it turn? The shaft inside the motor is covered with many electromagnets that turn with the shaft. Electric motors make power to run drills, vacuum cleaners, clocks, water pumps, and many other appliances that have parts that move.

What can all of these electrical appliances do?

How useful electricity is! It can make light and heat. When used in electromagnets, it can lift, pull, and turn things. By giving us electricity, God has given us a wonderful kind of energy. We can do many things with machines, which our grandparents needed to do by hand. We must use this good gift carefully and wisely.

Test Your Reading (Group B)

Choose the letter that would make a good ending.

10.	The center of an electromagnet	a.	strikes a gong to make a noise.
11.	Scrap metal can be moved	b.	make a stronger electromagnet.
12.	Electromagnets produce motion	c.	is wound on an iron center.
13.	The sound of a buzzer	d.	is a gift from God.
14.	Water pumps, drills, and clocks	f.	is made by a moving arm.
15.	The arm of an electric bell	g.	is made of iron.
16.	More turns of wire	h.	are run with electric motors.
17.	Useful electricity	i.	in an electric motor.
18.	The wire of an electromagnet	e.	with an electromagnet.

Group B

10. g
11. e
12. i
13. f
14. h
15. a
16. b
17. d
18. c

19. an iron center, insulated wire (2 points)
20. by turning off the switch
21. appliance

(22 points total)

Review Answers

1. circuit
2. a
3. true
4. c
5. false

(5 additional points)

Extra Activity Comments

2. You may be able to find a free source of insulated winding wire. Old solenoids, voltage regulators, and transformers are often a good supply of such wire. Avoid using overly thin or overly thick wire. If the wire is too thin, so little electricity will get through that the magnet will be very weak. If the wire is too thick, there will not be enough resistance. Then the wire will overheat, or it may ruin the source if you use a toy transformer.

Answer the following questions.

19. Besides a source and a switch, what two things do you need to make an electromagnet?
20. How can the load carried by an electromagnet be dropped?
21. Is an electromagnet the source, conductor, appliance, or switch of an electric circuit?

Reviewing What You Have Learned

1. Electricity must have a complete ——— to flow.
2. Which wire will give the greatest resistance to electricity?
   a. a long, thin wire
   b. a short, thick wire
   c. a long, thick wire
3. True or false? Switches are wired in series.
4. In parallel wiring, the electricity
   a. flows through the appliances one after the other.
   b. flows back and forth between two appliances.
   c. divides and flows through the appliances side by side.
5. True or false? The conductor part of a circuit has no resistance to the flow of electricity.

Extra Activities

1. Do research into how a fluorescent light is made and works. What is the gas inside the tube? What is the white coating? What does this white coating do? Why must a special box called a ballast be used? What does the starter do?
2. Make an electromagnet. Number 26 insulated wire works well for this. Winding wire with thin insulation that can be bought at an electrical supply store or a motor winding shop is best. Wrap 10 feet (3 meters) of insulated wire around a heavy nail or small bolt. Connect it to a dry cell battery or toy transformer. Be sure to scrape off the insulation from the end of the wire when making a connection. Touch the other end of the wire against the source for only a little so the wire does not become too hot. Try to lift some paper clips with your electromagnet. Now add another 10 feet (3 meters) of wire to

your electromagnet (after connecting the ends together). Again test the electromagnet. Why is it stronger? Why does it not get as warm? Another 10 feet (3 meters) will make the electromagnet even better. Be sure the insulation is removed when you make a splice. Twist the wires tightly together. **WARNING: NEVER CONNECT WHAT YOU MAKE TO AN ELECTRICAL OUTLET.**

Materials needed:

- 30 feet (9 meters) of #26 insulated wire
- heavy nail or small bolt
- dry cell battery
- paper clips
- wire pliers

3. The father of someone in the class may have a worn-out electric drill that he will allow to be torn apart. Take out the screws, and remove the shields. Find the electromagnets. Find the switch. Find the brushes that send electricity into the turning part. Can you find why the electric drill will not work? **WARNING: DO NOT PLUG THE DRILL INTO AN ELECTRICAL OUTLET.**

3. You may want to start a school collection of small appliances that are partly torn apart to show their inner workings.

Lesson 4

Using Electricity Safely

New Words

fuse (fyüz), a part of an electric circuit that melts when the electricity becomes too much.

receptacle (ri·sep′·tə·kəl), a thing with two or three holes into which a plug can be put to get electricity for an appliance.

shock, what you feel when electricity travels through your body.

short circuit, an electric circuit that has no appliance.

Electricity is a wonder given by God. It lets us do many things faster and better than we could if we did not have it. But just as it is with all other wonderful things God has made, we must be careful how we use it. We have already given some hints that electricity can be dangerous. In this lesson we shall learn how we can use it safely.

Appliances—using electricity safely. An appliance is necessary to use the electricity. In a circuit without an appliance, so much electricity will flow through the wire that it can become hot enough to start a fire. A circuit without an appliance is called a

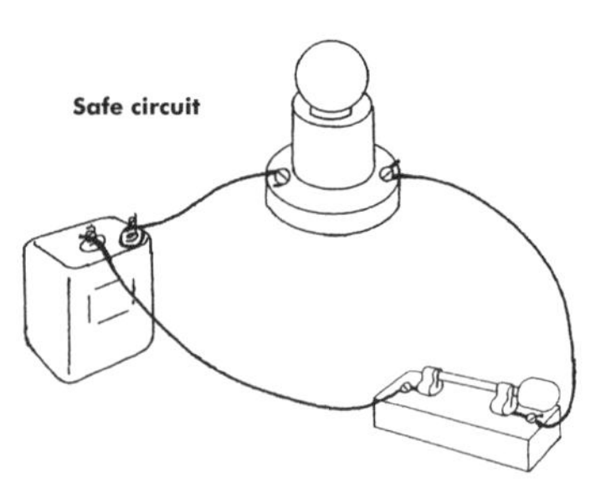

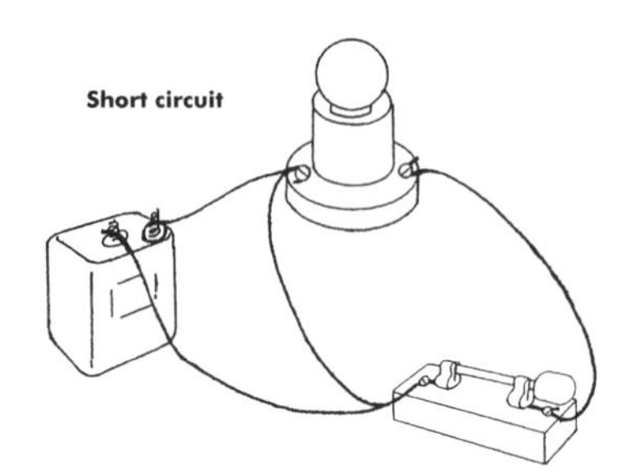

Electricity takes the path of least resistance. If a wire will complete the circuit, most of the electricity will go through the wire instead of the appliance.

Lesson 4

Concepts to Teach

- A circuit is not safe without an appliance.
- A circuit without an appliance is called a short circuit.
- Always remove a cord from a receptacle by pulling on the plug only.
- Wires with worn insulation can cause a short circuit.
- A short circuit can cause a fire.
- A fuse (or circuit breaker) protects a circuit from overload.
- You must avoid electric shock by not becoming part of an electric circuit.
- Many appliances have a third wire connected to the source and the ground to avoid electric shock.

Introducing the Lesson

Something with as much strength as electricity must be feared and respected. Several times God used lightning (a form of electricity) to cause people to be fearful (Exodus 9:23; 19:16; 2 Samuel 22:15). The account in 1 Samuel 12:14–18 would well illustrate this point. Perhaps the students know of cattle that have been killed or a building set on fire by lightning. Perhaps they know of a fire that was caused by faulty wiring. Persons have been killed with electricity.

Although electricity is a very useful gift from God, it must be used safely, or it will do us harm. We do not stop using electricity because of the damage it can do. We learn how to use it safely. That is the purpose of this lesson.

short circuit. Short circuits are very dangerous. Not only can they start a fire, but they can melt the wire or ruin the source. Never make an electric circuit without some kind of appliance.

Receptacles—getting electricity safely. A ***receptacle,*** sometimes called an outlet, has two or three holes into which a plug can be put to get electricity. A receptacle is not needed to make a complete circuit, but it makes an easy and safe connection between a source and an appliance.

There are two safety rules for using a receptacle. First, never put anything into a receptacle except a plug that is made to fit it. It is dangerous to put wires without plugs, paper clips, toys, and fingers into a receptacle. Sometimes receptacles have special covers to keep small children from putting something in them. Second, always remove a cord from a receptacle by pulling on the plug only. Never pull on the cord. Pulling on the cord can pull the wires loose inside the plug. If the wires touch each other, there will be a circuit without an appliance—a short circuit.

Cords—carrying electricity safely. Electric cords must also be used carefully. All electric cords have at least two wires inside. But they are kept separate with insulation. As long as the insulation keeps the two wires separated, the cord is safe. But if this insulation becomes broken or worn, the two wires can touch each other. Then the electricity will no longer travel all the way to the appliance and back again. Instead, it will jump across where the two wires touch,

Always remove a cord from a receptacle by taking hold of the plug.

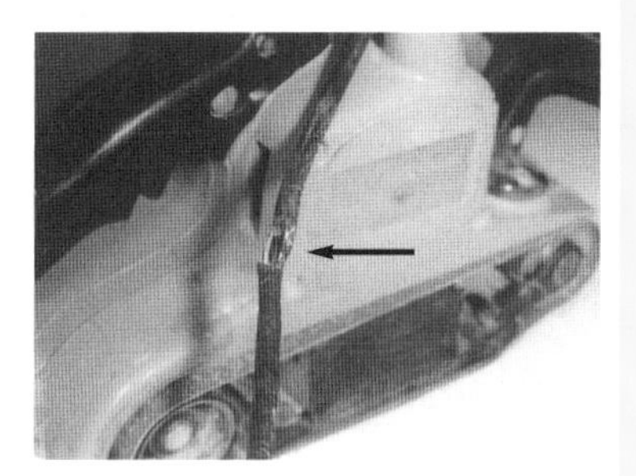

An unsafe cord in need of replacement or repair

Did you know—

...that an independent company, Underwriters' Laboratories, Inc., has been safety testing since 1894? Part of their work is testing electrical appliances and equipment. If an appliance passes their inspection, then the manufacturer may sell that appliance with the familiar symbol on it—UL in a circle. The customer can then have confidence that the appliance meets certain safety standards.

...that over 100 thousand fires are caused by electricity in the United States each year, causing well over 100 billion dollars' worth of damage?

...that current interrupters can be used in a circuit that will break the circuit when any stray voltage is detected? This happens so suddenly that a person will not get hurt if he contacts a hot wire or appliance case.

...that the size of wire determines the size of fuse (or circuit breaker) to use? A #14 wire requires a 15-ampere fuse; a #12 wire, a 20-ampere fuse; and a #10 wire, a 30-ampere fuse.

Quiz

Have the students say or write the correct New Word for each sentence below.

1. It is an electric circuit that does not have an appliance. *(short circuit)*
2. It is a place to get electricity by connecting with a plug. *(receptacle)*
3. It breaks the circuit if too much electricity flows through it. *(fuse)*
4. It happens when your body completes an electric circuit. *(shock)*

and there will be a short circuit. The place in a circuit where the wires touch and cause a short circuit is sometimes called a short.

To keep the insulation on electric cords in good condition, do not run over them with vehicles and machinery. Keep them away from hot things, such as light bulbs, and from moving parts of machinery, such as belts. When not in use, extension cords should be coiled neatly and hung up. These rules will not only keep the cord safe to use, but also help you be a good steward of what you have.

Never touch the prongs of a plug or the bare wires in a cord when it is plugged in. Your body is a conductor. So is the ground. When electricity passes through your body and completes a circuit, you feel what we call a ***shock.*** A small amount of electricity may only make you jump and say "Ow," but a large amount could kill you. You may also be shocked if you touch only one bare wire and the ground itself or a conductor that leads to the ground, such as a metal water pipe or water in a sink. Never touch bare wires unless you know there is no electricity in them. If you do not know, do not touch them!

Test Your Reading (Group A)

In the following sentences, the underlined words make the statements false. Write the word or words that will make each statement true.

1. Electricity is a wonderful gift from God, but it must be used carelessly.
2. A short circuit does not have a switch.
3. A short circuit can start a shock when the wire becomes very hot.
4. Always take hold of the cord when removing it from a receptacle.
5. You should put a wire into a receptacle.
6. Inside a damaged plug or cord, the wires can come apart to cause a short circuit.
7. When two wires get together to cause a short circuit, it is sometimes called a shock.
8. Keep cords against moving belts and hot light bulbs.
9. Running over a cord or walking on it is good for it.
10. Since your body is an insulator, you can get shocked if you touch bare electric wires.

Lesson 4 Answers

Group A

1. carefully (*or* safely)
2. an appliance
3. fire
4. plug
5. plug
6. together
7. short
8. away from
9. bad
10. a conductor

11. A shock may only make you jump, or it can please you.
12. You can be shocked if you touch one bare wire and a plastic water pipe.

11. kill (*or* injure)
12. metal

(12 points thus far)

Fuses—protecting an electric circuit. You learned earlier that a short circuit is dangerous because too much electricity flows through the wire. An appliance is necessary to use the electricity safely. As more appliances are added to the circuit, more electricity will flow through the wire. If too many appliances are on a circuit, however, the wire will get dangerously hot. Something is needed that will stop the electricity in these cases. A ***fuse*** is just what is needed in the circuit.

A simple kind of fuse is made of a special wire that will get hot and melt when too much electricity flows through the wire. When the fuse wire melts, it breaks the circuit and stops the flow of electricity. This protects the rest of the wires in the circuit from becoming too hot. A circuit needs a fuse to make it safe. When a fuse burns out, fix the problem and replace the fuse.

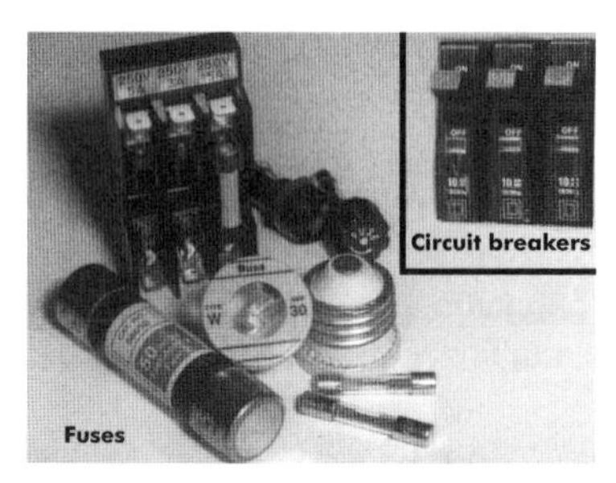

Safety switches for electrical circuits

Circuits in modern buildings often use special switches called circuit breakers to do the same thing as fuses. When they break a circuit, they can be reset like turning a switch on.

A third wire—carrying current away safely. It is possible to get shocked even if you do not touch a bare electric wire. Sometimes an appliance has a bad place in its wiring that lets some of the current stray out to the case. Then if a person touches the outside of the appliance and the ground itself or a material that conducts electricity to the ground, he completes the circuit and gets shocked.

Because of this danger, appliances often have a third prong on their plugs. The receptacle has a third place for that prong to go. This prong with its special wire connects the outside case of the appliance with the ground and the source.

Then if any electricity strays out to the case, it will go safely back to the source through the third wire instead of going through someone who touches the case.

Electricity is a wonderful gift from God. The way it works is marvelous. The many things it can do for us makes it very useful. As with any gift from God, we must use electricity wisely and safely. We must thank God for electricity.

What is the third prong for?

Test Your Reading (Group B)

Choose the best answer.

13. A fuse is really a special kind of
    a. source.
    b. appliance.
    c. switch.
14. Besides a short circuit, another way to have too much electricity flow is
    a. not having a source in the circuit.
    b. having too many appliances in a circuit.
    c. having the switch wired in series.
15. The purpose of a fuse is to stop the electricity
    a. before the wire gets too hot.
    b. before someone gets a bad shock.
    c. before the insulation on the wires becomes worn too badly.
16. The third prong on a plug
    a. allows the cord to carry more electricity.
    b. prevents a short circuit from happening.
    c. protects the one who uses the appliance from getting shocked.

Answer the following questions.

17. What needs to be done if a fuse burns out?

Group B

13. c
14. b
15. a
16. c
17. Fix the problem and replace the fuse.

18. What do some circuits have instead of a fuse that has the same purpose as a fuse?
19. What three places does the third wire connect?
20. What are two reasons we should praise God for electricity?

Reviewing What You Have Learned

1. True or false? An appliance gives resistance to the flow of electricity.
2. Electromagnets are useful because they can
   a. heat things.
   b. light things.
   c. move things.
3. The ——— light bulb gives off much heat.
4. The wire in an electromagnet must be
   a. thin and shiny.
   b. insulated.
   c. high resistance.
5. If one light in a circuit with ——— wiring burns out, the other light will not go out.

Extra Activities

1. With your teacher's help, learn how to replace a worn-out plug on an extension cord or appliance cord. It will be best for you to learn using a light 2-wire cord and a 2-prong plug. Be sure the cord is not plugged into a receptacle. Cut the old plug off. Some replacement plugs are made to fasten on to the wire without removing the insulation. Follow the instructions carefully that come with the plug.

   If the plug has screw fasteners, follow these instructions: Remove the insulation from ¾″ of the end of each wire. Lay the end of the wire on a board, and cut away from yourself in removing the insulation. Twist the strands of wire tightly. Wrap the wire around each screw in the same direction each screw is tightened. Be sure the two wires (or any strands of the two wires) do not touch after they are tightened under the screws. Have your teacher inspect your work before you plug the cord into a receptacle. (Even professional

18. a circuit breaker
19. the outside case of the appliance, the ground, and the source (3 points)
20. Electricity works in a wonderful way. Electricity does many useful things for us. (2 points)

(22 points total)

Review Answers

1. true
2. c
3. incandescent
4. b
5. parallel

(5 additional points)

electricians have inspectors check their work.)

Materials needed:

- light, 2-wire cord
- wire clippers
- knife
- board
- 2-prong plug
- screwdriver

2. **WARNING: THIS ACTIVITY SHOULD BE DONE ONLY WITH YOUR PARENT'S OR TEACHER'S SUPERVISION.** Use a neon light electrical tester to find which of the two slots of a receptacle is hot and which leads to the ground. Use a light extension cord that is long enough to go from a receptacle to some metal water pipes. Before plugging the extension cord into the receptacle, put one end of the tester into one of the slots of the extension cord. Hold the other end of the tester against a bare place on a metal water pipe. Have a friend plug in the extension cord. If the tester lights, you have the hot wire. If it does not light, you have the side of the circuit that is grounded. Go to the main electric box, or transformer, and try to find where it is grounded. The ground wire will disappear into the ground or be fastened to a rod driven into the ground.

A neon light electrical tester

Materials needed:

- neon light electrical tester
- extension cord

Extra Activity Comments

2. Neon testers can be bought at electrical supply stores. Quite likely, a father of one of the students will have one that could be used. If a receptacle for a three-prong plug is used, the one end of the tester can be put into the ground hole and the other end can be put into the other two slots in turn. The one that lights is the hot connection.

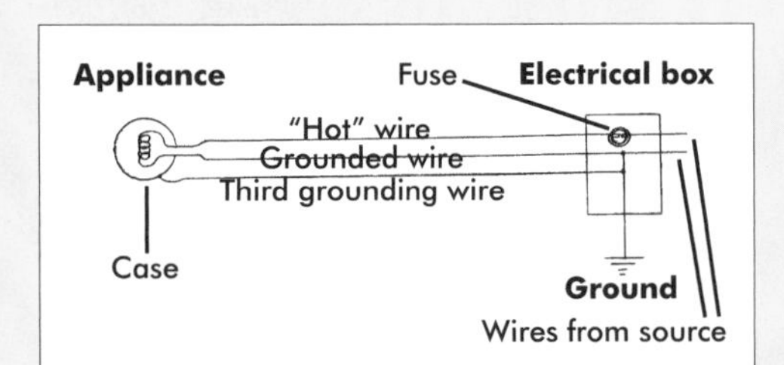

This diagram shows how the three wires are connected at the electrical box.

Lesson 5

Do You Remember?

Choose the correct letter from the list at the right to match with each phrase on the left.

1. A place in the wall to get electricity	a. appliance
2. Any material that stops electricity	b. conductor
3. Uses electricity	c. fluorescent light
4. Turns the flow of electricity on or off	d. fuse
5. Makes light with a hot wire	e. heating element
6. Any material that will carry electricity	f. incandescent light
7. A white tube with a special gas	g. insulator
8. Protects a circuit	h. receptacle
	i. switch

From the word box, find and write a word for each blank.

battery	motor	series
circuit	parallel	shock
electromagnet	resistance	short circuit

9. When electricity can return to the source without being used by an appliance, it is a ———.
10. When electricity travels through you, you feel a ———.
11. Electricity must flow through each bulb one after the other when they are wired in ———.
12. Slowing electricity down in a wire or appliance is called ———.
13. A ——— is one kind of source of electricity.
14. An ——— can lift things when electricity is passed through a wire that is wrapped around an iron center.
15. Electricity must have a complete ———, or it will not flow.
16. With ——— wiring, each bulb will light even if one of the others is missing or is burned out.

Lesson 5 Answers

1. h
2. g
3. a
4. i
5. f
6. b
7. c
8. d
9. short circuit
10. shock
11. series
12. resistance
13. battery
14. electromagnet
15. circuit
16. parallel

Lesson 5

Reviewing the Unit

To the students of our day, the subject of electricity is a familiar one. Even before they studied this unit, they knew that an appliance must be connected to a source. They knew that the plug has two prongs on it. They knew that the switch needs to be turned on to make it work. The study of a unit about electricity should have given them a better understanding of the whys and hows of using electricity. It should also help them to be more aware of the wisdom of God that makes our use of electricity possible.

This is a good time to do some chalkboard review. Draw a number of sets of circuit parts, leaving out the conductors between the parts (source, switch, appliance). Use the symbols shown below. Have each student "wire" each of the sets of parts to make complete circuits. Tell them to label the four parts of an electric circuit on their drawings. Have the other students say if the circuits are wired correctly.

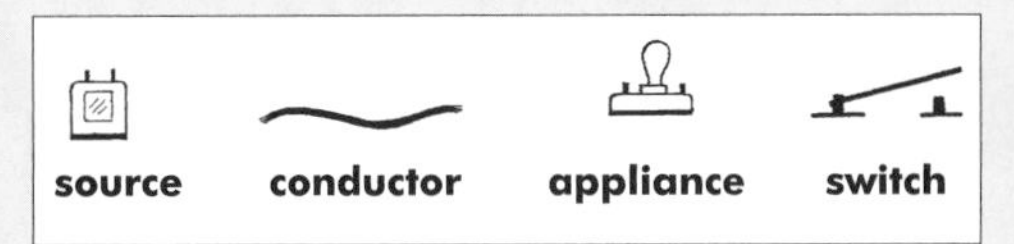

Make several identically arranged sets of circuit parts with two light bulbs in each set. (See examples on page 198.) Write *series* above one set in each pair. Write *parallel* above the other set in each pair. Have as many sets as students in the class. Assign a student to each set, to wire it according to the word above the set.

17. a
18. c
19. b
20. a
21. b
22. b
23. a
24. b

Choose the best answer for each sentence.

17. Aluminum, copper, and tin are all good
    a. conductors.
    b. heating elements.
    c. insulators.
18. Heating elements are used to
    a. move parts in a machine.
    b. lift heavy objects.
    c. cook food.
19. A fuse
    a. is a source of electricity in a circuit.
    b. is a switch in a circuit.
    c. is an appliance in a circuit.
20. If we wanted to keep electricity from passing from one wire to another, we would separate them with
    a. an insulator. b. a conductor. c. an appliance.
21. A switch
    a. uses electricity in a circuit.
    b. turns the flow of electricity on and off.
    c. keeps the wires in a circuit from getting too hot.
22. All of the following are parts of a complete circuit **except**
    a. a source.
    b. the insulation.
    c. an appliance.
23. If we wanted to put lights in a school building, it would be best to use
    a. fluorescent lights.
    b. incandescent bulbs.
    c. heating elements.
24. Which of the following has the most resistance?
    a. a short, thin wire
    b. a long, thin wire
    c. a short, thick wire

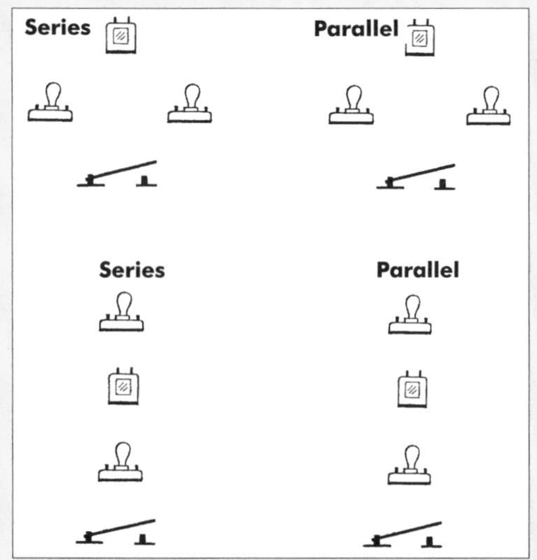

Possible solution of chalkboard exercises

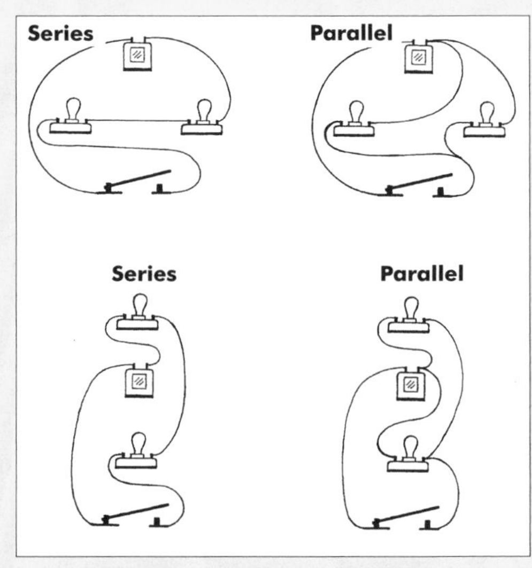

Possible solution of chalkboard exercises

25. All the following are true for series wiring except
    a. If one bulb is removed, all the others will go out.
    b. The electricity divides and then comes together again.
    c. Switches are wired in series.
26. When removing a cord from a receptacle, take hold of
    a. the plug. b. the receptacle. c. the cord.
27. Electricity must make a complete circuit
    a. without being used by an appliance.
    b. so the electrons will be able to flow.
    c. so that it must be used over again.
28. Which of the following would be the best insulator?
    a. water b. aluminum c. glass
29. Which of the following do **not** use electromagnets?
    a. buzzers
    b. heating elements
    c. motors

25. b
26. a
27. b
28. c
29. b

Write *true* if the sentence is true; write *false* if it is not true.

30. There can be a short circuit in an electric cord if the two wires touch each other.
31. Man, not God, should get the praise for modern electrical machines.
32. A heating element is useful because it uses electricity to make motion.
33. A third wire is a safe place for electricity to go that strays out of a circuit.
34. A battery and a generator are both appliances.
35. Plugs are the only thing that should be put in a receptacle.
36. Appliances use electricity to make light, heat, or motion.
37. If a circuit with bulbs is not complete, then only a few of the bulbs will light.
38. It will not hurt electric cords to run over them with cars or machinery.
39. If lights are wired in parallel, the switch must also be wired in parallel.

30. true
31. false
32. false
33. true
34. false
35. true
36. true
37. false
38. false
39. false

40. parallel
41. series
42. series
43. parallel
44. parallel

45. right
46. wrong
47. wrong

48–50. (Any three.)
Never make an electric circuit without some kind of appliance.
Never put paper clips, etc. into a receptacle.
Always pull on the plug when removing a cord from a receptacle.
Do not run over cords with machinery.
Do not let cords get against something hot.
Do not let cords get against moving parts of machines.
Coil and hang up cords when not in use.
Never touch the prongs of a plug or the bare wires of a cord that is plugged in.
(50 points total)

Write *parallel* if the drawing shows a parallel circuit. Write *series* if it is a series circuit.

40. 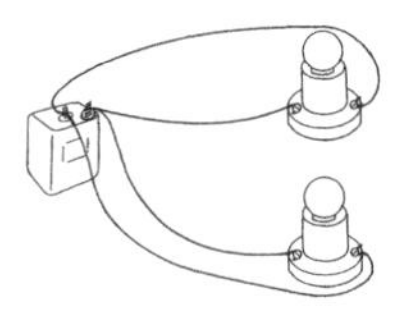

43. 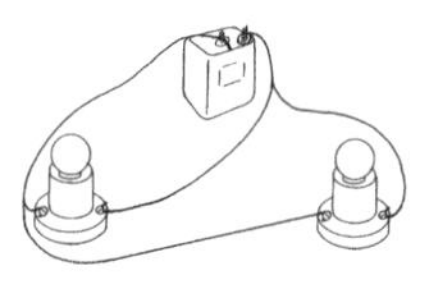

41. 

44. 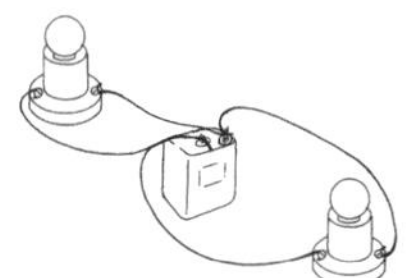

42. 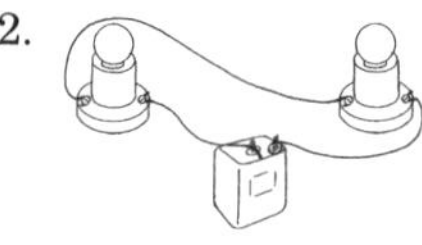

In which of the following circuits is the switch placed correctly? Write *right* if it is correct and *wrong* if it is not correct.

45. 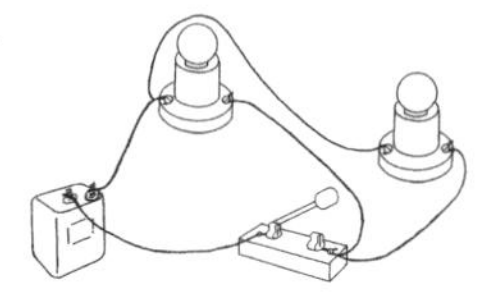

47. 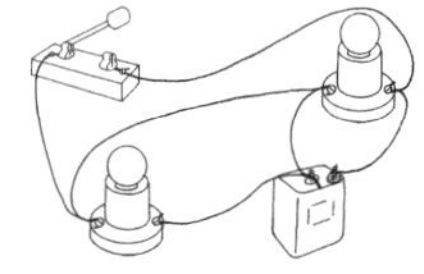

46. 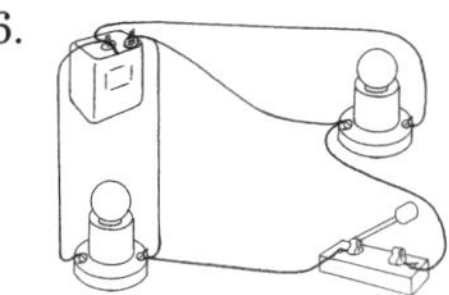

Answer the following question.

48–50. What are three safety rules to remember when we work with electricity?

Unit Seven

God Gave Us Plants

"And God said, Let the earth bring forth grass, the herb yielding seed, and the fruit tree yielding fruit after his kind, whose seed is in itself, upon the earth: and it was so" (Genesis 1:11).

What a wonderful thing is a seed! You can plant bean seeds or corn seeds or flower seeds in moist soil, and what happens? Soon tiny plants pop up and grow bigger and wider and taller. After a while you have great big plants just from tiny, little seeds. And these big plants make more tiny seeds to grow more plants.

Who would have ever thought of all this except God? Who could have ever done it except God? Just think of all the different colors and sizes and shapes of plants in the world. Think of the vegetables and mushrooms, the berries and fruit trees, the huge forest trees, the flowering and evergreen bushes, the spring bulbs, the grasses and mosses, and the waving fields of corn and wheat. God thought of each one and made it, or you would not see it today.

In this unit you will study groups of plants and how they are alike. You will learn names for the parts of plants. You will see that each part has an important work to do for the good of the whole plant. You will learn how a plant makes food. You will also see that there are other ways of raising new plants besides planting seeds.

God wisely created the plants for our good and His glory. Studying this unit should give us a greater reverence for God.

Unit Seven

For Your Inspiration

The references to plants in the Book of Job are wonderful object lessons of spiritual truth. In the following verses, for example, Job uses a tree as a word picture of death and resurrection.

For there is hope of a tree, if it be cut down,
  that it will sprout again,
  and that the tender branch thereof will not cease.
Though the root thereof wax old in the earth,
  and the stock thereof die in the ground;
Yet through the scent of water it will bud,
  and bring forth boughs like a plant.
But man dieth, and wasteth away:
  yea, man giveth up the ghost, and where is he?
If a man die, shall he live again?
  all the days of my appointed time will I wait,
  till my change come.
For I know that my redeemer liveth,
  and that he shall stand at the latter day upon the earth:
And though after my skin worms destroy this body,
  yet in my flesh shall I see God.

—Job 14:7–10, 14; 19:25, 26

Job saw Calvary "through a glass, darkly" by faith, for he did not have the advantage of looking back to it as we have today. In light of this, his understanding of God's work (as shown in the verses above) was commendable. His relationship with God and his faith in Him were outstanding for one living in his time.

If Job, living before Calvary, could endure severe trials without giving up his faith in God, how much more can we be found faithful by His grace!

Lesson 1

Seed-Producing Plants

New Words

annual (an′·yü·əl), one of a group of plants that lives only one year.

biennial (bī·en′·ē·əl), one of a group of plants that lives two years.

conifer (kon′·ə·fər), a cone-bearing bush or tree that has needlelike leaves year around.

perennial (pə·ren′·ē·əl), one of a group of plants that lives more than two years.

We eat seeds from seed-producing plants. "And there came a messenger unto Job, and said, The oxen were plowing" (Job 1:14). Why do you think Job's oxen were plowing? Why do farmers today plow the soil?

Job, like farmers today, plowed the soil before planting seeds of grain. Both wheat and barley were grains grown in Job's time (Job 31:40). Wheat and barley were eaten by people and animals.

Today people all over the world still eat more grain than anything else. Grain does not spoil easily and is one of the cheapest foods. The most common kinds of grain are rice, wheat, and corn. You eat grain whenever you eat foods such as bread, breakfast cereal, noodles, and corn chips.

Grains are really seeds. But what is a seed? It is a tiny plant inside a tough coating. The coating protects the living plant inside. It can stay alive for months or even years. Once, some wheat seeds sprouted that were 30 years old!

Along with the tiny plant in the

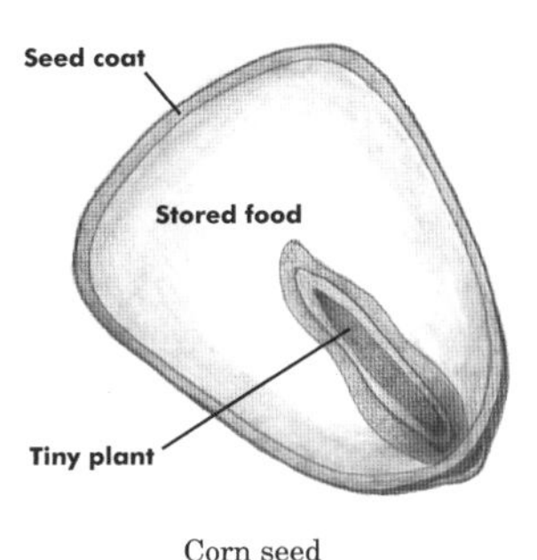

Corn seed

Plant Study for Unit Seven

This unit is best studied in the spring of the year when plants will be available for observation. However, since spring is the last part of the school year, plants started in the course of the study will not reach maturity in time for study. You may want to start a variety of plants earlier in the year so you will have more mature plants for study. Also check each lesson introduction because some of those suggestions need preparation ahead of time.

Unit Project: Growing Plants

Your students might enjoy helping to plant seeds and caring for young plants, such as lima beans, radishes, and marigolds. Other easy-to-grow choices would be peas and corn.

Plant the seeds in garden soil or potting soil if the plants will be raised to maturity. Sand or sawdust, however, can be used if they will not be raised beyond the seedling stage. One benefit of using sand or sawdust is that the plants cannot easily be overwatered by zealous, young gardeners. Another advantage is that the tender roots will sustain a minimum of damage from being uprooted, examined, and replanted.

Instead of ordinary pots, you could use some plastic peanut butter jars or some other clear, plastic containers. Be sure to punch a few holes in the bottom for drainage. Plant the seeds next to the clear plastic for easy viewing of germination and root growth.

Keep the pots in the dark except for one (to help them discover how light affects germination). Plant seeds both upside down and right side up in the same pot (to determine whether it makes any difference in which direction the roots grow). You could also put one pot in a cold place (to show the need for warmth). Another option is to plant some seeds in a jar without drainage holes and then to keep the soil soaking wet. (This, of course, would show the need for air.)

seed, there is some food for the plant to use when it sprouts. This stored food is what makes seeds so valuable for man and animals to eat.

Each year many new seeds sprout to produce new plants. The plants produce more seeds. The plants then die, but the seeds can be used to make new plants the next year. God planned it this way so that there are always plenty of plants on the earth. Plants are very important because every person and animal on earth gets its food from them. Even meat eaters, such as lions, depend on plants because they eat animals that eat plants.

Flowering plants are one group of seed-producing plants. Your family garden or flower beds are full of flowering plants. Most kinds of grass and many bushes and trees are flowering plants. Even thistles and prickly beggar ticks are flowering plants. Just because we might not call their flowers pretty does not mean they are not flowers.

Flowering plants can be put into two groups. The one group produces one-part seeds that have only one seed leaf. This group includes plants such as lilies, tulips, cattails,

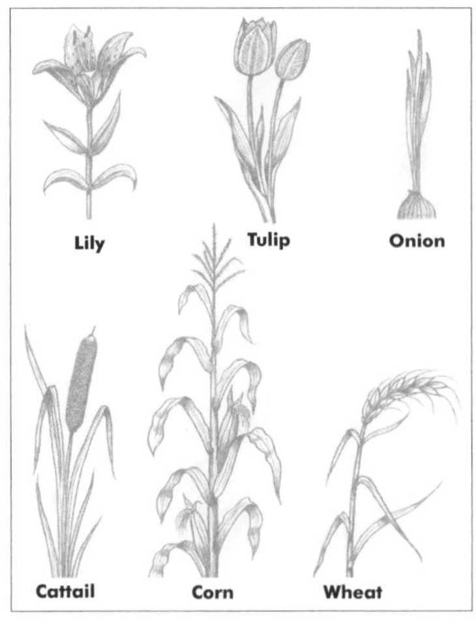

One-part-seed plants

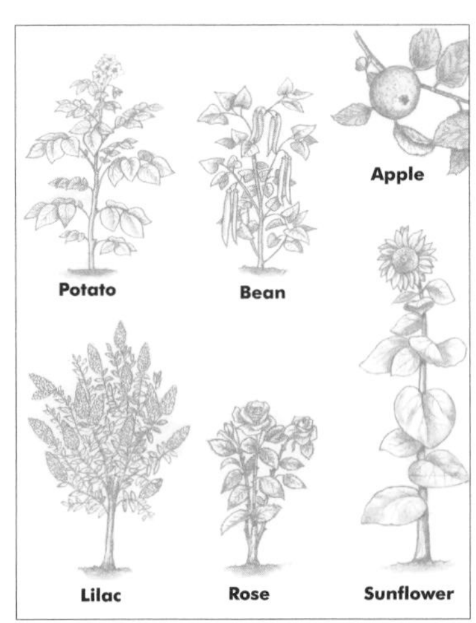

Two-part-seed plants

Lesson 1

Concepts to Teach

- A seed is a tiny plant inside a coating, which can protect the plant for a long time before it grows into a mature plant, along with food for the new plant to use when it sprouts.
- The flowering plants are divided into two groups: one-part-seed plants with bladelike leaves and two-part-seed plants with broad leaves.
- The seeds of conifers are produced in cones.
- Conifers have needlelike leaves that stay on the tree all year around. For this reason, they are sometimes called evergreen trees.
- Plants called annuals live only one year, biennials live two years, and perennials live more than two years.

Introducing the Lesson

Bring a variety of small plants or twigs from bushes or trees to illustrate the plant categories in this lesson. After a quick "tour" through the whole unit, show the plants and twigs. Then classify them as flowering plants versus conifers, one-part-seed plants versus two-part-seed plants, and annuals versus perennials or biennials. You could give a brief explanation of each group, but point them to the lesson text for more detail.

Materials needed:

- twigs from broadleaf and evergreen trees and bushes or shrubs
- houseplants, vegetable plants, or wildflowers

onions, and all grasses. Corn, wheat, and other grains are kinds of grasses, so of course, they are one-part-seed plants. The leaves of one-part-seed plants are narrow and bladelike. We talk about a blade of grass.

The other group of flowering plants has two-part seeds. You may have noticed when you shelled beans that the seeds can split in half. These two halves are the first leaves that come above the ground when the seeds sprout. Most vegetables and flowers that you plant have two-part seeds. Lilacs, roses, flowering bushes, and many trees belong to this group. Two-part-seed plants usually have broad, flat leaves.

Test Your Reading (Group A)

Complete the following chart to tell if the plants have one- or two-part seeds and if their leaves are blade or broad.

Plant	Seeds *one-part / two-part*	Leaves *blade / broad*
1. wheat	a. ———	b. ———
2. lilac	a. ———	b. ———
3. bean	a. ———	b. ———
4. corn	a. ———	b. ———

Answer the following questions.

5. What is most of the grain used for that is raised by farmers?
6. Every year many plants die. How did God plan that there would be more plants the next year?
7. What three things make up a seed?

The conifers are another group of seed-producing plants. ***Conifers*** make their seeds in cones instead of flowers. Pine, cedar, fir, and redwood trees are conifers. So are many kinds of shrubs planted in lawns and around buildings. These plants are also called evergreens because they stay green all year long.

It is not hard to tell conifers apart from flowering plants. Conifers have needlelike leaves, but flowering plants have blade or broad leaves. Another difference is the place where seeds are made. Conifers produce seeds in between the scales of their cones.

Lesson 1 Answers

Group A

1. a. one-part b. blade
2. a. two-part b. broad
3. a. two-part b. broad
4. a. one-part b. blade
5. Most of the grain is used for food.
6. God planned for the plants to make seeds that can grow into new plants the next year.
7. A seed is made of a protective coating, a tiny plant, and food to start the new plant. (3 points)

(13 points thus far)

Did you know—

...that rhododendrons and magnolias are flowering plants that are evergreens? Both conifers and flowering plants are evergreens in the tropics, of course, where temperatures stay warm.

...that many pine trees make food most efficiently in dim light?

...that the garden pepper plant, grown as an annual, is actually a perennial in warm climates?

...that the smallest flowering plant is the duckweed, measuring only 1/50 inch (½ mm) long and 1/63 inch (2/5 mm) wide?

Quiz

Write the New Words on the chalkboard. Ask the students to write the correct one for each sentence below. Remind them to use correct spelling.

1. One in this group lives for more than two years. *(perennial)*
2. One in this group has cones and needles. *(conifer)*
3. One in this group lives two years. *(biennial)*
4. One in this group lives one year. *(annual)*

Leaves and cones of a spruce tree

But flowering plants produce seeds inside fruits. These fruits grow after the flowers die.

How long do seed-producing plants live? Some plants live only one year. They are called ***annuals.*** Many vegetable plants, such as peas, radishes, and sweet corn, are annuals. They grow, flower, produce seeds, and die all in one season. Flowers such as marigolds, zinnias, and geraniums are also annuals. These bright flowers are favorites for flower beds.

Other plants, called ***biennials,*** live for two years. Some garden plants, such as beets and carrots, are biennials. The first year they store up food in their roots. The next year they use up the food while producing flowers and seeds. Of course, a gardener does not want a carrot's flowers or seeds. He wants the fat roots, so he digs up the roots the first year. Some other biennials in the garden are parsley and turnip plants.

The plants that live for more than two years are called ***perennials.*** Can you think of some perennial plants? Trees and bushes are perennials. Flowers such as

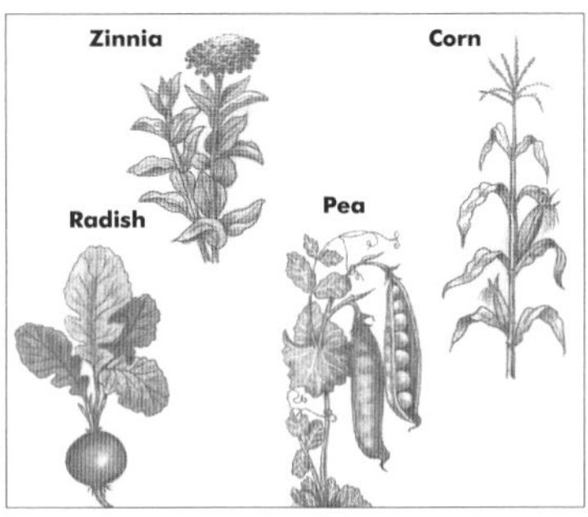

Annual plants

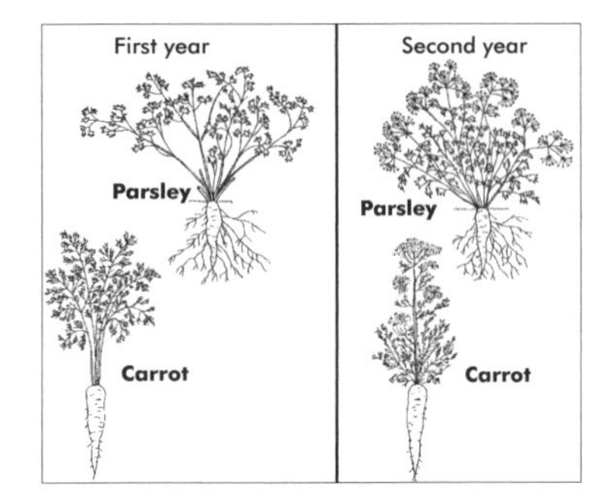

Biennial plants

lilies, tulips, and daffodils, which come up year after year, are also perennials. Raspberries and strawberries are perennial garden plants.

God has given us many different kinds of seed plants on the earth. Some have flowers, and others have cones. Some have blade leaves, some have broad leaves, and others have needle leaves. Some have one-part seeds, and some have two-part seeds. Some live one year, some live two years, and others live many years.

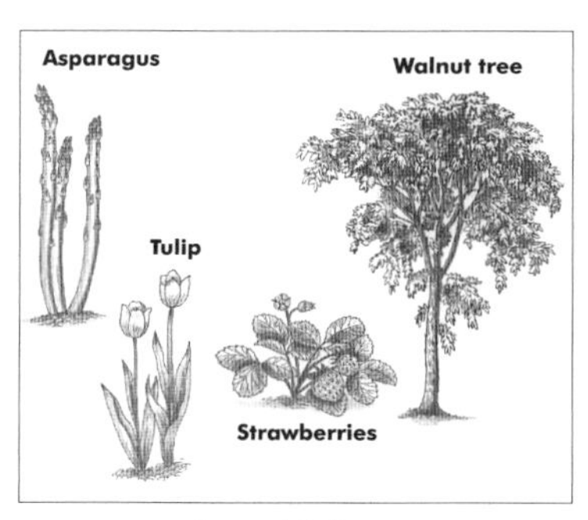

Perennial plants

With so many kinds of plants, we are sure to find one for whatever we need. Many plants like corn and beans are good for food. Some large grasses make good weaving material. Both broadleaf trees and conifers are used to make lumber and paper. Of course, we plant some plants just to enjoy their pretty flowers and leaves. Plants are indeed a wonderful gift from God!

Test Your Reading (Group B)

Tell whether the following plants are *annual, biennial,* or *perennial.*

8. carrots
9. strawberries
10. turnips
11. peas
12. maple trees
13. marigolds

Tell whether the following are *conifers* or *flowering plants.*

14. pine trees
15. maple trees
16. oak trees
17. fir trees

Group B

8. biennial
9. perennial
10. biennial
11. annual
12. perennial
13. annual

14. conifers
15. flowering plants
16. flowering plants
17. conifers

18. cones
19. evergreen
20. needles
21. biennial
22. annual
23. perennial
24. plants

(30 points total)

Write the missing words.

18. Conifers produce their seeds between scales in ———.
19. The conifers are ———, since they do not lose their leaves during the winter.
20. The leaves of conifers are shaped like ———.
21. A plant that produces a store of food in the roots one year and flowers and seeds the next year is called a ———.
22. Every year the farmer must sow seeds to get crops of corn, wheat, or soybeans because they are ——— plants.
23. A ——— plant like the apple tree will stay alive for 20 or more years.
24. God created many different kinds of ——— from which we get food, paper, lumber, and beauty.

Extra Activities

1. Study both one-part and two-part seeds. Maybe your parents have leftover corn, bean, and pea seeds from last year. It will make it easier to take the seeds apart if they are soaked overnight. Can you find the tiny seed plant in each? Can you see the two parts of the two-part seeds? Put some seeds between wet cloths in a warm place for several days. Study the sprouts.

   Materials needed:
   - corn, bean, and pea seeds
   - 2 cloths

2. If you live near a woods with conifer trees, you could ask for permission to hunt for cones there. You might also get a small twig with needles along with each cone.

   Then make a display for your classroom. Place the cones and twigs on a shelf or table, and label each pair neatly. You may need a tree guide or an encyclopedia to help you.

3. Ask your mother if you may look at food labels in her cupboards or refrigerator. Try to find out which kinds of plants were used to make the foods. Make a list of one-part-seed plants and two-part-seed plants that you find. Which list is longer? You may need a dictionary to understand some words.

Extra Activity Comments

2. This could be done as a class nature hike.

Lesson 2

Roots and Stems

New Words

absorb, to take in and make a part of itself.

bud, a small swelling at the tip of a stem that becomes a new stem, leaf, or flower.

cell, one of many tiny parts that make up each living thing.

root hair, one of many hairlike growths from the root of a plant.

sap, the liquid of water and minerals that flows through the stems of plants.

stem, the part of a plant from which flowers and leaves grow.

"His roots shall be dried up beneath, and above shall his branch be cut off" (Job 18:16). Does this make you think of a strong, healthy plant? Of course not. A plant without roots or branches will quickly die.

Plants are made of cells. Roots and stems are made of many tiny ***cells.*** In fact, anything alive is made of many cells. Your body is made of billions of cells, each too tiny to see without a microscope.

The size of a plant or animal depends on the number of cells it has. For example, the cells in a tall pine tree are hardly larger than those in a fern, but the pine tree has billions more of them.

Most of the cells in a plant have a boxlike shape. Although they may look alike, they do not all have the same job to do. Some of them store food, while others are lined up like a pipe to pass the food throughout the plant. All cells can grow and split to make new cells, but some

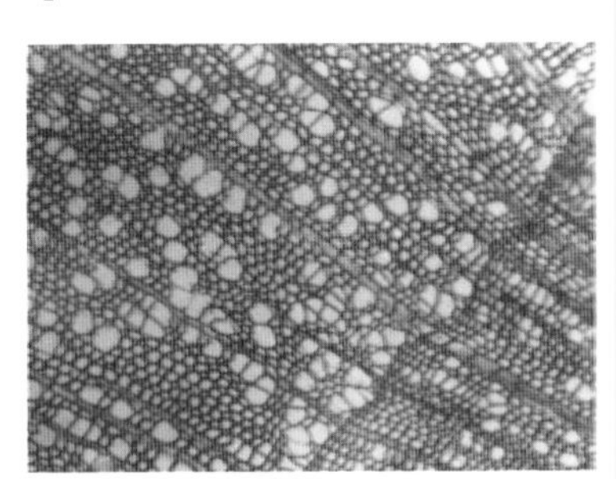

Cells of a plant stem

Lesson 2

Concepts to Teach

- Living things are made of small living parts called cells.
- Roots grow downward and toward water.
- Roots absorb water and minerals from the soil.
- Roots fasten the plant to the ground.
- Stems support the leaves and flowers of the plant and, in some plants, store food.
- Stems transport water, minerals, and food.
- In some stems, new cells produce growth around the stem, making a new ring each year.

Introducing the Lesson

Bring several plants with different kinds of stems and roots to class. Ask questions such as "Which stems do you think provide the most support? Which roots would be most useful in a dry climate? Which stems provide storage space?" Have a few students look for root hairs with a magnifying glass. They might not see any, for they are easily stripped off when the plant is uprooted.

If you have done the unit project as suggested on page 203, check to see whether the seeds have sprouted. If so, have the students gently uproot a sprout and look for root hairs with a magnifying glass.

Materials needed:

- several plants with different kinds of roots and stems
- tiny plant carefully uprooted
- magnifying glass

are able to multiply themselves much faster than the others.

For example, think of the roots of a maple tree. At the tip of each root are the cells that multiply quickly. They make the roots grow, pushing deeper and deeper into the soil.

Roots are important to plants. Roots always grow downward just as deep as they need to be to get enough water. A maple tree on a hill will usually have deeper roots than one beside a stream.

These roots fasten the plant firmly to the ground. You know how tightly roots can cling if you have ever pulled weeds in a garden. Those roots can make you work hard!

The root parts just behind the fast-growing tips are covered with many fine ***root hairs.*** One maple tree has billions of them. If the root hairs of one tree were all lined up end to end, the line would be hundreds of miles long.

Root hairs on radish seedlings

Each root hair is like a tiny mouth that drinks, or ***absorbs,*** water and minerals from the soil. They all keep taking in water and minerals, which become the liquid ***sap*** inside the maple tree.

The sap travels from the root hairs to the larger part of the roots. Next, the sap reaches the main stem, which is the tree trunk. The trunk sends the sap on up to the smaller branches. Every branch and leaf receives sap.

Test Your Reading (Group A)

Choose the best ending for each sentence, and write the letter on your paper.

1. All living things are made of tiny
   a. buds.
   b. cells.
   c. minerals.

Lesson 2 Answers

Group A

1. b

Did you know—

...that some plants get their moisture and nutrients from the air? Spanish moss and some ferns and orchids are such air plants. They cling to rocks and trees for support, but get moisture and nutrients from the air.

...that the African strangling fig starts out as an air plant in a tree, but later sends roots down into the soil? Meanwhile, it keeps winding itself around the tree, gradually choking it to death.

...that seaweeds called kelp have stems that grow 200 feet (60 m) long?

Quiz

Write the New Words on the chalkboard. Have the students write the correct one for each sentence below.

1. It is fastened to both the leaves and the roots. *(stem)*
2. All living things have lots of these. *(cells)*
3. It keeps drinking water and minerals. *(root hair)*
4. It means to gradually take inside. *(absorb)*
5. It is the beginning of a new branch or flower. *(bud)*
6. It is the liquid that flows through the stem. *(sap)*

2. The plant part that grows downward and toward water is
   a. the stem.
   b. the bud.
   c. the root.
3. The cells of a root grow and split to make new cells fastest
   a. at the tip of the root.
   b. in the middle of the root.
   c. on the outside of the root.
4. A root hair absorbs water and minerals. This means that it
   a. takes them inside the plant.
   b. stores them for later use.
   c. sends them through the stem.
5. A plant without roots will quickly die because
   a. there is nothing to hold up the stem.
   b. the plant cannot get water or minerals.
   c. the sap will run out of the bottom of the stem.
6. Besides the work of absorbing, roots also help the plant by
   a. fastening it to the soil.
   b. making food for the plant.
   c. giving an upward push to the stems.

2. c
3. a
4. a
5. b
6. a

(6 points thus far)

A stem is very important to a plant. You have just read how a ***stem*** or trunk helps to spread sap throughout a maple tree. All stems help to spread sap. They also spread the food a plant makes. God made this whole system work perfectly so that the whole plant gets all the food, water, and minerals it needs.

Sugar cane stalks can be up to 25 feet tall. The stems are a major source of sugar.

Stems also support the flowers of a plant and hold the leaves into the sunlight. The woody stems of trees are very strong so that giant trees can stand stormy weather.

Some stems also provide storage space for food. The stems of sugar cane contain much sugar and are a major source of the sugar we buy in stores. Potatoes also store food in their stems. These potato stems that we eat grow underground.

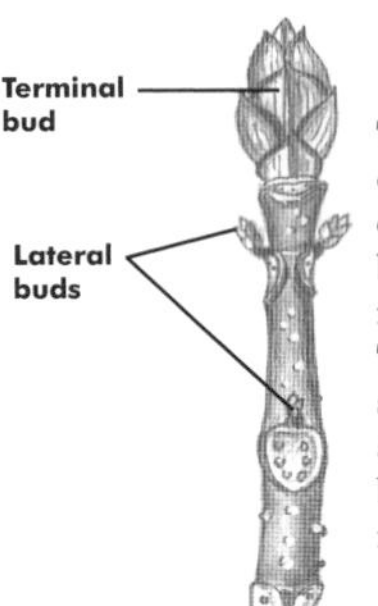

The bud on the end of a stem is called a terminal bud. *Terminal* means "end." The buds on the side of a stem are called lateral buds. *Lateral* means "side."

The underground stems of the potato plant are a good source of food.

Where a plant grows. You have already read how the cells at the tip of a root multiply quickly to make the root grow. The cells at the tip of a stem also multiply quickly to make the plant grow. The tip of a stem is called the ***bud.*** Some buds grow out the side of the stem to become stems, leaves, or flowers.

Many plants grow mainly at two places: at the root tips and at the buds. The plant grows taller or longer because of the cells multiplying in these two places. But some plants have fast-growing cells at a third place, around the stem. A tree trunk, for example, grows wider because of a special layer of fast-growing cells beneath the bark. As these cells grow, they make the rings inside the trunk that tell you how old a tree is. The tree makes a new ring every year. If you count the rings on a freshly-cut tree stump, you can tell how old it is.

Only God can make a plant. Since you have now finished reading this lesson, do you understand all about plants? Could you explain how the cells grow? Do you know how the sap rises? No, of course you cannot understand it all.

Not even Job could understand how God did it all. He did not know what to say when God asked, "Who hath divided a watercourse . . . to cause it to rain on the earth . . . and to cause the bud of the tender herb to spring forth?" (Job 38:25–27). But Job understood enough to humble himself before God. We should also learn enough to make us more amazed at our wonderful, wise Creator.

Test Your Reading (Group B)

Answer *true* if the statement is true. Answer *false* if the statement is false.

7. Stems make sap for the plant.
8. The leaves are held in the sunlight by the stems.
9. Some plants store food in stems that are underground.
10. When you eat a potato, you are eating one of the roots of a plant.
11. The cells of a bud grow fast like the cells of a root tip.
12. From a bud may come a new root.

Answer the following questions.

13. What part of the plant are you eating when you eat a potato?
14. What is the reason for the rings on a tree stump?
15. How can you tell how old a tree is when it is cut down?

Group B

7. false
8. true
9. true
10. false (*Note:* Because potatoes have buds [eyes], they are actually stems rather than roots.)
11. true
12. false

13. The potato you eat is a stem.
14. A tree trunk has a layer of fast-growing cells beneath the bark. Each year these cells make a new ring of growth.
15. The age of a tree can be found by counting the rings.

(15 points total)

Reviewing What You Have Learned

1. ——— have needles and cones.
2. An annual plant lives
   a. one year. b. two years. c. many years.
3. True or false? Two-part-seed plants have broad leaves.
4. A corn seed is an example of a
   a. one-part-seed plant.
   b. two-part-seed plant.
   c. many-part-seed plant.
5. True or false? A seed is a tiny plant with some stored food inside a tough coating.

Review Answers

1. Conifers
2. a
3. true
4. a
5. true

(5 additional points)

Extra Activities

1. You can see the work of a stem. Get some red or blue liquid food coloring and a stalk of celery with a few leaves on it. Celery that is

Extra Activity Comments

1. The reason for trimming the bottom of the stalk is to open any tubes that may be clogged. You as an adult may need to do this because a sharp knife should be used for best results.

   Discuss this experiment with your students. Express amazement that this seemingly helpless plant can pull the liquid upward and thus overcome the downward pull of gravity. (For your own information, scientists believe that this force is the cohesive attraction of the water molecules. As some evaporate at the surface of the leaf, they pull on those just below them. These, in turn, tug at the next ones and so on in a kind of chain reaction extending down to the roots.)

3. This could be a profitable class activity.

nearly white works best. Daffodils will also work. You will also need a small jar or cup of water.

First, put a few drops of the food coloring into the water. Then trim off the bottom of the celery stalk. Stand it on end in the colored water. Set the jar on a sunny windowsill for a few hours.

Now look at the celery stalk. Do you see any change? What does it show you about the work of a stem?

Materials needed:
- red or blue liquid food coloring
- stalk of celery with leaves
- small jar
- knife

2. Does a plant take in water through its leaves or its roots? You can see for yourself by doing this experiment. You need some aluminum foil and two plants that are nearly alike. (It could be two small seedlings recently sprouted.)

   Carefully fit the aluminum foil around the bottom of one plant. Arrange it so that no water can get to the soil. Sprinkle some water over the leaves of this plant every day. (Do this outdoors or over a sink to avoid a mess.) Water the other plant as usual, being careful not to wet the leaves.

   After a few days, compare the two plants. Which one is getting the water it needs? Do these plants receive water through their roots or their leaves?

   Materials needed:
   - aluminum foil
   - two potted plants

3. Go to a woods where tree stumps can be found. Look for one that was cut recently. Count the rings to find out how old the tree was. Someone may be able to bring a piece of a freshly cut log to school. Put needles with little flags in the ring of the year most of you were born, the year the school was built, and the years of other historical events. The rings of a tree can tell you about the weather in past years. A thin ring tells that the weather was dry. Read more about what the rings tell in an encyclopedia.

Lesson 3

Leaves Make Food

New Words

chlorophyll (klôr′·ə·fil), the green material that makes food in a plant cell.

transpiration (tran′·spə·rā′·shən), giving off water into the air from a leaf.

vein (vān), branching or parallel lines seen on a leaf.

Can you make your own food? What if you were to wake up one morning, feeling very hungry. "I want some breakfast," you tell your mother.

"Here is water," she answers, "and you have lots of air. Now use the water and air to make your own breakfast."

Could you make food from air and water? Of course not. But green plants do it again and again. They make food for themselves, for us, and for the animals.

You know why we need food. But why do plants need it? Plants need food for many of the same reasons we do. They need food in order to stay alive, to grow, and to do their work.

How does a plant make its own food? Plants are able to use air and water to make food. They also need two more things: ***chlorophyll*** and light. The plant has green chlorophyll inside its cells. That is what makes plants look green.

Chlorophyll gets its power from light. For most plants, the light is sunlight. But electric lights can be used for indoor plants.

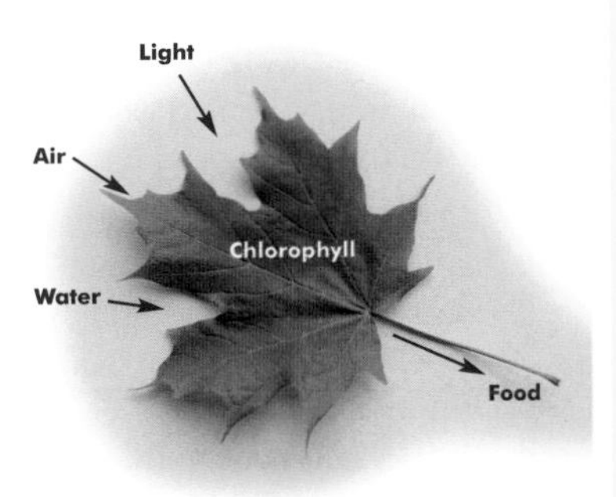

A green leaf is a food factory for itself, animals, and man.

Lesson 3

Concepts to Teach

- The green chlorophyll of leaves makes food when light shines on them.
- Guard cells regulate the flow of air and moisture into and out of the leaf by changing the size of the leaf openings.
- The water in the cells of a leaf produces its pressure. Without enough water, the plant loses its pressure and wilts.
- The leaves of a plant with one-part seeds have parallel veins; the leaves of a plant with two-part seeds have branching veins.
- Plants can be identified by their leaves.

Introducing the Lesson

Show both a fungus (mushroom is best for this) and a green plant. Ask the students to guess which one can make its own food. Invite speculation, but direct them to the lesson text for the answer.

Also show two leaves, one a monocot (parallel venation) and the other a dicot (branching venation). Ask the students to guess which is which. Again avoid giving the answer, pointing them to the lesson.

Materials needed:

- fungus such as mushroom or bracket fungus
- green plant
- leaves from monocot and dicot

Each leaf is like a busy factory with millions of chlorophyll workers. The food factories get busy each morning when the sun comes up. As soon as sunshine strikes the leaves, the chlorophyll starts catching it and making food. The brighter the sunshine, the faster the food is made. In the evening as the sunlight fades, food making is slower and slower. Finally, the leafy factories shut down for the night.

In places where the climate is warm the year around, the plants make food the year around. But in places with cold seasons, food making stops during the winter.

Where does a plant store its food? While the leaves of a plant are making food, the plant is using some of it and storing the rest away. The food can be stored in almost any part of a plant. For example, potato plants store food in their underground stems. Carrot and beet plants store food in their roots. Cauliflower and broccoli plants store food in their flowers. Corn and wheat plants store food in their seeds. Tomato plants, berry plants, and fruit trees all store food in their fruits.

So whatever you eat, you are eating the stored food of a plant. The apple you eat is made by the work of about 50 busy apple leaves. One peach is made by about 30 peach leaves, and a bunch of bananas is made by about 12 banana leaves.

Test Your Reading (Group A)

Match each letter to the correct number.

a. air and water
b. to live, grow, and work
c. plants
d. light
e. chlorophyll
f. at night
g. sun

1. Why living things need food
2. Green food-making material in leaves
3. Source of food-making light
4. Food making in plants cannot happen
5. Where man and animals get their food
6. What plants use to make food
7. The power used by plants to make food

Lesson 3 Answers

Group A

1. b
2. e
3. g
4. f
5. c
6. a
7. d

Did you know—

...that dogwood and poinsettia "flowers" are actually special leaves called bracts? Only the small yellow centers are the true flowers.

...that skunk cabbages and jack-in-the-pulpits have hoodlike leaves called spathes that help keep the plant warm?

...that an acre of corn gives off through transpiration about 4,000 gallons (15,000 liters) of water each day, which is almost enough to fill a milk truck?

...that a leaf on an apple tree has 47,000 stomata per square inch, while an oak leaf has over 100,000?

...that most of the oxygen in the air is a product of transpiration? Both water vapor and oxygen are released during transpiration, which is actually a part of photosynthesis.

Bulletin Board Idea

Have the students bring pictures of foods, especially vegetables and fruits. Arrange them around the bulletin board in groups with headings as suggested below. In large letters at the center, write *We eat different parts of plants.*

Seeds—wheat, corn, rice, beans, etc.
Fruits—green peppers, tomatoes, bananas, cherries, nuts, etc.
Leaves—lettuce, cabbage, spinach, parsley, onions, etc.
Stems—celery, white potatoes, rhubarb, asparagus, etc.
Roots—carrots, radishes, beets, sweet potatoes, etc.
Flowers—cauliflower, broccoli, cloves, artichokes

For some foods such as wheat, nuts, and cloves, it may be easier to display a sample of the food itself than to find a picture.

Match the plant with where it stores its food.

8. carrot	a. underground stems
9. corn	b. roots
10. tomato	c. flowers
11. potato	d. seeds
12. cauliflower	e. fruit

8. b
9. d
10. e
11. a
12. c

(12 points thus far)

What happens to the water in plants? Whenever leaves are busy making food, some water is used to make the food, but some is given off into the air. This is called ***transpiration.*** On a warm day, the leaves of a birch tree may give off over 70 gallons (265 liters) of water through transpiration. Some people believe that transpiration keeps a plant from overheating in bright sunlight, much like sweating keeps you from getting too hot.

Transpiration takes place mostly on the underside of a leaf. The water comes out of holes that are much too tiny for you to see without a microscope. A single leaf has many thousands of them.

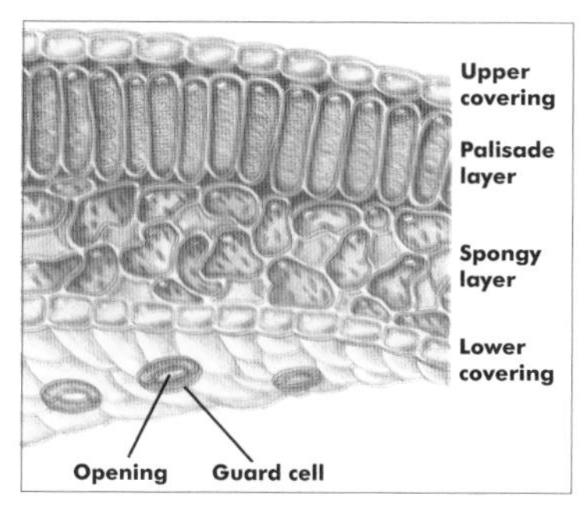

The guard cells control the air and water that enter and leave the leaf. Look at the photograph at the top of page 155. Can you find the four layers of leaf cells?

At night, guard cells close the holes. But during the day, while the "food factory" is busy, the guard cells keep the holes open. They let the right amount of water pass out of each opening. They also let air come inside the leaf. In this way the guard cells control the transpiration of each leaf and of the whole plant.

The plant must not lose too much water, or it will wilt. Every cell needs water to keep the right amount of pressure. The water pressure keeps the stems and leaves stiff.

You have often seen plants without enough pressure in their cells. Whenever you pick flowers, you know that they will wilt. The cells lose water from transpiration, and they are not getting more water from the roots. Then the flowers and

Quiz

Ask the students to write the correct New Word for each sentence below.

1. It is one of the many lines you see on a leaf. *(vein)*
2. It is a way green plants lose their water. *(transpiration)*
3. It makes food inside a leaf. *(chlorophyll)*

What is wrong with these petunia plants? What could be done to help them?

leaves soon hang down because they lose pressure inside their cells. If you put the stems in water, the cells keep some of their pressure. Then the flowers will not wilt quite as fast.

How can leaves help us know the kinds of plants? Sap flows through a leaf in its ***veins.*** You can see the veins easily on the underside of a large leaf. They look like patterns of lines on the leaf.

You can tell whether a plant has a one-part seed or a two-part seed just by looking at the veins on its leaves. If the leaf has one main vein in the center joined to smaller and smaller veins branching in all directions, that plant has a two-part seed. But if the veins all run side by side in one direction, that plant has a one-part seed. We say the veins of a one-part-seed plant are parallel because they run side by side. The veins of a two-part-seed plant are branching.

God made leaves with many interesting shapes. Many are shaped like feathers, but some are shaped like hearts, arrows, or flower petals. Oak and maple leaves look like fancy cutouts.

God also arranged leaves on

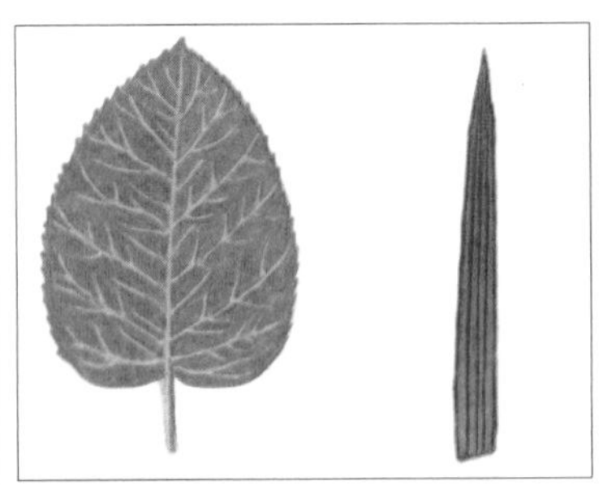
Leaves of two-part-seed plants have branching veins.

Leaves of one-part-seed plants have parallel veins.

God made leaves with a variety of interesting shapes.

their stems in different ways. A maple or an oak leaf has only one large blade, but a hickory leaf is made of a number of small blades, or leaflets. On the hickory leaf, the leaflets are fastened to the stem across from each other. But the leaflets of a willow leaf are fastened at different places on the stem.

These are only a few examples of the many interesting ways in which God designed leaves. If you notice such things carefully, you can soon tell trees and many other plants apart by their leaves. You can walk through a woods and say, "This is a birch tree" or "This is a jack-in-the-pulpit." Plants will become like friends to you.

The jack-in-the-pulpit has two sets of three leaves.

Test Your Reading (Group B)

Finish each sentence with the correct ending.

13. During transpiration, a plant ———.
14. Guard cells decrease the transpiration of a plant by ———.
15. A plant needs enough water inside each cell to keep up good ———.
16. After you pick a flower, it will wilt because ———.
17. The lines on a leaf are called ———.
18. A one-part-seed plant has parallel veins, but a two-part-seed plant has veins that are ———.
19. Learning leaf shapes and the ways leaves are arranged on the stems helps you to ———.

Reviewing What You Have Learned

1. Flowering plants with one-part seeds have
   a. broad leaves. b. bladelike leaves. c. needlelike leaves.

Group B

13. gives off water from its leaves
14. closing the openings
15. pressure
16. the cells lose pressure when they lose water from transpiration and they do not get more water from the roots
17. veins
18. branching
19. tell the plants apart by their leaves

(19 points total)

Review Answers

1. b

2. cells
3. c
4. bud
5. true

(5 additional points)

Extra Activity Comments

1. Your own enthusiasm for leaf identification will likely be reflected in your students. You may need to brush up on your knowledge of trees and wildflowers as well as cultivated plants.

   A class hike would be an excellent preparation for this activity. Of course, be sure to ask permission to hike in a woods, making sure to mention your plan to gather leaves.
2. The cards with leaves can also be used as flash cards for tree identification. Encourage the students to start with only one kind of oak, pine, or hickory leaf. When they have mastered the main kinds, then they could branch out to varieties such as white oak, red oak, and so on. Focus especially on the trees or plants that are abundant in your area.

2. All living things are made of ———.
3. Root hairs
   a. support and anchor a plant.
   b. carry water, minerals, and food.
   c. absorb water and minerals.
4. A ——— becomes a new stem or flower.
5. True or false? The stem of a plant can carry sap and store food.

Extra Activities

1. Make a leaf collection. You could use only tree leaves from a woods, or leaves from the plants in your yard and garden. It may be helpful to carry along a notebook, pencil, and tape as you gather the leaves. If there are several similar leaves, write the name of the plant, and tape the leaf right beside it to avoid getting mixed up. If you cannot name many of the plants, you could ask your parents to help you, or else get a book on tree or wildflower identification from a library.

   Make a poster with each leaf neatly labeled. If you have identified several different kinds of oak or pine trees, group them together on your poster.
2. Gather some leaves, and make a leaf memory game. For a quick one, cut out 20 cards large enough to hold the largest leaf you have gathered. On 10 of them, tape 10 different kinds of tree leaves. On the other 10 cards, write the names of the trees.

   Play this game just like the Memory game. Take turns picking up two cards at a time, trying to match each leaf with its name. The one who matches the most sets is the winner.
3. You can see how important sunlight is to a plant. Go outside and look for a large stone, board, or other object on top of the grass. Lift it and look at the grass underneath. Compare this grass with the other grass nearby.

Lesson 4

Flowers, Fruits, and Seeds

New Words

petal (pet′·əl), one of a set of colored parts inside the sepals of a flower.

pistil (pis′·təl), the part of a flower that makes plant eggs and seeds.

pollen (pol′·ən), fine powder from the stamen of a flower.

reproduce (rē′·prə·düs′), to produce offspring like itself.

sepal (sē′·pəl), one of a set of green, leaflike parts that cover a flower bud.

stamen (stā′·mən), the part of a flower that makes the pollen.

Will you help to tend a garden this summer? If so, perhaps you could pick a bunch of sweet corn flowers. Or how about picking some tomato flowers for your mother? Would she like that? No, your mother hardly wants you to pick these flowers, for then they cannot do their work.

What kind of work can a flower do? A tomato blossom helps to make a tomato with tomato seeds inside. Not every flower can produce a vegetable, but each kind makes seeds that can grow into new plants. In other words, flowers make seeds to ***reproduce*** again and again.

This work of making seeds is very important indeed. If plants were to stop making seeds for just one season, most living things and people would starve to death. Seeds are made in flowers. Flowers have four special parts: the ***sepals, petals, stamens,*** and ***pistils.*** Look at the drawing of a flower, and find each of these parts.

Before a rosebud opens, all you

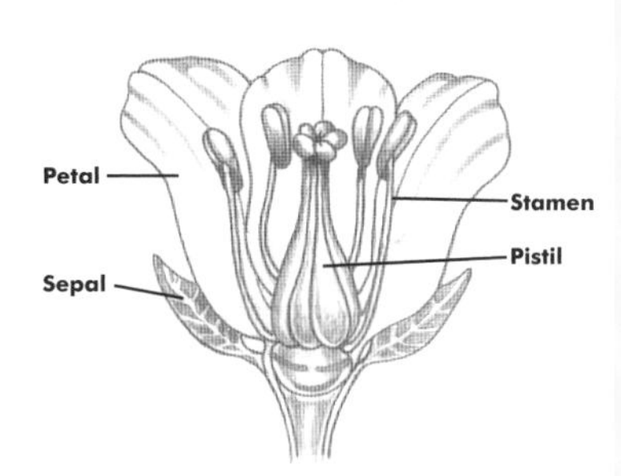

Parts of a flower

Lesson 4

Concepts to Teach

- Flowering plants reproduce by producing seeds.
- Flowers of one-part-seed plants have parts in multiples of three; flowers of two-part-seed plants have parts in multiples of four or five.
- Inside a flower, the stamens produce pollen and the pistils produce plant eggs.
- The pollen must unite with the plant egg in order to produce a seed.
- God has provided different ways for flowers to be pollinated.
- Fruits grow from special parts of the flower.
- God has provided various methods of seed dispersal.
- A seed contains a tiny plant, stored food, and a seed coating.
- A seed will grow into a new plant.

Introducing the Lesson

Dissect a flower to give your students a head start on their lesson. Choose a large blossom with a simple structure, such as a lily or tulip, not a compound flower, such as a daisy or dandelion.

With a pin, gently slit open one petal down to its base. Point out the sepals, petals, stamens, and pistil. Touch one or two stamens to white paper, calling attention to the powdery pollen. Encourage them to use a magnifying glass to examine it more closely. Then gently slit open the ovary. Have them examine the shiny, beadlike eggs with the magnifying glass.

Materials needed:

- lily, tulip, or other large flower
- straight pin
- magnifying glass

can see is its ***sepals.*** They protect the tender flower parts until the bud is ready to open. Then the sepals spread apart. Sepals usually look like little green leaves.

Inside the sepals is a circle of ***petals.*** God made petals in all kinds of bright colors that we enjoy. One-part-seed plants, such as irises, have petals and sepals in multiples of three (3, 6, 9, etc.). Two-part-seed plants, such as petunias, have petals in multiples of four or five.

Inside the circle of petals are the ***stamens.*** They usually look like stiff strings with little balls on top. The job of a stamen is to make many tiny grains of ***pollen.*** The pollen is made and stored in the little balls on top of the stringlike stamens.

A ***pistil*** is found at the very center of the flower. It looks like a tiny tube. The job of a pistil is to make little plant eggs at the bottom of the tube. It takes both the pollen and a plant egg to make a seed.

Test Your Reading (Group A)

Choose the best ending for each sentence.

1. Seeds allow flowering plants
2. Seeds are made
3. A flower needs sepals
4. A one-part-seed plant
5. A two-part-seed plant
6. The work of a stamen is
7. The work of a pistil is

a. may have 5 petals.
b. to make plant eggs.
c. to produce pollen.
d. may have 6 petals.
e. by eggs and pollen.
f. to reproduce again and again.
g. to protect the tender bud.

What are the numbered parts of this flower?

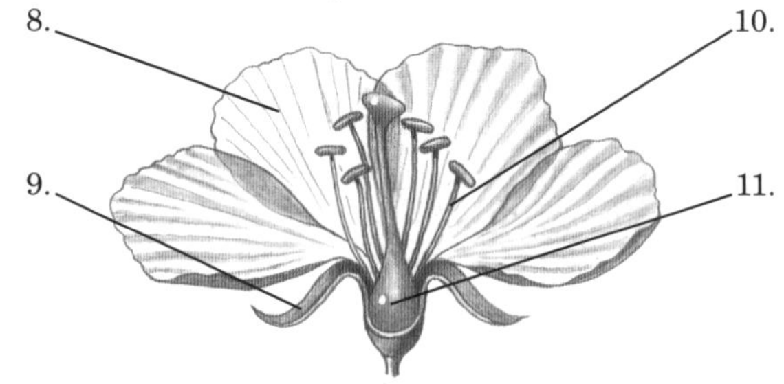

Lesson 4 Answers

Group A

1. f
2. e
3. g
4. d
5. a
6. c
7. b
8. petal
9. sepal
10. stamen
11. pistil

(11 points thus far)

Did you know—

...that some flowers give off their fragrance at night to attract night moths?

...that a dandelion head is actually a cluster of flowers called an inflorescence, and that it forms fertile seeds without being pollinated?

...that violet and witch hazel plants "shoot" their seeds away by an elastic contraction inside the pod?

...that hay fever in the United States is usually caused by windblown ragweed pollen?

...that a blackberry or raspberry is not a true berry, but a cluster of drupes? A true berry has its seeds inside the flesh of a single, juicy, enlarged ovary.

...that each blossom of a pea or bean plant has tightly closed petals to keep out pollen from other blossoms?

Unit Project Update

Have you done the unit project given on page 203? If so, check to see whether the seeds have sprouted. If they have, this would be a good time to discuss germination. Show the pot in the cold place and the pot without drainage to establish the need for warmth and air. Have them compare the upside-down seeds with the others to determine whether there is any difference. Also have them compare the pots kept in darkness with the one kept in normal lighting.

Then start another experiment to show that new seedlings do need their stored food in order to survive. Use three identical bean seedlings that have recently sprouted. Remove one seed half from one plant by bending it back gently. Remove both seed halves from the second plant. Leave the beans intact on the third plant as a control for the experiment.

How does pollen get to the pistil? Each kind of flower needs its own kind of pollen in order to make seeds. So how does the right kind of pollen get to each pistil? God planned several ways for this to happen. In some plants, the pollen from the stamens falls onto the pistil of that same flower. This may happen whenever the wind shakes the plant a little. This is what happens to cause the pollen of corn to fall from the tassel (the stamens) onto the silk (the pistils) of the ear. In other flowers, the stamens and pistils never ripen at the same time. So the wind carries the pollen between the flowers. Trees, shrubs, and grasses have large, feathery tips to catch the fine pollen blowing around.

The pollen of tulips, roses, lilacs, and other pretty flowers is carried by insects. Some of these flowers also make sweet-smelling nectar when their pollen is ripe. Their sweet smells and bright colors make it easy for the insects to find them. Bees, for example, like to drink the nectar from the flowers and eat the rich pollen. As a bee goes in and out of a flower, the pollen sticks to its fuzzy body. Some pollen from one flower is sure to brush off on the next one. In this way, much pollen is spread around from flower to flower.

The bees do not know that they are spreading pollen. And the flowers do not know that they are feeding the bees. But God knows. He made it all work together in His wonderful plan.

After the pollen gets to a pistil,

The stamen (tassel) and pistil (silk) are at different places on a corn plant.

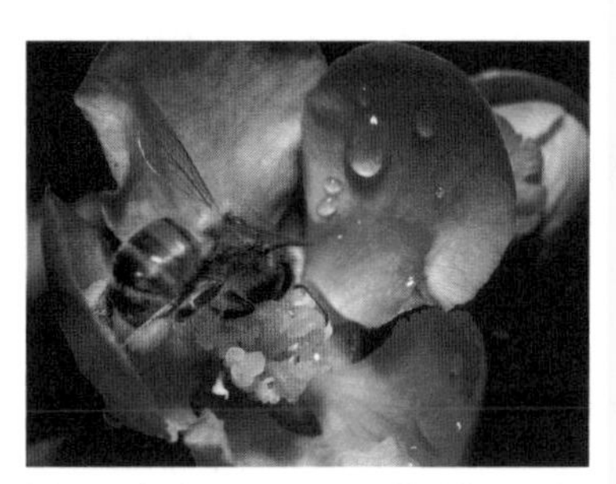

What is the bee doing for itself? What is the bee doing for the plant? Who designed that they help each other?

Water all three seedlings as needed, but keep them in darkness to avoid photosynthesis. Have the students check on the three plants every day, comparing the amounts of growth. Also ask them to check the size of the seed halves each day for about a week.

Quiz

Write the New Words on the chalkboard. Ask the students to supply the correct one for each phrase below.

1. The powdery material that helps to make seeds *(pollen)*
2. To make more like itself *(reproduce)*
3. One of the red parts of a rose *(petal)*
4. The green covering around a flower bud *(sepal)*
5. The part that makes pollen *(stamen)*
6. The part that makes plant eggs *(pistil)*

it unites with the plant eggs. Each egg starts growing into a seed. Meanwhile, the flower petals dry up and fall off. Their work is done. All that is left is the very center part of the flower. This center will grow into fruit that holds the seeds. The fruit and the seeds grow together. We eat the fruit of some plants, like the peach and pumpkin. We eat the seeds of other plants, like the beans and corn.

How are wild seeds scattered? You help to plant seeds in the garden. But how do all the wild seeds in the woods and meadows get planted? God has planned several ways for seeds to be scattered and planted in the wild.

The wind scatters many lightweight seeds. Dandelion and milkweed seeds, for example, are so light and fluffy that a little wind sends them sailing off. Maple and pine tree seeds have little wings to help them fly away with the wind.

Some seeds float on water. They fall into streams or rivers that carry them to new homes.

Some seeds travel with people or animals. They have tiny hooks or barbs to grab at anything that passes by. No doubt you yourself have helped to spread such seeds when you have taken a walk through a woods. You see those prickly burs and beggar ticks as just a bother and pick them off your clothes and drop them on the ground, but you are really helping to fulfill God's design for them to be scattered and planted.

How will the plant be helped if these seeds are pulled off and thrown away?

How does a seed grow into a plant? In Lesson 1, you learned that a seed is a tiny plant inside a tough outer coating. Besides this, a seed always holds a small supply of food for the baby plant.

When a seed falls into the ground, it soaks up water. The seed swells until the outer coat splits apart. Inside, a tiny stem and root start growing and using the stored food inside the seed. The food supply lasts long enough for the plant to grow its first leaves. Then the leaves start their normal job of making food in sunlight for the plant.

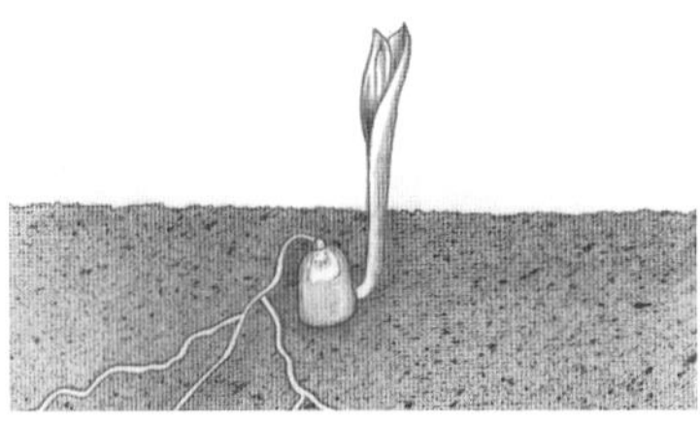
How does a corn seed know when to grow?

The new plant keeps on growing and making food. After a while, it makes flowers, fruit, and new seeds. In this way, all the flowering plants reproduce themselves year after year just as God in His great wisdom planned for them.

Test Your Reading (Group B)

Choose the best answer.

12. The pollen from the corn tassel gets to the silk of the ear when
    a. insects carry the pollen on their fuzzy bodies.
    b. drops of rain carry the pollen down.
    c. the wind shakes the tassel and the pollen falls down.
13. The main purpose of the petals and sweet nectar is to
    a. attract insects.
    b. encourage people to plant the flowers in their gardens.
    c. please us with beautiful sights and smells.
14. When you throw down a prickly bur, you are
    a. helping to carry pollen from the stamen to the pistil.
    b. keeping a plant from reproducing.
    c. helping a plant to spread.
15. Besides a tiny new plant, a seed contains
    a. a poison to keep animals from eating it.
    b. food for the new plant.
    c. something to keep the seed from rotting.

Answer the following questions.

16. Why do farmers with orchards like to see plenty of bees flying in the spring?
17. Why do the flowers and the bees help each other if they do not know that they are being helpful?
18. What two non-living things help to scatter seeds?
19. Why do the seeds not grow until they are put into the ground?

Group B

12. c
13. a
14. c
15. b

16. The bees are needed to carry and spread the pollen so that the trees can make fruit and seeds.
17. God made them to help each other.
18. Seeds may be scattered by the wind and water (*or* streams). (2 points)
19. The seeds must have water to soak up and swell and to start growing.

(20 points total)

Review Answers

1. false
2. c
3. Water
4. b
5. light (sunlight)

(5 additional points)

Extra Activity Comments

3. This project, like the one in Lesson 3, could be a by-product of a class nature hike in a nearby woods. If possible, take along a nature guide for plant identification.

When the pressed flowers are dry, have the students prepare their cards by twice folding an 8½-by-11-inch sheet of plain white paper. Or they could cut out a rectangle from posterboard and fold it.

Have each student arrange a simple bouquet of pressed flowers on the front of his card. Caution that the flowers are fragile and must be handled very gently. Each flower may be glued in place with small dots of "Tacky" glue or Elmer's glue along the stems. Use as little as possible to avoid discoloring the petals. Let the glue dry.

Next, cover the whole front of the card with clear Contact paper or clear plastic wrap, bringing it around to the back. If plastic wrap is used, it can be fastened with tape.

Finally, have each student write a note of cheer or appreciation inside his card along with an appropriate Bible verse. They could give their cards to some sick or elderly person or to their parents.

Reviewing What You Have Learned

1. True or false? Roots grow away from water.
2. Sap and food flow through a plant's
   a. guard cells. b. buds. c. veins.
3. ——— gives a plant its pressure so it can stand up.
4. During transpiration, a plant
   a. takes in water from the air.
   b. gives off water into the air.
   c. holds the water it gets from the air.
5. Chlorophyll needs ——— before it can make food from air and water.

Extra Activities

1. The next time you see an apple, look at the core end opposite the stem. There you see the dried-up remains of the pistil and stamens.
2. Make a seed collection. You could collect some seeds we eat, such as rice and dried beans. You could collect some seeds we throw away, such as watermelon and apple seeds or peach and cherry pits. You could also collect seeds from nearby trees and wild seeds, such as milkweed, cocklebur, and beggar tick seeds.

   Write the name of each seed on a slip of paper. Fasten each seed with its paper on posterboard or a bulletin board. You may need to ask your teacher or parents to help you.
3. Add pressed flowers to make your leaf collection (page 220) even more attractive. Or make pretty greeting cards from pressed flowers.

   You will need to find some pretty flowers that are not too thick. Tulips, petunias, and roses are not suitable for pressing. But violets, impatiens, and buttercups are fine choices.

   Spread the flowers out inside an old telephone book or newspaper. Put it in a dry place out of the way, and lay heavy books on top. Wait for a week or two. Then ask your teacher to help you make the card.

Lesson 5

Plants Can Multiply

New Words

bulb, a rounded, underground bud that grows into a plant such as a tulip or onion plant.

grafting, causing part of one plant to grow on another plant.

pruning, trimming buds or branches from vines or trees to get better fruit.

rooting, to cause to develop roots by placing the end of a stem in water or wet soil.

tuber (tü′·bər), a potato or other vegetable that is part of a thick underground stem.

Have you ever planted rose or tulip seeds? Or did you try apple, potato, or strawberry seeds? If you have ever raised plants from these seeds, you must be an unusual gardener. These seeds take longer to produce flowers or fruit than bean, corn, and marigold seeds do. In fact, if you were to plant some kinds of tulip seeds, you might have to wait seven years to see the first tulips!

Most gardeners can easily raise annual plants, such as peas, lettuce, and zinnias, from seeds. Some perennial flowers are not too hard to raise from seeds, either. But the best and fastest way to raise most perennial plants is by planting buds, stems, or other plant parts.

Some plants can multiply from bulbs. You raise tulips by planting tulip bulbs. A ***bulb*** is a rounded, underground bud. Inside is a tiny plant with plenty of stored food. On one end of the bud is a fast-growing tip. Here the plant cells multiply themselves quickly if

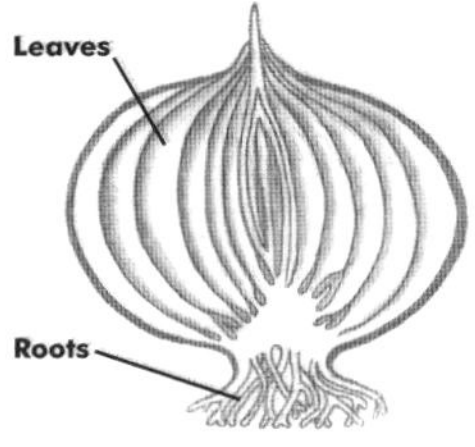

An onion bulb

Lesson 5

Concepts to Teach

- The stems of some plants will grow roots.
- Many plants spread from roots and underground stems.
- The white potato is an underground stem with buds.
- Strawberries spread by runners.
- Special trees can be multiplied by grafting.
- Some trees and grapevines must be pruned to yield large, perfect fruit.

Introducing the Lesson

Show the students some of the plants or plant parts mentioned in this lesson, such as a tulip bulb, a rooted cutting, a potato with growing buds, or a strawberry plant with a few runners. If you are ambitious, you could bring a small, wild seedling tree and a twig from another tree to demonstrate a simplified version of grafting. See "Grafting" in an encyclopedia for more details.

Materials needed:

- tulip bulb
- potatoes with growing buds
- rooted cutting from houseplant
- small strawberry plant with runners

Did you know—

...that at first strawberries were called *strewberries,* perhaps because the berries were "strewn" among the leaves?

...that the grapes in the northern states are a cross between the delicious European grape and the winter-hardy (but less flavorful) American grape? Furthermore, the vines are grafted onto rootstocks of native American grapes that resist the common insect pest, phylloxera.

the bulb is in warm, moist soil. Next, leaves and stems pop out from the tip of the bulb, and soon you see a tall tulip plant. Growing a tulip from a seed is much slower.

Onions are also grown from bulbs. The layers of the onion bulb are actually the lower ends of leaves.

Some plants can multiply from cuttings. What does your mother do when she wants a new houseplant or rosebush? She cuts off the top part of a few healthy stems. Then she puts the ends that were cut into a jar of water. For a rosebush or shrub, she might put the stems in wet soil. Then she tends the little cuttings for a few weeks, making sure they have enough water. Some of them may wither and die, but a few will likely grow their own roots. At last she is ready to plant her new plants into the soil where she wants them. She got some whole new plants by ***rooting*** some cuttings. Rooting is one way of multiplying plants without planting seeds.

Some plants multiply from underground stems. Many plants will multiply themselves without your help. They have underground stems and roots that keep spreading and sending up new shoots. Ferns, irises, and blueberries are only a few of the many plants that multiply in this way.

You have likely seen grass plants that spread and multiply. When you see newly planted grass, it looks thin and uneven. You can see many patches of brown soil. But soon the spreading stems make the grass thicker and thicker. It becomes a lush, green carpet that hides all the soil.

Some plants have special underground stems called tubers. A ***tuber*** is a thick underground

Willow trees can be easily multiplied by rooting.

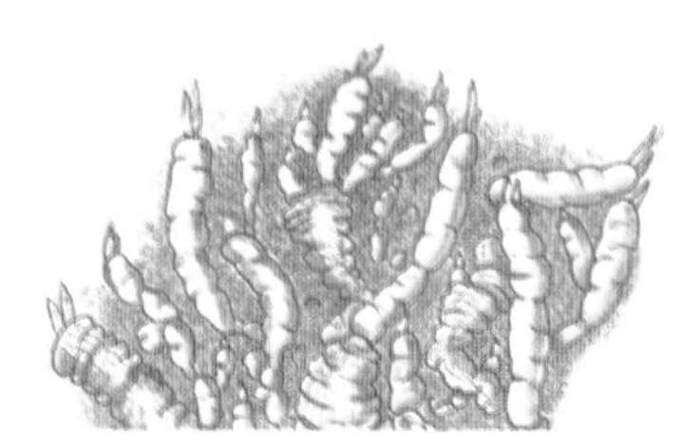

Irises spread by stems that grow underground.

...that the potato plant is closely related to the tomato, red pepper, and tobacco plant, but not to the sweet potato?

...that researchers have discovered that trees can defend themselves from invading insects? Once attacked, a tree begins to produce extra-high levels of bitter tannins to give the enemy indigestion, alkaloids to upset his nervous system, and fake amino acids to cause defective proteins in his body.

Field Trip Idea

A fruit farm or large orchard could prove to be an interesting field trip for the class. Ask to have someone available to explain how the different plants and trees are watered, fertilized, and pruned. Ask how the fruit is harvested. If grafting is done there, perhaps it could be demonstrated.

Quiz

Write the New Words on the chalkboard. Ask the students to say the one they think of when you read the phrases below.

1. A potato or its cousin *(tuber)*
2. A special bud to plant in the ground *(bulb)*
3. Cutting away the extra growth *(pruning)*
4. Joining a bud from one tree into another tree *(grafting)*
5. Getting a new plant from a cutting *(rooting)*

stem that stores food. It also grows buds that can start new plants.

The common white potato is one kind of tuber. The potato plant stores extra food inside its tubers, the potatoes. If you want this food, you eat a potato. If you do not eat it, the potato buds will!

The potato buds are the eyes of the potato. Whenever you see those white stems growing out of a potato, you know that the buds are eating. The potato becomes small and wrinkled because the buds are using up its stored food and water. Then you wish the buds would not grow.

But when you plant cut-up potatoes in your garden, you are glad that the buds grow. One bud can grow into a whole new plant that produces six big potatoes. Tubers with buds can produce new potato plants much faster than seeds can. God planned this way for potato plants to multiply.

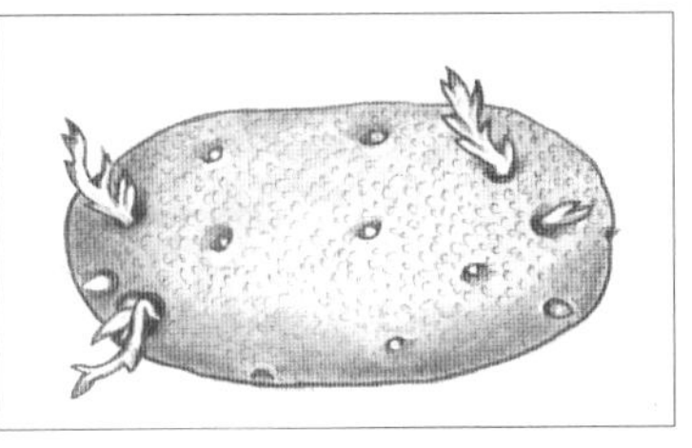

What can be done to a potato to make separate potato plants?

Test Your Reading (Group A)

Write the missing words.

1. Many plants are multiplied by planting parts of the plant because this is easier than growing them from ———.
2. A tulip is easily grown by planting a ———, which is an underground bud.
3. A new violet plant can be started by putting a ——— of a stem in water for several weeks.
4. When a stem grows roots to make a complete plant, that method of multiplying is called ———.
5. One grass plant can spread to cover a large area by sending up new shoots from ——— stems.
6. When you eat a potato, you are really eating food stored in a thick underground stem called a ———.
7. When potatoes are being cut into pieces for planting, each piece needs to have at least one ———, sometimes called an eye.

Lesson 5 Answers

Group A

1. seeds
2. bulb
3. cutting
4. rooting
5. underground
6. tuber
7. bud

(7 points thus far)

Some plants multiply from runners. God planned that strawberry plants could multiply themselves too. But instead of growing underground stems, they grow long stems above the ground. These long stems, called runners, produce many new strawberry plants.

If a runner lies on moist soil, it sends down tiny roots. The roots start sending sap upward to tiny new leaves. The new leaves soon start making their own food. Before long, the new plant could stay alive even if you were to cut it off from its parent plant. By next year it will be ready to produce juicy strawberries. It will also start sending runners in all directions to start more strawberry plants.

Ivy plants and some grasses also have spreading stems above the ground. They multiply the same way as the strawberry plant does.

Fruit trees are multiplied by grafting. If you plant a Red Delicious apple seed, you will get an apple tree that produces wild apples, not Red Delicious apples. Special fruit trees, such as Red Delicious, are multiplied by ***grafting.*** Although a number of different ways are used to do grafting, we shall describe only one. This kind of grafting is used to multiply special fruit trees and roses.

After these five steps are done, only the kind of branches and fruit grow on that tree that are like the tree from which the bud was taken. So if the bud came from a Red Delicious apple tree, the fruit from the graft will be Red Delicious. This is the way such special

A strawberry plant can spread with runners.

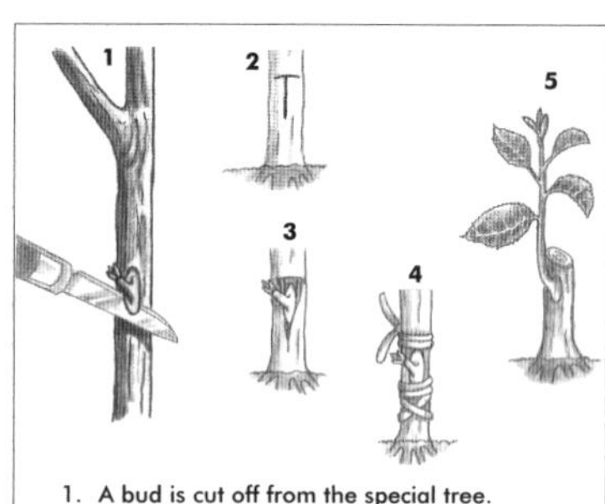

1. A bud is cut off from the special tree.
2. A slit is cut in the bark of a little tree.
3. The bud is pushed into the slit.
4. The bud is tied in place.
5. After the bud produces a leafy branch, the branches already on the little tree are cut off.

Steps of grafting

apple trees are multiplied.

A strong, healthy fruit tree or grapevine will not produce large, perfect fruits unless it receives regular pruning. ***Pruning*** is cutting off unnecessary buds or branches from a plant. This causes it to produce better fruit. If the tree has too much fruit, it is best to thin the fruit by removing some of it. A well-pruned and well-thinned peach tree will produce fewer peaches than an unpruned tree, but the peaches will be larger.

When an unpruned fruit tree is loaded with fruit, one or more large limbs may break off. This weakens the whole tree. But a well-pruned tree has branches that are thinned out. They are spaced so that they are unlikely to crack or break.

Seeds, bulbs, cuttings, underground stems, runners, and grafting are wonderful ways that God planned for plants to multiply. We cannot help but say what Job did about God's world: "I know that thou canst do every thing" (Job 42:2).

Well-pruned apple trees | Young peaches needing to be thinned | Same branch well-thinned

Test Your Reading (Group B)

Write *true* if the statement is true. Write *false* if the statement is false.

8. A runner is a long stem above the ground that can grow roots if it lies on the ground.
9. If you cut a runner, the new plant at the end of the runner will die.
10. If you have a tree that gives apples that you like, you can have more trees with that kind of apples by planting its seeds.
11. Grafting is done when the bud from one tree is pushed into a slit in the bark of another tree.

Group B

8. true
9. false
10. false
11. true

12. true
13. true
14. false

(14 points total)

12. After the graft produces a leafy branch, if the other branches of the tree are not cut off, the tree will give two kinds of fruit.
13. A fruit tree that gives only small fruit needs to be pruned.
14. A well-pruned tree will produce such big fruit that the branches will likely crack and break.

Review Answers

1. a
2. b
3. true
4. stamen
5. seeds

(5 additional points)

Reviewing What You Have Learned

1. A two-part-seed plant has
   a. branching veins in its leaves.
   b. veins that are side by side in its leaves.
   c. one vein in each leaf.
2. Stems
   a. fasten plants to the ground.
   b. carry water, minerals, and food.
   c. absorb water and minerals.
3. True or false? Guard cells control the transpiration of a plant.
4. A——— makes pollen.
5. Flowering plants reproduce by making ———.

Extra Activity Comments

2. The cuttings should be about five inches long, with the cut made just below the place where a leaf joins the stem. Remove the leaves from the lower half of the cuttings.

Extra Activities

1. If garden space is available, you might enjoy keeping a small berry patch of your own. Perhaps you could get some strawberry or raspberry starts from some friends or from your own family garden.

   Most gardeners with berry plants a few years old would be happy to have you dig up some starts because berry plants soon become too thick anyway. You might ask your parents or a gardener friend for tips on planting the starts. (For example, ask how deep and how far apart to plant them.)
2. Ask your teacher or parents to help you start some plants from cuttings as described in this lesson. Most kinds of vines are easy to start from cuttings, as well as geranium and begonia plants.
3. Read about grafting in the Bible. Find Romans 11:17–24, and read it several times. Ask your father or minister to help you understand the meaning of these verses. Write a few paragraphs about what you learned.

Lesson 6

Do You Remember?

Match each word on the right with a phrase on the left.

1. Has cones and needles
2. Lives one year
3. Lives two years
4. Lives more than two years
5. Absorbs water and minerals
6. Green food-making material

a. annual
b. biennial
c. chlorophyll
d. conifer
e. perennial
f. root hair

From the word box, find and write a word for each blank.

absorb	pruning	rooting
grafting	reproduce	transpiration
pollen		

7. A plant can ——— water and minerals from the soil.
8. A tree gives off many gallons of water through ———.
9. God caused most plants to ——— by producing seeds.
10. Bees and other insects spread ——— for many flowers.
11. Houseplants are often multiplied by ——— cut stems.
12. Special kinds of fruit trees are multiplied by ———.
13. Grapevines need regular ——— to produce good grapes.

Decide whether each sentence is true, and write *true* or *false*.

14. Most evergreens are plants with broad leaves that produce flowers, seeds, and fruit.
15. Roots fasten a plant to the ground and absorb water.
16. The wind spreads the pollen for pretty, sweet-smelling flowers.
17. Grass plants multiply by their spreading roots and underground stems.

Lesson 6 Answers

1. d
2. a
3. b
4. e
5. f
6. c
7. absorb
8. transpiration
9. reproduce
10. pollen
11. rooting
12. grafting
13. pruning
14. false
15. true
16. false
17. true

Lesson 6

Reviewing the Unit

Call attention to the lesson titles to help the students remember the main ideas of this unit. Drill the New Word quizzes and the key concepts as given in the Concepts to Teach sections of this teacher's guide. Be alert to student weaknesses, and repeat activities or quizzes as necessary.

Choose the best answer.

18. All living things are made of countless tiny
    a. seeds.
    b. buds.
    c. cells.
19. Leaves get the power for food making from
    a. water.
    b. light.
    c. heat.
20. The pressure a plant needs comes from the
    a. minerals in the soil.
    b. air inside its stem.
    c. water within its cells.
21. A tulip plant grows from a special underground bud called a
    a. bulb.
    b. tuber.
    c. stoma.
22. A tuber is an underground stem with buds, such as
    a. a potato.
    b. an onion.
    c. a radish.
23. Strawberry plants multiply by their
    a. fast-growing bulbs.
    b. long runners.
    c. underground stems.

18. c
19. b
20. c
21. a
22. a
23. b

Write the missing words.

24. The ——— of a plant grow downward toward water.
25. A radish ——— carries sap, stores food, and supports the leaves.
26. You can tell many trees apart by the shapes of their ———.
27. The ——— of a lily make tiny grains of pollen.
28. A rose has a ——— that makes plant eggs.
29. Pollen unites with the ——— to make seeds.
30. The pistil of a flower becomes the ——— that holds the seeds.
31. Every ——— has a tough coating, stored food, and a tiny plant.

24. roots
25. stem
26. leaves
27. stamens
28. pistil
29. plant eggs
30. fruit
31. seed

32. Guard cells control ——— by changing the size of the holes on the underside of a leaf.

Draw this picture.

33–38. Draw a picture of a large flower with these plant parts labeled neatly: *stem, veins, sepal, petal, pistil, stamen.*

Write the answers.

39. What are the leaves like of a one-part-seed plant?
40. What are the leaves like of a two-part-seed plant?
41. How many petals do the flowers have of a one-part-seed plant?
42. How many petals do the flowers have of a two-part-seed plant?

43–45. How do seeds travel away from the parent plants? Write three ways.

46–50. Write the five steps of grafting as given in the last lesson.

32. transpiration

33–38. (Drawings may vary, but they should have at least one of each part named.)

39. Leaves of one-part-seed plants have parallel veins (*or* are narrow and bladelike).
40. Leaves of two-part-seed plants have branching veins (*or* are broad and flat).
41. Flowers of one-part-seed plants have parts in multiples of three.
42. Flowers of two-part-seed plants have parts in multiples of four or five.

43–45. Seeds are scattered by the wind. They float in streams or rivers. They travel with people or animals.

46–50.
(1) A bud is cut off from the special tree.
(2) A slit is cut in the bark of a little tree.
(3) The bud is pushed into the slit.
(4) The bud is tied in place.
(5) After the bud produces a leafy branch, the branches already on the little tree are cut off.

(50 points total)

God's Inspiring World

Unit 1 Test **Score** ___________

Name ______________________________ **Date** ______________

Match the letter of each sentence ending to its correct beginning.

c 1. Climate
d 2. Polar
f 3. Atmosphere
a 4. A cyclone
g 5. A prevailing westerly
b 6. Humid air
e 7. Precipitation

a. is a circling air mass that brings us rain.
b. contains much water.
c. is the kind of weather from year to year.
d. is a climate that has cool, short summers.
e. is rain, sleet, snow, hail, dew, or frost.
f. is the air around the earth.
g. is a wide belt blowing over the same lands year after year.

Circle the letter of the best answer for each exercise.

8. The wind is caused by
   a. the difference in the height of the land above sea level.
   b. the rotation of the earth on its axis.
   (c.) the uneven heating of the earth by the sun.

9. Clouds are formed when
   (a.) humid air is raised.
   b. cold air mixes with warm air.
   c. water evaporates from the ocean.

10. The air in a cyclone is
   (a.) warm and moist. b. warm and dry. c. cold and dry.

11. A tornado is
   a. a slowly rotating mass of warm air.
   (b.) a fast wind in a small circle.
   c. a circling storm that covers a big area.

12. There may be rain in a few days if the direction of the wind changes and we see
   a. cumulus clouds.
   b. stratus clouds.
   (c.) cirrus clouds.

13. The kind of precipitation we get depends on
    a. the kind of clouds.
    (b.) the temperature of the air.
    c. the speed of the wind.

Fill each blank with a correct word from the box.

cumulus	front	snow
faith	frost	stratus
fear	sleet	temperate
fog		

14. God can use storms to test our ___faith___.
15. A ___front___ is the line where warm air meets cold air.
16. A ___temperate___ climate has a cold winter and a long-enough summer to grow crops.
17. The ___stratus___ clouds form a thick gray layer above us.
18. The fair-weather ___cumulus___ clouds look like piles of whipped cream.
19. A ___fog___ is a cloud that touches the ground and makes it hard to see.
20. You may find ___frost___ after a night when the ground is below freezing.
21. We shall get ___sleet___ during the winter when raindrops freeze.
22. We shall get ___snow___ if the precipitation is in the form of ice crystals formed in a cloud that is below freezing.

Write *true* if the sentence is true; write *false* if it is not true.

__true__ 23. The weather can be predicted because it is controlled by laws God made.

__true__ 24. A ring around the moon is caused by cirrus clouds.

__false__ 25. When cold and warm air meet, the cold air is pushed above the warm air.

__false__ 26. Trade winds blow from the south.

Label these pictures with the correct words.

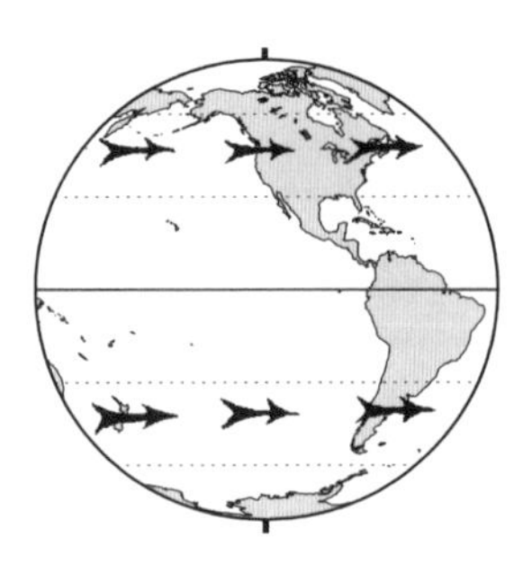

27. cirrus clouds 28. prevailing westerlies 29. thunderhead

Answer this question.

30–33. What four things make the kind of climate a land has?

the distance from the equator

the distance from the ocean

the height above sea level

the land around you

(Total: 33 points)

God's Inspiring World

Unit 2 Test **Score** ___________

Name ____ **Date** ______________________

Match the letter of each word on the right to its description on the left.

g	1. This is one bone in the backbone.	a.	down
b	2. This grinds up a bird's hard food.	b.	gizzard
a	3. This keeps a baby bird warm.	c.	octopus
d	4. This pearl maker has tasty meat.	d.	oyster
f	5. This kind of snail has no shell.	e.	segmented
e	6. The earthworm is an example of this.	f.	slug
c	7. This animal moves by shooting water.	g.	vertebra

Circle the letter of the best answer for each exercise.

8. Mammals, birds, reptiles, amphibians, and fish
   a. practice regeneration.
   (b.) have skeletons.
   c. are streamlined.

9. Two animals having exoskeletons are
   (a.) spiders and mosquitoes.
   b. lobsters and flatworms.
   c. butterflies and jellyfish.

10. A fish balances itself and slows down with its
    (a.) fins.
    b. gills.
    c. gizzard.

11. One animal with a one-part shell is the
    a. clam. b. slug. (c.) snail.

12. The two-part shells of mollusks are held together with
    a. arms lined with sucking pads.
    (b.) a strong muscle.
    c. a hatchet-shaped foot.

13. The animal that helps to fertilize the soil is the
    (a.) earthworm.
    b. leech.
    c. planaria.

14. The animal whose skeleton is used for cleaning is the
    a. clam.
    (b.) sponge.
    c. jellyfish.

15. A starfish feels, moves, and gets its food with its
    a. tentacles.
    b. vertebrae.
    (c.) tube feet.

Fill each blank with the correct word.

16. An exoskeleton is on the ____outside____ of an animal.
17. The tough ____backbone____ protects the spinal cord of a frog or turtle.
18. A bird cannot fly without stiff ____quills____ in its feathers.
19. A rooster can ____perch____ while it sleeps because of its ability to lock its toes around a branch.
20. A duck ____preens____ its feathers by smoothing them with its bill.
21. A fish moves forward by ____wagging____ its tail.

Write *true* if the sentence is true; write *false* if it is not true.

____false____ 22. Animals with backbones have exoskeletons.

____false____ 23. The body of a fish is covered with hard gills and a slippery material.

____false____ 24. Most fish use their air bladders to breathe air.

____true____ 25. An earthworm uses bristles to hold itself when making a tunnel in the soil.

____false____ 26. The planaria is a harmful insect that lives in streams.

____true____ 27. An octopus can hide itself with a dark cloud in the water.

____true____ 28. Jellyfish get their food by using stinging tentacles.

Answer these questions.

29. Why is it important for a bird to have hollow bones to be able to fly?

    Hollow bones cause a bird to be lightweight for flying.

30. Why is it important for a bird to have a streamlined body to be able to fly?

    A bird needs a streamlined body to move easily through air.

31. How can you attract birds to your house?

    You can attract birds by feeding them.

32. What is regeneration in an animal?

    Regeneration is the ability to grow missing body parts.

33. What is an animal that has the ability of regeneration?

    Starfish (*or* planaria, sponges, octopuses) have the ability of regeneration.

(Total: 33 points)

God's Inspiring World

Unit 3 Test **Score** ________

Name ______________________ **Date** ______________

Match the letter of each word on the right to its description on the left.

e	1. The sky directly overhead	a. constellation
b	2. The line where the earth and sky seem to meet	b. horizon
a	3. A star picture	c. observatory
c	4. A place that has a telescope	d. star guide
d	5. A map for finding the stars you can see	e. zenith

Label the pictures by finding and writing the correct name of each star group below.

Boötes	Hercules	Pegasus
Cassiopeia	Leo	Ursa Major
Cygnus	Orion	Ursa Minor
Gemini		

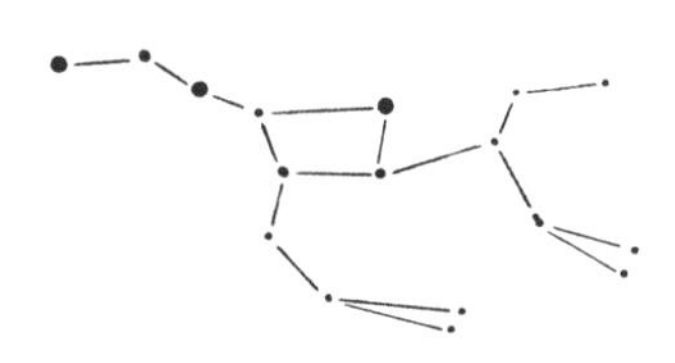

6. Ursa Major

8. Hercules

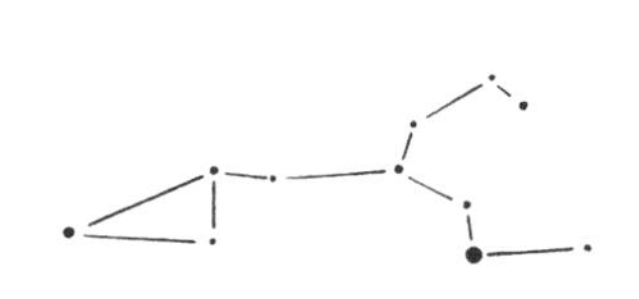

7. Leo

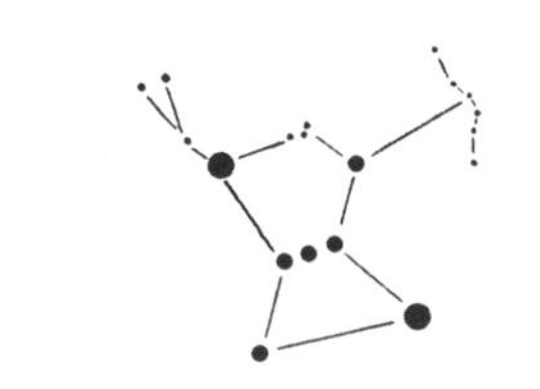

9. Orion

10. Boötes

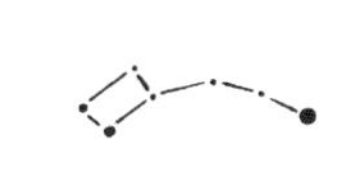

13. Ursa Minor

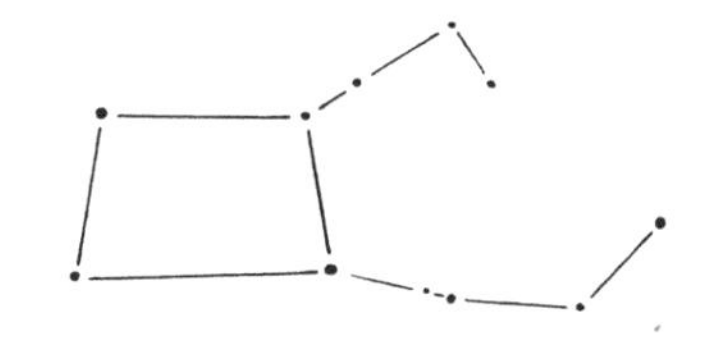

11. Pegasus

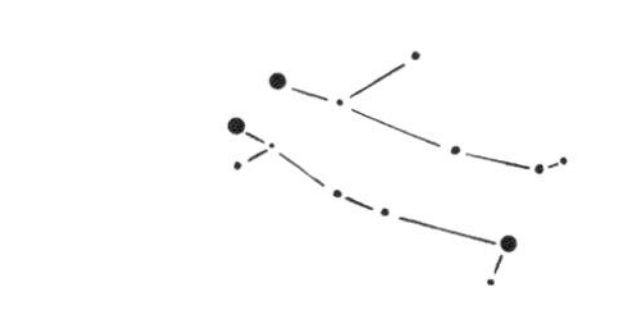

14. Gemini

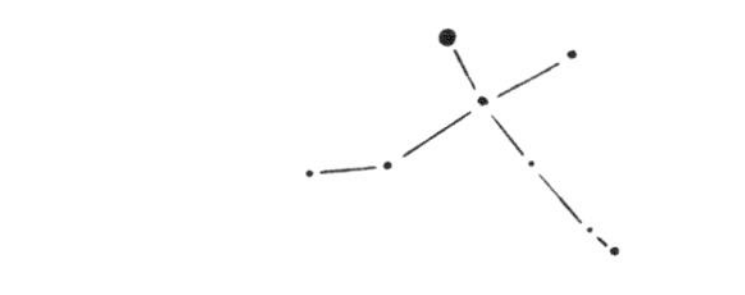

12. Cygnus

15. Cassiopeia

Circle which one of the three constellations listed is best seen in the season given.

16. *winter:*	Hercules	**Orion**	Boötes
17. *spring:*	Cassiopeia	Pleiades	**Leo**
18. *summer:*	**Cygnus**	Gemini	Pegasus

Fill each blank with the correct word.

19. Sirius is a bright star that rises about one hour after ____Orion____.
20. The star in Boötes that God mentioned to Job is ____Arcturus____.
21. Another name for Polaris is the ____North____ ____Star____.
22. The Northern Cross is part of the constellation ____Cygnus____.
23. We can see very faint stars with a ____telescope____.
24. A star is clearest when it is near the ____zenith____.

Circle the letter of the best answer for each exercise.

25. Twins is the common name for the constellation
    - (a.) Gemini.
    - b. Pegasus.
    - c. Hercules.
26. The common name for Orion is
    - a. giant.
    - (b.) hunter.
    - c. herdsman.
27. A sailor uses a sextant to find out
    - a. how deep the ocean is.
    - (b.) his position on the ocean.
    - c. the angle between a star and zenith.
28. You can find Hercules by looking for
    - (a.) a keystone shape.
    - b. a big square.
    - c. a sickle shape.
29. The stars circle the earth because
    - a. the stars revolve around the earth once each day.
    - b. the earth revolves around the sun once a year.
    - (c.) the earth rotates on its axis once each day.
30. The stars should not be used to
    - a. teach us the glory of God.
    - b. tell us when to plant our crops.
    - (c.) foretell the future.

Answer these questions.

31. What direction do most of the stars move?

    Most of the stars move from east to west. *or* The stars rise in the east and set in the west.

32. How could you use the stars if you were lost?

    You could find Polaris and know which direction was north.

33. What is a good way to learn the constellations? (Answers may vary.)

    A good way to learn constellations is to go star watching with someone who already knows some constellations (*or* . . . to use a star guide to find the zenith constellation and then other constellations nearby).

(Total: 33 points)

God's Inspiring World

Unit 4 Test **Score** ________

Name ______________________ **Date** ____________

Match the letter of each sentence ending to its correct beginning.

__e__ 1. Coughing and sneezing
__c__ 2. Vitamins and minerals
__a__ 3. Vaccines
__f__ 4. The skin and tears
__b__ 5. Cards and visits
__d__ 6. Prescriptions
__g__ 7. Antibodies

a. cause the body to make antibodies without becoming sick.
b. cheer the sick and help them get well.
c. are found in fruits and vegetables.
d. tell you how often to take medicines.
e. are common symptoms of colds and flu.
f. stop many germs before they get inside the body.
g. kill germs or make their poisons harmless.

Write *true* if the sentence is true; write *false* if it is not true.

__false__ 8. You cannot get germs from someone who is sick unless you touch him.
__true__ 9. Germs make you sick by multiplying quickly, making poisons, and destroying body cells.
__false__ 10. Being immune to chicken pox means that your body has never fought chicken pox germs.
__false__ 11. A sick person should drink fruit juice and hoe the garden.
__false__ 12. Being cheerful causes a sick person to get well more slowly than usual.
__true__ 13. We are kind to others when we have good health habits.
__true__ 14. God has given us medicines to help us get well.

Fill each blank with a correct word from the box.

antiseptic	diagnosis	flu
carrier	fever	sanitation
contagious		

15. A body temperature above normal is called a ___fever___.

16. Any ___contagious___ disease spreads from one person to the next.

17. After you tell a doctor the symptoms of your disease, he makes his ___diagnosis___ of your disease.

18. Having safe drinking water and clean food and milk, and properly getting rid of garbage are important parts of ___sanitation___.

Circle the letter of the best answer for each exercise.

19. A poor diet could cause you to get
    (a.) scurvy.
    b. mumps.
    c. leprosy.

20. You need a microscope to see
    (a.) germs.
    b. carriers.
    c. symptoms.

21. Infection is caused by
    a. sanitation.
    b. fever.
    (c.) germs.

22. Your body needs plenty of
    a. chips and ice cream.
    b. milk and cupcakes.
    (c.) fruits and whole-grain breads.

23. Tiny parts of your blood that will die by eating many germs are called
    a. infection carriers.
    (b.) white blood cells.
    c. antibodies.

24. When you bandage a wound, you may put
    a. a vaccine on it.
    (b.) an antiseptic on it.
    c. antibodies on it.

Complete the "Good Health Habits" with the proper word for each blank.
There are three blanks for each rule. One percent of credit can be given for each correct word.

25. Use a ___handkerchief___ to cover your ___nose___ and mouth when you ___sneeze___ or cough.
26. Wash your hands with ___soap___ before handling ___food___ and ___after___ using the restroom.
27. Use your own ___comb___, ___toothbrush___, and drinking ___glass___.
28. Wear ___clean___ clothes and take a ___bath___ at least ___twice___ a week.
29. ___Wash___ your hair at least ___once___ a ___week___.

Complete the "Rules During Sickness" with the proper word for each blank.

30. Be extra careful to ___follow___ the "Good ___Health___ ___Habits___."
31. Always keep tissues or ___handkerchiefs___ handy to catch ___coughs___ and ___sneezes___.
32. ___Wash___ your ___hands___ ___often___ with soap.
33. Stay ___away___ from others, especially ___babies___ and other ___sick___ people.

(Total: 33 points)

God's Inspiring World

Unit 5 Test **Score** ___________

Name ______________________________ **Date** ________________

Match the letter of each word on the right to its description on the left.

f	1. It reflects light evenly to see images.	a. cornea
d	2. It lets the right amount of light enter the eye.	b. eyepiece
e	3. It helps you see very tiny things.	c. eye socket
g	4. It is the colors of the rainbow.	d. iris
b	5. It is the part of the microscope that you look into.	e. microscope
h	6. It helps you see faraway things.	f. mirror
a	7. It is a protection over the front of the eye.	g. spectrum
c	8. It protects the eyeball from bumps.	h. telescope

Choose and underline the best answer for each sentence.

9. God made luminous things such as the (sun, moon, earth).
10. A (prism, convex, concave) lens can focus light.
11. A concave lens is (thinnest, thickest) at the center.
12. The black dot in your eye is the (pupil, iris, optic nerve).
13. Light travels through transparent (glass, metal, rock).
14. A brown roof (bends, reflects, absorbs) much light.
15. Both your convex lens and your (iris, cornea, retina) can adjust themselves by changing shape.
16. Your (pupils, eyelashes, irises) keep dust and dirt out of your eyes.

Write *true* if the sentence is true, and write *false* if it is not true.

false 17. God made light on the fifth day of Creation.

true 18. Light travels in rays to your eyes.

true 19. Reflecting light acts like a bouncing ball.

__true__ 20. The light that strikes a black coat is mostly absorbed and changed to heat.

__true__ 21. Light bends when it goes from the air into water.

__false__ 22. The slant of reflected light is greater than the slant the light strikes.

__false__ 23. You can judge distance better with one eye than with two.

__true__ 24. Both tears and blinking protect your eyes.

Fill each blank with the correct word.

25. God created the __sun__ to give us most of our light and heat.
26. The reflection of your face is turned __backward__ in the mirror.
27. A curved glass made to bend light is a __lens__.
28. Your eye's convex lens focuses light onto your __retina__.
29. Your __optic__ __nerve__ carries sight messages to the brain.

Write the answers to these exercises.

30–31. Name two ways that mirrors are useful to us. (Any two.)

Mirrors are used as looking glasses, rear-view mirrors, reflectors around search-lights and auto headlights, and in telescopes.

32–33. Name two ways in which we can use our eyes wisely. (Any two.)

We can keep sharp objects and strong chemicals away from them. We can avoid looking at bright lights. We can read good things. We can work to help others. We can help the blind.

(Total: 33 points)

God's Inspiring World

Unit 6 Test **Score** ___________

Name ________________________________ **Date** ____________________

Match the letter of each word on the right to its description on the left.

a. appliance
b. circuit
c. conductor
d. insulator
e. motor
f. parallel
g. resistance
h. series
i. shock
j. switch

__i__ 1. What you feel when electricity travels through you

__h__ 2. Connecting bulbs with wires so that all the electricity must pass through each bulb

__g__ 3. Slowing electricity down

__b__ 4. A complete path for electricity to follow

__j__ 5. Turns electricity on or off

__c__ 6. A material that carries electricity

__e__ 7. Uses electricity to turn something

__d__ 8. A material that keeps electricity from flowing

Circle the letter of the best answer for each exercise.

9. A light bulb, a refrigerator, a grinder, and a toaster are all
   a. conductors.
   b. motors.
   (c.) appliances.

10. Which of the following is **not** a cause of short circuits?
   a. worn insulation between two wires in a cord
   (b.) a burned-out fuse
   c. two bare wires touching each other

11. All switches must be wired in
   (a.) series.
   b. parallel.
   c. resistance.

12. A heating element can
   a. lift heavy objects.
   b. help you read.
   (c.) roast hot dogs.

13. All of the following are a source of electricity except
    a. a generator.
    (b.) a motor.
    c. a battery.

Fill each blank with a correct word.

14. A place to plug in for a source of electricity is called a ___receptacle___.
15. A ___fluorescent___ light is the best kind of light for a large building.
16. A ___fuse___ is a part in a circuit to keep the circuit from getting hot.
17. An ___electromagnet___ can be used to lift iron things from one place to another.
18. An ___incandescent___ light bulb gives off yellow light and much heat.
19. The third prong on a plug makes a ___safe___ way for stray electricity to get back to the source.

Write *true* if the sentence is true; write *false* if it is not true.

___true___ 20. A fuse works by melting.

___false___ 21. Electricity flows easier through a thin wire than through a thick wire.

___false___ 22. To keep electricity from going from one wire to another, they should be separated with a conductor.

___true___ 23. Every circuit must have an appliance to use the electricity.

___true___ 24. Electrons will travel through a conductor only when there is a complete circuit.

___true___ 25. A short wire has less resistance than a long wire.

___false___ 26. Buzzers and bells use heating elements to make sound.

Label the drawing, and circle the letter that answers each question. (1% each)

27. Give the names of the parts of an electric circuit that are marked with letters.

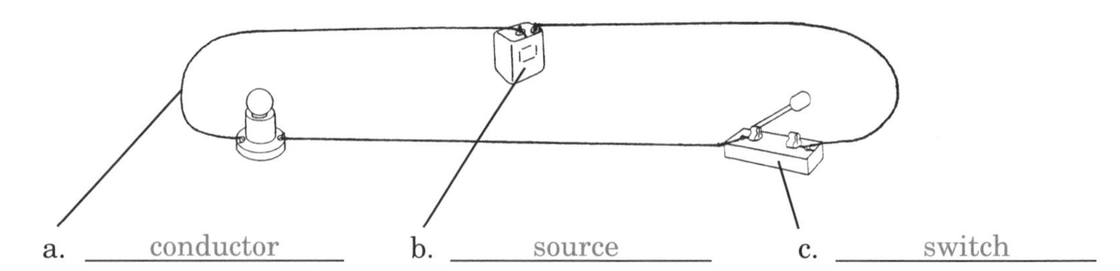

a. ___conductor___ b. ___source___ c. ___switch___

28. Which of the following drawings shows parallel wiring?

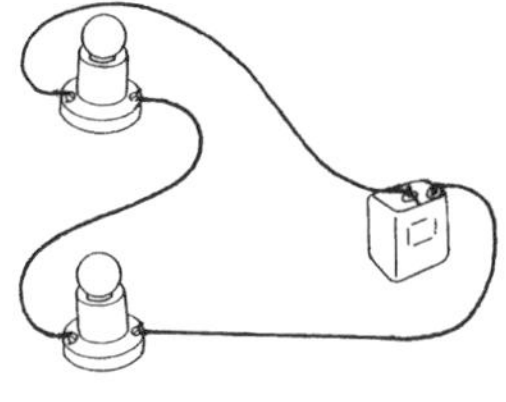

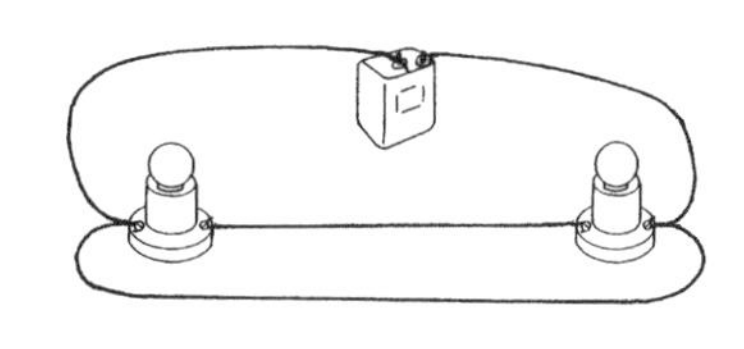
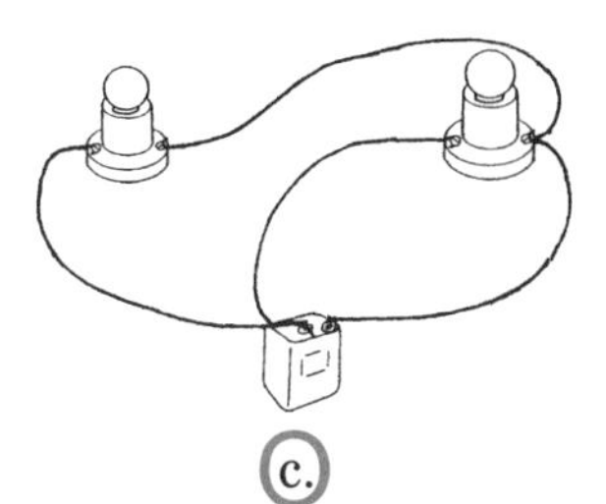

a. b. (c.)

29. Which of the following drawings would be a short circuit?

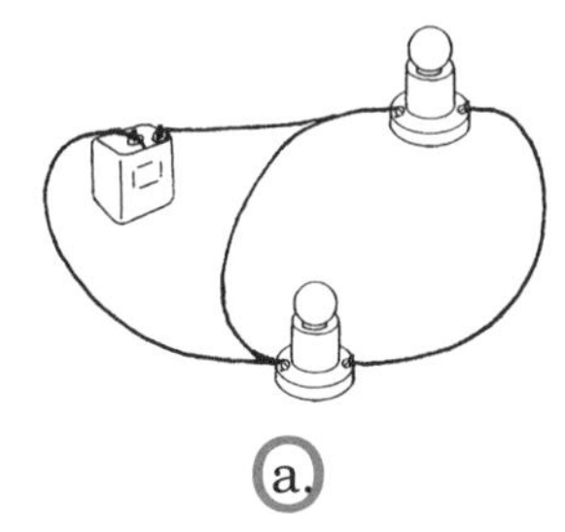
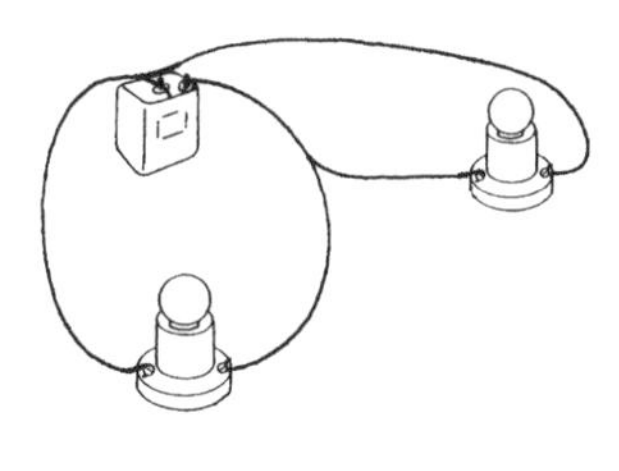

(a.) b. c.

30. Which of the three drawings shows the switch wired correctly?

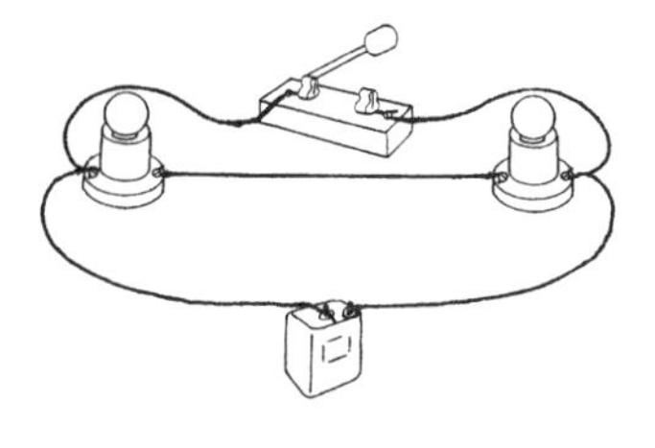
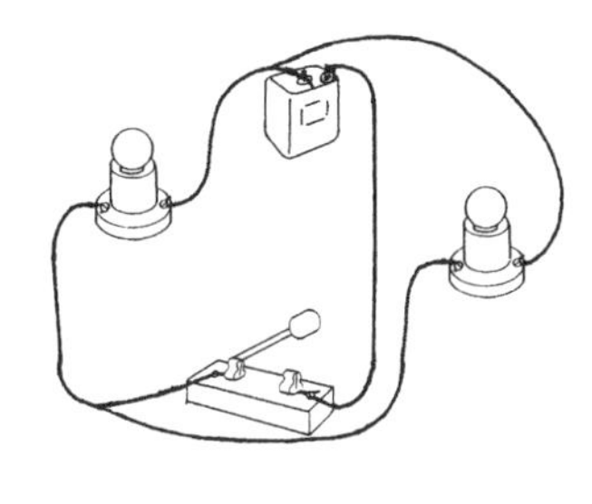
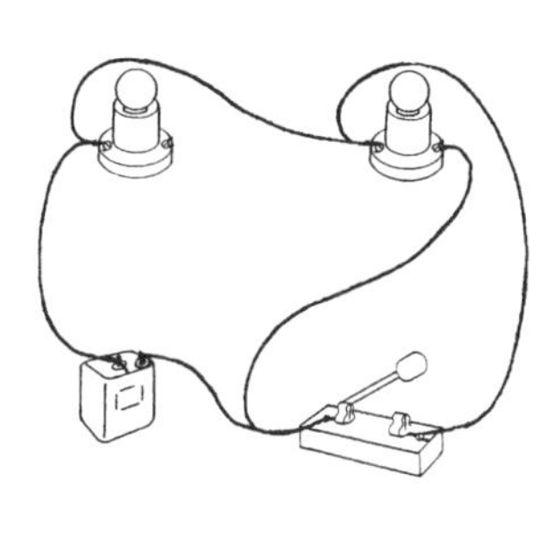

a. (b.) c.

Answer these questions in complete sentences.

31. How can you make an electromagnet?

An electromagnet is made by wrapping insulated wire around an iron nail or bolt.

32–33. What are two safety rules to remember when we use electricity? (Any two.)

Never make an electric circuit without some kind of appliance.

Never put paper clips, etc. into a receptacle.

Always pull on the plug when removing a cord from a receptacle.

Do not run over cords with machinery.

Do not let cords get against something hot.

Do not let cords get against moving parts of machines.

Coil and hang up cords when not in use.

(Total: 33 points)

God's Inspiring World

Unit 7 Test **Score** ________

Name ______________________ **Date** ______________

Match the letter of each sentence ending to its correct beginning.

f 1. Conifers
h 2. Buds
g 3. Roots
c 4. Stems
a 5. Two-part-seed plants
e 6. Cells
d 7. Root hairs
b 8. Guard cells

a. have broad leaves and flowers.
b. change the size of holes under a leaf.
c. carry water, minerals, and food.
d. absorb water and minerals.
e. make up each living thing.
f. have needles and cones.
g. fasten a plant in the ground.
h. become new stems or flowers.

Write *true* if the sentence is true; write *false* if it is not true.

true 9. All living things are made of cells.
false 10. Special fruit trees are multiplied by pruning.
false 11. A bud is a tough coating around a plant with stored food.
true 12. Many seeds are scattered by the wind.
true 13. A plant needs water to keep the right pressure inside its cells.
true 14. Many plants reproduce by bearing seeds.

Circle the letter of the best answer for each exercise.

15. A biennial plant lives
a. one year. (b.) two years. c. many years.

16. A corn seed is an example of a
(a.) one-part seed. b. two-part seed. c. many-part seed.

17. A thick underground stem with buds is called a
a. root. b. runner. (c.) tuber.

18. Giving off water through the leaves of a plant is called
    (a.) transpiration. b. pollination. c. reproduction.

19. Food is made by
    (a.) chlorophyll that receives light.
    b. water inside leaves and stems.
    c. underground stems that spread.

20. A flower with 6 petals is a
    a. conifer. (b.) one-part-seed plant. c. two-part-seed plant.

21. A tiny plant in a seed can start growing before it can make its own food because
    (a.) a seed has stored food in it.
    b. a seed swells with water.
    c. a seed gets food out of the ground.

22. A peach tree is pruned so that it
    a. bears more peaches.
    b. grows more quickly.
    (c.) produces larger peaches.

Label this picture by filling each blank with a word from the word box that names that part of the plant.

leaves	stamen
pistil	stem
roots	

23. stamen
24. pistil
25. stem
26. leaves
27. roots

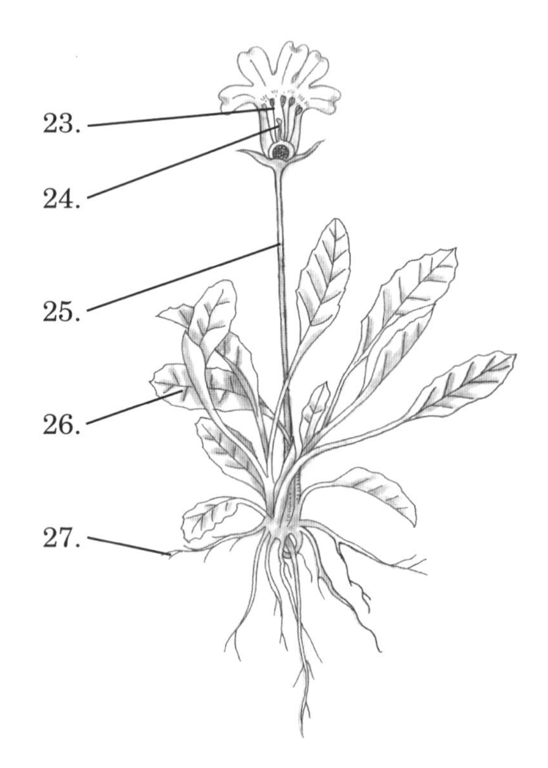

Write the answers to these exercises.

28–30. Choose three plant parts from the picture above. Write the work each one does for the plant. (Any three.)

A pistil makes plant eggs.

A stamen makes pollen.

The stem supports the plant (*or* carries sap *or* provides storage for food).

The leaves make food (*or* give off water).

The roots absorb water and minerals (*or* fasten the plant to the ground).

31–32. What are two ways in which pollen is spread? (Any two.)

Some flowers give pollen to themselves.

The wind spreads pollen for many flowers.

Bees and other insects spread pollen for many other flowers.

33. Explain how to use rooting to get a new plant.

Cut off a stem of the plant that is to be rooted and put the end of it in water or wet soil.

(Total: 33 points)

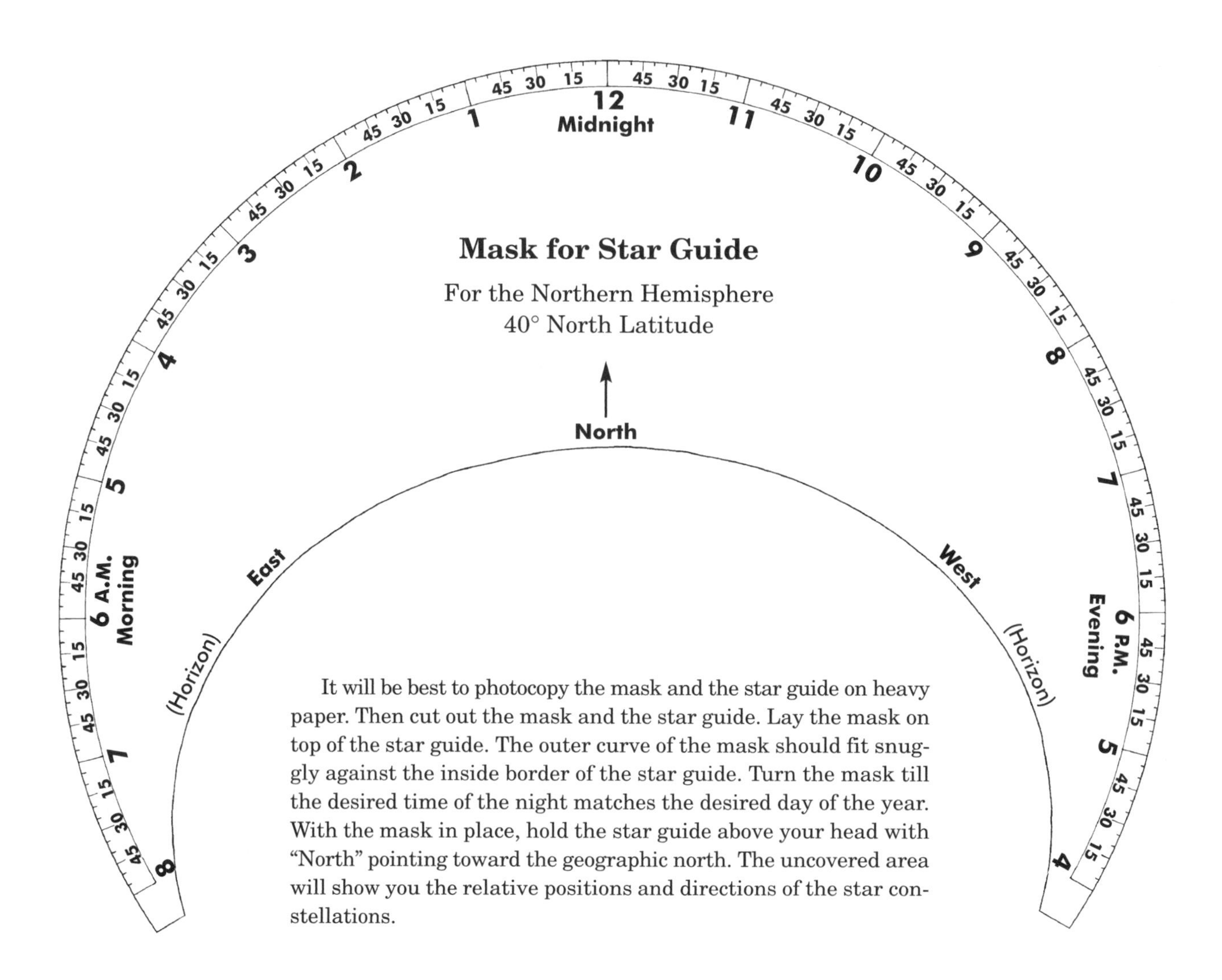

It will be best to photocopy the mask and the star guide on heavy paper. Then cut out the mask and the star guide. Lay the mask on top of the star guide. The outer curve of the mask should fit snuggly against the inside border of the star guide. Turn the mask till the desired time of the night matches the desired day of the year. With the mask in place, hold the star guide above your head with "North" pointing toward the geographic north. The uncovered area will show you the relative positions and directions of the star constellations.

Star Guide

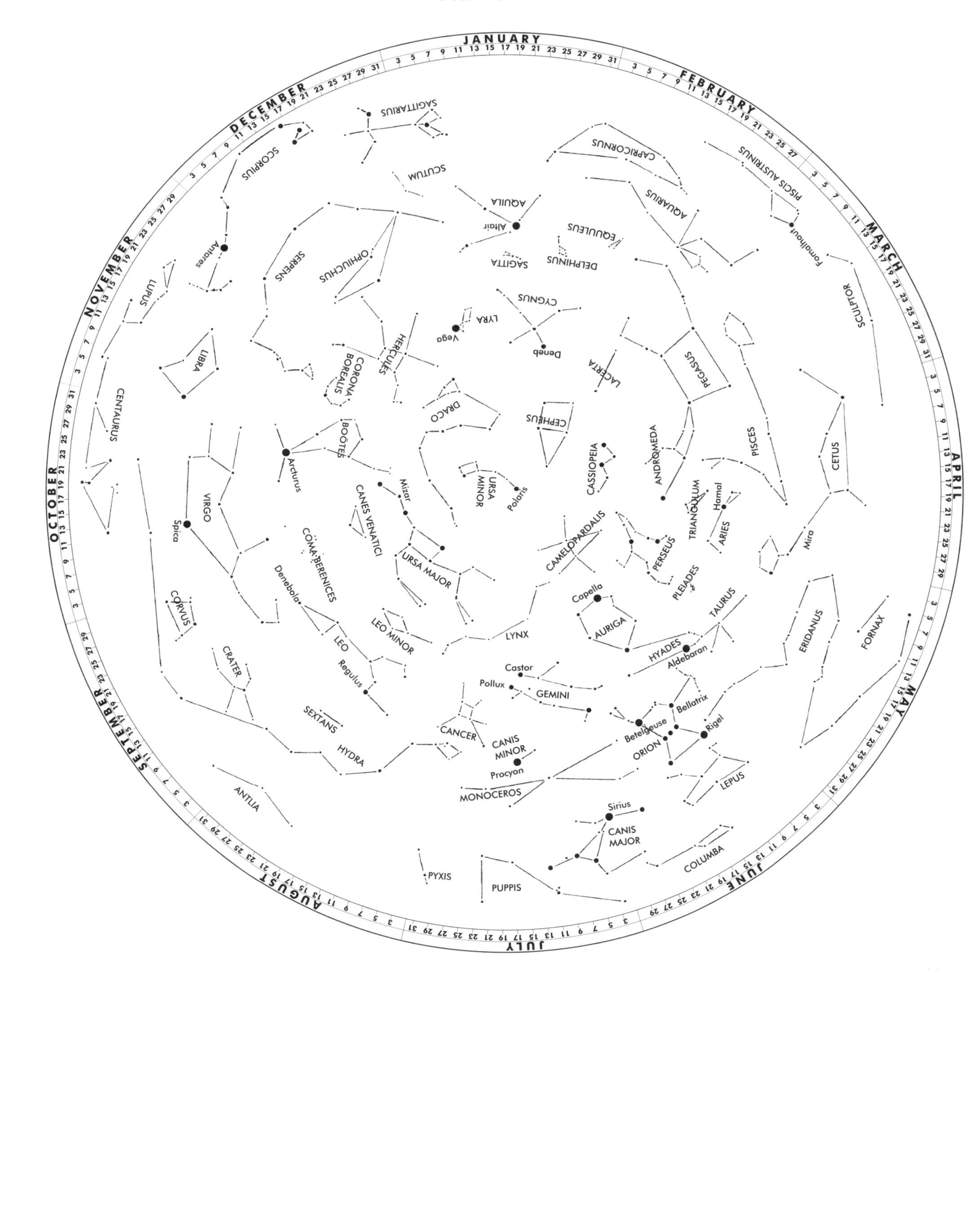
JANUARY
FEBRUARY
MARCH
APRIL
MAY
JUNE
JULY
AUGUST
SEPTEMBER
OCTOBER
NOVEMBER
DECEMBER
SAGITTARIUS
SCORPIUS
SCUTUM
CAPRICORNUS
PISCIS AUSTRINUS
AQUARIUS
AQUILA
Altair
EQUULEUS
Fomalhaut
Antares
SERPENS
OPHIUCHUS
SAGITTA
DELPHINUS
SCULPTOR
LUPUS
CYGNUS
LYRA
Vega
Deneb
LIBRA
HERCULES
CORONA BOREALIS
LACERTA
PEGASUS
CENTAURUS
DRACO
CEPHEUS
BOÖTES
Arcturus
CASSIOPEIA
ANDROMEDA
PISCES
CETUS
URSA MINOR
Polaris
Mizar
CANES VENATICI
VIRGO
Spica
TRIANGULUM
Hamal
ARIES
CAMELOPARDALIS
PERSEUS
Mira
COMA BERENICES
URSA MAJOR
PLEIADES
Denebola
Capella
CORVUS
TAURUS
LEO MINOR
AURIGA
LYNX
ERIDANUS
FORNAX
LEO
HYADES
Aldebaran
CRATER
Castor
Regulus
Pollux
GEMINI
Bellatrix
SEXTANS
CANCER
Betelgeuse
Rigel
CANIS MINOR
ORION
HYDRA
Procyon
LEPUS
ANTLIA
MONOCEROS
Sirius
CANIS MAJOR
COLUMBA
PYXIS
PUPPIS

Ursa Minor
Common name: Little Bear
Season: Year around

Ursa Minor
Common name: Little Bear
Season: Year around

Ursa Major
Common name: Big Bear
Season: Year around

Ursa Major
Common name: Big Bear
Season: Year around

Boötes
Common name: Herdsman
Season: Spring

Boötes
Common name: Herdsman
Season: Spring

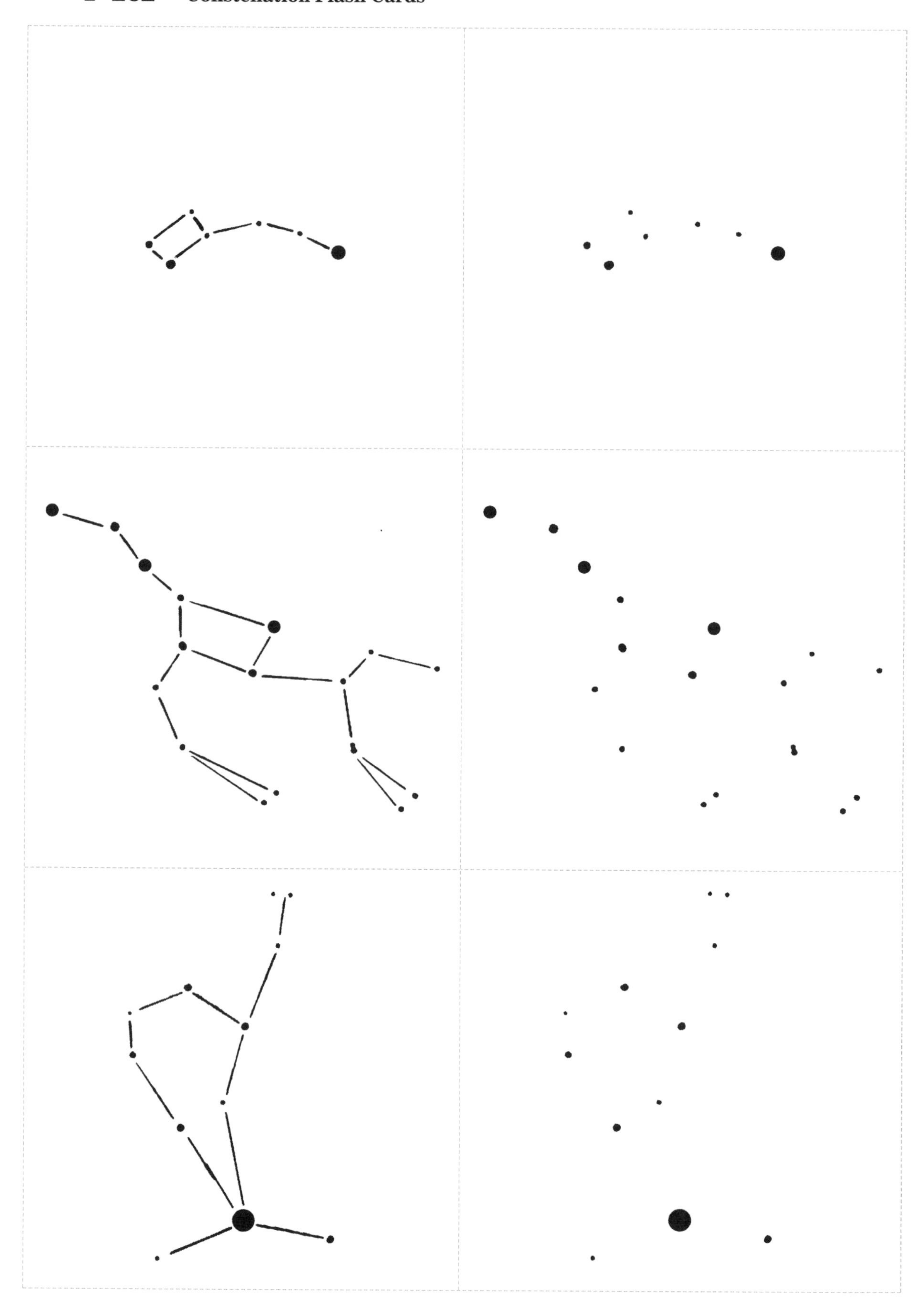

Orion
Common name: Hunter
Season: Winter

Orion
Common name: Hunter
Season: Winter

Gemini
Common name: Twins
Season: Winter

Gemini
Common name: Twins
Season: Winter

Pleiades
Common name: Seven Sisters
Season: Winter

Pleiades
Common name: Seven Sisters
Season: Winter

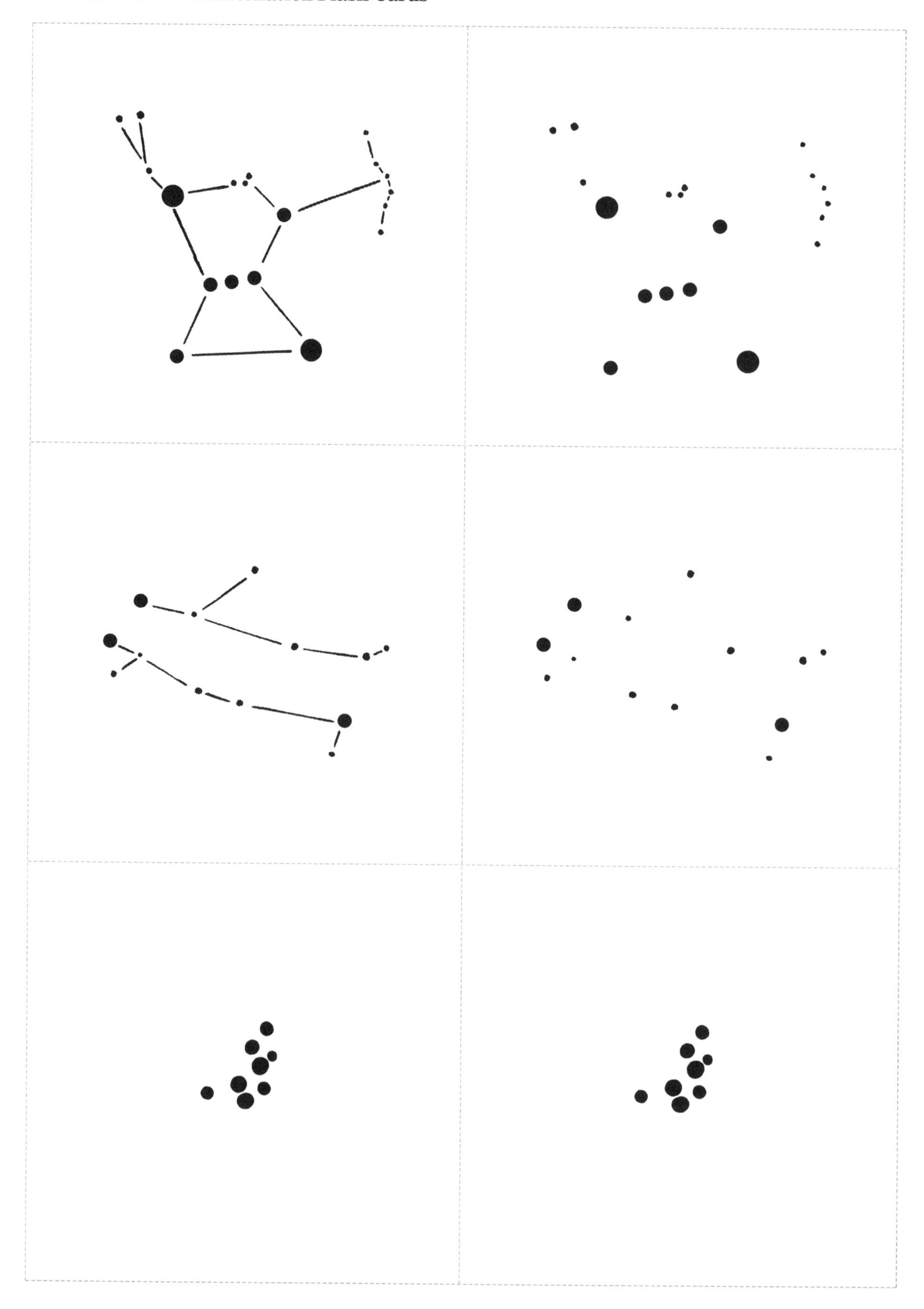

Leo
Common name: Lion
Season: Spring

Leo
Common name: Lion
Season: Spring

Hercules
Common name: Giant
Season: Summer

Hercules
Common name: Giant
Season: Summer

Cygnus
Common name: Swan
Season: Summer

Cygnus
Common name: Swan
Season: Summer

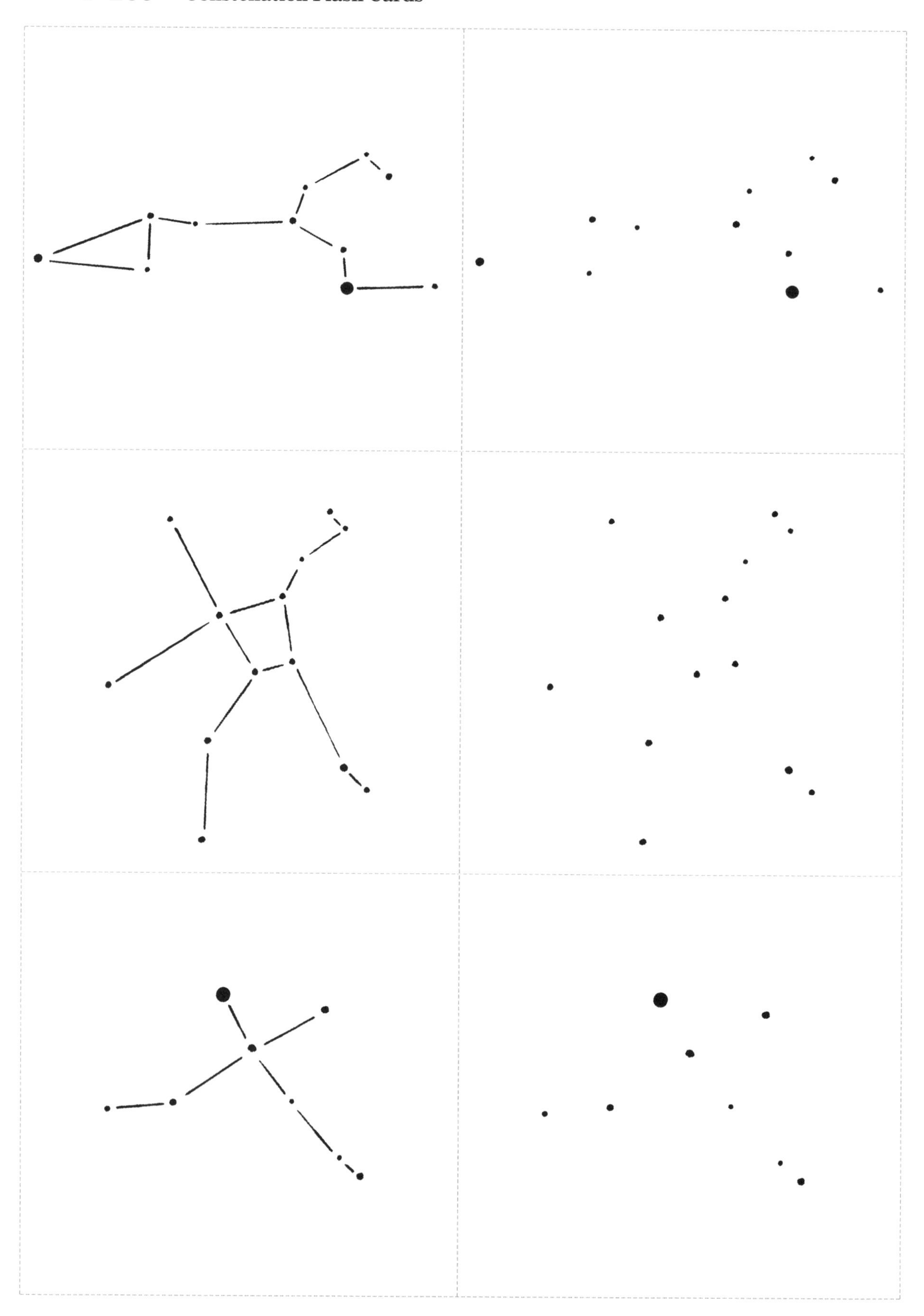

Cassiopeia
Common name: Queen
Season: Autumn

Cassiopeia
Common name: Queen
Season: Autumn

Pegasus
Common name: Winged Horse
Season: Autumn

Pegasus
Common name: Winged Horse
Season: Autumn

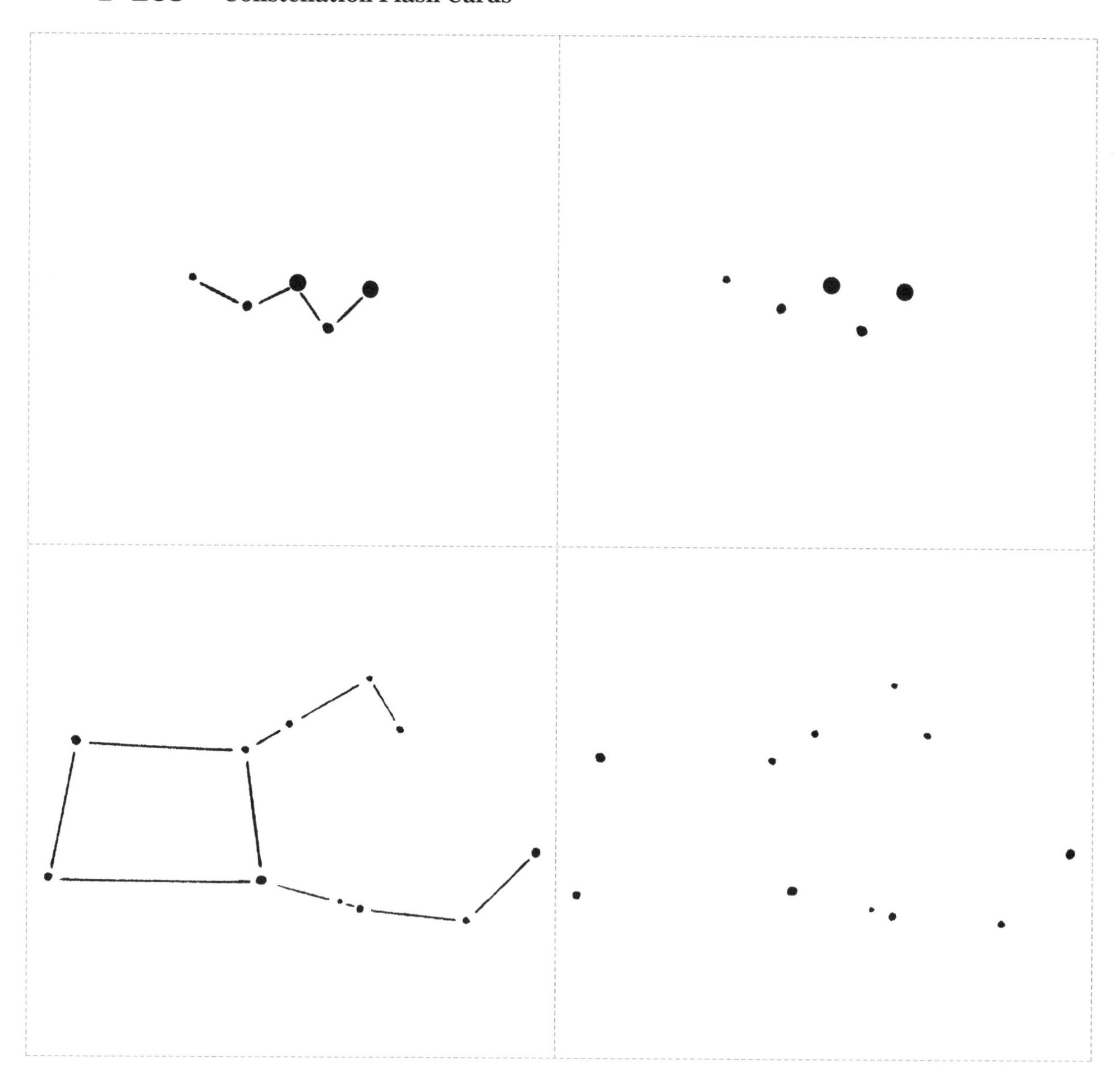

Index

Italics indicates vocabulary words and the pages on which the definitions are found. Illustrations are also indexed.

A

absorb, 141, 142, *209,* 210
absorbing light, 142
air bladder, 55, 57–58
amphibians, 44–45
animals, 40–71
  amphibians, 44–45
  birds, 44, 47–52
  cold-blooded, 45
  fish, 44, 55–59
  mammals, 44–45
  mollusks, 61–65
  reptiles, 44–45
  warm-blooded, 45
  with skeletons, 41–45, 47–52, 55–59
  without skeletons, 61–62, 64–65, 67–71
annual, 203, 206
antibodies, 113, 115–116
antiseptic, 123, 126
appliance, 169, 173, 190–191, 193
Arcturus, 83, 86–87, 90
arid climate, 11, 14, 16
atmosphere, 11, 12, 19
autumn constellations, 91

B

backbone, 41, 42–45
battery, 169, 172
beak, 47, 50–51
bending light, 147–150
biennial, 203, 206
Big Dipper, 77, 78, 80, 87, 90
binocular, 155
birds, 44, 47–52
bird watching, 52, 155
Boötes, 83, 86, 90, 93–94
bud, 209, 212
bulb, 227, 228
bulletin board ideas, 42, 216

C

calendars, 96–97
carrier, 123, 124, 127
Cassiopeia, 89, 91, 94
cell, 209, 210, 212
characteristic, 41, 44–45
charts
  animal groups, 44
  animals with skeletons, 44
  food guide, 109
  good health habits, 125
  rules during sickness, 125
  star-watching, 82
  weather, 23
  wind speed, 24
chlorophyll, 215
circuit, 169, 170–174, 177–181
circuit breaker, 193
cirrus clouds, 25, 28–29
clam, 61, 64
climate, 11, 12–16
clouds, 25–29
  cirrus, 28–29
  cumulus, 28
  stratus, 28
  thunderhead, 28
cold-blooded, 45, 59
cold light, 136
concave, 147, 150
conductor, 169, 171–173
conifer, 203, 205–207
constellations, 77, 78–81, 89–94, 261–268
  autumn, 91
  Big Dipper, 77–78, 80, 87, 90
  Boötes, 83, 86, 90, 93–94
  Cassiopeia, 89, 91, 94
  Cygnus, 89, 91, 93–94
  Gemini, 89–90
  Hercules, 89, 90, 93–94
  Leo, 89, 90, 93–94
  Little Dipper, 77–78, 83–84, 87
  Orion, 77–78, 80–81, 86, 89–90, 93–94
  Pegasus, 89, 91, 94
  Pleiades, 77, 80–81, 86
  spring, 86, 90
  summer, 90–91
  Ursa Major, 83, 87
  Ursa Minor, 83, 87
  winter, 86, 90
contagious, 123, 125

convection, 19
convex, 147, 149–150, 153
cornea, 159, 160, 162
cumulus clouds, 25, 28
cuttings, 228
cyclone, 18, 21
Cygnus, 89, 91, 93–94, 99

D

deserts, 14, 16
dew, 32, 34
diagnosis, 118, 120
diet, 107, 108
disease, 106–128
  contagious, 123, 125
  germs, 107, 110, 113–116, 123–124, 126–127
  healing of, 118–121
  protection from, 113–116, 123–128
  scurvy, 107–108
  symptoms of, 107, 110–111
doctors, 120–121
down, 47, 49–50

E

earth's revolution, 84–85
earth's rotation, 83–85
earthworm, 67, 68
electric bell, 186–187
electric circuits, 169–173, 177–181, 193
electric cords, 191–192
electricity, 168–194
  parallel circuits, 177–180
  parts of a circuit, 169–174
  series circuits, 177–179
  source of, 172
  to make heat, 185
  to make light, 184–185
  to make magnetism, 186
  to make motion, 186–187
  using safely, 190–194
electric motor, 184, 187
electromagnet, 184, 186–187
electrons, 169–174
equator, 15, 19
evaporation, 25, 27
exoskeleton, 41, 42
eyeglasses, 150, 153
eyepiece, 153, 154–156
eyes, 159–163

F

farsighted, 153
feathers, 48, 51–52
feet of birds, 51
fever, 107, 111
fins, 55, 56
first aid, 126
fish, 44, 55–59
flash cards, constellation, 79, 261–268
flatworms, 68
flowering plants, 204–207
flowers, 221–225
fluorescent light, 184, 185
focus, 147, 149–150, 153–155
fog, 25, 28
food, 215–219
food guide, 109
front, 25, 26
frost, 32, 34
fruits, 221–225
fuse, 190, 193

G

garbage, 127–128
Gemini, 89, 90
generator, 172
germs, 107, 110, 113–116, 123–124, 126–127
gills, 55, 58
gizzard, 47, 50
grafting, 227, 230–231
grains, 203
growth in plants, 212
guard cell, 217

H

hail, 32, 33–34
healing, 118–121
health habits, 125
heating element, 184, 185
Hercules, 89, 90, 93–94, 99
horizon, 89, 93
humid, 25, 26–27
hurricane, 18, 21

I

immune, 113, 115
incandescent light, 184, 185
infection, 123, 126
instinct, 47, 49
insulator, 169, 171
iris, 159, 160

J

jellyfish, 67, 70
Job, 7–10, 18, 21–22, 25, 32–34, 36, 41, 47, 49, 59, 69, 76–78, 81, 86–87, 94, 100, 106–108, 111, 118–119, 134–135, 163, 168, 171, 202–203, 209, 213, 231

L

lateral bud, 212
leaves, 215–219, 227–228
lens, 147, 149, 153–156, 160
Leo, 89, 90, 93–94
light, 134, *135,* 136–163, 215
    bending, 147–150
    rays, 137–138
    reflecting, 141–144
    source of, 135–136
    spectrum, 138
Little Dipper, 77, 78, 83–84, 87
luminous, 135, 136

M

magnetism, 186–187
magnifying glass, 149, 154
mammals, 44–45
man, 45
markings, 47, 52
medicine, 118, 120–121
microscope, 110, *153,* 154–156
minerals, 107, 108
mirror, 141, 142–144
mollusks, 61, 62–65
motor, 184, 187
multiplying plants, 227–231

N

nearsighted, 153
nectar, 223
North Pole, 15, 19, 84
North Star, 84

O

observatory, 96, 97
octopus, 61, 65, 71
one-part seeds, 204–205, 218
one-part shells, 61–62
optic nerve, 159, 160
Orion, 77, 78, 80–81, 86, 89–90, 93–94, 99
oxygen, 58
oyster, 61, 64

P

parallel circuit, 177, 178–180
pearls, 64
Pegasus, 89, 91, 94
perching, 47, 51
perennial, 203, 207
petal, 221, 222, 224
pistil, 221, 222–223
planaria, 67, 68, 71
plants, 202–231
    annuals, 206
    biennials, 206
    conifers, 205–207
    flowers, 221–225
    fruits, 224–225
    leaves, 215–219
    multiplying, 227–231
    perennials, 207
    roots, 210–212
    seeds, 203–207
    stems, 210–212, 228
Pleiades, 77, 80–81, 86
poems, 29, 40, 77,
polar climate, 11, 13
Polaris, 83, 84, 93
pollen, 221, 222–223
precipitation, 32, 33–34
    dew, 34
    hail, 33–34
    rain, 26–29, 32–33
    sleet, 32
    snow, 32–33
preen, 47, 51
prescription, 118, 121
prevailing westerlies, 18, 19–21
prism, 138
protection
    for circuits, 193
    for eyes, 162–163
    from disease, 113–116, 123–128
pruning, 227, 231
pupil, 159, 160
pus, 115

Q

quill, 47, 48

R

rain, 25–29, 32–33
rainbow, 148
rain gauges, 12
ray, 135, 137–138
rear-view mirror, 141, 143–144
receptacle, 190, 191, 193
reflect, 141
reflecting light, 141–144
regeneration, 67, 71
reproduce, 221
reptiles, 44–45
resistance, 177, 180–181
retina, 159, 160
root hair, 209, 210
rooting, 227, 228
roots, 209–212
rules during sickness, 125
runners, 230

S

safety
  for eyes, 162–163
  using electricity, 190–194
sanitation, 123, 127–128
sap, 209, 210–211
scales, 55, 56
scurvy, 107–108
seed-producing plants, 203–207
seeds, 203–207, 221–225
sepal, 221, 222
series circuit, 177, 178–179
sextant, 96, 98
shadow, 135, 137
shells, 62, 64
shock, 190, 192–194
short, 192–193
short circuit, 190, 191–193
sickness, 107–111, 113–116, 118–121, 124–125
sight, 159–163
Sirius, 96
skeleton, 41, 42–45, 61
sleet, 32
slug, 61, 62
snail, 61, 62
snow, 32–33
South Pole, 11, 15, 19
spectrum, 135, 138
sponge, 67, 68–69, 71
spring constellations, 86, 90
stamen, 221, 222–223
star calendar, 89–91, 96–97
star cluster, 80, 99
starfish, 67, 70–71
star guide, 78, 82, 89–91, 93, 258–259
stars, 76–100
  Arcturus, 86–87, 90
  constellations, 77–81, 89–94
  movement of, 83–86
  North Star, 84
  Polaris, 83–84, 93
  Sirius, 96
  uses of, 96–100
star study, 77–78, 80–82
stem, 209, 210–213, 228
storms
  hurricane, 21
  thunderstorm, 22, 28
  tornado, 21
stratus clouds, 25, 28
streamlined, 47, 48, 56
summer constellations, 90–91
sundogs, 29
switch, 169, 173, 179–180
symptom, 107, 110–111

T

telescope, 96, 97, *153,* 155–156
temperate climate, 11, 13
tentacles, 67, 70
terminal bud, 212
thermometer, 12, 111
thunderhead, 28
thunderstorm, 18, 22, 28
tornado, 18, 21
trade winds, 18, 20
transparent, 147
transpiration, 215, 217
tropical climate, 11, 13
tuber, 227, 228–229
two-part seeds, 205, 218
two-part shells, 64

U

Ursa Major, 83, 87
Ursa Minor, 83, 87

V

vaccine, 113, 116
vein, 215, 218
vertebra, 41, 42–43
vitamins, 107, 108

W

warm-blooded, 45
weather, 10, *11,* 12–34
  climate, 12–16
  clouds, 25–29
  dew, 34
  frost, 34
  hail, 33–34
  rain, 25–29, 32–33
  sleet, 32
  wind, 18–22
weather signs, 29
weathervanes, 12, 18
white blood cells, 113, 114–115
wind, 18–22, 24
  prevailing westerlies, 19–21
  trade winds, 20
winter constellations, 86, 90
wounds, 126

Z

zenith, 89, 93